The Catholicism of literature in the age of the Book of Common Prayer

Manchester University Press

The Catholicism of literature in the age of the Book of Common Prayer

Poetry, plays, works, 1558–1689

Thomas Rist

MANCHESTER UNIVERSITY PRESS

Copyright © Thomas Rist 2025

The right of Thomas Rist to be identified as the author of this work has been asserted in accordance with the Copyright, Designs and Patents Act 1988.

Published by Manchester University Press
Oxford Road, Manchester, M13 9PL

www.manchesteruniversitypress.co.uk

British Library Cataloguing-in-Publication Data
A catalogue record for this book is available from the British Library

ISBN 978 1 5261 8330 9 hardback

First published 2025

The publisher has no responsibility for the persistence or accuracy of URLs for any external or third-party internet websites referred to in this book, and does not guarantee that any content on such websites is, or will remain, accurate or appropriate.

EU authorised representative for GPSR:
Easy Access System Europe, Mustamäe tee 50, 10621 Tallinn, Estonia
gpsr.requests@easproject.com

Typeset
by New Best-set Typesetters Ltd

*To my children
Zachary and Rachel
with love always*

Contents

Introduction: Works of literature in the age of the Book of Common Prayer	*page* 1
1 Works, epitaphs, poetry	23
2 The Eucharist: Sacrificial works on stage	50
3 Purgatory and the stage	74
4 Catholic worship and devotional poetry	105
5 Mary of recusants and reform	140
6 What's in a name?: The Virgin Mary on stage	164
Concluding thoughts: Works of literature again	209
Bibliography	217
Index	246

Acknowledgements

For reading earlier drafts of this book, in whole or part, I would like to thank: David Aers, Ralph Houlbrooke, Lisa Hopkins, James Simpson and John Rist. Each brought a different expertise from which I have benefited, and I am deeply grateful for their thoughtfulness and time. I would also like to thank the anonymous readers for Manchester University Press: their comments too improved the work. Thank you to my editors, Michelle Houston and, too, Paul Clarke and Matthew Frost, and thank you also to Siân Chapman, Kate Hawkins, Michelle Gait, Rebecca Rist and Anna Rist. Above all, thank you to my family, Anna-Maija, Zachary and Rachel, who supported me at every step. I cannot thank you enough.

Introduction
Works of literature in the age of the Book of Common Prayer

This book demonstrates the continuity of Roman Catholicism in English literature from the accession of Elizabeth I in 1558 to the deposing of James II in 1689. I start with the view that, as much as Protestantism, English Catholicism was a religion of the book; and that the great gap left by sixteenth-century Protestant writing was filled by a rich, imaginative Catholic literature distributed from illegal presses.[1] Yet while studies of this process have focused on prose (with honourable attention to Robert Southwell), I focus mainly on poetry and plays. Scholars of recent years have increasingly debated the Catholic emphases of works of these kinds, sometimes extending their readings to conjectures of Catholic authorship. With poetry and plays the focus, this book is the first to argue for a continuing Catholic presence in English literature from 1558 to 1689.

The expressions of this Roman Catholicism are various and interrelated, but the book's topics fall broadly into four categories: the theology of works, Purgatory, Christian worship, and the Virgin Mary. The dominant category is the work of literature itself. Today, a 'work of literature' might seem almost a dead metaphor, meaning little more than 'a piece of writing'. Yet from medieval to present times, 'works' have denoted literary, as well as musical, compositions, especially in relation to their author, carrying what the *Oxford English Dictionary* defines as the primary connotations of work: action, labour and activity.[2] A work of literature, in these prime senses, is

---

1 See Alexandra Walsham, '"Domme Preachers"?: Post-Reformation Catholicism and the Culture of Print', *Past & Present*, 168 (2000), 72–123 (104, 122); also, 'Walsham, 'Preaching without Speaking: Script, Print and Religious Dissent', in *The Uses of Script and Print*, 1300–1700, ed. by Julia Crick and Alexandra Walsham (Cambridge: Cambridge University Press, 2004), pp. 211–34 (pp. 211–12); Earl Havens and Elizabeth Patton, 'Underground Networks: Prisons and the Circulation of Counter-Reformation Books in Elizabethan England', in *Early Modern English Catholicism: Identity, Memory and Counter-Reformation* (Leiden and Boston: Brill, 2017), pp. 165–89 (p. 168).
2 See *The Oxford English Dictionary*, 'works' (noun), definitions 1 and 16a.

one in which the work of the author (and, in the theatre, of actors) stands out. Chapters 1 and 2 attend to the theological implications of works thus understood in the literature of post-Reformation England. Establishing that, in their ideas of action, labour and activity, works of poetry and theatre engaged with theological ideas widely considered Roman Catholic from 1558 to 1689, these chapters frame English literature of the period in Roman Catholic terms. As subspecies of salvific works, the subsequent focuses of the book – Purgatory, Christian worship, and the Virgin Mary – extend this framing. It was the literary, as much as the personal, features of Southwell (1561–95), Robert Persons (1546–1610) and Edmund Campion (1540–81) which placed them at the centre of Roman Catholic culture in early modern England, both in its real and perceived forms.[3] Concerned with salvation, literary works on topics of Purgatory, Christian worship, and the Virgin Mary were extensions of this Roman Catholic, English reality.[4]

This Catholicism of works emerged against the backdrop of the Reformation, the replacement of an officially Catholic England under Mary Tudor with an officially Protestant England under Elizabeth I in 1558 and the Prayer Book of 1559. It is this Prayer Book to which 'the age of the Book of Common Prayer' in my title refers, for the Prayer Book of 1559 shaped the religion of England for centuries.[5] As a fundamental of the era, the Prayer Book of 1559 is bound up both with the Act of Supremacy (1559) and with Elizabeth I herself, since in the same year (1559), Elizabeth initiated England's religious transformation through the revised English liturgy.[6] The 'age of the Book of Common Prayer' therefore refers to an era in which Roman Catholic meanings in literature stood in contradistinction to English

---

3 Ronald Corthell, 'Writing Back: Robert Persons and the Early Modern English Subject', *Philological Quarterly*, 87/3 (2008), 277–97 (279); Thomas McCoag, '"Guiding Souls to Goodness and Devotion": Clandestine Publications and the English Jesuit Mission', in *Publishing Subversive Texts in Elizabethan England and the Polish Commonwealth*, ed. by Theresa Bela, Clarinda Calma and Jolanta Rzegocka (Leiden and Boston: Brill, 2016), pp. 93–109 (p. 94).

4 On the Catholic culture's concern with the salvation of souls, see Victor Houliston, 'Rehabilitating Robert Persons: Then and Now', in *Reformation Reputations: The Power of the Individual in English Reformation History*, ed. by David Crankshaw and George Gross (Cham, Switzerland: Palgrave Macmillan, 2021), pp. 421–47 (p. 429); Gerard Kilroy, *Edmund Campion: A Scholarly Life* (London: Routledge, 2015), p. 392. For more on the literary dimensions of this Catholic culture, see Houliston (2021), p. 428; Kilroy, pp. 187–91, 193, 383–90.

5 See Peter Blayney, *The Printing and the Printers of the Book of Common Prayer, 1549–1561* (Cambridge: Cambridge University Press, 2022), p. xvi; Timothy Rosendale, *Liturgy and Literature in the Making of Protestant England* (Cambridge: Cambridge University Press, 2007), pp. 34–69.

6 Blayney, p. 199.

religion, English law and the person of the monarch. For as we shall now see, the Prayer Book of 1559 had distinct things to say about imagination, plays and poetry and the cultural transformation which the Prayer Book produced aligned with a wider re-formation of English speech along Protestant lines. This context for the literature of the era needs attention.

The age of the Prayer Book: culture, religion, power

The Book of Common Prayer (hereafter the Prayer Book) is among the major literary monuments of early modern England. Presenting the established Church of England's order of service, it was designed to replace the Roman liturgy (in England, usually the Sarum rite) in English churches.[7] It established English as the vernacular language of the Church of England, simplifying and transforming Rome's Latin liturgy. Its attitudes to imaginative literature, which we shall come to, must be understood in these contexts. The book was authorised by Parliament in 1559, as part of a range of statutes. These formed the basis for much subsequent, coercive law relating to the established Church; the statutes required conformity to the Church of England whatever one's religious disposition.[8]

Estimates suggest that between 1549 and the 1730s there were over a million copies of the Prayer Book in circulation.[9] In the reign of James I, the Prayer Book flowed from the presses of the King's Printer, which was protected by a patent granting the 'privilege to print statutes, acts of Parliament, proclamations, injunctions, the Bible in English, service books and other books wholly or partly in English'.[10] The press thus carried out and sometimes initiated through its elite folios a royal political religious programme designed to promote an official idea of national culture.[11] Its predecessor, the Queen's Press, ran five printing presses from 1583, in contrast to the

---

7 See Aude de Mézerac-Zanetti, 'A Reappraisal of Liturgical Continuity in the Mid-Sixteenth Century: Henrician Innovations and the First Book of Common Prayer', *French Journal of British Studies*, 22/1, The Book of Common Prayer: Studies in Religious Transfer (2017), 1–11.
8 See Cyndia Clegg, 'The 1559 Books of Common Prayer and the Elizabethan Reformation', *Journal of Ecclesiastical History*, 67/1 (2016), 94–121 (94–5); Michael Questier, 'Historical Introduction', in *The Limits of Conformity in Elizabethan England: A Plea for a Priest*, ed. by Michael Questier, Camden Fifth Series, 48 (2015), 103–20 (103).
9 Brian Cummings, 'Introduction', *The Book of Common Prayer: The Texts of 1549, 1559 and 1662* (Oxford: Oxford University Press, 2011), pp. ix and x.
10 Graham Rees and Maria Wakely, *Publishing, Politics and Culture: The King's Printers in the Reign of James I and VI* (Oxford: Oxford University Press, 2010), p. 13.
11 Rees and Wakely, p. 13.

maximum two presses allowed to other printing shops in London.[12] Literary competition here is notable, as is the royal domination of English literary culture through the presses and the dominant role of the Prayer Book in that culture. In the literary milieu, the royal printers were 'eagles amongst the quarrelsome magpies and crows who otherwise represented the London book trade'.[13] Starker still is the contrast with Roman Catholic presses. Essential to the religion's survival, these were illegal and itinerant, depending for book distribution on prison networks, notably at Newgate and the Marshalsea.[14]

Yet the Prayer Book's success was gradual. Archbishop Cranmer's version of 1549 sparked rebellions in Devon and Cornwall and siege at Exeter.[15] The government's response was ferocious: 4000 insurgents were killed.[16] The 1552 Prayer Book was only briefly in use, but it was a competitive attempt to eradicate Catholic England for good and the version of 1559 contained just minor modifications.[17] Their effects were long-lasting.[18] Yet with minor revisions from the Hampton Court Conference (1604), the Elizabethan version of 1559, which had sought to restore Edwardian Protestantism, endured in England until the Ordinance for the Taking Away of the Book of Common Prayer in 1645.[19]

That reflects the continuing divide that dogged the Church of England. On the road to Civil War, there were two competing models of Christianity in the English Church.[20] The first entailed attending the local parish church or Cathedral, making use of its priest's ministrations and conformity to the

12 Rees and Wakely, p. 67.
13 Rees and Wakely, p. 66. The literary culture of the presses included the theatrical. See Lukas Erne, *Shakespeare and the Book Trade* (Cambridge: Cambridge University Press, 2013).
14 Havens and Patton, pp. 165–6; see also Kilroy, pp. 172, 259, 303.
15 Cummings (ed.) (2011a), p. xxxi.
16 Cummings (ed.) (2011a), p. xxxi; Mark Stoyle, *A Murderous Midsummer: The Western Rising of 1549* (London: Yale University Press, 2022).
17 See Cummings (ed.) (2011a), pp. xxxii and xxxiii–xxxiv; James Simpson, *Permanent Revolution: The Reformation and the Illiberal Roots of Liberalism* (Cambridge, MA and London: Harvard University Press, 2019), p. 33.
18 Cummings (ed.) (2011a), p. xxxiv.
19 See Charles Hefling, *The Book of Common Prayer: A Guide* (Oxford: Oxford University Press, 2021), p. 77; and Cummings (ed.) (2011a), p. xli. On the minor revisions of 1604, see Rees and Wakely, pp. 91–2. Cyndia Clegg writes: 'Grafton's book, the first 1559 Book of Common Prayer, was the product of a collaborative effort of Church and State, of learned divines and fit noblemen, of privy council and queen – and ultimately parliament – to restore the Church of England to Edwardian Protestantism'. See Clegg (2016), 121.
20 See Jeremy Morris, *A People's Church: A History of the Church of England* (London: Profile, 2022), p. 98.

Prayer Book: a 'conformist' position that became normal within two or three generations after 1559.[21] Conformity centred around Morning and Evening Prayer: adaptations from the five Latin 'hours', but in a new liturgy less unfamiliar.[22] The second model was the 'godly', in whom an adult 'conversion' might be expected and who rejected recreation, including drinking, dancing and singing.[23] This group rejected the liturgy, with its 'popish' residual signs and texts.[24] Beyond that were the 'recusant' Catholics, whose rising numbers in the mid-Elizabethan era show Roman Catholicism was not going to fade away.[25]

Between 1581 and 1603, a total of 191 Roman Catholics were judicially murdered; towards 80 suffered judicially sanctioned torture.[26] James I made a point only of associating rhetoric of the pope as anti-Christ with the papal claim to authority over secular princes; the Oath of Allegiance from 1606 gave Catholics the protection of the law, so long as they repudiated papal claims of authority to overthrow temporal rulers.[27] Yet this protection was limited by local Protestant magistrates.[28] Published by 150 different Roman Catholic and Protestant authors, above 500 pamphlets contributed to controversy between the churches of Rome and England between 1605 and 1625, with the King active in the anti-papalism distinguishing his reign's Protestant theology.[29] Anti-papalism ebbed as Charles I (reign: 1625–49) promoted Arminianism.[30] Among other reasons, this theology rejected Calvinist double predestination (the election of some to salvation and the reprobation of others to damnation) because: 'it represents God as decreeing something for a particular purpose that is not good, nor could it ever be good: namely that God created something for eternal damnation in order

---

21 Morris, pp. 98 and 74.
22 See Cummings (ed.) (2011a), pp. 690, 722 and 725.
23 Morris, pp. 96–7.
24 Morris, pp. 96–7. The group was also inclined to internal divisions. See Simpson (2019), p. 51; Poly Ha, 'Introduction', in *The Puritans on Independence: The First Examination, Defence and Second Examination*, ed. by Poly Ha (Oxford: Oxford University Press, 2017), pp. 6–25.
25 Peter Marshall, 'The Naming of Protestant England', *Past & Present*, 214 (2012), 87–128 (113); and Marshall, *Heretics and Believers: A History of the English Reformation* (New Haven, CT: Yale University Press, 2017), p. 526.
26 Diarmaid MacCulloch, *Reformation: Europe's House Divided, 1490–1700* (London: Penguin, 2003), p. 392; Simpson (2019), p. 36.
27 Morris, p. 96. See, also, MacCulloch (2003), pp. 513–14.
28 Morris, p. 96.
29 Anthony Milton, *Catholic and Reformed: The Roman and Protestant Churches in English Protestant Thought, 1600–1640* (Cambridge: Cambridge University Press, 1995), pp. 31–2.
30 MacCulloch (2003), p. 516; Milton, pp. 91–2, 119–20.

to praise his justice'.[31] Arminius (1560–1609) called this 'repugnant'.[32] Yet extreme Protestant positions characterised the English Church of Elizabeth I and James I.[33] In Elizabethan and early Stuart England, conformity depended entirely on the Church of England's coercive restraint of English subjects through state power.[34]

The reinstatement of the Prayer Book at the Restoration was accompanied by the harsh policy of actively excluding Catholics and dissenters from public office and freedom to worship.[35] Yet even here, where anti-Catholic ideology was fundamental, the situation was not completely resolved.[36] Although he was blocked by Parliament in 1662, and again in 1672, Charles II issued Declarations of Indulgence, suspending penal powers against both Catholics and dissenters.[37] The Duke of York's conversion to Roman Catholicism in 1668/9 (the heir to the throne, since there was no Prince of Wales) is other evidence of the era's religious irresolution, to which we turn in Chapter 6.

Why does this history matter for literary study? The answer is the continued, though disputed, authority of the Prayer Book for the period (excepting 1645–60) 1559–1689. The Prayer Book held a dominant cultural position in the reigns of Elizabeth I and James I, through their control of the presses and by law, and it was forcefully reasserted at the Restoration. Clarity about its religion is vital:

> Public prayer was constituted above all by the orders for morning and evening prayer, or Matins and Evensong. These were constructed by Cranmer from elements of the monastic offices – a sticking point for later critics who resented the retention of 'Popish' relics. But it is very doubtful that most people would have known this. Rather, these two offices were vehicles for the characteristically

---

31 Jacob Arminius, *The Theological Declaration* (1608), cited in *Arminius and his Declaration of Sentiments: An Annotated Translation with Introduction and Theological Commentary*, ed. by W. Stephen Gunter (Waco, TX: Baylor University Press, 2012), p. 113. The description of double predestination is from p. 103.
32 Gunter (ed.), p. 113.
33 Simpson (2019), p. 27. A 'spectacular Elizabethan violence' testifies to the extremity (Simpson, p. 36). England 'judicially murdered more Roman Catholics than any other country in Europe' (MacCulloch [2003], p. 391). 'No other Protestant state [except England] treated Catholicism as a capital crime': Alec Ryrie, *Protestants: The Radicals Who Made the Modern World* (London: William Collins, 2017), p. 96.
34 Ethan Shagan, *The Rule of Moderation: Violence, Religion and the Politics of Restraint in Early Modern England* (Cambridge: Cambridge University Press, 2011), p. 112.
35 Morris, p. 119.
36 Morris, p. 118; Shagan, p. 323. See also, Anthony Milton, *England's Second Reformation: The Battle for the Church of England, 1625–62*, Cambridge Studies in Early Modern History (Cambridge: Cambridge University Press, 2021), p. 485.
37 Morris, pp. 118–19.

English Protestant emphasis on good order and the reading of scripture. Scripture infused every page of the services, not just in the two readings, but in the psalmody, in the canticles such as the Jubilate (Psalm 100) and the Magnificat (Luke 146–55) and the Nunc Dimittis (Luke 2:29–32), and even in the quotations that helped to make up the responses. This combination of biblical weight and ordered uniformity was carried through into other services, chiefly those of the 'occasional' or pastoral offices of baptism, confirmation, marriage, visitation of the sick, and burial of the dead, as well as the Holy Communion. In the catechism, a reformed understanding of the sacraments is presented: there are only two sacraments, 'generally necessary to salvation', baptism and the Lord's supper; a sacrament is 'an outward and visible sign of an inward and spiritual grace given unto us, ordained by Christ himself'; bread and wine were the outward part of the communion, whereas the inward part, the 'thing signified', was the body and blood of Christ 'taken and received by the faithful'. It is true that the Prayer Book contained much that later generations could interpret or expand in a more traditional or 'Catholic' sense, but this was certainly not intended by Cranmer. The English liturgy was a Protestant liturgy: it gave expression to the key Reformation principles *of sola scriptura, sola fide,* and *sola gratia*.[38]

From a literary viewpoint, what stands out in this definition of Prayer Book religion is the reformed emphasis on 'good order and the reading of Scripture'. This message dispersed by the dominating royal printers shows the attempt of the Prayer Book to effect reformation by turning England into a country of obedient scripture readers.[39] This implies antipathy to other forms of literary expression, and we shall see that the Prayer Book addresses some of these forms directly. Yet it is worth noting the broader religious context of this literary putsch.

Along with the *Thirty-nine Articles of Religion*, the Prayer Book drew heavily on a recognisably reformed, continental model.[40] Opposition to the Catholic theology of works (Article 12, 'Of Good Works') is relevant, but more important at this stage is an implied attitude to literature. The Protestant stress on scripture meant each Reformation practice was traceable to this book.[41] The stress also intensified the 'basic aesthetic question' of how to present God through human artefacts without falling into idolatry.[42] Before

---

38 Morris, pp. 81–2.
39 See also Diarmaid MacCulloch, *The Later Reformation in England, 1547–1603*, 2nd edn., British History in Perspective (Basingstoke: Palgrave Macmillan, 2001), pp. 72–3.
40 Morris, p. 82; Diarmaid MacCulloch, *All Things Made New: Writings on the Reformation* (London: Penguin, 2017), pp. 142–45.
41 Simpson (2019), p. 262.
42 On this question, see Gary Kuchar, 'Poetry and Sacrament in the English Renaissance', in *A Companion to English Poetry*, ed. by Catherine Bates (Hoboken NJ; Chichester: Wiley Blackwell, 2018), pp. 51–62 (p. 51).

1640, Protestant writing was therefore at once dominated by the Bible and Biblicism: a domination largely to continue beyond 1650.[43] When Protestants wrote, in England, the ambition was texts that were patchworks or mosaics of scripture.[44] Genres were confined to diary-keeping, autobiographical writing, transcribing, commonplacing, paraphrasing or versifying scripture.[45] The Prayer Book is both a consequence and main cause of this Protestant English literary (if not Literary) culture.[46]

Signalling its scriptural values, most of the Prayer Book text derives verbatim from scripture.[47] The justification for this in the 'Preface' is a long list of alleged Roman Catholic corruptions, many of which are literary and in contrast with scripture: 'uncertain stories, Legendes, Respondes, Verses, vain repetitions, Commemoracions, and Synodalles'.[48] These literary and verbal forms stand starkly against 'God's worde', 'daily hearing of holy scripture read in the Church', 'bokes of holy scripture', 'the very pure word of God' and 'the holy scriptures'.[49] The Prayer Book is thus both an example of a scriptural mosaic and (in its Preface) a justification of scripture over rival literary forms. Since the rival forms are grouped as uncertain, vain, and Roman Catholic, the Prayer Book distinguishes between the sheep of scripture and the goat of alternative literature. It is a distinction expressing the anti-papalism of Thomas Cranmer, author of the Preface.[50] Yet embraced

---

43 Alec Ryrie, *Being Protestant in Reformation Britain* (Oxford: Oxford University Press, 2013), pp. 299–317; and (on the dates), p. 4; Thomas Fulton, *The Book of Books: Biblical Interpretation, Literary Culture, and the Political Imagination from Erasmus to Milton* (Philadelphia: University of Pennsylvania Press, 2021), especially pp. 233, 246 and 257.
44 Ryrie (2013), p. 304.
45 Ryrie (2013), pp. 299–317.
46 Within England's Protestant culture of the Bible, the distinction was only between Biblicism and 'anti-literalists'. See Simpson (2019), pp. 312–13. See also Susannah Brietz Monta, '"A Sweetness ready penn'd?" English Religious Poetics in the Reformation Era', in *A Companion to Renaissance Poetry*, pp. 63–77 (p. 70); Cummings observes that even biblical literature – even the psalms – were 'not uncontroversial', noting the 1539 Act of Six Articles as 'unpropitious for any act of literature'. See Brian Cummings, *The Literary Culture of the Reformation: Grammar and Grace* (Oxford and New York: Oxford University Press, 2003), p. 236. Elizabethan and Stuart writers became bolder with 'biblically inflected advice books of the previous generation' (Fulton, p. 257).
47 Hefling, p. 90.
48 'The Preface', *The Book of Common Prayer*, p. 4. As a 'proceeding from a synod' (*OED*, 'synodal', definition 1a), a 'synodal' has literary dimensions, so I include it among the other literary forms mentioned here.
49 'The Preface', *The Book of Common Prayer*, pp. 4–5.
50 On Cranmer's anti-papalism and authorship of the Preface, see Milton (1995), p. 31; Hefling, p. 83.

by Protestant archbishops of Canterbury from Cranmer (1489–1556) to George Abbot (1562–1633), anti-papal distinctions cut through every boundary in the English Church.[51]

Is there an acceptable or neutral space between scripture and Romanist writing in the Prayer Book? The very opening of the Preface rules this out in an axiomatic criticism of human creativity:

> There was never any thing by the wit of man so well devised, or so surely established, which (in the continuance of time) hath not been corrupted; as (among other thinges) it may plainly appere by the common prayers in the Church, commonlye called divine service …[52]

Presented as an axiomatic truth, failure in every form of wit and human imagination ('any thing by the wit of man devised') is the founding principle of common prayer, divine service, and their revision in the Prayer Book. The Prayer Book's founding argument for replacing Roman Catholic religion depends at once on a scripture-based opposition to that religion and a hostile presentation of other imaginative activity in general. This Protestant threat to poetry (and art) is the first principle of both the Prayer Book and the Church of England.[53]

In fact, the general objection to imagination in the Preface expands more specific objections to imaginative and verbal activity. In unabridged versions of the 1559 Prayer Book (which remained standard until the mid-seventeenth

---

51 Milton (1995), p. 31.
52 'The Preface', *The Book of Common Prayer*, p. 4. In the 1662 edition, these phrases appear under the new title 'Concerning the Service of the Church'. See *The Book of Common Prayer*, p. 212.
53 For more on this Protestant threat, see James Simpson, *Burning to Read: English Fundamentalism and its Reformation Opponents* (Cambridge, MA and London: Harvard University Press, 2007); Simpson, *Under the Hammer: Iconoclasm and the Anglo-American Tradition* (Oxford: Oxford University Press, 2010). The Protestant threat to 'poetry and art' was observed earlier by Gerrish. See B. A. Gerrish, *Grace and Gratitude: The Eucharistic Theology of John Calvin* (Minneapolis: Fortress Press, 1993), pp. 165–7. In a brief discussion, by contrast, Sophie Read claimed that Protestant fascination with the uses of rhetoric (especially as seen in the Prayer Book) produced a culture of poetry. Yet she considers none of the evidence from the Prayer Book presented here. Her approach derives largely from Cummings's *The Literary Culture of the Reformation: Grammar and Grace* (2003), so moving 'too quickly' (in Molly Murray's phrase) from the Protestant fascination with grammar to English poetry. See Sophie Read, *Eucharist and the Poetic Imagination in Early Modern England* (Cambridge: Cambridge University Press, 2013), pp. 29–30; Molly Murray, *The Poetics of Conversion in Early Modern English Literature: Verse and Change from Donne to Dryden* (Cambridge: Cambridge University Press, 2009), p. 98. In his most recent discussion, Simpson argues that Protestant alarm at poetry and art in England developed in three phases. See Simpson (2019), pp. 161–2.

century) the Preface follows the printed Act of Uniformity, which addresses 'Enterludes, Playes, Songs, Rimes' and 'open words' associated with them.[54] In the Act of Uniformity, these media are condemned only when 'in the derogation, depriving, or despising' of the Prayer Book. Yet placed before the Preface in the Prayer Book, these verbal, literary and dramatic media suggest salient examples of imagination's axiomatic corruption. While the Preface decries human imagination generally, in the Prayer Book the Act of Uniformity builds towards that condemnation through a more limited disapproval highlighting literature. In this the 1559 Prayer Book is evangelical: evangelicals detested imagination and opposed 'poetry'.[55]

Especially though not only through the Preface, then, Prayer Book religion seemingly contributed to an English Protestant culture promoting scriptural writing ('mosaics' and 'patchworks') over any other form. Together with the Act of Uniformity, the prefatory essays which open the Prayer Book are vital expressions of its status and purpose.[56] The question arising is why and how, nevertheless, the very wide-ranging literature of the era flourished. Yet before turning to that question, it is worth pondering quite how limited the disapproval of literature in the Act of Uniformity really was.

The Act foregrounds what was 'Enacted by the Queen's Highness, with the assent of the Lords and Commons of this present Parliament assembled, and by Authority of the Same'.[57] Punishments are threatened to transgressors, the first of whom are ministers of the church who stray from the Prayer Book's verbal formulae 'in such order and form, as they be mentioned, and set forth in the said Book'.[58] The second transgressors are the open words, plays, rhymes, songs and, broadly, literature aforementioned:

> And it is Ordained, and Enacted by the Authority aforesaid, That if any person, or persons whatsoever, after the Feast of the Nativity of Saint John Baptist next coming, shall in any Enterludes, Playes, Songs, Rimes, or by other open words declare, or speak any thing in the derogation, depriving, or despising of the same Book, or of any thing therein contained, or any part therof ... That then every such person, being thereof lawfully convicted in form abovesaid, shall forfeit to the Queen our Sovereign Lady, her Heirs, and Successors, Four hundred marks: And if any person, or persons, being once convict of any such offence, eftsoons offend against any of the last recited offences, and shall in form aforesaid be thereof lawfully convict; That then the same person, of offending and convict, shall for the second offence forfeit to the Queen our Sovereign Lady, Her Heirs and Successors, four hundred marks: And if any

54 *The Book of Common Prayer*, pp. 188–9.
55 Simpson (2007), p. 279.
56 Hefling, p. 76.
57 *The Book of Common Prayer*, p. 187.
58 *The Book of Common Prayer*, p. 187.

person, after in form aforesaid shall have been twice convict of any offence concerning any of the last recited offences, shall offend the third time, and be thereof in form abovesaid lawfully convict; That then every person so offending and convict, shall for his third offence, forfeit to our Sovereign Lady all his Goods and Chattels; and shall suffer imprisonment during his life; And if any person ...[59]

On the face of it, the concern here is to ward off satires of the Prayer Book. Yet to understand this fierce passage, one may need to consider its key terms closely. Especially where religion was concerned, the 'communicative space' between Elizabethan punishers and defendants routinely entailed 'a multiplicity of possibilities, of interpretations and appropriations, of meanings and understandings'.[60] The passage, then, is open to broader interpretation. Since the semantic field of English Protestants in 1558 grouped theatre with literature, black magic, popular superstition, idolatry and the Catholic Mass, broad understanding of the passage seems likely.[61]

What, then, do literary 'derogation, depriving, or despising' mean? And what do the terms mean in relation to the Prayer Book? 'Despising' implies viewing with contempt or scorn, and so satire.[62] Yet in relation to material things (like the Prayer Book) it also has a wider, figurative meaning: 'to set at nought'; to 'disregard'.[63] Disregarding the Prayer Book (very different

---

59 *The Book of Common Prayer*, pp. 188–9.
60 Photini Danou, 'Catholic Treason Trials in Elizabethan England. Complexities and Ambiguities in the Stage Management of a Public Show: The Case of William Parry', *Journal of Early Modern History*, 14 (2010), 393–415 (414). More generally, early modern England was deeply concerned with the construal of law. See Ian Williams, 'A Medieval Book and Early Modern Law: *Bracton*'s Authority and Application in the Common Law, c.1550–1640', *The Legal History Review*, 79 (2011), 47–80 (49–50). In sixteenth-century construal of acts of parliament, context and intent were deemed as important as literal meanings. See Denis Kurzon, 'Literal Interpretation and Political Expediency: The Case of Thomas More', in *Legal Pragmatics*, ed. by Dennis Kurzon and Barbara Kryl-Kastovsky, Pragmatics and Beyond New Series, 288 (Amsterdam and Philadelphia: John Benjamins Publishing Company, 2018), pp. 81–97 (p. 82). Context and intent are routinely important in this respect. See L. Millett, 'Construing Statutes', *Statute Law Review*, 20/2 (1999), 107–10; Nicholas Allott and Benjamin Shaer, 'Inference and Intention in Legal Interpretation', in *The Pragmatic Turn in Law: Inference and Interpretation in Legal Discourse*, ed. by Janet Giltrow and Dieter Stein, Mouton Series in Pragmatics, 18 (Boston and Berlin: De Gruyter Mouton, 2017), pp. 83–118. For good discussion of the context and intent of the Act of Uniformity, see Stephen Alford, *Burghley: William Cecil at the Court of Elizabeth I* (New Haven, CT, and London: Yale University Press, 2008), pp. 97–102.
61 On the semantic field, see Simpson (2019), p. 215.
62 On 'despising' in these terms, see 'despise' (verb) in the *OED*, definitions 1, 2 and 3.
63 See 'despise' (verb), definition 3b in the *OED*.

from satirising it) is thus in the purview of condemnation. Many works of literature of the era might have been said to 'despise' the Prayer Book in the sense of insufficiently regarding it.

'Depriving', too, has challengingly open connotations. To deprive persons of a thing (like the Prayer Book) means to divest, strip, or bereave them of that thing; to take it away from them.[64] The term has technical, ecclesiastical meanings too: to inflict deprivation of ecclesiastical office upon a person.[65] Yet no literature can forcibly take something from a person, so the meaning of 'deprived' is metaphorical. In relation to the Prayer Book, 'deprived' might therefore mean distracted from, connotating a spiritual deprivation. Many forms of literature (among the kinds named by the Act) might be open to charges of deprivation of the kind.

Most striking of all is the term 'derogation'. In the era, 'derogation' meant taking away (in part) the power or authority of a person or thing; weakening or impairing its (or their) authority.[66] Literature derogating the Prayer Book, therefore, is literature undermining the *authority* of the Prayer Book. Satire is one means to that end, yet it is authority, not the means of undermining it, which 'derogation' puts at stake. Since the authority of the Prayer Book extended from the Queen, the Lords and Commons to the ritual actions and theology which the Prayer Book propagated, any literary interlude, play, song, rhyme, or open words weakening that authority is within the scope of the Act of Uniformity.

The decisive question is what is meant in the passage by the Prayer Book: 'the same Book'. As Patrick Collinson observes, the Prayer Book, 'in the eyes of the law, was no more than an appendix to an act of parliament, the Act of Uniformity of 1559'.[67] In law, therefore, derogating, depriving or despising the Prayer Book meant disrupting the Act of Uniformity: the basis of Elizabethan Protestantism which (with the Act of Supremacy) defined Elizabeth as head of both church and state and was the foundation of her control of the press.[68] In Elizabeth's reign, at once, the passage from the Act of Uniformity opens the government's gradual tightening of control over theatre.[69] As part of the Act of Uniformity, the Prayer Book thus seems

---

64 See 'deprive' (verb 1a) in the *OED*.
65 See 'deprive' (verb) in the *OED*, definition 2.
66 See definition 2 of 'derogation', noun, in the *OED*.
67 Patrick Collinson, 'The Politics of Religion and the Religion of Politics in Elizabethan England', *Historical Research: The Bulletin of the Institute of Historical Research*, 82 (2009), 74–92 (75).
68 Cyndia Clegg, *Press Censorship in Elizabethan England* (Cambridge: Cambridge University Press, 1997), p. 30.
69 Simpson (2019), p. 224; Jonas Barish, *The Antitheatrical Prejudice* (Berkeley: University of California Press, 1981), p. 83.

an initial blast in the Protestant 'programme of social control' through speech reform of sixteenth- and seventeenth-century England.[70]

Yet how to explain, in this repressive culture, the flourishing of literature? How to explain Spenser and Milton? Already in his first collection of poems, the *Poems of Mr John Milton, both English and Latin* (1645), Milton recognised that his learning and Christian faith were contradictory.[71] He would come to see scripture alone as necessary for Christian education and every form of school as unnecessary and a barrier.[72] The principal source of *Paradise Lost* (first edition: 1667; second edition: 1674) is the Bible: the poem's relationship with scripture is more intimate than with any other work.[73] Like Milton's other late poems, *Paradise Regained* and *Samson Agonistes* (published 1671), *Paradise Lost* is a scriptural mosaic: of the utmost sophistication, yet in the Protestant tradition I have identified. In *Paradise Regained*, Milton makes Jesus maintain that classical learning can be entirely derived from scripture.[74] The broad trajectory from 1645 to the later poems shows that Milton resolved the contradictions he found in learning and scripture as a scriptural Protestant.[75]

Answers more fundamental are in Spenser (1552–99). Spenser was committed to scripture.[76] Driving his literary career, therefore, was a need to

---

70 Hugh Gazzard, 'An Act to Restrain Abuses of Players (1606)', *The Review of English Studies*, 61/251 (2010), 495–528 (522). For more on Protestant speech reform, see Simpson, pp. 261–4; 223–30; Peter Horsfield, *From Jesus to the Internet: A History of Christianity and Media* (Chichester: Wiley-Blackwell, 2015), pp. 192–207; Cyndia Clegg (1997); Clegg, *Press Censorship in Jacobean England* (Cambridge: Cambridge University Press, 2004); Clegg, *Press Censorship in Caroline England* (Cambridge: Cambridge University Press, 2008); Brian Capp, *England's Culture Wars: Puritan Reformation and its Enemies in the Interregnum, 1649–1660* (Oxford: Oxford University Press, 2012), pp. 87–109, 198–256. On Elizabethan authorities enforcing stretched legal definitions of forbidden words (of 1571 and 1581) to suit their purposes, see Mark Rankin, 'Richard Topcliffe and the Book Culture of the Elizabethan Catholic Underground', *Renaissance Quarterly*, 72 (2019), 492–536 (497–8).
71 Andrew Hui, 'The Soundscape of the Dying Pagan Gods in Milton's *Nativity Ode*', *Modern Language Quarterly* 78/3 (September 2017), 349–72 (369).
72 Matt Rickard, 'Milton and the Education Monopoly', *Studies in Philology*, 119/3 (Summer 2022), 495–525 (513).
73 Alasdair Fowler, 'Introduction', in *Milton: Paradise Lost*, 2nd edn (London and New York: Pearson Longman, 2007), pp. 1–48 (p. 10).
74 Rickard, 523.
75 See also Fulton, pp. 200–48. In biblical exegesis, Milton would eventually give some place to natural reason over Protestant literalism (Fulton, p. 246).
76 See Gillian Hubbard, 'Stoics, Epicureans and the "sound sincerity of the gospel" in book 2 of Spenser's *The Faerie Queene*', *Studies in Philology*, 111/2 (2014), 225–54. Hubbard contrasts her view to two older (and contradictory) views of Spenser: that he is a Thomist who sees nature as perfected by grace, or that he follows Melanchthon in keeping the domains of nature and grace separate (Hubbard, 226–7).

invent religious 'traditions', which would answer the consistent question from Catholics: 'Where was your religion before Martin Luther?'[77] Spenser is, thus, of a group of writers aiming to create a vernacular, learned, Protestant culture for England.[78] Yet *The Faerie Queen* is divided; so much so that it perhaps became unfinishable.[79] The contradiction centred on a medieval era 'when papistry as a standing pool covered and overflowed all England' (in Roger Ascham's words) and it provided militant Protestants, including the poets of Spenser's circle, with a dichotomy for centuries.[80] The answer to the question 'How did English Literature flourish among scripture-centred Protestant poets?' is now clear: the poets resisted the reductively scriptural biases in the Prayer Book and wider Protestantism through proto-Catholic inventions.

In Protestant poetics, this fictional medievalism gave rise to resistances both cultural and political.[81] The resistance included classical culture: Protestants made an explicit equation between medieval Catholicism and the heathen religion of the Gentiles; and medieval Roman Catholicism (which was not Biblicist) made room for pagan ideas within reason, especially in Aquinas.[82] Since we shall later turn to Roman Plays and Purgatory (ascribed

---

77 Andrew Hadfield, 'Spenser and Religion – Yet Again', *Studies in English Literature*, 51/1 (Winter 2011), 21–46 (21).

78 Christine Hutchins, 'English Anti-Petrarchism: Imbalance and Excess in "the English straine" of the Sonnet', *Studies in Philology*, 109/5 (2012), 552–80 (558).

79 See Richard Helgerson, *Forms of Nationhood: The Elizabethan Writing of England* (Chicago and London: The University of Chicago Press, 1988), p. 54; Gary Waller, *The Virgin Mary in Late Medieval and Early Modern English Literature and Popular Culture* (Cambridge: Cambridge University Press, 2011), p. 120. Still more recently, Andrew Carlson shows how the Spenserian stanza 'habitually generates figures of its own failure'. See Carlson, 'Monstrous Length in Spenser's *Faerie Queene*', *English Literary History*, 86/2 (2019), 441–65 (461).

80 Helgerson, p. 42 (quoting Ascham) and p. 62. On Spenser's circle as militantly Protestant, see p. 59. The contradiction seems also to have troubled earlier Protestant poets, for example the Neo-Latinist John Parkhurst. Parkhurst had moral reservations about his poetry but overcame them especially at the example of (Roman Catholic) Thomas More. As bishop of Norwich, Parkhurst seems later to have regretted his poetry. He died in 1575. See James Binns, 'John Parkhurst and the Traditions of Classical Latin Poetry in Sixteenth-Century England', *International Journal of the Classical Tradition*, 1/1 (Summer 1994), 52–61 (54–5, 61).

81 Helgerson, p. 60.

82 See Alexandra Walsham, *The Reformation of the Landscape: Religion, Identity, and Memory in Early Modern Britain and Ireland* (Oxford: Oxford University Press, 2011), p. 85; Justin Anderson, *Virtue and Grace in the Theology of Thomas Aquinas* (Cambridge: Cambridge University Press, 2020), pp. 222–47; James Arthur, *A Christian Education in the Virtues: Character Formation and Human Flourishing* (London: Routledge, 2021), pp. 25 and 40.

Introduction 15

by English Protestants to pagan 'fantasies') this medieval distinction from Protestant Biblicism bears emphasis.[83]

Yet add to the proto-Catholic purview the early modern Catholic continuities we have observed so far in England (viz., the rise of recusancy under Elizabeth I, prompts from Persons and Campion, the partial support for Catholicism under James I on the road to Civil War and the attempts at Catholic toleration of Charles II) and English literature 1558–1689 looks far from Protestant, especially by the Prayer Book's scriptural definition of literature. Add further, by contrast, such influential Catholic figures as Southwell and Queen Henrietta Maria and this same English literature begins to seem a proto-Catholic, Roman Catholic blur. Clarifying the Roman Catholic is the aim of this book. It is time (despite advances) that the substantive basis of English literature 1558–1689 in Roman Catholicism is recognised.[84]

Not everyone has interpreted proto-Catholicism in this era as resistance. Keith Thomas, notably, saw the 'fabulous past' of Elizabethan England as nostalgia.[85] Yet the claim is misleading. Since Protestant England began well after the accession of Elizabeth I (as Collinson and Eamon Duffy agree) one should not assume reading practices of the era were uniform.[86] Study of Elizabethan reading confirms this.[87] Yet so does Spenser. From the 1590 edition, and with the Geneva Bible his main field of reference, the Elizabethan John Dixon read the first book of *The Faerie Queen* as an allegory of England's Reformation.[88] Yet a reader of Spenser's 1611 edition

---

83 On English Protestants ascribing Purgatory to the pagans, see Peter Marshall, *Beliefs and the Dead in Reformation England* (Oxford and New York: Oxford University Press, 2002), p. 143. I return to pagan religion in relation to Pope Pius II (and Roman plays) in Chapter 2. I return to (very rare) exceptions to Church of England Biblicism in Chapter 1; see, too, the concluding chapter.

84 Advances have especially arisen since Alison Shell's *Catholicism, Controversy and the English Literary Imagination, 1558–1660* (Cambridge: Cambridge University Press, 1999); many of them are cited in this book.

85 Keith Thomas, 'The Perception of the Past in Early Modern England', in *The Creighton Century, 1907–2007*, ed. by David Bates, Jennifer Wallis and Jane Winters (London: University of London Press, Institute of Historical Research, 2009), pp. 185–218 (pp. 187, 202).

86 See Patrick Collinson, *The Birthpangs of Protestant England* (Basingstoke: Palgrave Macmillan, 1988), p. ix; Eamon Duffy, *Saints, Sacrilege and Sedition: Religion and Conflict in the Tudor Reformations* (London, Berlin, New York, Sidney: Bloomsbury, 2012), p. 6. See also, Marshall (2017), p. 538.

87 See Margaret Connolly, *Sixteenth-Century Readers, Fifteenth-Century Books: Continuities of Reading in the English Reformation*, Cambridge Studies in Palaeography and Codicology (Cambridge: Cambridge University Press, 2019), pp. 243–4; see also Rosendale (2007), p. 110.

88 Fulton, p. 169.

contemptuously perceived in it Catholic representations.[89] Neither reader is nostalgic; they are 'polarised by religious zeal'.[90] Together with disputes over the words of institution at the Eucharist, the Bible made post-Reformation culture fundamentally hermeneutical.[91] The effect was felt in every direction.[92] It made literature (in general) a major locus of theology.[93]

Monuments, works, chapters

At the centre of Spenser's uncertainty were monuments, from which in his poetry arise tensions between paganism, Christianity, iconoclasm, and idolatry.[94] The tensions are of the age. In 1582, the Jesuit Robert Persons observed the monuments of England 'yet extant to the world' as follows:

> our forefathers the sainctes of God, were most diligent and carefull in doinge good workes in their daies ... the infinite monumentes of their almes deedes, yet extant to the worlde, are sufficient testimonies of the same ... so manye bishopprickes, deaneryes, archdeaconeryes, Cannonyres, prebends, chauntyres, and the like: ... so many Abbayes, Nunries, Priaries, hermitages.[95]

Persons's text was influential: it is linked with Robert Greene, William Shakespeare, Thomas Nashe, Thomas Middleton, and John Donne.[96] Published in 1584, a Calvinist version scrupulously removed its mentions of salvific works, including the ecclesiastical monuments listed here.[97] Yet the landscape of England was replete with memorials. Around them swirled myths, oral and written, of the pagan and Roman Catholic past. Iconoclasm, propaganda

---

89 Fulton, p. 168.
90 Fulton, p. 169.
91 Fulton, p. 249; Rosendale (2007), pp. 133–4.
92 Rosendale (2007), p. 176.
93 Fulton, p. 256.
94 Andrew Hui, *The Poetics of Ruins in Renaissance Literature* (New York: Fordham University Press, 2017), pp. 177–8.
95 Robert Persons, SJ, *The Christian Directory (1582), The First Book of the Christian Exercise Appertayninig to Resolution*, ed. by Victor Houliston (Leiden, Boston and Cologne: Brill, 1998), p. 33.
96 On the links to these authors, see Houliston (ed.), pp. xi–xiv; John Yamamoto-Wilson, 'Robert Persons's Resolution (1582) and the Issue of Textual Piracy in Protestant Editions of Catholic Devotional Literature', *Reformation & Renaissance Review*, 15/2 (2015), 177–98 (192); Hannibal Hamlin, *The Bible in Shakespeare* (Oxford: Oxford University Press, 2013), pp. 314–19.
97 See Brad Gregory, '"The True and Zealous Service of God": Robert Persons, Edmund Bunny, and the First Book of the Christian Exercise', *Journal of Ecclesiastical History*, 45/2 (1994), 238–68 (248, 252).

Introduction

and the disciplinary initiatives of bishops, ministers and elders conspired radically to reconstitute, if not to sever, those myths.[98] 'Monuments', a word punctuating Spenser's career, reveal reformed England's paradox.[99]

They also reveal attitudes to works, theological and literary. Monuments, works, and literature are of similar connotation and share intellectual terrain. As 'things made', monuments, like works of literature, are material.[100] Monuments and literature present figures: of speech and matter. In literature, the work is revealed in studies of early modern translation, where the intermediate state of the translator, between an original text and its translation, focuses attention on the translator's work as that of an artifex.[101] Yet as training in the writing and delivering of speeches, rhetoric is important.[102] Training, schooling, learning – each entail work. Without deep study, 'studia humanitatis' is impossible. Yet the humanist work of rhetoric was transformed in northern Europe, especially by Philipp Melanchthon (1497–1560).

Friend of Luther and author of that fundamental statement of Lutheran doctrine, the Augsburg confession (1530), Melanchthon was also the dominant rhetorician of north European humanism.[103] His rhetorical influence continued in the seventeenth century; in England almost every sixteenth-century rhetoric echoed him after 1530.[104] Yet his effect on rhetoric was a 'drastic alteration of function'.[105] Wedded to *sola scriptura*, Melanchthon turned rhetoric towards hermeneutics, so making rhetoric the communal key, for Protestants, for interpreting scripture's singular and literal meaning.[106] To Melanchthon, then, in large part goes credit for Protestant Biblicism in England, including in the Prayer Book. *Sola scriptura* its origin, his hermeneutic rhetoric of the Bible defined Protestant writing communities. Yet despite its theological inflections from the reigns of Elizabeth I to Charles II, English Literature

---

98 Walsham (2011), pp. 471–72.
99 On 'moniments' punctuating Spenser's career, see Hui (2017), p. 177. Hui seeks to pinpoint where Spenser stood amid the paradoxes; the reading is offset by Stuart Mottram, *Ruins and Reformation in Spenser, Shakespeare and Marvell* (Oxford: Oxford University Press, 2019), pp. 24–91.
100 See *OED*, 'works' (noun), definition 12.
101 Jaimie Goodrich, *Faithful Translators: Authorship, Gender and Religion in Early Modern England* (Evanston, IL: Northwestern University Press, 2014), p. 9.
102 On rhetoric so defined, see Peter Mack, *A History of Renaissance Rhetoric* (Oxford and New York: Oxford University Press, 2011), p. 1.
103 Mack, pp. 104 and 106.
104 Mack, p. 129; Michael Kearney, 'Melanchthon's Dialectic Genre and the Rhetoric of Reformation', *Rhetorica*, 40/1 (2022), 23–42 (27).
105 Kearney, 25; Hans-George Gadamer, 'Rhetoric and Hermeneutics', trans. Joel Weinsheimer, in *Rhetoric and Hermeneutics in our Time*, ed. by Walter Jost and Michael Hyde (New Haven, CT: Yale University Press, 1997), p. 48.
106 Kearney, 38; Mack, p. 119.

(capital E, capital L) was never regularly reducible either to Biblicism or to the Bible.[107] Wider in scope, English Literature worked to different ends.

The work of literature is therefore the dominant literary category of this study. Examining the shared intellectual terrain of literary works and monuments, Chapter 1 closely considers the relation of epitaphs to poetry. Beginning in the reign of Elizabeth I, the chapter shows that epitaphs reflected on their literary and material work theologically, while readers recognised and imagined the theological meaning. In *The Works of Ben Jonson*, the poet (a Roman Catholic from 1598 to 1610) adapted and developed this monumental theology, leaving a legacy of literary work still heard in John Dryden at the end of the seventeenth century.

Chapter 2 turns to sacrificial works in the memorial of the Eucharist on stage. Of particular importance here is Augustine's *City of God*. The edition of Juan Luis Vives, which was the canonical text from 1529 to *c*.1680, stresses the importance of the works of the faithful in the Sacrifice of the Mass. The chapter explores the conjunction of works, monuments, drama and Christian sacrifice in three plays: Jonson's *Sejanus his Fall* (1603), Shakespeare's *Julius Caesar* (1599), and John Ford's *Love's Sacrifice* (published 1633). The Jonsonian emphasis on works in Chapter 1 thus develops into Jonson's Eucharistic works in Chapter 2, but the wider display of this second chapter is theological theatre in Jacobean, Elizabethan and Caroline England.

The dominant category of works thus established in poetry and drama, the book turns to subordinate matters of literary theology. Chapter 3 considers Elizabethan drama in the context of Article 22 of the Church of England ('Of Purgatory'), especially its capacious definition of 'Romish doctrine'. Through this legal and religious definition of the realm, the chapter interprets English theatre in a period roughly corresponding with Spenser's literary career. The theatre emerging is haunted by Catholicism. By the Protestant standards of the day defined by Article 22, histories, comedies and revenge tragedies on stage in the period are Romish, in contravention to England's established religion.

Chapter 4 examines the Church of England through the attitudes to worship of four of its priests. The poetry is by Richard Crashaw (1612–48), George Herbert (1593–1633), Robert Herrick (1591–1674) and John Donne (1572–1631). Deeply influenced by Robert Southwell, among other Catholic

---

107 On English Literature's theological inflection in the period, see Timothy Rosendale, *Theology and Agency in Early Modern Literature* (Cambridge: Cambridge University Press, 2018). For a still wider purview, see David Aers, *Versions of Election: From Langland and Aquinas to Calvin and Milton*, ReFormations: Medieval and Early Modern (Notre Dame, IN: Notre Dame University Press, 2020); Aers, *Salvation and Sin: Augustine, Langland, and Fourteenth-Century Theology* (Notre Dame, IN: Notre Dame University Press, 2009).

sources, this poetry spanning the sixteenth and seventeenth centuries conveys forms of worship contravening Church of England sermons like 'Against the Peril of Idolatry' in the *Book of Homilies*. As the chapter shows, the poetry also stands in a problematic relation to emerging Laudianism and is not sufficiently explained by this Church of England variant. The forms of worship found in this clerical poetry shows Roman Catholic deviations in the heart of the developing Church of England.

Chapters 5 and 6 focus on the Virgin Mary as a counter-definer of the Reformation. Chapter 5 considers sixteenth- and seventeenth-century poetry about Mary in the light of Protestant iconoclasm, removal of Mary from English prayer and the restricting of Protestant views of Mary to the evidence of scripture. The poetry of Henry Constable and Richard Verstegan, both recusants, stands out in this respect, as does the recusant Jonson of 'On my first daughter' (1600) and his 'An Epigram to the Queen' of 1630. By contrast, Protestant presentations of Mary limit her along scriptural lines, but in poems after 'The Wracks of Walsingham' the limits also signal crises in national religion.

Chapter 6 presents Marian figurations in the different theatres of Elizabethan, Jacobean, Caroline and Restoration England. In Anthony Munday's Robin Hood plays, the figurations stand out in Maid Marian and the convent. Some of these aspects of Robin Hood remain in *The Roaring Girl* (1611) and still more in Robert Davenport's *King John and Matilda*, which was performed around 1630 and printed in 1655. Dekker and Middleton's city comedy develops 'Moll' along lines of the English Ladies of Mary Ward (1585–1645), as well as of popular transvestite saints of medieval Europe like St Margarita-Pelagius. Davenport, by contrast, argues for England's religious obedience to Rome as a member of Queen Henrietta Maria's players. On stage and elsewhere, this 'Maria' vigorously promoted convents and Catholic figurations of Mary, while Margaret Cavendish and Thomas Killigrew, both members of the queen's circle before the Civil War, differently echo the figurations later in the century. The chapter ends with theatre in the Exclusion Crisis (1679–81) and the Popish Plot (1678–81). In Aphra Behn's *The Rover* (based on Killigrew's *Thomaso*) and *The Younger Brother* (probably from the late 1680s; published 1696), Marian figurations through convents express both libertine and recusant meanings at the close of the seventeenth century.

Through different times and moments, *The Catholicism of literature in the age of the Book of Common Prayer* thus demonstrates the continuity of Roman Catholicism in English Literature from the accession of Elizabeth I in 1558 to the deposing of James II in 1689. Just four more points of introduction are needed.

The first is a clarification of terms important in early modern debates about salvation. We have already noted Protestant 'Arminianism': an anti-Calvinist theology in which grace-enabled free will meant people participated in their own salvation.[108] Still focused on salvation, we also understand the following: 1. Pelagianism. Condemned at the councils of Carthage (AD 418) and Ephesus (AD 431), this asserts the sufficient goodness of human persons to move to God by virtue and free choice of the will; 2. Lutheranism. Derived from Martin Luther (1483–1546), this maintains that faith in Christ, not human merit, is the only means of salvation; 3. Calvinism. Named after John Calvin (1509–64), this adds to Luther's view of faith the doctrine of double predestination: that every person is predestined to heaven or to hell;[109] 4. Laudianism. Referring to William Laud (Archbishop of Canterbury, 1633–45) and his followers, this term, still debated by historians, links the ceremonial policies of the 1630s Church of England with Arminianism.[110] Of course, early modern word usages were not absolute: we will occasionally encounter variants.

The next point concerns nomenclature. In what follows, I save words by referring to Roman Catholicism as 'Catholicism' or 'Catholic'. This is historically justified. We have already seen that despite later 'Catholic' interpretations, the English liturgy was a Protestant liturgy expressing the key principles of *sola scriptura*, *sola fide* and *sola gratia* (scripture alone, faith alone, grace alone).[111] The same emphases are in the two *Books of Homilies* (1547 and 1562) and the *Thirty-nine Articles of Religion*. The *Thirty-nine Articles* draw heavily on Continental reformed models.[112] Of special relevance to this study are that human beings have *no* power in themselves to do good works 'without the grace of God by Christ preventing [i.e. going before] us' (Article 10, 'Of Free Will'); and that only through the merit of Christ could we be 'accounted righteous before God' (Article 11, 'Of the Justification of Man').[113] The *Books of Homilies*, meanwhile, show 'consonance' with the main points of Reformation soteriology, confirming a late sixteenth-century Church of England 'essentially aligned to north European Protestantism' in its theology.[114]

How far even Protestant poetics were from this model is the third point. In complete contrast to Articles 10 and 11, in the *Apology for Poetry* Sir

---

108 See Roger Olson, 'Arminianism', in *The Cambridge Dictionary of Christian Theology*, ed. by Ian McFarlane, David Ferguson, Karen Kilby and Iain Torrance (Cambridge: Cambridge University Press, 2011), pp. 34–5.
109 Definitions derived from *The Cambridge Dictionary of Christian Theology*, especially pp. 161, 292, 378.
110 See Anthony Milton, 'Arminians, Laudians, Anglicans and Revisionists: Back to Which Drawing Board?', *Huntington Library Quarterly*, 78/4 (2015), 723–42 (726).
111 See above (citing Morris, p. 82); see also Simpson (2019), p. 27.
112 Morris, p. 82.
113 See Morris, p. 82.
114 Morris, p. 83. See also MacCulloch (2017), pp. 359–60.

Philip Sidney claimed the poet 'is lifted up with the vigour of his own invention'.[115] Since poetry for Sidney is (in Robert Maslen's words) the art of the fallen world, the claim to be able to lift oneself up, in poetry, challenges English religion. It does so the more when Sidney asserts that poetry's 'final end is to lead and draw us to as high a perfection as our degenerate souls are capable of'.[116] Here the invited questions are: how high is that perfection; how degenerate are we; and how capable are we of escaping the degeneration? The *Thirty-nine Articles* are clear on this point; Article 10 states that the condition of man after the fall of Adam 'is such, that he cannot turn and prepare himself by his own natural strength and works to faith and calling upon God'.[117] Sidney's self-propelling image of the poet challenges this.[118] The poet 'lifted up with his own invention' defies the Church of England by asserting the potentially redemptive power of a poet's works.

Sidney dwells on those works:

> Neither let it be deemed too saucy a comparison to balance the highest point of man's wit with the efficacy of Nature: but rather give right honour to the heavenly Maker of that maker, who having made man to His owne likeness, set him beyond and over all the works of that second nature; which in nothing he showeth so much as in Poetry, when with the force of a divine breath he bringeth things forth surpassing her doings, with no small arguments to the incredulous of that first accursed fall of Adam: since our erected wit maketh us know what perfection is, and yet our infected will keepeth us from reaching unto it.[119]

In late sixteenth-century England, it is small wonder Sidney thought 'few' would grant these saucy claims.[120] In the fallen world, humans 'know what

---

115 See *An Apology for Poetry, or The Defence of Poesy: Sir Philip Sidney*, ed. by R. W. Maslan, 3rd edn (Manchester and New York: Manchester University Press, 2002), p. 85. On Protestant poetics, see Barbara Lewalski, *Protestant Poetics and the Seventeenth Century Religious Lyric* (Princeton: Princeton University Press, 1979), especially (for Sidney), p. 9. Lewalski's claim for significant 'biblical poetics' in early modern England based on Patristic and medieval sources (Lewalski, p. 7) is importantly corrected by three studies cited: Simpson (2007), Simpson (2019), and Fulton (2021). These studies (especially Fulton) show English Protestantism from Tyndale to late Milton was overwhelmingly Biblicist. Claiming the study was 'often not possible or profitable' (Lewalski, p. 11), Lewalski also largely sidestepped the Prayer Book, including its Preface and the Act of Uniformity of 1559.
116 *Apology*, p. 88.
117 See Cummings (ed.) (2011b), p. 676.
118 According to Williams, the poet 'exists as a kind of discrete totality in relation to his physical and psychic environment'. See James Williams, 'Erected Wit and Effeminate Repose: Philip Sidney's Postures of Reader-Response, in *The Modern Language Review*, 104/3 (July 2009), 640–58 (656).
119 *An Apology for Poetry, or The Defence of Poesy: Sir Philip Sidney*, ed. by R. W. Maslen, rev. 3rd edn (Manchester and New York: Manchester University Press, 1973; repr. 1989), p. 86.
120 *Apology*, p. 86.

perfection is' by their own 'erected wit'. Likened to the Maker, moreover, makers of poetic works have 'the force of a divine breath'. Brian Cummings rightly observed that Sidney takes 'extraordinary theological risks' in this passage.[121] Yet it is wrong to confine those risks to the pressures on literary culture from 'puritanism'.[122] Given its essential theological alignment with north European Protestantism, it is the Church of England that Sidney here defies through poetic works. The ground of experience in Sidney was the Holy Roman Empire: holy in 'many different ways, Roman in its heritage, and an empire in its always surprising capacity to hold the incompatible together'.[123]

The fourth point of note is the imagery of 'erected wit' describing the poetic person. It is a monumental image of intelligence developed by Sidney in the *Apology* through repeated images of the poet's works. Poetry, says Sidney, 'in the most excellent work is the most excellent workman'.[124] The poet builds, 'as Amphion was said to move stones with his poetry to build Thebes'.[125] In these images, poets work monumentally.[126] It is time to attend more closely to their creativity.

---

[121] See Cummings (2002), p. 270; and, similarly, Lauren Shufran, 'At Wit's End: Philip Sidney, *Akrasia*, and the Postlapsarian Limits of Reason and Will', *Studies in Philology*, 115/4 (Fall, 2018), 679–718 (682). In this passage, Sidney echoes the claims to divinity of Italian Renaissance humanists such as Pico: 'Thou shalt have the power … to be reborn, into the highest forms, which are divine.' See Pico, 'Oration on the Dignity of Man', cited in Ayesha Ramachandran, 'Humanism and its Discontents', *Spenser Studies: A Renaissance Poetry Annual*, 30 (2015), 3–18 (9).

[122] Cummings (2002), p. 270.

[123] Roger Kuin, 'Philip Sidney's Travels in the Holy Roman Empire', *Renaissance Quarterly*, 74 (2021), 802–28 (825). Note: 'Curious as it seems, he [Sidney] left no statement of personal religion. He translated Mornay and De Bartas; he versified the Psalms; but nowhere does one get a clear sense of his beliefs' (Kuin, 821).

[124] *Apology*, p. 96.

[125] *Apology*, p. 82.

[126] See Scott Newstok, *Quoting Death in Early Modern England: The Poetics of Epitaphs Beyond the Tomb*, Early Modern Literature in History (London: Palgrave Macmillan, 2009), p. 120.

1

Works, epitaphs, poetry

Our introduction considered the Church of England as expressed in the Prayer Book, showing its competitive hostility towards less scriptural, more imaginative literatures, as well as the Prayer Book's grouping of these other literatures with Catholicism. Supported by critics like Timothy Rosendale and Molly Murray, we began also to see Catholic continuities which persisted in the literature of sixteenth- and seventeenth-century England.[1] This chapter turns to the 'epitaphic situation' of sixteenth- and seventeenth-century literature, in which all sorts of writing were 'permeated with epitaphs'.[2] The epitaphic writing was monumental; yet it was also an ambiguous testing ground for reformers' debates on the eradication of Roman Catholic phrases, terms and practices, and it was still recognised as such in Restoration England.[3] A pamphlet of 1605, for example, published the burial of a recusant called Alice Wellington. When the vicar refused to bury her, proclaimed the pamphlet, friends buried her by night with the full, memorial panoply of saint's bell, crucifix and burning tapers in the churchyard.[4] Here is an example of memorial objects and ritual becoming controversial memorial literature. At least until 1640, there are many records of recusant burials of the kind.[5]

These textual epitaphs bear witness to the intense consciousness in early modern England of theological meanings in epitaphic literature; they imply

---

1 Timothy Rosendale, *Theology and Agency in Early Modern Literature* (Cambridge: Cambridge University Press, 2018); Molly Murray, *The Poetics of Conversion in Early Modern English Literature: Verse and Change from Donne to Dryden* (Cambridge: Cambridge University Press, 2009; repr. 2011).
2 Scott Newstok, *Quoting Death in Early Modern England: The Poetics of Epitaphs Beyond the Tomb*, Early Modern Literature in History (London: Palgrave Macmillan, 2009), p. 8.
3 Newstok, pp. 17–18.
4 Daniel Swift, *Shakespeare's Common Prayers: The Book of Common Prayer and the Elizabethan Age* (Oxford: Oxford University Press, 2013), pp. 187–8.
5 See Christopher Haigh, *The Plain Man's Pathways to Heaven: Kinds of Christianity in Post-Reformation England, 1570–1640* (Oxford: Oxford University Press, 2007), pp. 194–5.

the capacity of texts of the era to signal theological meanings and the capacity of readers to understand those meanings.[6] In this chapter, I observe the persistent Catholic meanings in epitaphic poetry which readers of the kind looked for and understood. I show that epitaphic treatments of the Catholic theology of works underpinned the 'landmark in authorial presence' that was *The Works of Ben Jonson*: constructing Catholic ideas of creative authorship to last through the seventeenth century.[7] Jonson was a recusant from 1598 to 1610 and was certainly aware of the theological significance of the word 'works' in his self-memorialising title *The Works of Ben Jonson*. In this, Jonson's memorial volume aimed at posterity, 'works' gave a Catholic accent to imaginative literature. It added the inflection to the memorial model of Horace, on whom Jonson modelled himself.[8] As I show, later authors (Catholic and Laudian) drew on Jonson's model in their own memorial works. They therefore affirmed the connection of Catholicism with imaginative literature propagated by Jonson yet already in the Prayer Book, while undercutting that book's hostility to more-than-scriptural imagination. From Jonson, therefore, a distinct literary identity arose in the seventeenth century which was Catholic in tenor. I begin with 'works', their theological significance, and the monumental status of theology.

'Works', theology and the theological monument

When the Elizabethan divine William Perkins published his *A golden chain, or the description of theology* in 1591, he began as follows:

> Christian reader, there are at this day four several opinions of the order of God's predestination.
>
> The first is of the old and new Pelagians, who place the cause of God's predestination in man, in that they hold that God did ordain men either to life or death according as he did foresee that they would by their natural free will either reject or receive grace offered.
>
> The second, of them, who (of some) are termed Lutherans, which teach that God, foreseeing how all mankind, being shut up under unbelief, would therefore reject grace offered, did hereupon purpose to choose some to salvation

---

6 On 'textual epitaphs', see Newstok, pp. 35–7. See also Eamon Duffy, *A People's Tragedy: Studies in Reformation* (London: Bloomsbury, 2020), pp. 114–15.
7 Martin Butler and Jane Rickard, 'Introduction: Immortal Ben Jonson', in *Ben Jonson and Posterity: Reception, Reputation, Legacy*, ed. by Martin Butler and Jane Rickard (Cambridge: Cambridge University Press, 2020), pp. 1–22 (p. 9).
8 On Jonson as at once Catholic and modelling himself on Horace, see Victoria Moul, *Jonson, Horace and the Classical Tradition* (Cambridge: Cambridge University Press, 2010), pp. 1–2.

of his mere mercy, without any respect of their faith or good works, and the rest to reject, being moved to do this because he did eternally foresee that they would reject his grace offered them in the Gospel.

The third, of semi-pelagian Papists, which ascribe God's predestination partly to mercy and partly to men's foreseen preparations and meritorious works.

The fourth, of such as teach that the cause of God's predestination is his mercy in Christ, in them which are saved; and in them which perish, the fall and corruption of man; yet so, as that the decree and eternal counsel of God concerning them both hath not any cause beside his will and pleasure. Of these four opinions, the three former I have laboured to oppugn as erroneous, and to maintain the last, as being a truth which will bear weight in the balance of the Sanctuary.[9]

Perkins's view that salvation 'hath not any cause beside his [God's] will and pleasure' shares the view of the Lutherans, here, that salvation is 'without any respect ... of faith or good works'. There is difference between these Protestants regarding God's 'mercy' and His 'will and pleasure', but the bigger difference of the passage is with those who affirm the value of works in salvation: the Pelagians and the Catholics (called 'semi-pelagian Papists' by Perkins). In broad terms, the Lutherans' theology would re-emerge in the seventeenth century as 'Arminian'; yet Perkins's own theological position presents that of the leading Calvinists on the continent and the fashionable majority-position of Elizabethan theologians.[10]

What needs also to be observed is the monumentality of Perkins's text. Perkins is describing theological positions 'at this day', but he is also remembering theological positions in words. The mention of Pelagius (AD 354–418) is perhaps the passage's most evidently memorial feature, but Martin Luther (remembered in 'Lutherans') had died in 1546 and the 'Pelagian' debate (picked up by Luther) centrally involved Augustine (AD 354–430). Perkins's text, therefore, monumentalises both a swathe of Christian history and major figures from it. It also serves as a reminder that, elucidating the thoughts of earlier authors, the greater part of theological writing in this era is monumental.

9 'A golden chain', in *Religion in Tudor England: An Anthology of Primary Sources*, ed. by Ethan Shagan and Debora Shuger (TX: Baylor University Press, 2016), p. 291.
10 Shagan and Shuger (eds), pp. 288–9. On Lutheran and Arminian connections in more detail, see Anthony Milton, *Catholic and Reformed: The Roman and Protestant Churches in English Protestant Thought, 1600–1640* (Cambridge: Cambridge University Press, 1995), pp. 384–95, 426–7, 439–44. On terminology, see Milton, 'Arminians, Laudians, Anglicans, and Revisionists: Back to Which Drawing Board?' in *Huntingdon Library Quarterly*, 78/4 (2015), 723–43 (724–5); Calvin Lane, 'John Milton's Elegy for Lancelot Andrewes (1626) and the Dynamic Nature of Religious Identity in Early Stuart England', *Anglican and Episcopal History*, 85/4 (2016), 468–91 (468).

It is inconceivable, therefore, that Jonson, collecting writings in a memorial volume he called *The Works of Ben Jonson*, was unaware of theological features in his chosen title. Jonson carefully designed the folio, omitting, among other things, the poems he had written to Catholic friends soon after his conversion to Catholicism in 1598.[11] Implied is an author very careful of his religious presentation; and Jonson took seriously the theology of works. In 1604, the first authorised edition of *The Passions of the Mind* by the Catholic priest, Fr Thomas Wright, was published with a tributary sonnet to the author by Jonson.[12] In flat contradiction to the Prayer Book, where the General Confession states 'there is no health in us', *The Passions of the Mind* argues that the passions are a force for good in spiritual life rather than just for evil; and that the human faculty of reason is also a good, since it orders the passions correctly.[13] Yet Wright's book, which in the following twenty-five years went through five more editions, is still more theologically forthright than this.[14] Reflecting that 'all natural creatures contend extreamely [sic] to win their ends, and to procure the means they conceyve necessary for their good', Wright asks what the proper end is for humanity – a question he answers immediately:

> What is our end? God: what is the meanes? to fly vice and follow Vertue: Let us now discourse over the world and try what extreme diligence men use in procuring riches, honours, pleasures, and what exorbitant negligence in providing vertues and good works to come to God.[15]

This sharp contrast of virtue and vice across the world speaks to Jonson's 'global satire'.[16] More importantly, for present purposes, the means to God in this Catholic book celebrated by Jonson is to follow virtue and 'good works'. Commemorating himself and his 'works', in early modern literature's epitaphic situation, Jonson gave a theologically Catholic face to literature. The memorialising Perkins would have defined it as Pelagian or 'semi-pelagian Papist', but those like Wright would have recognised its Catholicism.

The obvious objection to this claim is that Jonson's 'works' are not aimed at salvation. Yet this is not correct, and the objection is reductive. For pious

---

11 Ian Donaldson, *Ben Jonson: A Life* (Oxford and New York: Oxford University Press, 2011), p. 332.
12 Donaldson, p. 141.
13 For this description of *The Passions of the Mind*, see Donaldson, p. 142. For the phrases of the 1559 General Confession, see *The Book of Common Prayer: The Texts of 1549, 1555, and 1662*, ed. by Brian Cummings (Oxford: Oxford University Press, 2011), p. 103. Wright's view echoes Aquinas (who evokes Augustine against the Stoics). See Robert Miner, *Thomas Aquinas on the Passions: A Study of Summa Theologiae 1a2ae 22–48* (Cambridge: Cambridge University Press, 2009), pp. 289–91.
14 Donaldson, p. 141.
15 Thomas Wright, *The Passions of the Mind in generall* (London: 1604), p. 342, *in Early English Books Online* (hereafter *EEBO*; accessed 2.7.2021).
16 On 'global satire', see Donaldson, pp. 145–74.

Christians of every kind, in early modern England, life was a preparation for death.[17] All Protestant writing in England had death in mind, and by 1616, when *The Works of Ben Jonson* was published, Jonson was outwardly Protestant.[18] Yet *The Works of Ben Jonson* not only memorialises Jonson; it also memorialises his 'works'. In the age of the Prayer Book, the combination is important. The memorialisation of the man, Jonson, and his imaginative work is in monumental contrast with the memorialisation of scripture in the Prayer Book, its opposition to imaginative memorials and its claim that such literary memorials are Catholic.[19] Nor are these the only points of strong contrast between Jonson's monument and the Prayer Book's.

Material and conceptual aspects of monuments always risked idolatry for Reformers.[20] Yet rather than toning down memorial in his folio, Jonson maximised it. Until *The Works of Ben Jonson*, folios were largely reserved for elite genres and dead authors.[21] Certainly, therefore, Jonson's folio made very grand claims for his works and for himself; yet it also placed his works and person largely among the dead, in a monumental construction of authorship and literature. In this intensely epitaphic context, the theological import of 'works' stands out. Death was the door to the afterlife in the era; to emphasise one's works, in the context, was to suggest their utility in salvation.[22]

For epitaphic writing in England did not need to be explicit about the utility of works in salvation to indicate that belief. Various kinds of example demonstrate this. Consider, for instance, this memorial ambiguity, in an epitaph of 1580 to one William Lambe:

> So that I may conclude of him, as needes conclude I must,
> If works may simply of themselves, make righteous men and just,
> (Which I denie, for unto faith this office is assigned:)
> Then is he sanctified from sinne, and cleansed in hart and minde.[23]

---

17 See Alec Ryrie, *Being Protestant in Reformation Britain* (Oxford: Oxford University Press, 2013), p. 460.
18 Ryrie (2013), p. 312.
19 On these points, see the Introduction to this book.
20 Newstok, pp. 16–18.
21 Lynn Meskill, 'Ben Jonson's 1616 Folio: A Revolution in Print?' in *Études Épistémè: Revue de literature et de civilisation (XVI-XVIII siècle*s), 14 (2008), https://doi.org/10.4000/episteme.736 (accessed 7.6.2021); Stephen Orgel, *The Idea of the Book and the Creation of Literature* (Oxford: Oxford University Press, 2023), p. 72.
22 On death being important due to its consequences in the afterlife, see Ryrie (2013), p. 461. We shall observe a similar connection of death and consequences in the theologically Catholic *Everyman*.
23 Reference and following citations to this epitaph are from 'An Epitaph, or funeral inscription, upon the godlie life and death of the Right worshipfull Maister William Lambe Esquire, Founder of the new conduit in Holborne, &C. Deceased the one and twentieth of April, and intumbed in S. Faiths Church under Powles, the sixt of Maie next and immediately following. Anno. 1580. Devised by Abraham Fleming', STC (2nd edn) / 11038, in *EEBO*, lines 80–3 (accessed 13.7.2018).

Clearly, this is an epitaph concerned with theology, but which theology it adheres to is a puzzle. The passage protests the author's Protestant *sola fide*, but it also imagines Lambe's salvation through his good works. The epitaph is, thus, another example, beyond those observed already, of monumental writing, but one not signalling certainty about salvation. The author claims to deny salvation through works, and (in the passive voice, in which his personal affirmation disappears) the author also says salvation 'is assigned' to faith. Yet the conclusion that Lamb 'is sanctified' depends on the hypothetical proposal that 'works may simply of themselves, make righteous men and just'. That sounds hopeful – but it is certainly not Protestant at all.

It is just possible that aimed at here was the covenant theology of mid-sixteenth-century Heidelberg Calvinists, but it is unlikely: the epitaph dates from 1580 and covenant theology was only fully expressed in England in 1585.[24] Yet even if covenant theology was the aim, it did not remove ambiguity from epitaphs like Lambe's. The so-called 'covenant of grace' constantly risked over-emphasising works as products of faith, which left covenant theology wide open to the charges of Pelagianism which Protestants levelled at Catholics.[25] Quite where Lambe's epitaph stands theologically in this mix is ambiguous. Yet the epitaph challenges readers to interpret the ambiguity. This is the epitaphic context for Jonson's *Works*: silences and evasions around a crucial, theological word imbue it with challenging meanings, even when those meanings are partly withheld.[26]

Sometimes, in the era, epitaphic works not only withhold a theologically Catholic meaning, but they are entirely silent about it. This did not stop contemporaries from recognising the meanings in the writings. When Raphael Holinshed gloated at the destruction of the shrine of Thomas Becket ('Where be the shrines that were erected in this church and that chappell for perpetuities of his name and fame?') he quoted in Latin the first five lines of Horace's ode *Exegi monumentum*.[27] There is nothing, of course, in Horace's ode concerning Catholic memorial theology; but in Holinshed's account, the ode nevertheless comes to stand for Catholic memorial hubris. Seeing Catholicism where it is absent also occurs in a second example, an epitaph of around 1648 designed to be fastened on the door of St Paul's:

> Reader,
>   Within this Church Sir Philip Sidney lies

---

24 Diarmaid MacCulloch, *The Later Reformation in England, 1547–1603*, British History in Perspective, 2nd edn (Basingstoke: Palgrave, 1990), p. 76.
25 MacCulloch (1990), pp. 76–7; Milton (1995), p. 211.
26 See also lines 55–7 of Lambe's Epitaph. Contrast their claim that human deeds 'accord' with God's will with Article 10 of the *Thirty-nine Articles of Religion*.
27 Newstok, pp. 97–8.

> Nor is it fit that I should more acquaint,
> Lest superstition rise,
> And men adore,
> Souldiers, their Martyr; Lovers, their Saint.[28]

'Superstitious' is one of the terms used in the Preface to the Prayer Book to describe literary Catholicism; and in view of the standard associations of epitaphs with idolatry in the era it is easy to see these lines as an extended warning against Catholic idolatry.[29] Of course, Sidney's resting place bespoke no Catholic memorial theology of any explicit kind, but that no more stopped Catholic interpretation of the site than it stopped Holinshed linking *Exegi monumentum* with the cult of Thomas Becket. Scott Newstok explains why: epitaphs arrested physical motion to inspire emotional and behavioural moving.[30] Literary epitaphs *worked* that effect: the genre is implicitly theological.

This implicit theology it is that Jonson played up in *The Works of Ben Jonson*. By making 'works' the titular centre of his project, Jonson not only linked a challenging theological term with a genre associated with the dead (the folio), but he also gave emphasis to epitaphic literature as a memorial genre seeking to work effects on readers. Moreover, since readers inferred Catholicism from epitaphic effects even when Catholicism was not present, there is every reason to believe that Jonson – a recusant from 1598 to 1610 – intended that his folio would have a theologically Catholic effect in its title.

Two other points need emphasis. The first is that Renaissance drama and poetry were by no means divorced from the theological differences of agency and predestination which divided Christendom at the Reformation. Poetry and drama enacted this theology time and again in early modern England. In one view, the distinctive feature of the enactments was the 'questions' they raised, making English Literature theologically Catholic, Protestant, or an indistinct blend of both.[31] Yet this analysis fails to observe the competition between Protestant literature as scriptural mosaics and more imaginative literatures, as seen in our Introduction. That distinction between literary kinds means that imaginative literatures opposed Protestant ideas of writing *before* they addressed questions of agency and salvation; and that in so far as they presented those questions in a Catholic way, they did so *in addition*

---

28 Newstok, p. 130.
29 On 'superstitious' in the Prayer Book, see *The Book of Common Prayer*, p. 5.
30 Newstok, p. 30. Notably, this epitaphic idea of moving informs major analyses of poetry of the period, including Sidney's *Defence of Poetry*. See Newstok, pp. 109–34.
31 Rosendale (2018), p. 224, discussed in the Introduction on p. 18, note 107. See also Rosendale (2018), p. 108.

to being anti-Protestant, imaginative literatures linked to Catholicism. As the Introduction showed, the Prayer Book reinforced English Protestant distinctions between scriptural mosaics (which were acceptable) and more imaginative writings (which were unacceptable and identified with Catholicism). To signal theologies of salvation through works in imaginative writings, therefore, was less to raise theological questions than to intensify widespread Protestant perceptions of literary Catholicism.

In this respect, Jonson's imaginative *Works* stands in distinctive contrast with Protestant *Works* by Tyndale, Frith and Barnes (1573), Edward Dering (1614) and William Perkins (1631); for these and similar Protestant works attend to scripture, theology, controversy and prayer, but they by no means attend to works of literary imagination of Jonson's kind.[32] For example, when Perkins's *Works* addresses the imagination, in 'A Treatise of Man's Imagination', the subtitle is telling: 'Shewing his Natural Evil Thoughts. His Want of Good thoughts: The Way to Reform them'.[33] The first two of these phrases echoes the Prayer Book's claim 'there is no health in us'. Evangelicals like Perkins operated well within the bounds of the established Church.[34] Needless to say, Perkins's reform is not through poetry or theatre. Words, actions and thoughts must be in 'subjection' to God, and Perkins is clear that 'no work of man can be accepted of God, unless the person of the worker be approved of him'.[35] Celebrating human works, *The Works of Ben Jonson* is a high watermark of imaginative literatures grouped with Catholicism by the Prayer Book in Protestant England (as observed in the Introduction). Rejecting Melanchthon's scriptural hermeneutics, too, it stands strikingly in contrast with the works of Perkins as a leading evangelical.

The second point to emphasise is that Jonson's memorialisation of works does not end with the title of his folio. In the next chapter, we shall observe this memorialisation at length and in complex detail in Jonson's play *Sejanus his Fall*. Yet Jonson thought of labour as fundamental for the cultivation of virtue and contemporaries marvelled at his literary labour.[36] Four briefer

---

32 See *The Whole Workes of W. Tyndall, John Frith and Doct. Barnes* (London, 1573); *M. Derings Works* (London, 1614); and *The Workes of that Famous Worthy Minister of Christ in the University of Cambridge, M . William Perkins* (London, 1631), in *EEBO* (accessed 5.5.2021).
33 Perkins, p. 426.
34 Karen Bruhn, 'Pastoral Polemic: William Perkins, The Godly Evangelicals, and the Shaping of a Protestant Community', *Anglican and Episcopal History*, 72/1 (2003), 102–27 (104). See also James Simpson, *Permanent Revolution: The Reformation and the Illiberal Roots of Liberalism* (Harvard, MA and London: Harvard University Press, 2019), p. 27.
35 Perkins, p. 477 and p. 17.
36 See Steven Hrdlicka, 'Labourious Ben Jonson', *The Ben Jonson Journal*, 26/1 (2019), 21–39 (24–5).

and more easily surveyed forms of evidence than *Sejanus* attest the theological meaning of *The Works of Ben Jonson*. The first evidence is from the 1616 folio and largely implicit; the second is also from this folio and largely explicit; the third is from the 1640 folio and entirely explicit.[37] The fourth is from John Donne's poem on Jonson, *Amicissimo & meritissimo* (1605).

The first evidence is from Jonson's plays *Every Man in his Humour* and *Every Man out of his Humour*. They are the first plays listed in the folio's 'Catalogue' and the first full works to appear in the folio after the encomia. The two *Every Man* plays, thus, are the first substantial, literary works to appear in *The Works of Ben Jonson*. This is significant. *Every Man out of his Humour*, especially, had striking religious resonance. For the first performance, Jonson had used the new Globe Theatre to depict the vast cathedral of St Paul's as a microcosm of the world.[38] Yet religion emanates from both *Every Man* plays, especially in their distinctions between pre-Reformation prayers and their unthinking use in fashionable swearing: for example, 'By'r Lady' and 'Marry'.[39] More immediately, through their titles each *Every Man* play recalls the late medieval play *Everyman*: a moral play intensely concerned with salvific works.[40] From title to opening plays, therefore, the structure of Jonson's 1616 folio builds on and develops suggestions of theology.

For reasons normally ascribed to traditionalism and atavism, Jonson turned frequently in his writing to medieval drama.[41] In *Everyman* (printed *c.*1520), salvation is shown to depend not just on the seven sacraments of Catholicism, but also on the personified character Good Deeds. Finding nothing else helps in his hour of death, Everyman turns to Good Deeds, who tells him: 'Your book of count now full ready had be. / Look, the books of your works and deeds eke, / As they lie under the feet / To your soul's heaviness!'[42] For salvation, Everyman realises he must take Good Deeds to the afterlife 'Or else I am forever damned, indeed'.[43] Everyman's

---

37 On the new, Jonsonian works in the second collection of his *Works*, including 'Underwoods', see Eugene Giddens, 'The Final Stages of Printing Ben Jonson's Works, 1640–1', *The Papers of the Bibliographical Society of America*, 97/1 (March 2003), 57–68 (57–8).
38 Donaldson, p. 156.
39 John Cox, 'Stage Prayer in Marlowe and Jonson', *Comparative Drama*, 50/1 (2016), 63–80 (71–5).
40 Jonson's debt to medieval drama is well known. See, for example, Ineke Murakami, *Moral Play and Counterpublic: Transformations in Moral Drama, 1465–1599* (New York and London: Routledge, 2011), especially the discussion of *Every Man Out of his Humour* (pp. 127–54).
41 Murakami, p. 128.
42 *Everyman*, in *Three Late Medieval Morality Plays: Mankind, Everyman, Mundus et Infans*, ed. by G. A. Lester (London and New York: Norton, 1981), p. 84, lines 502–5.
43 *Everyman*, p. 84, line 510.

first good deed is going to Confession and doing penance, upon which Good Deeds is sufficiently revived to help Everyman face judgement:

> I thank God! now I can walk and go,
> And am delivered of my sickness and woe;
> Therefore with Everyman I will go, and not spare.
> His good works I will help him to declare.[44]

In *Everyman*, the Catholic theology of works is explicitly and emphatically necessary for salvation. Recalling the medieval *Everyman* in their titles, *Every Man in his Humour* and *Every Man out of his Humour* implicitly reflected this theology, especially when immediately following the all-embracing title, *The Works of Ben Jonson*. In the light of the medieval *Everyman*, indeed, Jonson's title for his *Works* can be said to reflect precisely on *Everyman*'s 'book of your works', making the folio, *The Works of Ben Jonson*, a seventeenth-century reiteration of Catholic, theological literature.

The second evidence of theological meaning in *The Works of Ben Jonson* comes from poems of the 1616 and 1640 folios. Readers of these poems will find it hard to deny a theology of works in the title, *The Works of Ben Jonson*, for the poems link 'works' to theology explicitly. As works of literature on the topic of theological works, each poem implies an extended pun aligning literature with theology.[45] The pun breaks down distinctions between the fields of theological and literary works, aligning the works of literature evident in *The Works of Ben Jonson* with works pertaining to salvation.

The first poem is 'Of Life, and Death'. Much like *Everyman*, it sees life as a journey through which man 'makes his way'. On this journey, death and sin contrast with life, good deeds and 'merit'. Those who fail to see that it is 'in his powers' for man 'to make his way', and so to 'front death', are condemned as 'wilful blind':

> The ports of death are sinnes; of life, good deeds:
> Through which, our merits leads us to our meeds.

---

44 *Everyman*, pp. 89–90 (lines 619–22).
45 I focus here on an important pun, but for discussion of 'political theology within the domain of rhetoric', see Graham Hamill, 'Blumenberg and Schmitt on the Rhetoric of Political Theology', in *Political Theology and Early Modernity*, ed. by Graham Hamill and Julia Reinhart Lupton (Chicago and London: University of Chicago Press, 2012), pp. 84–103 (p. 84).
46 See *The Workes of Beniamin Jonson* (London, 1616), pp. 790–1, in *EEBO* (accessed 30.3.2020).
47 See Joshua Scodel, *The English Poetic Epitaph: Commemoration and Conflict from Jonson to Wordsworth* (Ithaca and London: Cornell University Press, 1991), p. 39.
48 See Richard Rex, *The Making of Martin Luther* (Princeton and Oxford: Princeton University Press, 2017), pp. 61–2; Milton (1995), p. 210.

Works, epitaphs, poetry

> How wilful blind is he then, that would stray,
> And hath it, in his powers, to make his way!
> This world deaths region is, the other lifes;
>   And here, it should be one of our first strifes,
> So, to front death, as men might judge us past it.
>   For good men but see death, the wicked tast it.[46]

So intense are the claims for salvific works in this poem that Joshua Scodel mooted it was Pelagian.[47] William Perkins would no doubt have thought it at least 'semi-pelagian Papist'. Yet formally, there were no Pelagians in early modern Europe. The pejorative term 'Pelagian' arose in the Reformation from Luther's analysis of Catholicism; Church of England Calvinists (preferring to call Catholics semi-Pelagian) reserved the label mainly for Arminians.[48] Yet Catholics acknowledged neither the label nor Pelagian theology; and today we recognise how very important Catholicism was in Jonson's creative development.[49] 'Catholic', therefore, seems the precise, historical label for 'Of Life and Death', a poem explicitly giving *The Works of Ben Jonson* a theological facet.

The third evidence is from the second volume of Jonson's *Works* (1640). Though published after Jonson's death, this volume containing almost half of the first printings of Jonson's writings is vital for Jonson studies.[50] It is also inextricable from recusancy, since its editor, Kenelm Digby, converted to Catholicism between 1637 and 1638.[51] Among the new features of this *Works of Ben Jonson* is the collection of poems 'Underwoods' and especially the poem 'The Sinner's Sacrifice'. This makes Jonson's Catholic theology of works explicit in the poem's analysis of the Trinity:

> Eternal Spirit, God from both preceding
> Father and Son, the Comforter in breeding
> Pure thoughts in man: with fiery zeal them feeding
> For acts of grace
>
> Increase those acts, o glorious Trinitie,
> Of persons, still one God in Unitie
> Till I attaine the long'd for mysterie,
> Of seeing your face.
>   ('The Sinner's Sacrifice', 29–36)

---

49 See Donaldson (2011).
50 Giddens, 57.
51 For standard discussion of the conversion (and some of Digby's Catholic associates, English and continental) see 'Death of Venetia, Reconversion, and life in France', in Michael Foster, 'Digby, Sir Kenelm', in *Oxford Dictionary of National Biography* (online; accessed 10.8.2022).

Proceeding from God the Father and Son, here the Holy Spirit breeds pure thoughts in man, feeding him with 'zeal' for acts of grace. The depiction of humanity is a world away from that of the Prayer Book, where there is 'no health in us'. Praying, in the second stanza, for graceful acts to be increased in him, Jonson here affirms a Catholic theology of works; and this theology intensifies in the suggestion that the 'acts' lead to salvation ('seeing your face').[52] Like 'Of Life and Death', these stanzas from 'The Sinner's Sacrifice' bring a Jonsonian example of literary work together with a theology of works, in an extended and pointed pun.

The fourth evidence, Donne's *Amicissimo & meritissimo* (1605), strikingly illustrates contemporary perceptions of Jonson's theology of works. I come to Donne fully in Chapter 4, but his family connections with Catholicism are well known. These include Henry, Donne's brother, who died in Newgate prison for harbouring a seminary priest; Jasper, Donne's maternal uncle, who headed a Jesuit mission to England in 1581–83; and Ellis, another maternal uncle of the Society of Jesus.[53] In *Amicissimo & meritissimo*, Donne says of Jonson: 'Priscis, ingenium facit, labórque / Te parem; hos superes, ut & futuros, / Ex nostra vitiositate sumas, / Qua priscos superamus, & futuros' [Genius and toil put you on a level with the ancients; excel them, so that you may raise a new race from our wickedness, in which we surpass both past and future ages]. Such is the forceful effort of Jonson's writing, here, that it can save humanity 'from our wickedness'. If others imitated Jonson the poet, moreover, 'O omnes saperemus ad salutem' [we all should have the wisdom needed for salvation]. Both these statements make clear that humans, and especially Jonson and his writing, have the power to attain salvation through their works. The title of the poem, *Amicissimo & Meritissimo* sharpens these theological points by emphasising Jonson as 'most full of merit'.[54]

From the first and second folios, our three examples of Jonson addressing theological works indicate a punning understanding of 'works' (as at once theology and literature) in *The Works of Ben Jonson*. As we have seen, too, *The Works of Ben Jonson* contributed to a body of literary works of the era frequently addressing salvific works. That means that Jonson's title gave

52 For similar theological reading of these lines, in the broader context of Jonson's religion, see Alison Searle, 'Ben Jonson and Religion', *The Oxford Handbook of Ben Jonson*, ed. by Eugene Giddens (Oxford: Oxford University Press, 2014; online repr. 2015).

53 Michael Martin, *Literature and the Encounter with God in Post-Reformation England* (London and New York: Routledge, 2016), p. 47.

54 For parallel discussion, see Hrdlicka, p. 25. Yet Hrdlicka here translates Donne's title as 'Greatest friend & most deserving', missing the clear, theological import of 'meritissimo'.

focus to literary-theological concerns, rather than inventing them. It suggests, too, that audiences and readers were sufficiently familiar with Jonson's literary theology to recognise it. Donne's commentary on Jonson in *Amicissimo & meritissimo* is a clear illustration of this recognition. Since Jonson was a recusant in 1605, the poem also celebrates an explicitly Catholic literary theology.

By the time Jonson's second folio arrived, its Catholic meanings had been monumentalised elsewhere, albeit discontentedly. In a poem of 1629, the clergyman Nicholas Oldisworth called for Jonson to die because he was a threat to English religion: 'Die Johnson: crosse not our Religion so'.[55] The poem continues: 'Thy doome / Will do as much good, as the Fall of Rome, / 'Twill crush an Heresie'; and it builds to the claim that 'Thou and the Pope' are England's obstacles to truth. This hostility memorialises Jonson as a Catholic writer. Jonson, claimed Oldisworth, was a working threat; not, presumably, in his person, which was ageing, but in the enduring potency of his works. As it was for Donne in 1605, it was evidently still easy to see 'works of Ben Jonson' as Catholic in 1629.

Although he condemns Catholicism regularly, Oldisworth could write more gently of recusants.[56] What enraged him, seemingly, was Jonson's highly visible, literary Catholicism. Yet by no means every seventeenth-century Protestant who remembered the works of Jonson was as hostile to their Catholicism; some were frankly admiring. One such admirer was Robert Herrick. His short poem, 'His Prayer to Ben Jonson', which was published in *Hesperides* in 1648, monumentalises Jonson and his Catholicism together:

> When I a verse shall make
> Know I have pray'd thee,
> For old religion's sake
> Saint Ben to aid me.
>
> Make thy way smooth for me
> When I, thy Herrick,
> Honouring thee, on my knee,
> Offer my lyric.
>
> Candles I'll give to thee,
> And a new altar,

---

55 See 'A Letter to Ben Johnson, 1629', in *Ben Jonson: The Critical Heritage*, ed by D. H. Craig (Routledge 1995) ProQuest Ebook Cenral, http://ebookcentral.proquest.com/lib/abdn/detail.actoin?docID+179680 (accessed 6.9.2018), pp. 137–8.
56 See John Gouws, 'Nicholas Oldisworth, Richard Bacon, and the Practices of Caroline Friendship', *Texas Studies in Literature and Language*, 47/4 (2005), 366–401; Gouws, 'Nicholas Oldisworth and William Davenant: Moors and Slaves in Early Modern England', *Notes & Queries*, 57/1 (2010), 36–7 (37).

> And thou, Saint Ben, shall be
> Writ in my psalter.[57]

Amid altar, candles, sanctity and 'old religion', Jonson here is evidently Catholic.[58] The claim in line 2 to have 'pray'd thee' may even suggest prayer for the dead. Yet the Catholic Jonson is from the very first line Herrick's inspiration 'When I a verse shall make'. Although Herrick was a clergyman of the English Church, the poem happily monumentalises a Jonson whose Catholicism is a literary inspiration. The contrast with the Prayer Book, where literary Catholicism is roundly condemned, is stark; so, what is happening?[59] The answer is in the last line's contention that Herrick will write the Catholic Jonson 'in my psalter': a book for which the Prayer Book prescribed 'Proper Psalms on certain days'.[60] Writing the Catholic Jonson into Herrick's psalter means finding a place for Jonson's literary religion within the ritual of Herrick's Church of England.

We should not get too excited about that. Historians now insist that Anglicanism did not exist before 1662, one claiming that even then the movement was just the largest of new 'sects' in the Church of England.[61] While it may seem hard to keep the distinctions clear, 'A Prayer to Ben Jonson' is not an expression of Anglicanism. While the last line introduces the Catholic Jonson to the Church of England, the poem's earlier lines present the literary Catholicism of Jonson distinctly; and a force of the poem depends on the juxtaposition of each religion, of Jonson and the English Church, distinctly. Nevertheless, there is, at the end of this poem published in 1648, a small entry of Jonsonian Catholicism into the scriptural orbit of the English Church upheld by Herrick which suggests contemporary rapprochements with Catholicism. Kenelm Digby was a 'Blackloist' Catholic: arguing that only reliance on the traditional wisdom of the Church could guarantee certainty

---

57 *The Complete Poetry of Robert Herrick*, 1, ed. by Tom Cain and Ruth Connolly (Oxford: Oxford University Press, 2013), p. 201. In their introduction, Cain and Connolly repeatedly cite Herrick's 'To the Reverend Shade of his Religious Father', which refers to his father's suicide and begs forgiveness 'I did never come / To do the rites to thy religious tomb' (1–2). Rites for the dead were vital to Herrick and 'His Prayer to Ben Jonson' details them.
58 'For Robert Herrick, Jonson was an object of devotion for those of the "old religion"'. Donaldson, p. 434.
59 On the Prayer Book's condemnation of literary Catholicism, see the Introduction, pp. 8–13.
60 *The Book of Common Prayer*, p. 221.
61 See Alec Ryrie, *Protestants: The Radicals Who Made the Modern World* (London: William Collins, 2017), pp. 130–1. On 'Anglican' before 1662, see also MacCulloch: 'I have consistently discouraged students from using the word at all in that earlier context, though I still constantly notice the usage in places beyond my control'. See Diarmaid MacCulloch, *All Things Made New: Writings on the Reformation* (Falkirk: Penguin, 2017), p. 218. See also Morris, p. 101; Milton (2015), 737, 739.

in matters of religion; yet also seeking to bring Protestants and Catholics closer together through claims that some elements in Catholicism difficult for Protestants were not true to Catholic tradition.[62] Though Blackloism largely failed, Digby would have a lasting impact on English Protestants troubled less by Catholicism than by seventeenth-century atheism.[63] Yet even earlier than 1648, the 'Works' of Jonson were receiving special attention among English Protestants, especially under the guidance of one of Digby's correspondents, Bishop Brian Duppa of Salisbury and, later, Winchester.[64]

Duppa's monument to Jonson

The collection of poems of 1638 called *Jonsonus Virbius* illustrates Jonson's distinct idea of literary labour, as well as the widespread recognition of this feature of Jonson's work by his contemporaries. Yet most critics today associate this literary labour with means of production, leaving the theology of works to one side.[65] In view of the theological currency of 'works', this is surprising, especially since (like Donne) *Jonsonus Virbius* hails Jonson as 'our poet first in merit'.[66] It is the more surprising since the collection appeared at a highpoint for seventeenth-century Catholics: 1636 had been the first year since the accession of Elizabeth I in which no work of anti-papal polemic seems to have been printed in England.[67] Yet the omission is remarkable when one turns to theological statements by Bishop Duppa, the editor of *Jonsonus Virbius*.

Despite connections with Lancelot Andrewes, Archbishop Laud, Charles I and Charles II, little attention is given to Duppa (1588–1662) today. Yet the seventeenth century remembered this unambiguous Laudian for his charity and linked it with salvation.[68] Celebrating prominent English divines

---

62 Hans Thomas Adriaenssen and Laura Georgescu, 'Introduction: The Digbean Way, or Navigating Between the Old and the New', in *The Philosophy of Kenelm Digby, 1603–65*, ed. by Laura Georgescu and Hans Thomas Adriaenssen, International Archives of the History of Ideas (Cham, Switzerland: Springer, 2022), pp. 1–33 (p. 3). For more on the rapprochements, see Milton (1995), p. 126; and (with focus on prayer for the dead) Anthony Milton, *England's Second Reformation: The Battle for the Church of England, 1625–1662*, Cambridge Studies in Early Modern British History (Cambridge: Cambridge University Press, 2021), p. 425.
63 John Henry, 'Sir Kenelm Digby, the Immortality of the Soul, and Philosophical Theology in Seventeenth-Century England', in *The Philosophy of Kenelm Digby*, pp. 89–112 (p. 103).
64 On Digby's correspondence with Duppa, see Donaldson, p. 432.
65 See Hrdlicka, 25–6.
66 See Donaldson, p. 431.
67 Milton (1995), p. 92.
68 On Duppa's Laudianism, see Milton (2021), p. 176.

including Richard Hooker, in 1670 *A Remembrancer of Excellent Men* by Clement Barksdale (an irenic 'post-Laudian') recalled Duppa for his 'good deeds'.[69] Strikingly, Duppa's good deeds included founding an almshouse and 'large bounty to the College, of which I am a member', wrote Barksdale, who summarised Duppa's charity as follows:

> In short, when he had but *two Coats* left, to give one to the Naked; when he had hardly more than *one dish,* to make the poor his guests; to see him walk on the *Hill* with not much money in his purse, and return back with none: But then to think of laying up *treasures* in Heaven, when he had so little left on earth, was a *Charity* which raised in me a *Religious admiration,* and lookt something like the *Miracle* wrought by our Saviour in the Gospel, where *Multitudes* were fed with two fishes, and five loaves.[70]

A range of biblical allusions underpin this celebration of Duppa's Christian example. Yet connecting works of charity with 'laying up treasures in Heaven' is using scripture (Matthew 6:20) to imply that works lead to salvation. *A Remembrancer of Excellent Men* celebrates Duppa for a theology which in 1591 William Perkins had termed 'semi-pelagian Papist'.

Barksdale's remembrance of Duppa's theology is no mere fiction. Ten years after *Jonsonus Virbius*, Duppa published distinct views on the relation of works to salvation in a sermon called *Angels rejoicing for sinners repenting* (1648).[71] The celebration of Christian repentance suggests an interest in salvific works, which becomes explicit in the sermon's address to the devil and mankind. In Duppa's sermon, the devil says of man: 'see where he is fallen, how deep, how dangerously fallen, how still he lies in his foul sins, without any motion left, any sense of grace'. This echoes the already noted confession of the Prayer Book: 'there is no health in us'. Yet in Duppa's sermon, the devil receives a response: 'For though a sinner be fallen, though fallen into the depth of sinne, he is not become like one of you'. This leads Duppa to important distinctions:

> for you fell *nullo tentante*, without a Tempter, damned are you therefore, *nullo reparante*, without a Saviour. But this fall'n sinner ... fell by another's malice, and shall rise by another's merit. They were some of the black crue that helped

69 See Clement Barksdale, *A Remembrancer of Excellent Men* (London: 1670), pp. 112 and 113, in *EEBO* (accessed 29.6.2021). On Barksdale as an 'irenic post-Laudian', see Marco Barducci, 'Clement Barksdale, Translator of Grotius: Erastianism and Episcopacy in the English Church, 1651–1658', *The Seventeenth Century*, 25/2 (2013), 265–80 (267).
70 Barksdale, pp. 112–13.
71 Brian Duppa, *Angels rejoicing for sinners repenting, Delivered in a sermon by the Right Reverend Father in God, Brian Duppa, now Bishop of Salisbury* (London, 1648), in *EEBO* (accessed 10.5.2021). Further citations from this work are from this edition.

to throwe him downe; the Son of God shall help him up againe: For though sinne hath been his poyson, yet repentance may be his antidote; though his sins have made the Devil sport, yet his repentance may breed his Angels joy: A sinner is no good prospect, but at the sight of a repentant sinner Heaven opens all her windows; the Text is warrant enough for such a Doctrine, *for there is joy in heaven over one sinner that repenteth*.[72]

Duppa's distinction between the fallen angels and fallen man is traditional. It is in Anselm and Augustine, even as it is here reinforced by scripture (Luke 15:7).[73] Duppa is careful to ascribe salvation to 'the Son of God'. Yet for the 'poison' of man's sin, says Duppa, 'repentance may be his antidote'. Here the human work of repentance has a role in salvation. The point is repeated in the claim that 'at the sight of a repentant sinner Heaven opens all her windows'; and it is repeated in still stronger terms soon after: 'without sorrow on the earth, I am confident there is no joy in heaven'.[74] Here the work of sorrowful repentance becomes necessary for salvation. Citing Bellarmine, Saint Bernard and Andreas Vega ('this sad friar'), Duppa is clearly here thinking along Catholic lines.[75]

This is important for Jonson studies. Duppa's proposal that theological works (here, explicitly, repentance) are necessary for salvation is a context helping to explain the bishop's promotion of Jonson's literary works in *Jonsonus Virbius*. *Jonsonus Virbius* constantly celebrates the virtue of Jonson's laborious writing and sometimes celebrates it as a mark of sanctity. *Jonsonus Virbius* can therefore be seen as an extension of Duppa's promotion of Catholic theologies of works into the field of literature, with Jonson (who already combines literary and theological works) the appropriate figure to celebrate for that project. *Jonsonus Virbius* upholds the link between writing and labour proverbial for Jonson in the era, recalling Jonson's own theological statement in *Discoveries*: 'Many might go to heaven with half the labour they go to hell, if they would venture their industry the right way.'[76] Yet what is worth stressing in *Jonsonus Virbius* is the link between literary and moral work on one hand, and the link of literary and salvific work on the other.

---

72 Duppa, *Angels rejoicing*, p. 13.
73 See John Rist, *Augustine Deformed: Love, Sin and Freedom in the Western Moral Tradition* (Cambridge: Cambridge University Press, 2014), pp. 97–9. Duppa cites Augustine: *Angels rejoicing*, p. 15.
74 See *Angels rejoicing*, p. 15.
75 See *Angels rejoicing*, p. 14. The Catholic influences are important. Alec Ryrie notes that English reasoning 'in which repentance is an inverted image of grace, is scarcely Protestant, but it was nevertheless widespread'. For Protestant pastors, he adds, the relation of deathbed repentances to 'works' was 'a recurring theological headache'. See Ryrie (2013), pp. 60 and 421.
76 See Hrdlicka, 21 and 31.

The moral aspect is seen, for example, in the memorials of Henry King and Lord Falkland. According to King, Jonson 'reformed ... the Stage' with a comedy that 'purged *sense*'.[77] Audiences, says Lord Falkland, 'did rather chuse / To taxe their Judgements then suspect his Muse'.[78] The moral work effected through Jonson's works is an expanding theme:

> How no spectator his chaste stage could call
> The cause of any crime of his, but all
> With thoughts and wils purg'd and amended rise,
> From th' Ethicke Lectures of his Comedies,
> Where the Spectators act, and the sham'd age
> Blusheth to meet her folies on the stage.[79]

Since *Angels rejoicing* identified repentance as a salvific work, the emphasis here on creating moral shame in spectators (making them blush) is especially germane to Duppa's theological project; and there are other parallels between the bishop and the playwright. For example, when Duppa recalls Saint Ambrose to define repentance as '*Laboriosum Baptismum*, a laborious a painfull Baptism', the emphasis on labour and its association with moral Christianity are both Jonsonian in tenor.[80] Like Nicholas Oldisworth's poem of the late 1620s and Herrick's poem of the late 1640s, *Jonsonus Virbius* monumentalises a Catholic aspect of Jonson especially found in his literature; like Donne and Jonson himself, *Jonsonus Virbius* also links Jonson's literary work with salvific works. Punning on sheets of paper and winding sheets, for example, Henry King (a close friend of Donne's, who preached at Duppa's funeral) writes: 'Thou *wrapt* and *shrin'd* in thine own *sheets* wilt lye / A *Relique* fam'd by all *Posterity*'.[81]

All of this points to a theologically Catholic understanding of imaginative works of literature enduring until the mid-seventeenth century. This confirms the association of imaginative literature with Catholicism seen in the Prayer Book, as described in the Introduction. Yet especially under the auspices of Duppa, a bishop, it also suggests the fledgling adoption of Catholic literary ideas within the Church of England. In this respect, it is notable that first editions of the poetry of John Donne and George Herbert (both Church of England ministers) were published in 1633. The date conveniently suggests a watershed when, despite the continuing link between imaginative literature

---

77 Henry King, 'Upon BEN. JOHNSON', *Ben Jonson: The Critical Heritage*, p. 187.
78 Falkland, *Ben Jonson: The Critical Heritage*, p. 182.
79 Falkland, *Ben Jonson: The Critical Heritage*, p. 183.
80 On Jonson's moral Christianity ('the Christian note in Jonson's art'), see Hrdlicka, 25; on '*Laboriosum Baptismum*', see *Angels rejoicing*, p. 14.
81 See King, 'Upon BEN. JOHNSON', in *Ben Jonson: The Critical Heritage*, p. 188. 'Relique', here, implies sanctity. I address the seventeenth-century resonance of such imagery directly below.

and Catholicism in the Prayer Book, imaginative literature clearly linked with the Church of England arrived in the public domain.[82] How distinct that identity was is for discussion in Chapter 4. For the present, the legacy of Jonson's imaginative literature working for salvation is the theme.

Jonsonians

Seventeenth-century admirers of Jonson maintained his connection of virtue with salvation; and connecting these in imaginative, literary works, they also kept up his idea of salvific literature. Striking examples of this continuity are to be found in John Dryden, who converted to Catholicism in 1686, but who had presented Jonson as the hero of English culture as early as 1668, in the hugely influential *An Essay of Dramatic Poesy*.[83] Yet Jonson's literary celebrity persisted through most of the seventeenth century.[84] Anticipating Dryden, then, it is briefly worth noting a few, earlier examples of poetic works attached to salvation in the Jonsonian style.

One example is found in Richard Lovelace, whose style in *Lucasta* was designed to evade Parliamentary and Presbyterian licensors of the 1640s; and whose poetic career was defined by the religion and politics associated with the Civil War.[85] The works in *Lucasta* work against the prevailing Presbyterianism, conveying Jonson's salvific idea of imaginary 'works'.

82 Asking how poets might overcome 'the basic aesthetic questions posed by scripture: how does one experience God through human artefacts without devolving into idolatry?', Gary Kuchar begins with Herbert. Yet even this poet published in 1633 suffers monumental anxieties: 'The desire to "engrave" God's love subtly betrays the [Herbert's] speaker's fear that poetry might deaden rather than convey divine mystery.' See Gary Kuchar, 'Poetry and Sacrament in the English Renaissance', in *A Companion to English Renaissance Poetry*, ed. by Katherine Bates (Hoboken, NJ, and Chichester: Wiley Blackwell, 2018), pp. 50–61 (p. 50). I broadly agree with Kuchar that intellectual history relating to religion and poetry from the Reformation 'might be better articulated with reference to an ongoing dialectic of enchantment and disenchantment, one that did not begin at a particular historical moment' (Kuchar, p. 61), and I therefore stress 1633 as a 'convenient' watershed. I would add, though, that poets did not seek spiritual sustenance through 'a living church' (Kuchar, p. 53). Rather, they sought it through many iterations of the Church and indeed many Churches often hostile to one another. As shown in the Introduction, the Prayer Book makes strong distinctions with Roman Catholicism, including strong literary distinctions.
83 See Nicholas McDowell, 'Early Modern Stereotypes and the Rise of English', *Critical Quarterly*, 48/3 (January 2006), 25–34 (26–7).
84 See Jane Rickard, 'Seventeenth-Century Readers of Jonson's 1616 Works', in *Ben Jonson and Posterity*, pp. 85–104 (p. 103); and Jennifer Chalindor, 'Jonson's Ghost and the Restoration Stage', in *Ben Jonson and Posterity*, pp. 105–24 (p. 108).
85 See Randy Robertson, 'Lovelace and the "barbed Censurors": Lucasta and Civil War Censorship', *Studies in Philology* (January 2006), 465–98.

Commemorating 20 January 1639, for instance, the poem called 'An Elegie: Princesse KATHERINE, born, christened, buried in one day' calls for festival triumphs for a daughter of Charles I and his queen, Henrietta Maria, 'as when a Saint we canonize'.[86] This imagery implies salvation, even if Lovelace here stops short of affirming Katherine is saved.

The elegy to Princess Katherine commemorates a specific occasion, but the contexts for other poems in *Lucasta* are less clear. This does not mean the Catholic terminologies they work with are without significance. 'That a line or phrase participates in a topos or recites a sententia does not render it empty or inert.'[87] In and beyond Lovelace, therefore, we can take seriously seventeenth-century connections between literary works and salvation.

These abound in literature of the period. Literary images of sanctity are worked into poems by Lovelace including 'An Elegie: On the death of Mrs Cassandra Cotton, Only Sister to Mr cotton' and 'On the Death of Mrs Elizabeth Filmer. An Elegiacall Epitaph'.[88] Margaret Cavendish, the wife of Jonson's patron, William Cavendish, works saintly imagery into her poem of 1653, 'An Elegy on a Widow', as well as into 'An *Elegy* on my brother, Killed in these unhappy Warres'.[89] In his Jonson-echoing *Works* of 1673, William Davenant (also patronised by Cavendish) linked sainthood with actions in 'Epitaph On Mrs Katherine Cross *buried* in France'. Through her looks, says Davenant, the saint 'Persuaded more then [*sic*] others by their speech: / Yet more by Deeds than words she loved to teach.'[90] Explicitly, here, it is the works (deeds and words) which define Katherine's celebrated sanctity. Yet in every Jonson-echoing work, a theological resonance can be presumed. Early modern literature abounds with highly mediated and multi-layered connections of this kind, depending on them for its meanings.[91] When a later, literary work echoes Jonson, therefore, it echoes his theological

---

86 See *Lucasta epodes odes, sonnets, songs &c. To which is added Aramantha, A Pastorall. By Richard Lovelace, Esq.* (London, 1649), pp. 20-3, in *EEBO* (accessed 6.6.2020). The elegy to Princess Katherine had earlier been published in the Oxford University Collection of verse *Musarum Oxoniensium Charisteria* (1639).

87 See James Loxley, 'Echoes as Evidence in the Poetry of Andrew Marvell', *Studies in English Literature 1500–1900*, 52/1, The English Renaissance (Winter 2012), 165-85 (169).

88 *Lucasta*, pp. 112-15 and pp. 46-8.

89 For these poems by Cavendish, see *Poems, and fancies written by the Right Honourable, the Lady Margaret Newcastle* (London: 1653), pp. 94 and 96, in *EEBO* (accessed 31.3.2020).

90 See 'Epitaph On Mrs Catherine Cross *buried* in France', in *The Works of Sir William Davenant, Kt. Consisting of those which were formerly published and those which he design'd for the press: now published out of the authors originall copies* (London: 1673), pp. 301-2, in *EEBO* (accessed 31.3.2020).

91 Loxley, 173.

understanding of literary works; and when the later, literary work adds to its Jonsonian echo some further idea of salvation (for example, an image of sanctity), it builds on Jonson's connection between literary and theological works and intensifies the connection.

John Dryden

When Dryden came to write, therefore, there was already a sustained idea of imaginative works of literature conveying a theology of works. Dryden brought both ideas of works together strikingly in the Preface to *Religio Laici* (1682), a poem written before his conversion to Catholicism but thought to ventriloquise Catholic, Protestant and deist positions.[92] Acknowledging his poem's topics 'belong to the Profession of Divinity', Dryden writes in the Preface that some (though not all) of his 'helps' in the poem have come from Church of England divines:

> I will ingeniously confess, that the helps I have used in this small Treatise, were many of them taken from the Works of our own Reverend Divines of the Church of England; so that the weapons with which I combat irreligion, are already Consecrated.[93]

Combined here are the theological works of 'Divines' with the literary work of the poet. Yet while the Church of England divines are passive, Dryden is active: he has 'used' their help and 'taken' from their works. As a 'weapon' meant to 'combat irreligion', moreover, Dryden's poetic work is actively theological.

This poetic activity is itself submitted to theological scrutiny. Deploying notably monumental metaphors, Dryden writes:

> They who wou'd prove Religion by Reason, do but weaken the cause which they endeavour to support: 'tis to take away the Pillars from our Faith, and to prop it onely with a twig: 'tis to design a Tower like that of *Babel*, which if it were possible (as it is not) to reach Heaven, would come to nothing by the confusion of the Workmen. For every man is Building a several way; impotently conceipted [sic] of his own Model, and his own Materials[94]

This affirms that, like the Tower of Babel, the poem is an impious construction which cannot reach Heaven, but – like the builders of Babel's tower – it also imagines a 'possible' way into heaven by human means. That 'every man

---

92 See Michael Prince, '*Religio Laici* v. *Religio Laici*: Dryden, Blount and the Origin of English Deism', *Modern Language Quarterly*, 74/1 (March 2013), 29–66 (29).
93 John Dryden, 'The Preface', *Religio Laici, or a Layman's Faith* (London, 1682), unpaginated, in *EEBO* (accessed 17.6.2021).
94 Dryden, 'The Preface', *Religio Laici* (unpaginated).

is Building a several way' affirms the energy of this project; and that these people (including Dryden) are 'Workmen' reinforces Dryden's connection between literary and theological works. At stake in these monumental works, literary and otherwise, are the 'Pillars' of the Church of England ('our faith').

The central question, theologically, is whether literary works of the kind entail agencies in any way salvific. Dryden's opening address to the topic states, 'we have not lifted up ourselves to God, but he has been pleasd [*sic*] to descend to us', seemingly sidestepping the question; for while it is regular, in Christianity, that Christ saves us, Dryden leaves unanswered the vital question of whether we have *any* role in that process through our works. Soon after, Dryden sounds carefully Protestant: 'Let us be content at last, to know God, by his own Methods; at least so much of him, as he is pleas'd to reveal to us, in the sacred Scriptures'.[95] Yet he then adds: 'to apprehend them [the Scriptures] to be the word of God, is all our Reason has to do; for all beyond that is the work of Faith'.[96] Suddenly, here, the human faculty of reason emerges as necessary for 'the work of Faith' and, especially, as a faculty which 'has to do'; that is, as an active agent. Turning a Protestant reliance on faith and scripture ('sola fide, sola scriptura') on its head, the work of human reason (of which the poem will soon be a theological expression) becomes necessary for salvation.

That is extraordinary. Only in Milton's *A Treatise of Civil Power in Ecclesiastical Causes* of 1659 (and there only on the topic of obedience to civil magistrates interpreting Romans 13) did literate Protestants in England at last allow in their writing an explicit role for reason in scriptural interpretation.[97] Since Dryden maintains that reason underpins faith, a chasm yawns between the Protestant writing and the poet's Preface.

---

95 Dryden, 'The Preface', *Religio Laici* (unpaginated).
96 Dryden, 'The Preface', *Religio Laici* (unpaginated).
97 Thomas Fulton, *The Book of Books: Biblical Interpretation, Literary Culture, and the Political Imagination from Erasmus to Milton* (Philadelphia: University of Pennsylvania Press, 2021), pp. 247–8. I emphasise 'explicit' Protestant writing here, since it has been argued that Hooker saw the relationship between reason and scripture differently. For example, Nigel Voak argues that: 'In the *Lawes*, Hooker is implicitly assigning to demonstrative reasoning a principial religious authority, in addition to the principial authority of Holy Scripture as the sole source of divinely revealed laws.' Nevertheless, 'Hooker never states this explicitly.' Moreover, the view took Hooker 'decisively outside the Reformed tradition'. See Nigel Voak, 'Richard Hooker and the Principle of *Sola Scriptura*', *Journal of Theological Studies*, 59/1 (2008), 98–139 (136–7). Irregularity occasionally occurs elsewhere. A subtle distinction between reasoning and Biblicist religion was held by the Cambridge Platonist Benjamin Whichcote (1609–83); in the difficult 1650s the Platonist's view had a limited political appeal. Yet Whichcote's claim for reason was 'unorthodox theological opinion': 'All such proposals foundered, and they ceased to be live political options at the Restoration and the Passing of the Act of Uniformity of 1662'. See Paul Helm, *Calvin at the Centre* (Oxford and New York: Oxford University Press, 2010), pp. 85–6.

The poem that follows is a maze of theological positions. Presenting an argument originally made against Luther, Scripture is found to provoke subjectivity rather than truth: 'every Sect will rest [Scripture] a several way'.[98] The importance of tradition is considered ('Oh but says one, Tradition set aside, / Where can we hope for an unerring Guid[e]?'); and tension between traditional and personal belief emerges.[99] Tradition gives authority to religious interpretation, as the 'partial Papists' affirm; yet they are 'partial' in assuming 'with wondrous Art / Themselves to be the whole [Church], who are but *part*'.[100] All of this is largely familiar. Yet when Dryden considers the problem of interpreting Scripture, he distinctly speaks out, in the voice of *Religio Laici*'s layman:

> Shall I speak plain, and in a Nation free
> Assume an honest *Layman's Liberty?*
> I think (according to my little Skill,)
> To my own Mother-Church submitting still)
> That many have been sav'd, and many may,
> Who never heard this Question brought in play.
> Th'*unletter'd* Christian, who believes in *gross,*
> Plods on to *Heaven;* and ne'er is at a loss ...

From the myriad theological positions here, at last, the question of salvation emerges explicitly. This salvation is emphatically not a matter of what one believes or argues, but of what one does: how one 'Plods on to Heaven'. The observation chimes strikingly with Christopher Haigh's claim that ordinary English Protestants (often illiterate) maintained a faith in salvation through works long after the theology had been formally abandoned.[101] As importantly, Dryden, who has contrasted himself with professional theologians from the Preface, here presents himself as the poem's layman articulating the layman's faith in salvation through his works.

Yet it is not just the layman's theology proposed here that is important. Just as important is the literary speech-act ('I speak plain') and its accompanying

---

98 Dryden, *Religio Laiti*, p. 19.
99 *Religio Laiti*, pp. 17 and 19.
100 *Religio Laiti*, p. 22.
101 See, originally, Christopher Haigh, *English Reformations: Religion, Politics and Society under the Tudors* (Oxford: Oxford University Press, 1993; repr. 2012), pp. 281–4. Haigh has more recently shown that versions of this popular belief in salvific works were increasingly present in theological writings of the era: 'between 1675 and 1680 fifty-three works relating to the justification controversy were published, by thirty-four different authors'. See Haigh, '"Theological Wars": "Socinians" v. "Antinomians" in Restoration England', *Journal of Ecclesiastical History*, 67/2 (April 2016), 325–50 (341). Yet by 1683, Protestant 'unity against popery' had brought these debates to a close 'for the time being'. See Haigh, 'Theological Wars', 348 and 350. In the concluding chapter of this book, I return to the matter of widespread popular illiteracy.

thought: 'I think (according to my little Skill)'. The stress on articulation (the heart of a literary project) connects theological with literary works; and while there will be more theological musing, it is with literary work that the poem largely ends:

> Thus have I made my own Opinions clear:
> Yet neither Praise expect, nor Censure fear:
> And this unpolish'd, rugged Verse, I chose;
> As fittest for Discourse, and nearest Prose:
> For, while from *Sacred Truth* I do not swerve,
> Tom Sternhold's, *or* Tom Sha—ll's Rhimes *will serve*.[102]

Here theology ('Opinions' 'Sacred Truth') stands side by side with literature ('rugged verse', 'Discourse' and 'Rhymes'), in a blend of works at once theological and literary. The deep admirer of Jonson has recognised his hero's theological point about imaginative literature and brought the point out sharply. Even the styles of Sternhold and Shadwell 'serve' because (despite their inferiority) they are styles of literary work.

To that extent, the poem is tolerant.[103] Yet the targets are apt. In his comic hand, the two Toms (Sternhold and Shadwell) present an alternatively plodding '*unletter'd* Christian' to Dryden's lay persona. A regular target of Dryden, the Whig Shadwell's anti-Catholic polemic *The Lancashire Witches* was censored in 1681.[104] Extolling the Popish Plot, the play is irrational.[105] Yet 'Tom Sternhold' (Thomas Sternhold, 1500–49) is equally sharp. Superseded by *A New Version of the Psalms of David* (1696), in the seventeenth century his Psalms in the common metre were disdained.[106] Yet the Church of England had resounded with Sternhold's plodding scriptural work since the early reign of Elizabeth I.[107] Like the two Toms, Dryden suggests, in the Church of England scripturalism and irrationality are of a kind.

The larger point, in this closing emphasis on literary works, is that in pursuing a range of theological positions and arguments, *Religio Laici* in its entirety has challenged our faculties of reason. As we have seen, the Preface maintained that to apprehend scripture, we have reason and faith: 'to apprehend

---

102 *Religio Laiti*, p. 28.
103 Jonathan Koch, '"The Phanaticks Tyring Room": Dryden and the Poetics of Toleration', *Studies in Philology*, 19, 116/3 (Summer 2019), 539–66 (541).
104 See 'Thomas Shadwell', in *Oxford Dictionary of National Biography* (online; accessed 10.3.2022).
105 See Eric Pudney, *Scepticism and Belief in English Witchcraft Drama, 1538–1681* (Lund: Lund University Press, 2019), p. 297.
106 See Elisabeth Jones, 'From Chamber to Church: The Remarkable Emergence of Thomas Sternhold as Psalmist for the Church of England', *Reformation and Renaissance Review*, 11/1 (2009), 29–56 (30–1).
107 Jones, 30.

them [the Scriptures] to be the word of God, is all our Reason has to do; for all beyond that is the work of Faith'. Taking readers through contrasting theological arguments and positions, *Religio Laici* constantly engages the reason of readers, requiring them to be 'beyond' the work of faith, where reason has 'to do'. Work transfers to readers, imbuing their theology.

In *Religio Laici*, Dryden was still of the Church of England: 'To my own Mother-Church submitting still'. Yet the poem's Jonsonian combination of literary and theological works, and its broader association with 'Workmen', anticipates the Catholic theology explicit in Dryden's writings after his conversion, even as it developed his earlier, literary principles. Following the celebration of Jonson in *An Essay of Dramatic Poesie*, in 1668 Dryden had explained those principles stridently:

> Judgement is indeed the Master-workman in a Play: but he [Judgment] requires many subordinate hands, many tools to his Assistance. And verse I affirm to be one of these: 'Tis a rule and line with which he keeps his building compact and even, which otherwise lawless imagination would raise either irregularly or loosely.[108]

From as early as 1668, Dryden not only monumentalised Jonson, works and indeed literary monuments ('his building compact'), but he also celebrated the reasoning faculty of judgement as a 'Master-workman' in plays and verse. Turning to the active 'work of faith', *Religio Laici* developed these Jonsonian, literary principles in a direction at once religious and Catholic.

After Dryden's conversion, the theology of works becomes both extensive and crystal clear. Concluding that souls like that of the Marquis are both 'mighty patterns given / To earth' and 'meant for ornaments to heaven', for example, Dryden's 'Epitaph on the Monument of the Marquis of Winchester' celebrates action as the means to salvation:

> He who in impious times untained stood
> And mist rebellion durst be just and good
> Whose arms asserted, and whose suffering more
> Confirmed the cause for which he fought before,
> Rests here, rewarded by a heavenly prince,
> For what his earthly could not recompense.[109]

Works in this life (to 'be just and good') clearly earn reward in the next.

---

108 John Dryden, 'An Essay of Dramatic Poesie', in *The Dramatic Works of John Dryden, in Three Volumes* (London, 1695), p. 48, in *EEBO* (accessed 18.6.2021).
109 *The Works of John Dryden: Illustrated with Notes, Historical, Critical and Explanatory and a Life of the Author, by Sir Walter Scott, revised and corrected by George Saintsbury* (London: William Paterson, 1882–92), p. 152, in *Literature Online* (accessed 1.4.2020).

Works are equally rewarding in heaven in Dryden's 'An Epitaph on Sir Palmes Fairbourne's Tomb in Westminster Abbey'.[110] Addressing 'sacred relics', here 'Great actions great examples must attend' and these lead the way to heaven: 'Still nearer heaven his virtue shone more bright ... / ... The martyr's glory crown'd the soldier's fight'. A final example of Dryden's promotion of theological works is *Eleonora: A Panegyrical Poem, Dedicated to the Memory of the late Countess of Abington* of 1692. In its 377 lines, this epitaph unswervingly emphasises that sainthood derives from practical acts of charity. The poor, for example, will miss Eleonora because:

> Such Multitudes she fed, she cloath'd, she nurs'd
> That she, herself, might fear her wanting first.
> Of her Five Talents, other five she made;
> Heav'n, that had largely giv'n, was largely pay'd
> ...
> Nor did her Alms from Ostentation fall,
> Or proud desire of Praise; the Soul gave all:
> Unbrib'd it gave; or, if a bribe appear,
> No less than Heaven; to heap huge treasures, there.[111]

As in the entire poem, acts of charity here earn and lead to salvation: Catholic Dryden asserts a Catholic theology.

Yet for literary history, what is striking is the continuity between *Eleonora*, of Dryden's Catholic phase, and *Religio Laici*, from Dryden's days in the Church of England. Though *Eleonora* does so more emphatically, both poems assert the sanctification of persons through their works. Like *Religio Laici*, moreover, *Eleonora* emphasises literary works as theological works, concluding: 'Thy Reliques (such thy Works of Mercy are) / Have in this poem been thy holy care.' Works of theology and literature ('this poem') combine here, much as they combined in *Religio Laici*; as they combined, too, in the writing of Dryden's hero, Ben Jonson; and as they combined, as well, in the writings of the Jonsonians between.

In *The Works of Ben Jonson*, Jonson defined the Catholicism of seventeenth-century English Literature. Yet as we have seen, he had his sources. While the Prayer Book condemned imaginative writing other than scriptural mosaics, English literature of the sixteenth and seventeenth centuries asserted the value of its monuments through a challenging, theological language of works. Not all imaginative literature, perhaps, sought to participate in the challenge. Yet linked with traditions of literary works to flower in Jonson, and in view

---

110 Quotations from this poem are from *The Works of John Dryden*, pp. 157–8.
111 'Eleonora: A Panegyrical Poem Dedicated to the Memory of the Late Countess of ABINGTON', in *The works of Mr John Dryden* (London: 1691), pp. 2–3, in *EEBO* (accessed 1.4.2020).

of the oppositions to plays, verse and imagination of the Prayer Book, imaginative literature irreducible to scripture could not escape Catholic reference.

Following the thread from Jonson to Dryden, I have looked in this chapter at English poetry largely to the exclusion of theatre. To compensate, Chapter 2 looks steadily and at length at three English plays: Jonson's *Sejanus his Fall* (1603), Shakespeare's *Julius Caesar* (1599), and John Ford's *Love's Sacrifice* (published 1633). Looking in detail at these sixteenth- and seventeenth-century plays reveals the intensity with which imaginative literature of the theatre attended at once to salvation and works. In the theatre, too, Eucharistic theology will stand out.

My link of literary monuments with salvation also invites wider literary questions of attaining salvation. Regarding Purgatory and prayer for its souls, both the Prayer Book and less scriptural, more imaginative literature had answers. They are the subject of Chapter 3.

2

The Eucharist: Sacrificial works on stage

In this chapter I develop my focus on works through detailed readings of Jonson's *Sejanus his Fall*, Shakespeare's *Julius Caesar* and John Ford's *Love's Sacrifice*. Having attended to Jonson and his successors, I begin with *Sejanus* (1603), before turning to the somewhat earlier *Julius Caesar* (1599) and the later *Love's Sacrifice* (published in 1633). The effect is to show how intensely these plays of the sixteenth and seventeenth centuries focused on works. Jonson's emphasis on works in *Sejanus* complements his partly theological use of the term in *The Works of Ben Jonson*; yet each of the plays show theologically Catholic understandings of works connected to salvation and the Eucharist.[1] As ever, 'works' continue to imply theological monuments. In the era, the term 'works' referred to the construction of buildings, especially the construction and repair of churches.[2] The connotations of the related noun 'church work' (which the *Oxford English Dictionary* dates from 1225) were constructions of a church, work undertaken for a church, work for the Church, and works of charity.[3]

These churchly works might seem far from the Roman plays *Sejanus* and *Julius Caesar*, but they are not. Drawing heavily on classical sources, Roman plays are not, certainly, the widespread scriptural mosaics of England's Protestant writers. The plays convey Christianity of another kind. Critics have long been aware of Christian dimensions in Shakespeare's Roman plays. As Maurice Hunt observes, the plays are compound: metaphysically combining Christian elements with ancient rituals and beliefs.[4] *Julius Caesar* not only presents Christian allusions and overtones, but it enhances them. While the eponymous character has the Saviour's initials, in Shakespeare's play the number of Caesar's stab wounds is not twenty-eight, as in Plutarch's *Life*,

---

1 I discussed the theological meaning of *The Works of Ben Jonson* extensively in Chapter 1.
2 See the *OED*. definition 6a of 'works'.
3 See the *OED*. definitions 1 and 2 of 'church work' (noun).
4 Maurice Hunt, 'Jonson vs. Shakespeare: The Roman Plays', *The Ben Jonson Journal*, 23/1 (2016), 75–100 (84).

The Eucharist: Sacrificial works on stage 51

but thirty-three: the age of the crucified Christ.[5] Irreducible to mainstream Protestant writing, *Julius Caesar* and similar Roman plays convey Christian meanings.

The context of Christian meanings in Roman plays is threefold. Since Caesar was regarded as the founder of the universal empire inherited by the popes, to connect Caesar with the papacy, and ancient Rome with Catholicism, was commonplace in Elizabethan England; in this respect, ancient Rome conveys Roman Catholicism.[6] Analogical habits of mind, more generally, encouraged Elizabethans to interpret persons and events typologically, as part of the Christian drama of salvation.[7] Lastly, Tacitus was yet another means of connecting early modern England with ancient

---

5 Hunt, 77. More recently still, Lisa Hopkins also shows that Christian allusions and overtones 'pervade' *Julius Caesar*. See Hopkins, 'Beautiful Polecats: The Living and the Dead in *Julius Caesar*', *Shakespeare Survey*, 72 (2019), 160–70. I turn to other recent commentators on this topic below.

6 Domenico Lovascio writes: 'Caesar frequently functioned more or less explicitly as a type of the papacy, since Rome had become the bastion of Catholicism.' See Lovascio, 'Rewriting *Julius Caesar* as a National Villain in Early Modern English Drama', *English Literary Renaissance*, 47 (2017), 218–50 (245). See also David Kaula, '"Let Us be Sacrificers": Religious Motifs in *Julius Caesar*', *Shakespeare Studies*, 14 (1981), 197–214 (202). As Kaula here noted, the connection between Caesar and the papacy is evident in editions of the Geneva Bible from 1595, especially its commentaries on Revelation. See, similarly, Daniel Streete, *Apocalypse and Anti-Catholicism in Seventeenth-Century English Drama* (Cambridge: Cambridge University Press, 2017), p. 27. I address Kaula's specific question of sacrifice in *Julius Caesar* in this chapter. Lisa Hopkins highlights several Renaissance plays connecting ancient Rome with Roman Catholicism. See Hopkins, *The Cultural Uses of the Caesars on the English Renaissance Stage* (Aldershot and Burlington, VT: Ashgate, 2008), pp. 4–5. Hopkins also notes here that the choice of classicising names like Pius and Julius by successive popes invited the analogy between Rome and Roman Catholicism, with Pope Pius II (the 'second Caesar') a particular example. The connection is extensively explored by Emily O'Brien, in 'Arms and Letters: Julius Caesar, the *Commentaries* of Pope Pius II and the Politicization of Papal Imagery', *Renaissance Quarterly*, 62/4 (Winter 2009), 1057–97. Clearly Catholics, as well as Protestants, connected the popes and Caesars. I return to Pius II in the sections that follow.

7 Lovascio therefore refers to Caesar as a 'type' of the papacy' (Lovascio, 202). For broader discussion of this early modern habit of analogical thinking, see Helen Cooper, *Shakespeare and the Medieval World* (London and New York: Bloomsbury, 2010), pp. 106–8. Hopkins observes that critics have found 'several points of similarity with both mystery plays and a general medieval sensibility'. See Hopkins (2019), 163; she considers Caesar 'a flawed type of Christ' (Hopkins, 2019, 170). Patrick Gray has provided a reading of *Julius Caesar* along analogical lines in 'Caesar as Comic Anti-Christ: Shakespeare's *Julius Caesar* and the Medieval English Stage Tyrant', *Comparative Drama*, 50/1 (Spring 2016), 1–31. Yet the focus on the 'stage tyrant' is reductive (compare Kaula, Hunt, Lovascio, and Hopkins) and the article ignores the tendency of medieval and early Tudor England to present sympathetic portraits

Rome: 'The principal fear of Tacitean historiography lay in its capacity to compare past and present times, and to reflect adversely, through the subtle use of historical parallelism, on current political rulers, polices, and systems of government.'[8] Jonson frequently used ancient Rome to comment on Elizabethan society.[9] In the case of *Sejanus*, for which Jonson was charged with 'popery and treason', the result was striking: Catholic communities of late Elizabethan and early Jacobean London closely resemble the society of *Sejanus*.[10]

In the Catholic milieu, Jonson's treatment of 'works' is pointed. The treatment integrates dramatic action, monuments and actions linked with salvation. As I here argue, it also integrates an attention to Christian sacrifice that has been observed in *Julius Caesar* and in *Sejanus*.[11] It does so, especially, through the association of works with Christian sacrifice visible in texts like Juan Luis Vives's critical edition of Augustine's *City of God*. *City of God* expresses Augustinian soteriology, which is fundamental to the Reformation's dilemmas and causes.[12]

---

of Caesar (Lovascio, 221–2). Gray's observation of the Shakespearean critical tradition of 'two Caesars', and of the 'insubstantial, mirage-like uncertainty' about Shakespeare's Caesar, itself speaks against the article's reductive tendency (Gray, 2; Hopkins, 2019, 165–6). I turn to *Julius Caesar* directly below.

8 Ian Donaldson, *Ben Jonson: A Life* (Oxford: Oxford University Press, 2011), p. 187.
9 See Warren Chernaik, *The Myth of Rome in Shakespeare and his Contemporaries* (Cambridge: Cambridge University Press, 2011), pp. 108–34.
10 Donaldson, p. 192. On Catholicism in *Sejanus*, too, see Peter Lake, 'Ben Jonson and the Politics of "Conversion": *Catiline* and the Relocation of Roman (Catholic) Virtue', *The Ben Jonson Journal*, 19/2 (2012), 163–89 (163–8).
11 On Christian sacrifice in *Julius Caesar*, see especially Kaula, 197–214; Hunt, 77, 81; Hopkins (2019), 165–6. Hopkins here notes further critics who have observed parallels between Christ and Caesar, including sacrificial and martyrological parallels. On *Sejanus* and the Christian communion ritual, see Hunt, 82. Hunt also observes a 'conspirator's "sacrament" of blood and wine' in Jonson's *Cataline* (Hunt, 80).
12 On Augustinian soteriology and the Reformation, see Diarmaid MacCulloch, *Reformation: Europe's House Divided, 1490–1700* (London: Allen Lane, 2003), p. 110. Yet MacCulloch misreads Augustine's soteriology. Compare his claim that 'All the saved must be predestined to salvation (and though Augustine rarely said this explicitly, all the damned to damnation)' (MacCulloch, p. 109) with John Rist: 'Fallen men … are not wholly corrupt; fallen angels are. […] For fallen men, or at least some of them … God has something to work on. This 'something' … depends on the fact that human beings are created in God's image and that some spark (*scintilla*) of that image remains after the fall (*City of God* 22:24) […] Augustine does not believe that human beings are totally depraved.' See John Rist, *Augustine Deformed: Love, Sin and Freedom in the Western Moral Tradition* (Cambridge: Cambridge University Press, 2014), pp. 48–9. Notably, Augustine's distinction between fully fallen angels and largely (but not completely) fallen humans was also bishop Brian Duppa's in Chapter 1 (see pp. 38–9). Duppa, in this respect, was properly Augustinian.

There is every reason to think Jonson was familiar with Vives's critical edition of the *City of God*. Jonson owned Vives's *Opera Omnia* (Basel, 1555).[13] Moreover, Vives's edition of the *City of God* was the canonical text for a century and a half after its publication in 1529, going through 25 editions in the sixteenth century and a further 18 editions in the seventeenth century.[14] His text was translated into French in 1570 and into English in 1610.[15] Vives was of particular interest in England, having dedicated the *City of God* to Henry VIII, been tutor to Mary I, and as a friend of Erasmus, Thomas More and Catherine of Aragon.[16] Vives's commentary on the *City of God* has been called 'the hallmark of the Renaissance work on the text' and 'a marvellous exemplar of a humanist commentary on an early Christian writer, which is still unsurpassed in many respects'.[17] Not just Jonson – eventually celebrated as 'Our third, and richest university' – but also many others in England would have known Vives's *City of God*.[18] As Michael Sloan writes, 'rarely was it ignored'.[19]

Vives's *City of God* therefore provides an explanatory context for Roman plays like *Sejanus*. Deeply sensitive to Reformation debates, Vives's text addresses Christian works of sacrifice.[20] These are defined in the opening emphasis on works in chapter 6: 'Every work tending to effect our beatitude … is a true sacrifice'; 'the works of mercy referred unto God … are true sacrifices'.[21] For these reasons, the body of the true Christian Church is a sacrificial body: 'Truly it followeth that the whole and holy society of the redeemed and sanctified Citty, bee offered unto God by that great Priest who gave up his life for us to become members of so great a head.'[22]

13 See David McPherson, 'Ben Jonson's Library and Marginalia: An Annotated Catalogue', *Studies in Philology*, 71/5 (December 1974), 1–106 (98).
14 See Charles Fantazzi, 'Vives, Juan Luis', *The Oxford Guide to the Historical Reception of Augustine*, Volume 3, ed. by Willemien Otter (Oxford: Oxford University Press, 2013), pp. 1876–8 (1876).
15 Fantazzi, p. 1876.
16 See Michael Sloan, 'Modern Reception: *De Civitate Dei*', in *The Oxford Guide to the Historical Reception of Augustine*, pp. 257–60 (p. 258); Fantazzi, p. 1876; McPherson, 98.
17 Sloan, p. 258; Fantazzi, p. 1878.
18 Donaldson, 87.
19 Sloan, p. 258.
20 On the sensitivity to Reformation debates, see Arnoud Visser, 'Juan Luis Vives and the Organisation of Patristic Knowledge', in *Confessionalisation and Erudition in Early Modern Europe*, ed. by Nicholas Hardy and Dmitri Levitin (Oxford: Oxford University Press, 2019), pp. 96–114.
21 See St. Augustine, *Of the Citie of God with the learned comments of Io. Lod. Viues. Englished by I.H.*(London: 1610), p. 368, in *EEBO* (accessed 13.6.2019). All following citations from the 'City of God' are from this edition.
22 *City of God*, p. 368.

Crucially, the Church is therefore identical to the sacrifice of the Eucharist at the altar:

> This is the christians sacrifice: wee one body with Christ, as the church celebrateth in the sacrament of the altar, so well known to the faithyfull, wherein is shewed that in that oblation, the church is offered.[23]

Vives's single, marginal note, 'The sacrament of the altar', beside this passage stresses the importance of the altar in the Church's sacrificial process. It also stresses the integrity of the good works of the faithful in the altar's sacrifice. This last is important, both for English religion and early modern drama. Elizabethan England largely swept away the altars of English churches, a privation legally confirmed in the Jacobean canons of 1604.[24] Vives's 'works', meanwhile, pertain to drama: a medium where personal action is on show.

In a play as conscious of Catholic England as *Sejanus*, this is important. The historical Sejanus lived from *c.*20 BC to AD 31, making him a contemporary of Christ. The play's emperor, Tiberius, is of the gospels (Luke 3:1; John 6:1; John 6:23). As in Shakespeare's *Cymbeline*, the temporal setting of *Sejanus* draws attention to Christian topics.[25] Combining pagan and biblical focus, *Sejanus* (like *Julius Caesar*) is the very opposite of what the *Prayer Book* calls 'the very pure Word of God', for the play prominently includes much that the Prayer Book calls the 'superstitious'.[26] The temporal setting of *Sejanus* presents parallels and also distinctions between Christian and pagan Rome. As I now show, *Sejanus* stresses the morality of action (including the morality of Christian action: works) in relation to altars, sacrifice and salvation.

Sejanus: works, sacrifice and salvation

The stress on works in *Sejanus* is part of its Roman–Christian milieu. The emphasis in the text emerges in two ways. The first is verbal. The frequency of the word 'works' – and of associated words like 'acts' and 'labours' – brings

---

23 *City of God*, p. 369.
24 Kenneth Fincham and Nicholas Tyacke, *Altars Restored: The Changing Face of English Religious Worship, 1547–c.1700* (Oxford: Oxford University Press, 2007), p. 39.
25 *Cymbeline* was written around 1610. The importance of its setting, in the time of Christ, has been extensively discussed. See recently, for example, Julia Reinhart Lupton, *Shakespeare Dwelling: Designs for the Theatre of Life* (Chicago and London: The University of Chicago Press, 2018), p. 153.
26 See 'Concerning the Service of the CHURCH', in *The Book of Common Prayer*, ed. by Brian Cummings (Oxford: Oxford University Press, 2011), p. 213.

a twist to the familiar idea that theatre entails action. From Luther and Calvin to mid-seventeenth-century England, Protestant theologies sought a language to express humanity's total dependence on God for salvation.[27] Eradicating agency, and so ensuring grace appeared only as a gift, was key.[28] Standard methods of doing this were threefold: a persistent use of the passive voice; a complex use of conditional clauses; and the use of a modal grammar of imperatives, asking God to fulfil a need not otherwise fulfillable.[29] Almost entirely, Jonson's grammatical perspective in *Sejanus* is different.

Meaningful human action is emphatic in *Sejanus*, for works, acts and labours pervade the play. The terms already stand out in the Quarto's address 'To the Readers' and in 'The Argument' of Jonson's *Works*. 'To the Readers', thus, opens with 'the voluntary labours of my friends, prefixed to my book'.[30] 'The Argument', in turn, presents a Sejanus who 'labours to marry Livia, and labours (with all his engine) to remove Tiberius from the knowledge of public business'. Using Macro, Sejanus then 'underworketh' – seemingly a Jonsonian coinage meaning 'works secretly' – to obtain his ends.[31] Even as a synopsis of events, 'The Argument' constructs its play for readers as a series of works, one after another, in which agents like Sejanus or Macro do things and then do more things. For example:

> Against whom, he [Sejanus] raiseth (in private) a new instrument, one Sertorius Macro, and by him underworketh, discovers the other's counsels, his means, his ends, sounds the affections of the Senators, divides, distracts them ... he trains him from his guards, and with a long doubtful letter, in one day, hath him suspected, accused, condemned, and torn in pieces.[32]

The frequency of active verbs (raiseth, discovers, divides, sounds, distracts, trains, hath him suspected, accused, condemned, torn) places dramatic emphasis on consequential human actions.

---

27 See Brian Cummings, *The Literary Culture of the Reformation: Grammar and Grace* (Oxford: Oxford University Press, 2002), pp. 326–7.
28 Cummings (2002), pp. 320–21.
29 Cummings (2002), p. 324.
30 *Ben Jonson: Sejanus his Fall*, ed. by W. F. Bolton (London: Benn, 1966), p. 5. All quotations from *Sejanus* are from this edition.
31 'Works secretly' is Bolton's gloss on 'underworketh' (Bolton, p. 7, note 33) and makes sense both in the context of 'The Argument' and the play. Yet 'underworketh' is not in the *OED* and the dictionary's first reference to 'underwork' is from Fletcher's *Christ's Victorie* of 1610, where the definition given is 'undercurrent'. There are in fact very few references to 'underwork' in the *OED*. Milton uses the term to mean 'subordinate or inferior work' in 1645 and Addison uses it similarly in 1708. The *OED*'s first instance of 'underwork' meaning 'underhand or secret work' – the meaning ascribed to it by Bolton – is from 1814, meaning Jonson's 'underworketh' is original and extraordinary.
32 Bolton (ed.), pp. 7–8.

It is important to note how intensely stressed is the language of works. In an opening example of 'underworks', Sabinus describes princes jealously moving against a popular rival: they detract from his 'greatest actions' and 'work to put him out / In open act of treason' (1.1.170–2). The play will show several instances of Tiberius and others working in this way, for as Sejanus says, in another summary bringing works out, 'the license of dark deeds protects / Even states most hated' (2.2.183–4). Less summary examples abound. 'Send him to me, I'll work him' (1.1.24), Sejanus advises, adding in a later soliloquy: 'Thou has the way, Sejanus, to work out / His secrets' (1.1.370–1). Tiberius will 'work to satisfy' the Senate (3.1.152) and Macro is 'the organ, we must work by now' (3.2.649). He is enjoined to 'great work' (3.2.674) since Sejanus 'hath a spirit too working' (3.2.655). Of the affections and passions, Tiberius wonders: 'Which way, and whether they will work' (3.2.697).

Pointing to works in a change of register, Agrippina must: 'do some action' (3.1.36). He advises his sons: 'though you do not act, yet suffer nobly' (4.2.74). Opsius longs 'for such an action' (4.3.99). For Latiaris: 'It must be active valour must redeem / Our loss' (4.3.157–8). In the Epistle of Tiberius, revealing his underworks, 'the openness of their actions, declared them delinquents' (5.6.582). Indeed, for its stress on works and workings (strange or otherwise) the simple 'Strange act!' (5.6.881) speaks volumes for *Sejanus*, as does this exclamation: 'See, see, see, their action!' (3.1.21). Yet working is not just a matter of developing plot or meta-theatre. As 'instruments' (4.3.226 and 'The Argument'), dramatic characters are to be worked and worked upon. Characters exist to 'abide our opportunity: / And practise what is fit' (1.1.431); those 'who will search the reasons of their acts' (1.1.539) understand the psychology of the characters. Sejanus calls Eudemus 'a man, made, to make' (1.1.351): a pithier claim that action is a man's purpose is hard to imagine.

Since Protestants sought to reflect God's grace through grammatical choices, the connection of agency with doing evil in many of these examples could be mistaken (in the Christian and Catholic contexts identified) for a theological critique of Catholicism. It is, therefore, vital to stress the examples of virtuous action of the play. Agrippina and Opsius link action with nobility, whereas Latiaris believes in the redemptive qualities of 'valour'. Other characters, too, imply the virtue of actions. Arruntius sets the scene, asking in Act 1, Scene 1, who 'durst be good, / When Caesar durst be evil' (1.1.90–1). Here the distinction between being good and bad is a matter of one's actions and the moral distinctions are absolute. Arruntius's broad complaint that 'we are base, / Poor, and degenerate from th'exalted strain / Of our great fathers' (1.1.87–9) makes similarly strong distinctions between those who do better and those who do worse.

It is not the view of *Sejanus*, then, that actions are inherently evil: that (in the words of the *Prayer Book*) 'there is no good in us'. Rather, people can do good, but they often choose to do evil. Part of the distinction is illuminated by Agrippina, who claims that 'Virtue's forces / Show ever noblest in conspicuous courses' (2.3.456–6). Openly striking and challenging the underworking Sejanus, therefore, Drusus receives acclaim. To Arruntius, he is 'A noble prince!' (1.1.574) and a 'Good! Brave! Excellent brave Prince!' (1.1.565). To everyone else on the stage ('All'), he is even greater: 'A Castor, a Castor, A Castor!' (1.1.575). The deification brings us to the second means of addressing works in the play.

The second means of emphasising works in *Sejanus* is through its treatment of monuments. This treatment is verbal and visual, and it brings further contrasts between Drusus and Sejanus. Celebrating Drusus as Castor is monumentalising him as a god, which is what Sejanus wants for himself. Yet in contrast to Drusus, who is metaphorically celebrated by others, Sejanus seeks materially to monumentalise himself. In the opening scene, Tiberius agrees 'To our Sejanus, to advance his statue / In Pompey's theatre' (1.1.520). The significance is noted by Cordus in 'Great Pompey's theatre was never ruined / Till now' (1.1.542–3), but Drusus highlights a Christian criticism: this is 'to heave / An idol up with praise!' (1.1.549–50). In the pagan and Christian Rome of *Sejanus*, the opening dispute between Drusus and Sejanus arises, in part, on Christian grounds.

These grounds are important. Sejanus will later be named 'his idol lordship' (5.5.451), but Rome, more generally, is an empire of monuments. Tiberius considers Senate proposals 'for the suit of Spain, t'erect a temple / In honour of our mother and ourself' (1.1.454–5). He compares the proposals to similar ones for 'the Asian cities' (1.1.459), as well as to a temple that 'deified Augustus ... built, at Pergamum' (1.1.461–2). For the Forum, Tiberius endorses 'repairing the Aemilian place, / And restoration of those monuments' (1.1.512–3). When Sejanus falls, 'his images and statues' are pulled down (5.4.701) in the temple 'of Apollo' (5.1. SD). The Rome of *Sejanus* combines pagan images and Christian criticisms.

It also contrasts Christian forms of sacrifice with pagan. By Act 4, the monumentalised Sejanus is 'raised ... to side the gods, / And have his proper sacrifice in Rome: / Which Jove beholds' (4.4.406–8). To Sejanus, 'new statues are advanced' (4.4.429) and 'More altars smoke to him, than all the gods' (4.4.433). Yet challenging Sejanus in Act 1, Drusus speaks a different religious language. He tells Sejanus:

> I'll advance a statue,
> Of your own bulk; but 't shall be on the cross:
> Where I will nail your pride, at breadth, and length ...
> (*Sejanus his Fall*, 1.1.570–2)

The alternative monument Drusus proposes is of Sejanus crucified. The self-glorification of Sejanus is to be humiliated and the humility is Christian in tenor. With its definite article, 'the cross' recalls Christ's crucifixion and the seventeenth-century overtones of 'nail your pride' are also Christian, especially in a play set in Christ's lifetime. Amid Rome's pagan religion, Christianity, especially the sacrifice of Christ, peeps out here, as it peeped out in the play's language of idolatry. Yet the context for these Christian ideas is the play's much more pervasive language of works, which Vives's *City of God* – rarely ignored in the era – identified with beatitude, true sacrifice, and the Christian 'body with Christ, as the church celebrateth in the sacrament of the altar.'[33] It is in its language of works, especially, that the Christian dimensions of *Sejanus* stand out.

These dimensions are theologically Catholic, as the Roman setting underlines. They come together in Act 5, Scene 3, which foregrounds an altar, an 'image' of Fortune (5.3.185; 207) and a 'pious rite' (5.2.190) performed by three ministers and a Flamen, who is called a 'scrupulous priest' (5.3.190). Visually, the Roman rite might itself have justified the charge of popery Jonson faced for the play. As we have seen, altars were removed from English churches at the accession of Elizabeth I. They remained deeply contentious in the early seventeenth century and Jonson's sacrificial rite at the altar, performed by the priest, does little to diminish the Catholic associations.[34] Beside the altar, for example, the 'pure vestments' (5.3.174) of the priest and ministers are suspect. Though monarchical policy produced vestiary conformity in the English church, Protestants widely thought priestly vestments remnants of Catholic idolatry to be removed.[35] Moreover, Jonson augments the priest's rite. Washing vessels, ministering purified milk and honey to himself, Sejanus, and others around, the priest presents 'an ancient equivalent of Communion'.[36]

To those familiar with Jonson's major source for the scene, Giraldus's *De Deis Gentium*, the Communion connotation would have been still stronger: in the source, the sacrifice is of milk, honey and blood.[37] Yet most controversial in the scene is the image of Fortune. Protestants would normally have identified this with idolatry and Catholics could easily have agreed. Yet not all Catholics did so. Famously dividing opinion, for example, the Renaissance

---

33 I discussed these points about works in Vives's translation, as well as the text being 'rarely ignored', earlier in this chapter (see pp. 53–4).
34 On the contentiousness of altars deep into the seventeenth century, see Fincham and Tyacke, *Altars Restored* (2007).
35 Su-Kyung Hwang, 'From Priests' to Actors' Wardrobe: Controversial, Commercial and Costumized Vestments', *Studies in Philology* (January 2016), 282–305 (304–5).
36 Hunt, 82.
37 See John Kuhn, '*Sejanus*, the King's Men Altar Scenes, and the Theatrical Production of Paganism, *Early Theatre*, 20/2 (2017), 77–98 (83).

Pope, Pius II (known as the 'second Caesar') placed statues of classical gods within the Vatican precincts. For this he received criticism from, among others, Martin Luther and Girolamo Savonarola, but the statues were also a source of awe, and they were defended by the papal court.[38] The rationale for the defence was humanistic: 'In the pope's view … the pagan gods of antiquity were allowed to share the sacred space of the Vatican with the holy symbols of Christianity, exactly as the pagan philosophers were permitted to face the Church Fathers in the frescoes of the pope's private library and office, the Stanza della Segnatura.'[39] Syncretic Catholicism of this kind helps to explain the combined Christian and pagan imagery of Roman plays, especially Act 5, Scene 3 of *Sejanus*. Set in the moment that Rome's empire gives rise to Christianity, Act 5, Scene 3 implies continuities between pagan and Christian religion, especially in images, altars, and works of sacrifice.

Fortune is not evil in the scene. Jonson's priestly ritual is neither inefficacious nor false, but rather a holy relief from the public rites of Rome elsewhere.[40] The ritual sacrifice at the altar is attentive to works. Through a series of verbs, Jonson's stage direction emphasises the agency of the 'scrupulous priest' in the sacrifice:

> *While they sound again, the Flamen takes of the honey, with his finger, and tastes, then ministers to all the rest: so of the milk, in an earthen vessel, he deals about; which done, he sprinkleth upon the altar, milk; then imposeth the honey,*

---

38 See Ada Palmer, 'Gods in the Garden: Visions of the Pagan Other in the Rome of Julius II', *Journal of Religion in Europe*, 12/3 (2020), 285–309. Pius II is no Catholic outlier. The Piccolomini Library in the Cathedral of Siena remains famous for its 'epic series of historical narrative murals' commemorating his life. See Susan May, 'The Piccolomini library in Siena Cathedral: A New Reading with Particular Reference to Two Compartments of the Vault Decoration', *Renaissance Studies*, 19/3 (June 2005), 287–324 (287). The Italian city of Pienza is largely a monument to Pius II. See Charles Mack, 'Beyond the Monumental: The Semiotics of Papal Authority in Renaissance Pienza', *Southeastern College Art Conference Review*, 16/2 (December 2012), 124–50.

39 Palmer, 293. Augustine's view of pagan statues was complex: 'He does not appear to instigate the destruction of statues, but he suggests instead that idols had to be removed from the heart of the pagans so that they would destroy their idols themselves'. See Anne Leone, *The End of the Pagan City: Religion, Economy and Urbanism in Late Antique North Africa* (Oxford: Oxford University Press, 2013), p. 10. Medieval attitudes to pagan statues ranged from the contemptuous to the marvelling. Master Gregorius, who appreciated pagan statues, claims pious pilgrims to Rome sometimes crawled under the obelisk in St Peter's square to 'be cleansed of their sins'. He condemns this. See C. David Benson, 'Statues, Bodies and Souls: St Cecilia and some Medieval Attitudes to Ancient Rome', in *Medieval Women and their Objects*, ed. by Jenny Adams and Nancy Mason Bradbury (Ann Arbor: University of Michigan Press, 2017), pp. 267–89 (pp. 269–70).

40 See Kuhn, 83. Hunt claims *Sejanus* 'vaguely endorses' Fortune's 'reigning deity' (Hunt, 83).

and kindleth his gums, and after censing about the altar placeth his censer thereon, into which they put several branches of poppy, and the music ceasing, proceed.
(*Sejanus his Fall*, 5.3.177. SD)

The numerous verbs describing the priest's action emphasise his agency in the central, sacrificial action of the scene: he 'takes', 'tastes', 'ministers', 'deals', 'sprinkleth', 'imposeth', 'kindleth', 'censors[s]' and 'put[s]'. The priest's actions, too, suggest those works of mercy that Vives identified with the altar and Christian community. Following the peripatetic scene, the fall of Sejanus is a mercy to Rome.

The mercy is complex. Theologically, it presents, 'the god / That wants not, nor is wearied to bestow / Where merit meets his bounty' (5.4.332–4). Since audiences hear words rather than read them, 'god', here, is indistinguishable from God. Yet Sejanus signally fails to meet the 'bounty' of God through merit. In Act 1, Tiberius described Sejanus as 'a man / Whose merit more adorns the dignity [of office] / Than that can him' (1.2.524–5). Yet by Act 5, Sejanus has duped and betrayed Tiberius and demeaned his office. Theologically, by the end, God has withdrawn his bounty from a man whose works failed to meet standards.

The result, of course, is damnation. Yet by the seventeenth century, a visual hell on stage was ripe for parody: a mode assuming audience understanding of what is parodied.[41] Jonson gives us a damnation altogether more horrifying than anything that could be staged. It is spoken by Terentius, and it recalls Sejanus's *damnatio memoriae* in AD 31.[42] Jonson's immediate source for the speech was Juvenal's Tenth Satire.[43] Yet the practice of *damnatio memoriae* continued through the Christian middle ages and the Renaissance and was frequently linked to excommunication.[44] Since worthy Christians were rewarded with conscious efforts of remembrance, it stood to reason that the unworthy dead were punished by equally conscientious acts of forgetting.[45] This is what happens to Sejanus, following his execution:

> These mounting at his head, these at his face,
> These digging out his eyes, those with his brain,

---

41 Helen Cooper, p. 84. As Cooper here notes, Jonson's *The Devil is an Ass*, which opens in Hell, exemplifies this parody.
42 For details, see Frank Madsen, 'Damnatio Memoriae', in *Europe in Crisis: Crime, Criminal Justice and the Way Forward: Essays in Honour of Nestor Courakis*, ed. by C. D. Spinellis, Nikolaos Theodokaris, Emmanoüil Billis, George Papadimitrakopoulos (Athens: Ant. N. Sakkoulas Publishers, 2017), pp. 1217–33 (p. 1223).
43 See Appendix A, in Bolton (ed.), pp. 123–4.
44 Dyan Elliott, 'Violence against the Dead: The Negative Translation and Damnatio Memoriae in the Middle Ages', *Speculum: A Journal of Medieval Studies* (October 2017), 1020–55; Tracy Robey, '*Damnatio Memoriae*: The Rebirth of Memory in Renaissance Florence, *Renaissance and Reformation / Renaissance et Réforme*, 36/3 (Summer 2013), 5–32.
45 Elliott, 1021.

> Sprinkling themselves, their houses, and their friends;
> Others are met, have ravished thence an arm,
> And deal small pieces of the flesh for favours;
> These with a thigh, this hath cut off his hands:
> And this his feet, these fingers; and these toes;
> That hath his liver, he his heart: there wants
> Nothing but room for wrath, and the place for hatred!
> What cannot oft be done, is now o'erdone.
> The whole, and all of what was great Sejanus,
> And next to Caesar did possess the world,
> Now torn, now scattered, as he needs no grave,
> Each little dust covers a little part:
> So lies he nowhere, and yet often buried!
> (*Sejanus his Fall*, 5.6.821–35)

The destruction of Sejanus's corpse leads to a man with 'no grave' who lies 'nowhere', pointing, in Jonson's Christian era, to the unworthy dead: the dammed. Compounded with Christian meaning throughout, Jonson's story of Sejanus ends with a pagan damnation that was also recognisably Christian. Vitally, this damnation hinges on the intensely observed 'works' of its protagonist. The pagan Terentius, who has the last word, brings out a moral in which, as ever, pagan and Christian works combine:

> Let this example move th'insolent man,
> Not to grow proud, and careless of the gods:
> It is an odious wisdom, to blaspheme,
> Much more to slighten, or deny their powers.
> For, whom the morning saw so great, and high,
> Thus low, and little, 'fore the even doth lie.
> (*Sejanus his Fall*, 5.6.901–6)

Condemning pride (long associated with desire for God's omnipotence) and, also, those careless of the gods, Christianity and paganism combine here once more.[46] The combination defiantly affirms the humanistic Catholicism (in the spirit of Pius II) of Act 5, Scene 3.[47] The premise of the defiant message is that one's works are paramount. Terentius condemns carelessness, blasphemy, slighting gods, denying them and pride, each of which Sejanus has illustrated in word and deed. Terentius therefore condemns a set of actions that, as the play has shown, lead to a terrible damnation. The didactic point of 'this example' is that we, the audience, are to see the connection between salvation (the alternative to damnation) and what we do.

---

46 The association of pride with desire for God's omnipotence dates back at least as far as Augustine. See John Rist, p. 44.

47 I here part company with Hunt, who claims that 'All that one can conclude' is that Jonson endorses the importance of 'worshipping a powerful reigning deity in which one is lucky enough to believe' (Hunt, 83).

The para-dramatic aim to 'move th'insolent man / Not to grow proud' connects this soteriology with dramatic working on the audience. Moral working of this kind (often in the context of salvation) was standard in medieval drama, and it remained entirely recognisable in Jonson's day.[48] Yet the connection between works and salvation had more recently been broached to English audiences in another Roman play, Shakespeare's *Julius Caesar*. By the time Shakespeare wrote that play, he had met Jonson, acted *in Every Man in His Humour*, and begun a relationship with the younger playwright that would be mutually influential.[49] As a play about ancient Rome, *Julius Caesar* implied Catholicism for the analogical and historical reasons we have observed.[50] Considering *Julius Caesar* beside *Sejanus* brings out the differences and, also, the commonalities of the plays.[51] The commonalities between the plays and playwrights include, broadly, their audience.

Julius Caesar: sacrifice, works, and the providential audience

The Christian significance of sacrifice in *Julius Caesar* has been well-observed. In his much-cited article 'Let Us Be Sacrificers: Religious Motifs in *Julius Caesar*', David Kaula connected sacrificial motifs with Catholicism as an expression of Shakespeare's typological mode.[52] His view that 'Shakespeare is applying contemporary [early modern] religious notions to the situation in Rome' was developed in another major study: Naomi Conn Liebler's *Shakespeare's Festive Tragedy: The Ritual Foundations of Genre*.[53] For Liebler, *Julius Caesar* is grounded in sacrifice from its first scene to its last, but English audiences understood this focus through an early modern prism.[54] In particular, the Lupercalia which open the play suggest the 'between forty

---

48 See Helen Cooper, pp. 77 and 106.
49 Donaldson, pp. 128–31.
50 Notice that these analogical and historical reasons are not a question of (in Kastan's phrase) 'the stylistic requirement of a [Catholic] faith that dares not speak its name'. Much more prosaically, Shakespeare's analogical meanings are a result of his playwright's debt to medieval theatre. The point about religious faith (as established in the Introduction) is that England's mainstream Protestants did not write this way. See David Scott Kastan, *A Will to Believe: Shakespeare and Religion* (Oxford: Oxford University Press, 2013), p. 39.
51 Hunt (2016), 96.
52 See Kaula, '"Let Us Be Sacrificers": Religious Motifs in *Julius Caesar*' (1981), 14, 197–214 (212). For recent citations, see Lovascio (2017), 245; Hopkins (2019), 161 and 164.
53 Quotation from Kaula, 198.
54 Naomi Conn Liebler, *Shakespeare's Festive Tragedy: The Ritual Foundations of Genre* (London: Routledge, 1995; repr. 2002), pp. 105 and 109.

and fifty' Catholic holy days requiring church attendance, which Protestant England abolished; the 'sacred body' of sacrificed Caesar inverts parodies of Catholic relics such as in John Heywood's *The Four PP* (1544), and 'Antony represents the sacramental system invented by Caesar'.[55] We have already observed the precise connection of Caesar's thirty-three wounds to Christ; yet Caesar's death 'About the ninth hour' also echoes the death of Christ 'at about the ninth hour' (Matthew 27:46).[56] There is an intimate connection between sacrificial tragedy and the sacrificial Mass.[57] The connection suggests theological works, for *Julius Caesar* stresses human motives and action.[58]

Not everyone concedes Catholicism in *Julius Caesar*. Much as I observed analogical and typological meanings in Roman plays, Hannibal Hamlin observes the 'figurative' meaning of Caesar's sacrifice: 'The strain inherent in the metaphor is intensified and underscored by the contrastive allusions to the genuine Christian sacrifice. Rather than saving the Roman people, Caesar's death plunges Rome into a protracted and bloody civil war that results not only in thousands of human deaths but, ultimately, in the death of the republic.'[59] Yet for a figurative reading, this is remarkably literal. Study of the use of 'like' in *Julius Caesar* reveals the word 'constantly activates an idea of uncanniness and doubleness': neither the play nor Caesar's sacrifice can be reduced to its material consequences.[60] In a recent phrase: 'the play shows us each of the central characters unlearning the lessons of (pagan) philosophy, or Roman virtue and republican honour; coming, in fact, to believe in what Calpurnia calls "ceremonies" and what, at the end of the play, Cassius calls "things that do presage" and nearer the beginning "superstition"'.[61]

This Roman superstition betokens the operations of providence.[62] Yet as we have seen, superstition is the very opposite of what the Prayer Book

---

55 Liebler, p. 101.
56 Hannibal Hamlin, *The Bible in Shakespeare* (Oxford: Oxford University Press, 2013), p. 189.
57 See Regina Schwartz, 'Tragedy and the Mass', *Literature and Theology*, 19 (June 2005), 139–58.
58 Timothy Rosendale, *Theology and Agency in Early Modern Literature* (Cambridge: Cambridge University Press, 2018), p. 1.
59 Hamlin, p. 192.
60 Hopkins (2019), p. 170. We have noted 'superstition' denoting Catholicism in the Prayer Book, but the term was, of course, very widely used in this way.
61 Peter Lake, *How Shakespeare Put Politics on the Stage: Power and Succession in the History Plays* (New Haven, CT, and London: Yale University Press, 2017), p. 495; see also Lake, 'Shakespeare's *Julius Caesar* and the Search for a Usable (Christian?) Past', in *Shakespeare and Early Modern Religion*, ed. by David Lowenstein and Michael Whitmore (Cambridge: Cambridge University Press, 2015), pp. 111–30.
62 For superstition as providence, see Lake (2017), p. 496.

calls 'the very pure Word of God', and the Prayer Book connects superstition with Catholicism. Since almost all anti-Catholic literature of the era made the same connection, the providence of *Julius Caesar* looks popish.[63] From a different starting point, Catholics could come to broadly the same conclusion. For educated medieval and Counter-Reformation Catholics, the word 'supernatural' (in distinction from 'preternatural') denoted God and the activity of his grace.[64] Providence is precisely that.

Salvation may elude the pre-Christian works of *Julius Caesar*, but the play's popish and Catholic providence suggests constantly where salvation lies, and this is not merely (in Hunt's phase) metaphysical. Superstitious understanding resides with the audience: its panoptic view of a providential pattern of events unfolding is far fuller than any character's.[65] Popish providence resides, then, outside pagan Rome yet in relation to it. Though pagan works will produce no salvation on earth, Rome's analogue in the theatre, the Christian audience, partakes in the working providence of the play.[66] The Christian thought process is exposed by Hamlin in his lengthy identification of saintly and Christo-centric images in the play:

> Summing up, Brutus wants to be called a 'sacrificer' or a 'purger' rather than a 'butcher', and wants Caesar's death to be not a squalid assassination but a necessary, noble sacrifice to redeem Rome. Caesar's blood, by this logic, should in fact save the Republic, whereas it paves the way for Rome's imperial era instead. Brutus and Cassius hope that the blood ritual they enact (or wish to think they are enacting) will be repeated by Romans in years to come, in commemoration of the original act, suggesting the sacrifice of Christ regularly commemorated when participants in the Eucharist consume the 'saving blood' of Christ. But Caesar is no Christ, nor even a saint, because though his death does superficially benefit the Roman citizens, they get only seventy-five drachmas and some public walks rather than eternal salvation.[67]

This passage exposes why Caesar cannot be taken either for Christ or a saint. Yet it also exposes the thought process of analogy. Repeated reference

---

63 On superstition as Catholicism in 'virtually all anti-Catholic literature of the period', see Francis Young, *English Catholics and the Supernatural 1553–1827* (Oxford and New York: Routledge, 2016), p. 32. In this respect, *Julius Caesar* certainly does not present 'a nationally self-congratulatory religious argument'. Nevertheless, Shakespeare does present a 'career-long pattern of pre-Christian deities' and paganism 'evokes some aspects of England's Old Religion'. See Tiffany Grace, 'Paganism and Reform in Shakespeare's Plays', *Religions* 9/7 (2018), 214, https://doi.org/10.3390/rel9070214, pp. 1–2.
64 Young, p. 32.
65 Lake (2017), p. 496.
66 As Lake observes, it is as 'orthodox Christians' that 'the play constructs its audience'. See Lake (2017), p. 498.
67 Hamlin, p. 194.

to what pagan Rome is not evoke the Roman Catholic alternatives: Eucharistic sacrifice and the saints. These Roman Catholic features exist in the play by contradistinction.

The example of reliquary sufficiently illustrates the point. Attending to Caesar's 'mantle' (3.2.168), his 'vesture wounded' (3.3.194) and 'himself marred' (3.3.195) presents a cult of 'relics' (2.2.89).[68] The cult eventually becomes extensive:

> And they would go and kiss dead Caesar's wounds
> And dip their napkins in his sacred blood,
> Yea, beg a hair of him for memory,
> And dying, mention it within their wills,
> Bequeathing it as a rich legacy
> Unto their issue.
> (*Julius Caesar*, 3.3.134–9)[69]

At least until the 1580s, English crowds at the executions of Catholic priests and missionaries collected body parts, clothing and the blood-stained earth as relics. There was a rage for dipping handkerchiefs in a martyr's blood.[70] Caesar, of course, is no Catholic martyr and pagan Brutus, the speaker, is manipulative. The blood of the martyrs exists by contradistinction.

It is worth noting that analogical thinking based in contradistinction is at the heart of the play's treatment of sacrifice. In the pagan sacrifice of the 'priests' (2.2.5), the entrails of the 'beast' (2.2.40) stand for the question of whether Caesar should go to the Senate. In the same way, Christ, the Eucharist, the Catholic saints, martyrs and relics are Christian contradistinctions to pagan Rome that are recognisable to the audience. If there is, perhaps, some paradox in this link of pagan and Christian forms of sacrifice, it is part of the wider fascination: 'the play, of course, is not about Christians, but about exponents of a pagan philosophy'; yet in notions of liberty, justice, nobility and honour, the pagan philosophy presents Christian audiences with recognisable moral goods.[71]

These moral goods extend to the treatment of works, though always by analogue. *Julius Caesar* emphasises action, the basis of drama, through its

---

68 See the first definition of 'relic' (1a) in the *OED*: 'In the Christian Church, esp. the Roman Catholic and Orthodox churches: the physical remains (as the body or parts of it) of a saint, martyr, or other deceased person, or a thing believed to be sanctified by contact with him or her (such as a personal possession or piece of clothing), preserved as an object of veneration'.
69 All citations from *Julius Caesar* are from *The Oxford Shakespeare: The Complete Works*, ed. by Stanley Wells and Gary Taylor (Oxford: Clarendon Press, 1988; repr. 1995).
70 Hamlin, p. 193.
71 Lake (2017), p. 497.

shape and its language of works. The play divides between actions leading to Caesar's death and actions after. Remembering when Cassius 'first did whet me against Caesar' (1.3.61), Brutus describes an 'interim' (1.3.64): 'Between the acting of a dreadful thing / And the first motion' (1.3.63–4). On the day of the killing, he then observes, 'But this same day / Must end that work the ides of March begun' (5.3.113–4). Brutus thus divides the play into distinct actions: before and after March 15th. Yet the actions here have been matters of 'work'.

Julius Caesar is fine-grained with this language. The play opens with Flavius asking what the commoners on holiday do for a living. The cobbler answers he is a 'workman' (1.1.10). Adding that his trade makes 'a safe conscience' (1.1.13), he links his work with moral goods. That his moral works save 'soles' (1.1.4) is a Catholic pun. To the charge that holidays make one 'idle' (1.1.1), his witty response is they make 'more work' (1.1.30). Since 'idle' and 'idol' are homonyms, theological wit resonates on the holy day from line 1, but each homonym's witty contradistinction (soles/souls, idle/idol, holiday/holy day) primes the audience in contradistinctive thinking. The audience is thus prepared to interpret by contradistinction the morally serious and religious works ahead.

From Scene 2, the focus on works develops in the great theme of what to do about Caesar. Cassius observes 'virtue' in Brutus (1.2.92), who recognises instantly the work Cassius wants of him: a killing of Caesar he protests 'is not in me' (1.2.67). Yet gradually worked on by Cassius, he finds he can do it. Brutus highlights the work of Cassius: 'What you would work me to I have some aim' (1.2.164). Importantly, here, persuasion is a work. Like action, on the stage, persuasion is everywhere.

In speeches, famously, Brutus and Antony work the crowds in Act 3, Scene 2, yet the play is full of examples of smaller, but similarly persuasive, works. Since 'persuasion of his augurers' (2.1.200) might keep Caesar from the Senate, Decius must work to persuade him: 'Let me work, / For I can give his humour the true bent' (2.1.208–9). Soon after, Brutus says he will 'fashion' (2.1.219) Ligarius into a conspirator by speaking to him. Central in the killing of Caesar and the action thereafter, persuasion works wonders. From the contested actions of the tradesmen in Scene 1 to the play's last battles, and encompassing all the decisions between, 'the work we have in hand' (1.3.128), though first referring to killing Caesar, describes the dramatic action in word and deed.

This theatre of works shines brightly in moments of meta-theatre. 'But bear it as our Roman actors do / With untired spirits and formal constancy' (2.1.225–6) suggests a Stoic version of the moral good. Elsewhere, in the play, the concern with works risks pedantry: 'Do so: and let no man abide this deed / But we the doers' (3.1.94). Elsewhere, again, the text emphasises the work involved in simple movements: 'Fly not! Stand still!' (3.1.82). Doings of every kind are registered by the text as effortful works, from such small plans and actions to the central killing of Caesar – 'our present act', where 'You see we do' (3.1.167–8) – and to the speeches, combats and actions beyond. All of this, as we have seen, is pagan futility. Yet as elsewhere, the futility of pagan works faces the Christian audience sensible to Catholic contradistinctions. Amid the martyrs, saints, relics and Body and Blood of Christ so distinguished, works, which are futile in pagan Rome, have a Christian and Catholic meaning. Though pagan works are unredemptive, Christian, Catholic works are not.

That Catholic message confirms the wit of the opening cobbler, whose works save 'soles' (1.1.4).[72] Yet it also confirms the far weightier authority of Augustine in the *City of God*. Making strong distinctions between pagan and Christian sacrifice, as we saw, this too affirmed (in Vives's edition) the agency of humans in both sacrifice and salvation: 'This is the christians sacrifice: wee one body with Christ, as the church celebrateth in the sacrament of the altar.' That the Church 'celebrateth' the sacrament stresses the agency of Christians in the Sacrament of the Mass and the salvation it offered. In *Julius Caesar*, no Christian altar is visible to the Christian audience, but it does not need to be. By contradistinction with pagan works, Christian works of sacrifice stand out, especially in Christ, his martyrs, relics and saints.

John Ford: *Love's Sacrifice* (published 1633)

Relics and saints stand out in the third play of this chapter, *Love's Sacrifice*, and works stand out with them. Set in Renaissance Italy, the play has no need of the analogical processes of *Julius Caesar*, but it makes its Catholicism clear. Performed by the Queen's Men, the play's Catholic outlook reflects the personal patronage of Henrietta Maria on the company in the late 1620s and 1630s.[73] Henrietta Maria promoted probable Catholic playwrights like

---

72 As observed in the Introduction, the *Book of Common Prayer* and *Thirty-Nine Articles* make clear the English Protestant position that works cannot save. For relevant discussion of Protestant attitudes more widely, see *A Companion to the Eucharist in the Reformation*, ed. by Wandel Lee Palmer (Leiden and Boston: Brill, 2014). For discussion of 'vehement' opposition to the Sacrifice of the Mass by Luther, Lutherans and Reformed, see Thomas Schaffauer, 'From Sacrifice to Supper: Eucharistic Practice in the Lutheran Reformation', pp. 205–30, especially p. 213; Raymond Mentzer, 'Reformed Liturgical Practices', pp. 231–50, especially p. 231.
73 On the personal patronage, see Lucy Munroe, 'The Queen and the Cockpit: Henrietta Maria's Theatrical Patronage Revisited', *Shakespeare Bulletin*, 37/1 (Spring 2019), 25–45 (42).

James Shirley and William Davenant.[74] Ford's coterie (which included Penelope Devereux, Thomas Howard, Earl of Arundel, John Mordaunt, Earl of Peterborough and William Cavendish, Earl of Newcastle and friend to many Catholics) evokes a further, Catholic context for *Love's Sacrifice*.[75]

The play presents the stage sacrificially in ways both unique and typical of revenge tragedy. A distinct feature is the play's valediction. That is given to the Abbot of Monaco, so that closure depends visibly and audibly on the Catholic religious. The Abbot of Monaco stands out in three other ways. Abbots (unlike monks) are highly unusual in Renaissance drama. At the start of *Love's Sacrifice*, moreover, Ford's Abbot of Monaco is heading to Rome to be made a cardinal: the valediction belongs to an abbot close to the papacy. As a religious celibate, the Abbot of Monaco is largely detached from the sexual desires and corruption of the play's laity. He avoids the commonly staged criticism that priests fail to live up to the virtue implied in their vestments.[76]

As we shall see, it is also the Abbot's work that pulls the end of the play back from complete tragedy. Yet this unusual feature revolves round two other works: those of mercy and repentance. These works primarily concern Fiormonda, whose name means 'worldly flower'. Sister to Caraffa, the duke of Pavy, she is in love with his friend, Fernando. Yet Fernando, in love with Bianca (Caraffa's wife), is uninterested in Fiormonda, who is angered by the rejection. The intricate emphasis on desiring the unavailable is typical of Italianate tragedy, and is seen, too, in Bianca's desire for Fernando and Roseilli's play-long desire for Fiormonda.[77]

During the play, the angered Fiormonda deceives her brother (Caraffa), provoking the murder of Bianca and, thence, the suicides of Caraffa and

---

74 See Rebecca Bailey, *Staging the Old Faith: Queen Henrietta Maria and Theatre of Caroline England* (Manchester: Manchester University Press, 2009).

75 On the 'markedly Catholic leanings' of Ford's coterie, see Lisa Hopkins, *John Ford's Political Theatre* (Manchester and New York: Manchester University Press, 1994), p. 14. Newcastle enjoyed 'cordial and relaxed' relations with English and continental Catholics. Besides Ben Jonson, his intellectual circle 'numbered several priests and lay papists, including Richard Flecknoe, whose Enigmaticall Characters (1658) contains commendatory verses by Newcastle, Endymion Porter, Sir Kenelm Digby, Marin Mersenne, René Descartes, François Derand, and Beatrice de Cusance'. See Lynne Hulse, 'Cavendish, William, First Duke of Newcastle upon Tyne', in *Oxford Dicctionary of National Biography Online* (January 2011; accessed 21.5.2020).

76 As Hwang notes, the focus of dramatic representations of Catholic priests is not on 'the wickedness of the vestment itself, but the potential for its abuse'. See Hwang (2016), 299–300.

77 On Italianate tragedy in these terms, see *The Duchess of Malfi* and *The White Devil*, as discussed by Gabriel Rieger, in *Sex and Satiric Tragedy in Early Modern England: Penetrating Wit* (New York: Routledge, 2016), p. 6.

Fernando. Roseilli, the new duke, is now free to marry Fiormonda. Yet surprisingly, given his long-held passion, he marries Fiormonda while dismissing the 'mutual comforts of our marriage bed' (5.3.157).[78] That is Fiormonda's punishment or 'desert' (5.3.161). Yet it is also a chance for Fiormonda to 'Learn to new-live', so that with time and contemplation she can 'make ... peace with heaven' (5.3.158–60). It is a striking transformation of English revenge tragedy. In *The Spanish Tragedy*, violence on stage already departed from classical decorum and the genre was, if anything, more violent thereafter.[79]

Roseilli's verdict on Fiormonda is a punishment, yet it is also a forgiveness. Approving the judgement in his penultimate speech, the Abbot explains the logic: "Tis fit: / Purge frailty with repentance' (5.3.162–3). For English Protestants, this is deeply problematic. English Protestants advocated repentance in two forms. One, which Alec Ryrie rightly calls 'scarcely Protestant', since it ascribes agency to the work of repentance, held that repentance leads to salvation.[80] Just how scarcely Protestant this view of repentance is Ford's Catholic Abbot here reveals. The second, Protestant view of repentance correctly held that penitence was a sign that God was at peace with the sinner.[81] Yet the Abbot's claim that repentance 'purges', which ascribes agency to the work of repentance, goes well beyond that. In the mouth of an abbot, the Catholicism of purging repentance is patent. Instead of death, which precludes further works, *Love's Sacrifice* ends with monastic works of repentance in tandem with the judicial work of Roseilli. Since he has always desired Fiormonda, Roseilli's judicial work – the last of the play – is a sacrifice of love.

The idea that good works, especially the work of sexual abstinence, are sacrifices is foundational in Christianity.[82] Yet the last, sexual abstinence of Roseilli and Fiormonda resounds deep themes in *Love's Sacrifice*. The play's crux is the decision of Bianca and Fernando not to consummate their love. A tertiary, Fernando seeks to 'live a single life' (1.2.164) as a 'religious vow'

---

78 This and the following quotations from *Love's Sacrifice* are from *Love's Sacrifice: John Ford*, ed. by A. T. Moore, The Revels Plays (Manchester and New York: Manchester University Press, 2002).
79 For standard discussion, see Tanya Pollard, 'Tragedy and Revenge', in *The Cambridge Companion to English Renaissance Tragedy* (Cambridge: Cambridge University Press, 2010), pp. 58–72, especially the section on 'Violence'.
80 See Alec Ryrie, *Being Protestant in Reformation Britain* (Oxford: Oxford University Press, 2013), p. 60.
81 See Ryrie (2013), pp. 60–1.
82 See Moshe Blidstein, *Purity, Community, and Ritual in Early Christian Literature*, Oxford Studies in Abrahamic Religions (Oxford: Oxford University Press, 2017), pp. 135–41.

(2.2.225). Abstaining from sex with Bianca, he fulfils this vow, while she fulfils her vow of marriage. Love, for each, is a sacrifice. Yet showing how acutely Bianca and Fernando desire each other, the play highlights the hard work of these vows. Fernando's lengthy pursuit of Bianca, in which he threatens to perjure himself, illustrates this, as does Bianca's eventual revelation that she rejected him despite herself. Bianca's brief decision in Act 2 to 'give up my body to thy embraces' (2.4.50), even though the shame will kill her, brings out the hard work that keeping her vow of marriage requires. Seeing her pain, Fernando's consequent decision to 'master passion' (2.4.85), and his several, subsequent demonstrations of what that self-mastery costs, also illustrate the hard work of abstinence.

For Bianca, the shows of hard work culminate in open questioning of the 'iron laws' of marriage and the question, 'What's a vow?" (5.1.6–7). Yet her death in Act 5 precludes the sexual work which might follow, and her murder is called a 'martyrdom', since 'Earth was unworthy of thee' (5.1.73–4). In the Christian context, the constant emphasis on resisting sexual desire has justified these claims, for like sexual abstinence, martyrdom is a sacrifice. The extreme passion Bianca expresses in the play suggests a desire few could resist, moreover, so heaven, instead of earth, is her sphere. Striking as she is, Bianca exemplifies the ideal wife of Christian manuals like the *Handbook of Gregoria*, where martyrdom is an *imitatio Christi* coming through daily works of endurance.[83]

Always regarding works, Christian exemplarity does not end there. The murder of Bianca leads to the suicide of besotted Fernando. Since it demonstrates his passion, that too shows the work abstinence has entailed. Yet it also shows a weakness in the tertiary, whose pursuit of Bianca, against his vow, always meant dubious works. It falls to the Abbot to note his 'desperate end' (5.3.98) with theological precision. As *Dr Faustus* showed to the seventeenth century, and as earlier moral plays had taught, suicide was a work of despair leading to damnation. *Love's Sacrifice*, therefore, ends with three contrasting responses to love: suicide (Fernando, quickly followed by Caraffa); perilous mastery (Bianca); and complete mastery (Roseilli). The first and third of these, especially, illustrate contrasting works of sacrifice: that of the saint; and, it is suggested, that of the damned, who fail in 'Christendom' (1.2.201) to endure.

---

[83] On this form of wifely martyrdom in Christian history, see Kate Cooper, '"Only Virgins Can Give Birth to Christ": The Virgin Mary and the Problem of Authority in Late Antiquity', in *Virginity Revisited: Configurations of the Unpossessed Body*, ed. by Bonnie MaLachlan and Juidth Fletcher (Toronto, Buffalo and London: University of Toronto Press, 2007), pp. 100–15 (pp. 107–8). Saints who renounce sexuality are common in medieval culture. See Ilse Friesen, 'Virgo Fortis: Images of the Crucified Virgin Saint in Medieval Art', in MacLachlan and Fletcher (eds), pp. 116–27 (p. 118).

In 'To my Friend Mr John Ford', James Shirley, who probably converted to Catholicism, called *Love's Sacrifice* a 'sweet pile' and its theatre 'this altar'.[84] The play's sacrificial emphasis explains this, especially in its culmination. The backdrop is the 'sacred tomb' (5.1.40) of Bianca, whose 'blessèd bones [are] inhearsed within' (5.3.39). For her works of self-denial, the martyred Bianca is here proclaimed a saint. Her blessed bones recall 'the blessed bones / Of good Saint Francis' (1.2.253–4), as well as 'Holy Saint Bennet' (3.4.26). Presided over by an abbot and pointing to the Eucharist, the scene is altogether Catholic. Unlike Protestant communion tables, Catholic altars, on which the sacrifice of Christ took place, were the shrines of saints. Bianca's relics and saintly tomb indicate, therefore, the Catholic Eucharist: the last meaning of 'Love's Sacrifice' is the Sacrifice of Christ in the Mass.

The stage directions emphasise a reverence. Amid 'sad sound and soft music', the 'tomb is discovered'. Next, the stage direction presents a procession: 'Enter four with torches, after them two Friars; after, the Duke in mourning manner; after him, the ABBOT, FIORMONDA, COLONA, JULIA, ROSEILLI, PETRUCCIO, NIBRASSA and a Guard, D'AVOLOS, following behind.' The ceremonial is marked; and it is soon marked again: 'Coming near the tomb they all kneel, making show of ceremony.'[85] Yet ceremony consists of actions by individuals. Assigning roles to actors, the stage direction shows several works of piety.

The contrasting works of Act 5, Scene 3, namely the suicides of Fernando and Caraffa, stand out impiously, but not identically. Differently, both characters say they will join Bianca in death. Fernando states, 'I come Bianca' (5.3.95), while Caraffa says: 'Bianca, thus I creep to thee' (5.3.125–6). This last, especially, suggests that Caraffa pulls himself to Bianca's tomb, having fallen to the floor, and Fernando may do the same, providing a striking tableau at the saint's tomb. Yet Caraffa's 'creep' to Bianca (metaphorical or real) shows a Christian humility absent from Fernando's dying words. While Caraffa regrets his self-harm (5.3.118–19), praying 'Now heavens, wipe out / The writing of my sin' (5.3.125–6), Fernando comes in 'spite of hell' (5.3.78) and he is (in sharp contrast to Bianca) a 'man of darkness' (5.3.70). Exploring 'hot flames' as he dies (5.3.96), the suggestion is that he is going to hell. Though neither that fact nor the salvation of Caraffa are confirmed, the contrasts between the two men give focus to their actions,

---

84 See James Shirley, 'To my Friend, Mr John Ford', in Moore (ed.), p. 114. On Shirley's likely conversion to Catholicism, see Rebecca Bailey, 'James Shirley', in *The Encyclopedia of English Renaissance Literature*, ed. by Alan Stewart and Garrett Sullivan (Malden, Oxford and Chichester: Wiley-Blackwell, 2017); Eva Griffith, '"Till the State Fangs Catch You." James Shirley the Catholic: Why it does not matter (and why it really does), *The Times Literary Supplement*, 2 (April 2010), 14–15.
85 *Love's Sacrifice*, 5.3.35. SD.

not just in relation to salvation but in the presence of Bianca's blessed bones and her martyr's tomb. Works of love, abstinence, anger and repentance brought Bianca, Caraffa and Fernando to Act 5, Scene 3 and the final scene aligns these works with salvation inextricably. Replete with Catholic imagery, *Love's Sacrifice* affirms the role of works in salvation through its structure.

Dramatic theology

This chapter has demonstrated the importance of theological works in three plays: *Julius Caesar* (1599), *Sejanus his Fall* (1604) and *Love's Sacrifice* (c.1633). Through detailed study of *Sejanus*, we have seen the interconnection of theological and dramatic works in one of the major plays eventually published in *The Works of Ben Jonson*: further, sustained evidence of the theological meaning of 'works' in that title. In *Julius Caesar* and *Love's Sacrifice*, we have also established a much wider context combining dramatic and theological works. From Elizabethan England to well into the reign of Charles I, the plays of this chapter show that works continually had theological implications that were Catholic in tenor on the Renaissance stage. The plays presented the theology through varying perspectives and an admirably engaging versatility. The objection to 'plays' of the Prayer Book (observed in the Introduction) may owe something to the fact that, as a medium based in action, drama is easily adapted to ideas of salvation based in works. Medieval moral plays had demonstrated this, and while Renaissance drama diverged in many ways from its medieval predecessor, the later drama retained much of the former's ethical foundation.[86] It was part of the ingenuity of authors, as they worked on plays, to place that ethical foundation in varied contexts: pre-Christian Rome (*Julius Caesar*), Rome in Christ's era (*Sejanus*), Renaissance Italy (*Love's Sacrifice*) and other locations beyond the scope of this study. The reason for this bears repetition. As a medium based in action, theatre is amenable to Catholic ideas of salvation based in works; for if actions connect with salvation, or even the idea of it, a Catholic theology of works is latent. Given the ban on this theology in the *Thirty-nine Articles* (and the intense objection to it in wider Protestantism) one must infer this latent meaning was recognised and intended: the inherent theology of dramatic work.

Something else emerges from the dramatic theology of this chapter, especially from *Sejanus* and *Love's Sacrifice*. While Jonson's play ends with *damnatio memoriae*, Ford's ends with the sanctified monument of Bianca's tomb. As we have seen, these alternatives for the dead were consistent in

---

86 Kate Cooper, p. 108.

Christian (and before that, pagan) thinking; since worthy Christians were rewarded with conscious efforts of remembrance, it stood to reason that the unworthy dead were punished by equally conscientious acts of forgetting.[87] In fact, *damnatio memoriae* is a frequent punishment for reprobates on the English stage. In Kyd's influential play *The Spanish Tragedy*, for example, Pedringano is executed, but his body is left 'unburied'. 'Let not the earth by choked or infect', says the executioner, 'With that which heaven contemns' (3.6.110–12).[88] In *Julius Caesar*, a fate similar to that of Sejanus awaits Cinna, whose name suggests 'Sinner'.[89] In *Love's Sacrifice*, devilish D'Avolos is condemned to die unburied (5.3.146–8).[90] On the Renaissance stage, it seems, burial and non-burial of the dead held Christian meaning.[91] Yet as we shall see in the next chapter, these Christian rites of memory were at odds with burial ritual in the Prayer Book.

---

87 I discussed this point earlier in the chapter. See p. 60.
88 See *The Spanish Tragedy, by Thomas Kyd*, ed. by Clara Calvo and Jesus Tronch, Arden Early Modern Drama (London: Bloomsbury: 2013), pp. 218–19.
89 Hopkins (2019), 163–4.
90 For discussion of the import of names in Renaissance drama and associated literature, see Alasdair Fowler, *Literary Names: Personal Names in English Literature* (Oxford: Oxford University Press, 2012), especially pp. 12–116.
91 Burial and non-burial also held important Christian meanings in the wider society. See Bill Angus, 'The Night, the Crossroads and the Stake: Shakespeare and the Outcast Dead', *in Reading the Road, from Shakespeare's Crossroads to Bunyan's Highways*, ed. by Lisa Hopkins and Bill Angus (Edinburgh: Edinburgh University Press, 2019), pp. 51–70 (p. 51–6).

3

Purgatory and the stage

'The Romish Doctrine concerning Purgatory, Pardons, Worshipping and Adoration as well as Images, as of Reliques, and also Invocations of Saints, is a fond thing, vainly invented, and grounded upon no warranty of Scripture, but rather repugnant to the word of God.'[1] So, succinctly, states Article 22 ('Of Purgatory') of the Church of England's *Thirty-nine Articles of Religion* (1571). It brings together some features of English Protestantism observed already in this book: the necessity for that religion to be grounded in Scripture; the 'repugnance' of religious views without scriptural warrant and grounding; the opposition to relics, images, worshipping and, additionally, Purgatory. The expansive category, encapsulating all these features, is 'Romish Doctrine'. Noting the term is frequently derogatory, the *Oxford English Dictionary* defines 'Romish' as: 'Of, relating to, or belonging to the Roman Catholic Church; adhering to or favouring Roman Catholic doctrine, practice etc.'[2] Importantly, here, being 'Romish' is not identical with being Roman Catholic. Article 22 of the Church of England uses 'Romish' as an adjective to describe or modify the noun 'Doctrine', implying a distinction between Roman Catholic doctrine and things which pertain to that doctrine. In Article 22 of the Church of England, it is not just Roman Catholic doctrine that was repugnant to the word of God, but rather the things that pertain, or relate, to that doctrine. Article 22 details these things as Purgatory, pardons, worshipping and adoration, as well as images, relics and the invocation of saints. In 'Of Purgatory', Purgatory stands for each of these things inclusively, even as 'Romish' points not just to doctrinal Catholicism but to things associated with it: what we can broadly call

---

1 'The Thirty-nine Articles of Religion' (hereafter, the *Thirty-nine Articles*) in 'Appendix B', *The Book of Common Prayer*, ed. by Brian Cummings (Oxford: Oxford University Press, 2011, pp. 674–85 (p. 679).
2 See the *OED* definition 2 of 'Romish'. Notably, definition 1 refers to ancient Rome. Clearly definition 2 is what is mainly at stake in Article 22, but definition 1 is also worth noting, since two plays in Chapter 2, *Sejanus* and *Julius Caesar*, address ancient Rome as well as Roman Catholicism.

'Catholic culture'.[3] This chapter shows that the larger part of Renaissance drama was 'Romish' and 'of Purgatory' in the inclusive senses in which those terms are used in the *Thirty-nine Articles*.

In part, this is a nonempirical, theoretical claim. It is evidently beyond the scope of this chapter (or of many books) to demonstrate empirically that every Renaissance play was either Romish or 'Of Purgatory'. Since Article 22 of the *Thirty-nine Articles* uses the terms Romish and 'of Purgatory' relationally, nevertheless, the claim that drama (or poetry) relating to Catholicism or Purgatory were included in the Church of England's understanding of those terms stands to reason. We may recall, too, that deep into the seventeenth century, the writing of mainstream English Protestants extended no further than to scriptural mosaics, since there was little scriptural warrant for writing.[4] That is a view enshrined in the *Thirty-nine Articles*. The emphasis on scriptural warrant and grounding in Article 22 suggests it, but this emphasis in fact develops earlier, more absolute statements on the topic. For having asserted that 'As the Church of Jerusalem, Alexandria, and Antioch have erred: so also the Church of Rome hath erred' (Article 19), Article 20 states:

> The Church hath power to decree Rites or Ceremonies and Authority in Controversies of Faith; and yet it is not lawful for the Church to ordain any thing contrary to God's word written.[5]

Only the Gospel ('God's word written') is an acceptable literary form for the Church of England, as indeed for Elizabeth I, the bishops of the Upper House and the 'whole Clergy of the Nether House' who ratified the articles in 1571.[6] All other literary forms are unacceptable. Like the Church of Rome in Article 19, forms which are alternative to the Gospel err 'in matters of Faith'.[7] This chapter details the Romish erring in matters of faith promoted by a wide range of purgatorial drama.

Purgatory and Drama: *Hamlet* and *Dr Faustus*

Purgatory and the Mass were 'the first pillar' of medieval Catholic culture and religion.[8] So when Reformation historian Peter Marshall put *Hamlet*,

---

3 Diarmaid MacCulloch calls the Mass and Purgatory 'the first pillar' of medieval Catholic culture. See MacCulloch, *Reformation: Europe's House Divided, 1490–1700* (London: Allen Lane, 2003), pp. 10–16, and below.
4 I discussed this point (following Alec Ryrie) in the Introduction. See p. 8.
5 See articles 19 and 20, in Cummings (ed.) (2011b), p. 679.
6 See 'The Ratification', in Cummings (ed.) (2011b), p. 685.
7 Article 19, Cummings (ed.) (2011b), p. 679.
8 MacCulloch (2003), pp. 10–16.

especially its Ghost, at the centre of Reformation history, it was clear that Renaissance drama and Reformation history overlapped, with much to say to each other.[9] Even critics claiming religious interpretation comes 'too quickly' to *Hamlet* acknowledge its importance.[10] *Hamlet* 'is intensely saturated with religious language, religious practices and religious ideas'.[11]

That the religious practices and ideas are theatrical bears emphasis. While religion matters in the play, Marshall argues that the play matters in the history of religion. That is true in various ways. First, the form taken by religion in *Hamlet* is dramatic. Second, as Article 22 of the *Thirty-nine Articles* implies, Purgatory and its associated, Catholic culture is 'vainly invented': it was an article of belief of the Church of England that Romish and purgatorial religion were mistaken imagination, so as a work of dramatic imagination, *Hamlet* responds to Article 22. This is specifically the case in the passage outlining the Ghost's purgatorial claims:

> I am thy father's spirit,
> Doomed for a certain term to walk the night,
> And for the day confined to fast in fires,
> Till the foul crimes done in my days of nature
> Are burnt and purged away. But that I am forbid
> To tell the secrets of my prison-house
> I could a tale unfold whose lightest word
> Would harrow up thy soul, freeze thy young blood,
> Make thy two eyes like stars start from their spheres,
> Thy knotty and combined locks to part
> And each particular hair to stand on end
> Like quills upon the fretful porcupine.
> (*Hamlet*, 1.5.9–20)[12]

The theatricality of the scene here is as important as the Ghost's claim that he is temporarily 'purged' in the afterlife. In a microcosm of the play's wider theatricality, here the Ghost performs his role and speech to Hamlet's audience, going so far as to suggest the still greater 'tale' he could tell and the moving effects it would have. Indeed: 'Hamlet's complex response to the Ghost models the vulnerability and responsibility of theatrical spectatorship itself.'[13]

---

9 See Peter Marshall, *Beliefs and the Dead in Reformation England* (Oxford and New York: Oxford University Press, 2002), p. 232.
10 See David Scott Kastan, *A Will to Believe: Shakespeare and Religion* (Oxford: Oxford University Press, 2014), pp. 119 and 143.
11 Kastan, p. 143.
12 All quotations from Shakespeare in this chapter are from *The Oxford Shakespeare*, ed. by Stanley Wells and Gary Taylor (Oxford and New York: Oxford University Press, 1988; repr. 1995).
13 Sarah Outterson-Murphy, '"Remember Me": The Ghost and its Spectators in *Hamlet*', *Shakespeare Bulletin: The Journal of Early Modern Drama in Performance*, 34/2 (Summer 2016), 253–75 (254).

While Article 22 of the *Thirty-nine Articles* made Purgatory and Romish culture a matter of imagination, *Hamlet*, especially in Act 1, Scene 5, makes Purgatory a matter of the imaginative performances of theatre and the responsiveness of audiences.

Unlike Article 22, *Hamlet* makes no clear statement that this imagination is vain. The Ghost's presentation runs counter to the English Church's official ideology.[14] Yet while *Hamlet* is the best-known example of Renaissance theatre connected with Purgatory, the connection is more explicit in Marlowe's *Dr Faustus* (1588).[15] In Marlowe's play, Faustus visits the Vatican invisibly, where he is mistaken for 'some ghost, newly crept out of purgatory, come to beg a pardon of your holiness'.[16] This explanation is accepted by the Pope, who initiates a 'dirge to lay the fury of this ghost' (Scene 8, 75–6), a ritual including signs of the cross and 'bell, book and candle' (Scene 8, 82). Exposed once more (though here by the damnable Faustus) is the theatrical religion of Catholics, especially the Romish rituals of Purgatory. From a perspective perhaps less sympathetic, *Dr Faustus* is here like *Hamlet*, Act 1, Scene 5: both scenes not only dramatise Purgatory, but they also imply it is theatrical.[17] To audiences, the suggestion is that their present commitment, theatre, is a Romish pastime. How plausible would that claim have seemed?

From the abundance of recent criticism detailing Catholic features on the stage, the short answer would seem not just 'entirely plausible', but 'just about certain'.[18] There has been a widespread rejection of claims that theatre

---

14 Peter Lake, *Hamlet's Choice: Religion and Resistance in Shakespeare's Revenge Tragedies* (New Haven, CT, and London: Yale University Press, 2020), p. 89.

15 For the date, see *British Drama, 1533–1642: A Catalogue*, 2, 1567–1589, ed. by Martin Wiggins (Oxford: Oxford University Press, 2012), p. 419. Wiggins's 'best guess' is 1588; upper and lower limits are 1587–89. Dates for the pre-Shakespearean plays of this chapter are normally from this catalogue.

16 See *Christopher Marlowe: The Complete Plays*, ed. by Frank Romney and Robert Lindsey (London: Penguin, 2003), Scene 8, 73–4), p. 375. Unless stated otherwise, all subsequent quotations from Marlowe are from this edition.

17 I note *Dr Faustus* is only 'perhaps' less sympathetic because the scene (and the play) is fraught with ironies, including, here, that Faustus mocks Catholic ritual as a damned man visibly working with a (dramatic representation of) a devil. Today scholars note the play's two-sided attitude to religion. See, for example, John Cox, 'Stage Prayer in Marlowe and Jonson', *Comparative Drama* (January 2016), 63–80 (67–8); Barbara Parker, '"Cursed Necromancy": Marlowe's Faustus as Anti-Catholic Satire', *Marlowe Studies*, 1 (2011), 59–77 (76–7); Gillian Woods, 'Marlowe and Religion', in *Christopher Marlowe in Context*, ed. by Emily Bartels and Emma Smith (Cambridge: Cambridge University Press, 2013), pp. 222–31 (222). This chapter helpfully elucidates significant aspects of the theatricality of *Dr Faustus* (Woods, 229–30).

18 Lake notes that the 'entire audience – even (especially) those who were themselves Catholic – would have been acutely aware' of the Catholic connotations of *Hamlet* in 1604. See Lake (2020), p. 89.

undermined belief.[19] Some now argue that, between religion and an emerging secularity, theatre occupied a 'vexed middle ground', where standard uses of religious language and ideas could be accompanied by dissociation.[20] Yet religion thrived in the provincial dramatic culture of England connected to London's theatres.[21] Assessing early modern performance culture as a whole, through detailed study of performance environments, occasions, reception histories, shared dramaturgical practices and audiences responses, Matthew Smith's verdict is categorical: theatricality was 'intertwined with the religious'.[22] *Hamlet* and *Dr Faustus* illustrate this theatrical religion, but they do so with special reference to Purgatory and its Romish rituals. We shall shortly assess how deep-rooted Romish theatre of the kind was. Yet a word on English rituals of burial brings the Romish performance into focus. Literary scholars today are used to a post-Reformation England dissociated from dead parents or grandparents; where some were confused, others conflicted, and others shared in Reformed zeal.[23] It is important to put this medley of outlooks in its political framework. Legally defining attitudes to the dead, the Prayer Book is vital.

Disrespect for the dead is enshrined in the Prayer Books of 1549 and 1559, where 'The Order of the Burial of the Dead' presents 'our vile body'.[24] The backdrop is a Lutheran and Calvinist lexicon where 'human', obstructing the divine and placed against it, was consistently a term of abuse.[25] Exemplified by the corpse, the Prayer Book's 'vile body' belongs to 'our' humanity; as the Prayer Book says elsewhere, 'no fleshe is righteous in thy [God's] sight'; 'there is no health in us'.[26] More broadly, the burial services of 1549 and

---

19 See Brian Walsh, *Unsettled Toleration: Religious Difference on the Shakespearean Stage* (Oxford: Oxford University Press, 2016), p. 6.
20 See Walsh, pp. 6–8, who here highlights parallels between Cummings and Dawson. See Anthony Dawson, 'Shakespeare and Secular Performance', in *Shakespeare and the Cultures of Performance*, ed. by Paul Yachnin and Patricia Badir (Aldershot: Ashgate, 2008), p. 84; Brian Cummings, *Mortal Thoughts: Religion, Secularity and Identity in Shakespeare and Early Modern Culture* (Oxford: Oxford University Press, 2013), p. 10.
21 See Paul Whitfield White, *Drama and Religion in English Provincial Society, 1485–1660* (Cambridge: Cambridge University Press, 2008).
22 Matthew Smith, *Performance and Religion in Early Modern England: Stage, Cathedral, Wagon, Street*, Re-Formations: Medieval and Early Modern (Notre Dame, IN: University of Notre Dame Press, 2019), p. 2.
23 Stephen Mullaney, *The Reformation of the Emotions in the Age of Shakespeare* (Chicago and London: University of Chicago Press, 2015), p. 13.
24 *The Book of Common Prayer*, pp. 83 and 172.
25 James Simpson, *Permanent Revolution: The Reformation and the Illiberal Roots of Liberalism* (Cambridge, MA, and London: Harvard University Press, 2019), p. 58.
26 See Morning Prayer (1559), in *The Book of Common Prayer*, p. 103. My comments here are particular to the Prayer Book and its lexical context. Funeral monuments (the religious sensitivity of which I observed in Chapter 1) are a different thing. Yet

1559 cut out any implied reference to Purgatory and excluded intercession for the dead.[27] Yet there are significant differences between the 1549 and 1559 services. While the 1549 rite contains a 'CELEBRACION [sic] of the holy communion when there is a burial of the dead', the 1559 rite has entirely removed the communion celebration.

One effect was to cut further any association of the church ritual with a Mass for the dead. Another effect was a shorter funeral ritual. The ritual of burial of 1559 is about half the length of that of 1549.[28] It shows a determination by Elizabethan, religious authorities to reduce church ritual for the dead and the comfort rituals offer.[29] The relevant context, here, is the very positive attitude to godly discipline of Reformed Protestants.[30] Emphasising scripture (Matthew 18:15–22), these Protestants thought discipline should come from within, both individually and in the Church community.[31] Of special note, from the Prayer Books, is the removal from the 1559 burial service of the closing Epistle of 1549, in which the minister stresses the need to 'comforte youre selves'.[32] This contraction of the minister's role attests the advancement of godly discipline. Yet it also testifies that the bereaved needed comfort in early modern England, producing intense arguments over the scale and duration of appropriate grief.[33] Even the godly, like Lady Grace Mildmay, were tormented by the thought that others, including her Catholic parents, would be damned.[34] Mildmay's solution was to cheat 'a bit', easing from strict Calvinism into a

---

the ranks of honour in post-Reformation England aimed in these monuments at a continuity of memory replacing the individual. See Nigel Llewellyn 'Honour in Life, Death and in the Memory: Funeral Monuments in Early Modern England', *Transactions of the Royal Historical Society*, 6 (1996), 179–200 (180). Heraldic funerals are similar. See Jennifer Woodward, *The Theatre of Death: The Ritual Management of Royal Funerals in Renaissance England, 1570–1625* (Woodbridge: Boydell Press, 1997), p. 61.

27 Cummings (ed.) (2011b), *Book of Common Prayer*, p. xxviii.
28 Compare the services in the Prayer Book: Cummings (ed.) (2011b), pp. 82–90 and 171–4.
29 Social sciences 'have long agreed that rituals and emotionality are interconnected'. See *Emotion, Ritual and Power in Europe: Family, State and Church*, Palgrave Studies in the History of the Emotions, ed. by Merridee Bayley and Katie Barclay (Cham, Switzerland: Palgrave Macmillan, 2019), p. 293. Yet, notably, the European Reformation 'set out to create a more thoroughly doctrinal mode' (Merridee and Baylee (eds), p. 285).
30 On this attitude, see MacCulloch (2003), p. 591.
31 MacCulloch (2003), p. 593.
32 *Prayer Book*, p. 90.
33 See B. Capp, '"Jesus Wept" But Did the Englishman? Masculinity and Emotion in Early Modern England', *Past and Present*, 224 (2014), 75–108 (88).
34 Mullaney, p. 15.

covenant theology that allowed her to think her parents might be saved.[35] Objections to godly discipline go beyond failures to understand the past by modern 'liberal' historians.[36]

Much more vocally than the Prayer Book early modern drama cried out for comfort for the dead. Alongside Romish rituals we shall observe, the theatre thus objected in a Romish style to godly discipline in mourning. For this objection, in the theatre, there were three general precedents. Classical tragedy encouraged a mourning emphasis on the Renaissance stage.[37] With a Catholic colouring, medieval drama encouraged and developed this emphasis.[38] Through humanist curricula, classical rhetoric produced an 'emotional inculcation' in actors which defied godly discipline.[39] Yet well before *Hamlet* or *Dr Faustus*, mourning on the Elizabethan stage had already gained Christian emphases deemed Romish by the Prayer Book.[40] The following discussion considers some striking, earlier examples.

Earlier tragedy and mourning: *Gorboduc*

When in *The Defense of Poesie* Sir Philip Sidney denounced England's pre-Shakespearean theatre, the one play 'of these that I have seen' which he admired was Thomas Sackville and Thomas Norton's *Gorboduc*.[41] First

35 Mullaney, p. 16.
36 On modern liberal historians not understanding, see MacCulloch (2003), pp. 591–2.
37 For discussion of Renaissance theatre's debt to classical ideas of mourning, see Tanya Pollard, 'What's Hecuba to Shakespeare?', *Renaissance Quarterly*, 65/4 (2012), 1060–93. For a useful view of the centrality of mourning in classical tragedy (a topic on which much has been written), see Olga Tazidou, *Tragedy, Modernity and Mourning* (Edinburgh: Edinburgh University Press, 2004). Wider connections between the Renaissance and classical theatres were well established by John Kerrigan, in *Revenge Tragedy; Aeschylus to Armageddon* (Oxford: Clarendon Press, 1996).
38 See Katharine Goodland, *Female Mourning in Medieval and English Renaissance Drama: From the Raising of Lazarus to King Lear* (Aldershot: Ashgate, 2005); Goodland, 'Female Mourning, Revenge and Hieronimo's Doomsday Play', in *The Spanish Tragedy: A Critical Reader*, Arden Early Modern Drama Guides, ed. by Thomas Rist (London: Bloomsbury, 2016), pp. 175–96. We observed other, wider debts to medieval drama in Renaissance theatre in Chapter 2 and we shall observe further debts below.
39 See John Wesley, 'Quintilian's Forensic Grief and *The Spanish Tragedy*', *Studies in English Literature*, 1500–1900, 60/2 (Spring 2020), 209–28 (222).
40 This chapter revises and significantly develops my article 'Those Organnons by which it Mooves', Shakespearean Theatre and the Romish Cult of the Dead', in *Shakespeare Survey* (2016), 228–42. The discussion of comedy is entirely new.
41 See 'The Defense of Poesie', in *Sir Philip Sidney: The Major Works*, Oxford World Classics (Oxford: Oxford University Press, 2008), p. 243.

performed in 1561/62, *Gorboduc* is the first printed English tragedy and the first in blank verse.[42] Sidney may have liked it for its treatment of Queen Elizabeth's succession. The play's opposition to foreigners is taken to prefer a marriage of Elizabeth to Lord Robert Dudley rather than King Eric of Sweden.[43] The opposition to foreigners has also been taken to refer to Mary 'Queen of Scots', though less persuasively. Mary's claim, and that of her supporters, rested on the Tudor blood (originally Welsh) she shared with Elizabeth. Thomas Sackville, notably, was not against aligning the English throne with foreign Catholics. He campaigned actively for Elizabeth to marry Hapsburg and French Catholic princes.[44]

We need not dwell on *Gorboduc*'s uncertain view of Catholic rule, beyond noting the national and religious contexts at stake. Politics, in *Gorboduc*, is deeply equivocal, for collaborative plays of the Inns of Court normally expressed competing interests.[45] Much more clearly, the appreciation of *Gorboduc*, in the *Defense*, aligns with Sidney's connection of tragedy and funeral. Sidney's argument against the theatre of his day is that it failed to distinguish 'right comedies' from 'right tragedies', so matching 'hornpipes and funerals'.[46] As we shall see, comedy did indeed contain important funerary

---

42 See Jessica Winston, 'Gorboduc Now!': The First English Tragedy in Modern Print in Performance', *English*, 68/261 (2019), 184–283 (185).

43 See Jessica Winston, 'Expanding the Political Nation: *Gorboduc* at the Inns of Court and Succession Revisited', *Early Theatre*, 8/1 (2005), 11–34 (15–16).

44 While promoting English Protestantism in Sussex parishes, moreover, Sackville, who lost a son fighting for the Protestant Henri of Navarre, also 'quietly supported and promoted some very active committed Catholics among his own children and grandchildren'. See Rivkah Zim, 'A Poet in Politics: Thomas Sackville, Lord Buckhurst and first Earl of Dorset (1536–1608), *Historical Research*, 79/204 (2006), 199–223 (200–1). As Zim remarks, there have been two images of Sackville: 'one created by university departments of English, the other created by History departments' (Zim, 199). For Zim, Sackville also exemplifies the Elizabethan inner circle, where policy was 'fluid and subject to changing circumstances'. See Zim, 'Thomas Sackville, Lord Buckhurst's letters from the Low Countries, the 'quarrels of my Lord Leicester' and the rhetoric of political survival', *Historical Research*, 92/255 (February 2019), 73–96 (96).

45 On the equivocal politics, see Doyeeta Majumder, "Absolutism Without Tyranny in *Gorboduc*: The Changing Poetics of Tudor Political Drama', *Renaissance Studies*, 32/2 (2017), 201–18 (218); on the collaboration and competing interests, see Winston (2005), 11.

46 See 'The Defense of Poesie', p. 244. The significance of Sidney's association of tragedy and funeral was first observed by Michael Neill in 'Feasts Put Down as Funeral', in *True Rites and Maimed Rites: Ritual and Anti-Ritual in Shakespeare and His Age*, ed. by Linda Woodbridge and Edward Berry (Urbana, IL, and Chicago: University of Illinois Press, 1992), pp. 47–74 (p. 48), and has been frequently noted since.

elements. Yet the tragedy of *Gorboduc*, which Sidney admired, is intensely concerned with funeral. A second observer also made this clear.

The eyewitness account of *Gorboduc* in the Yelverton Collection of the British Library also notes the play was a 'tragedie'.[47] The eyewitness stresses the play included an entrance of 'mourners' and repeats the funereal emphasis in his dramatic interpretation:

> The shadowes were declared by the *chore*. First to signyfie unytie. The 2. howe that men refused the certen and tooke the uncerten, whereby was ment that yt was better for the Quene to mary with the L.R. knowne than with the K. of Sweden. The thryde to declare yt cyvill disccntion bredeth mourning.[48]

According to the eyewitness, mourning is central in the three identified ways that *Gorboduc* 'signifies'; it is also the only feature of the play mentioned repeatedly.

There are just six eyewitness accounts of London plays from 1567 to 1642.[49] The conjunction of mournful action with tragedy in Sidney and the anonymous eyewitness strikingly suggest connections between mourning and tragedy which are widespread in the genre. That Sackville and Norton placed mournful action in a dumbshow also merits comment: in a static play of long sentientious speeches, the elaborate spectacle and movement of the dumbshows (the first known of in English drama) were the most memorable parts of the play.[50] Projecting mourning through a dumbshow, Sackville and Norton gave it a prominence: one answering to Sidney and the eyewitness accounts of its tragedy. Since godly discipline had removed ritual 'comfort' from the burial service of the 1559 Prayer Book, and since theatricality was inextricable from religion, here, in *Gorboduc*, is an example of Romish mourning crying out on the English stage.

The outcry presents a form of moral politics, especially in the Chorus and dumbshow which separate each act. Chorus and dumbshows work in tandem. While the Chorus is replete with moral maxims, the dumbshows are unusually full, stressing their meaningfulness for the play through a repeated heading: 'The Order and Signification of the Dumb Show'. Thus structured, the play is not just 'full of stately speeches and well-sounding

---

47 Citation from the Yelverton Collection are from Norman Jones and Paul Whitfield White, '*Gorboduc* and Royal Marriage Politics: An Elizabethan Playgoer's Report of the Premier Performance', *English Literary Renaissance*, 16/1 (1996), 3–17 (3–4).
48 Citation from Jones and White, p. 4. We may notice, here, that while the King of Sweden is evoked in this account, Mary Queen of Scots is not.
49 Jones and White observe five eyewitness accounts of London drama of the period including that of the Yelverton collection (p. 3). Sidney's insistence that he has seen *Gorboduc*, and other plays, makes a sixth.
50 Jones and White, pp. 5 and 16.

phrases, climbing to the height of Seneca's style' (in Sidney's phrase) but also 'as full of notable morality'.[51] Yet inextricable from this structured and emphatic morality is mournfulness. An example is illustrative.

The Chorus ending Act 3 precedes the dumbshow which opens Act 4. Quoted in full, the Chorus illustrates its extensive intervention in the dramatic meaning, its means of arguing from moral maxims and its interconnection of these features with mourning:

> CHORUS.
> The lust of kingdom knows no sacred faith,
> > No rule of reason, no regard of right,
> No kindly love, no fear of heaven's wrath;
> > But with contempt of gods and man's despite,
> Through bloody slaughter doth prepare the ways
> > To fatal sceptre and accursed reign.
> The son so loathes the father's lingering days,
> > Ne dreads his hand in brother's blood to stain.
>
> O wretched prince, ne dost thou yet record
> > The yet fresh murders done within the land
> Of thy forefathers, when the cruel sword
> > Bereft Morgan his life with cousin's hand?
> Thus fatal plagues pursue the guilty race,
> > Whose murderous hand, imbrued with guiltless blood,
> Asks vengeance still before the heaven's face
> > With endless mischiefs on thy cursed brood.
>
> The wicked child thus brings to woeful sire
> > The mournful plaints to waste his very life.
> Thus do the cruel flames of civil fire
> > Destroy the parted reign with hateful strife.
> And hence doth spring the well from which doth flow
> > The dead black streams of mourning, plaints, and woe.[52]

Dramatic moralising here begins with the chaos falling on kingdoms where individuals lust for power, but it ends with a kingdom in mourning. Funerary performance and 'mourning' are inseparable from this political theory.

In the following 'Order and Signification of the Dumb Show Before the Forth Act', political theory and mourning trade places. Instead of moving

---

51 'The Defense of Poesie', p. 243. For more on 'moral commentary' in the play, see Jones and White, pp. 4–5.
52 This and all citations from *Gorboduc* are from *Gorboduc or Ferrex and Porrex*, ed. by Irby Cauthen, Regents Renaissance Drama Series (London: Edward Arnold, 1970).

from the political to the funerary, the dumbshow moves from the funerary to the political:

> *The Order and Signification of the Dumb Show*
> *Before the Fourth Act*
>
> First, the music of hautboys began to play, during which there came forth from under the stage, as though out of hell, three Furies, Alecto, Megaera, and Tisiphone, clad in black garments sprinkled with blood and flames, their bodies girt with snakes, their heads spread with serpents instead of hair, the one bearing in her hand a snake, the other a whip, and the third a burning firebrand, each driving before them a king and a queen which, moved by Furies, unnaturally had slain their own children. The names of the kings and queens were these: Tantalus, Medea, Athamus, Ino, Cambises, Althea. After that the Furies and these had passed about the stage thrice, they departed, and then the music ceased. Hereby was signified the unnatural murders to follow; that is to say, Porrex slain by his own mother, and of King Gorboduc and Queen Videna, killed by their subjects.

Clad in black garments, the three furies bring to life the funeral imagery of 'dead black streams of mourning, plaints and woe' concluding the Chorus. Yet by the dumbshow's end, this imagery has become explicitly political in the 'signified ... unnatural' murders of Gorboduc, Videna and Porrex. From the beginning of the Chorus to the end of the dumbshow the meta-theatrical commentary has swirled from political theory to funerals and from funerals back again to political theory. Besides illustrating their immediate dramatic centrality, *Gorboduc* here begins the process of making English political theory and funerals inseparable on the English stage. The focus on 'vengeance' and 'Fury' points especially (though not exclusively) towards English revenge tragedy. The presentation of funerary remembrance as an agent in historical development points to the history play. Both forms received significant development by the playwrights and friends Christopher Marlowe (1564–93) and Thomas Kyd (1558–94).[53]

Earlier tragedy and history: *Tamburlaine II* and *The Spanish Tragedy*

Marlowe's history *Tamburlaine Part 2* (hereafter *Tamburlaine II*) appeared in 1587.[54] Like Part, 1, the play surrounds Tamburlaine with figures living

---

53 For discussion of Marlowe's friends, including Kyd, see Lisa Hopkins, *Christopher Marlowe: A Literary Life* (Basingstoke: Palgrave, 2000), p. 47; see also Sarah Dewar-Watson, 'Marlowe's Dramatic Form', in Bartels and Smith (eds), pp. 49–56 (p. 53).

54 On the Tamburlaine plays as history, see Linda McJannet, *Dialogue in English Plays and Histories about the Ottoman Turks* (New York: Palgrave, 2006), especially pp. 63–90; also, Charles Melville, 'Visualising Tamerlane: History and its Image', *Iran: Journal of the British Institute of Persian Studies*, 57/1 (2019), 83–106.

Purgatory and the stage 85

and dead.[55] Yet a contrast of the Prologues from these plays exposes differences. While both plays address brutal conquest, the Prologue to *Tamburlaine* promises a 'stately tent of war' backed by the 'high astounding terms' of its hero. The Prologue to Part 2 is distinct:

> The general welcome Tamburlaine received
> When he arrivèd last upon our stage
> Hath made our poet pen his second part,
> Where death cuts off his progress in his pomp
> And murd'rous Fates throws all his triumphs down.
> But what became of fair Zenocrate
> And with how many cities' sacrifice
> He celebrated her sad funeral,
> Himself in presence shall unfold at large.
> (*Tamburlaine II*, Prologue)

The first sentence addressing the audience presents Tamburlaine supplanted by death. Retaining death's emphasis, the second sentence initially moves away from Tamburlaine entirely. Instead, it makes sacrifice and the 'sad funeral' of Zenocrate the emphasis, only readmitting Tamburlaine to the drama as its narrator. Conjuring a very different audience response from the Prologue of *Tamburlaine*, death, funeral and sacrifice are the dramatic focus of *Tamburlaine II*. The subtitle to *Tamburlaine II* reinforces this. Often ignored, the subtitle reads: 'With his impassionate fury, for the death of his Lady *and* Love, fair Zenocrate: his form of exhortation and discipline to his three sons, and the manner of his own death.'[56] This makes the deaths of Zenocrate and Tamburlaine central. It also makes Zenocrate's death in Act 2, Scene 4 the motive for the 'impassionate fury' of Tamburlaine which follows.

Funeral indeed becomes the dramatic theme with the death of Zenocrate. Act 2, Scene 4 ends with Tamburlaine mourning her:

> For she is dead? Thy words do pierce my soul.
> Ah, sweet Theridamas, say so no more:
> Though she be dead, yet let me think she lives
> And feed my mind that dies for want of her.
> Where'er her soul be, thou shalt stay with me,
> Embalmed with cassia, ambergris, and myrrh,
> Not lapped in lead but in a sheet of gold;
> And till I die thou shalt not be interred.
> Then in as rich a tomb as Mausolus',

---

55 See Kathryn Shwartz, 'Marlowe and the Question of Will', in Bartels and Smith (eds), pp. 192–201 (p. 197).

56 See *Tamburlaine the Great … The Second Part*, in EEBO (accessed 16.8.2022); the subtitle quoted here modernises the original spellings.

> We both will rest and have one epitaph
> Writ in as many several languages
> As I have conquered kingdoms with my sword.
> This cursèd town will I consume with fire
> Because this place bereft me of my love.
> The houses, burnt, will look as if they mourned,
> And here will I set up her stature,
> And march about it with my mourning camp,
> Drooping and pining for Zenocrate.
> (*Tamburlaine II*, 2.4.125–42)

Various points need emphasis from this speech developing the Prologue and subtitle. Rather than the 'thirst of reign' of *Tamburlaine* (2.6.12), conquest and violence are here expressions of mourning.[57] This is clear in the images of the burnt houses 'as if they mourned' and from Tamburlaine's 'mourning camp' on the march. According to the speech and later evidence, this second image will be lasting. Extending mourning for the term of the play, Tamburlaine here states that rather than burying her, Zenocrate will accompany his march across the world. At least from Act 2, Scene 5, *Tamburlaine II* is an anguished cry for comfort at the loss of a beloved queen and wife.

As a ritual of memory for Zenocrate, the play thus stands against the foreshortening burial rituals of 1549 and 1559 we have observed, as well as the godly discipline which de-emphasised comfort, especially in the burial rubric of 1559. Far from being compressed or internalised, mournful images of funeral develop in *Tamburlaine II*. Act 3, Scene 2 presents this stage direction and scene: '[Enter] TAMBURLAINE *with* USUMCASANE, *and ... four [*SOLDIERS*] bearing the hearse of* ZENOCRATE, *and the drums sounding a doleful march, the town burning.*' In the last scene, Tamburlaine again recalls a funeral procession for Zenocrate: 'fetch the hearse of fair Zenocrate. / Let it be placed by this my fatal chair / And serve as parcel of my funeral' (5.3.210–12). Climaxing the play, Tamburlaine looks on the hearse, his last speech celebrating 'eyes [that] enjoy your latest benefit' (5.3.224), but the play has consistently enabled us to enjoy these sights.

Worship and adoration of relics are what Article 22 defined as 'of Purgatory' and 'Romish Doctrine'. *Tamburlaine II* extensively illustrates this Romish worship, and it adds another prohibited feature: 'Images'. Protestants allowed sacred pictures in the home and images of the Holy Land in the English Geneva Bible were an unprecedented example of sacred imagery in Protestant

---

57 Thirst of reign is part of Marlowe's attack on ideas of place, belief and status, on which critics have 'overwhelmingly agree[d]'. See James Siemon, 'Marlowe and Social Distinction', in Bartels and Smith (eds), pp. 155–68 (pp. 155 and 159).

books.[58] Yet Article 22 integrates Romish doctrine, Purgatory, relics, worship and adoration, and 'Images'. By contrast, Act 3, Scene 2 of *Tamburlaine II* selects and dwells on images of commemoration:

> [*Enter*] TAMBURLAINE *with* USUMCASANE, *and his three* SONS ...
> *four* [SOLDIERS] *bearing the hearse of* ZENOCRATE, *and the drums sounding a doleful march, the town burning.*
> TAMBURLAINE. So burn the turrets of this cursed town.
> Flame to the highest region of the air
> And kindle heaps of exhalations
> That, being fiery meteors, may presage
> Death and destruction to th' inhabitants;
> Over my zenith hang a blazing star,
> That may endure till heaven be dissolved,
> Fed with the fresh supply of earthly dregs,
> Threat'ning a dearth and famine to this land!
> Flying dragons, lightning, fearful thunderclaps,
> Singe these fair plains, and make them seem as black
> As is the island where the Furies mask,
> Compassed with Lethe, Styx, and Phlegethon,
> Because my dear Zenocrate is dead!
> CALYPHAS. This pillar, placed in memory of her,
> Where in Arabian, Hebrew, Greek, is writ:
> 'This town being burnt by Tamburlaine the Great,
> Forbids the world to build it up again.'
> AMYRAS. And here this mournful streamer shall be placed,
> Wrought with the Persian and Egyptian arms
> To signify she was a princesses born
> And wife unto the monarch of the East.
> CELEBINUS. And here this table, as a register
> Of all her virtues and perfections.
> TAMBURLAINE. And here the picture of Zenocrate,
> To shew her beauty, which the world admired –
> Sweet picture of divine Zenocrate,
> That, hanging here, will draw the gods from heaven
> And cause the stars fixt in the southern arc,
> Whose lovely faces never any viewed
> That have not passed the centre's latitude,
> As pilgrims travel to our Hemi-sphere,
> Only to gaze upon Zenocrate.
> (*Tamburlaine II*, 3.2.1–33)

Reiterating the funereal image of the burnt-black landscape, in this dialogue Tamburlaine initially also repeats both his and the subtitle's logic of conquest:

---

58 MacCulloch (2003), p. 560.

'Because my dear Zenocrate is dead'.[59] Implying material memorials onstage, Calyphas then alludes to 'this pillar, placed in memory of her'. Further commemorative materials emerge in the mournful streamer, the 'table' registering Zenocrate's virtues and the 'picture of Zenocrate / To show her beauty'. As part of the wider treatment of conquest as funeral, this unusually developed and, also, focused use of stage properties transforms the procession of victories originating in *Tamburlaine* into a vast, Romish funeral procession which is actively endorsed by those on stage. The Romish endorsement includes the Middle Eastern setting. Article 19 of the *Thirty-nine Articles* identifies the Church of Rome with the Christian errors of Jerusalem, Alexandria, and Antioch, as we have seen.[60]

A parallel process of endorsement is visible in Kyd's revenge tragedy *The Spanish Tragedy* (1587).[61] Here the Spanish setting gives Romish focus to memorials in the 'bloody handkerchief' passed between characters.[62] In this play too, a hero, Hieronimo, keeps a beloved family member unburied to the end. Emphasising his grief and suffering, Hieronimo's laments are more sustained than laments in *Gorboduc* and much more sustained than in *Tamburlaine II*. Yet the dramatic motif of the corpse preserved from burial until the denouement shows a collaboration of ideas between Marlowe and Kyd. In *The Spanish Tragedy*, the unburied family member is a son, Horatio, rather than a wife, and Horatio does not receive even the partial ritual of a hearse accorded to Zenocrate. Yet the combination of withheld funeral ritual with bloodthirstiness, in which violent language and action express a memorial lacking comfort, is the same in each play. As Tamburlaine produces Zenocrate's hearse before dying, therefore, Hieronimo produces his son's corpse:

> I see your looks urge instance of these words.
> Behold the reason urging me to this!
> *Shows his dead son.*
> See here my show; look on this spectacle!
> (*The Spanish Tragedy*, 4.4.86–8)[63]

---

59 As noted, the play's subtitle said fury arose 'for the death of his Lady'.
60 Catholicism is widely involved in depictions of the Middle East on the English stage. See Jane Hwang Degenhardt, *Islamic Conversion and Christian Resistance on the Early Modern Stage* (Edinburgh: Edinburgh University Press, 2010); for specific discussion of Marlowe in this respect, see pp. 155–61 and 167–73. Since I now turn to Kyd, it is noteworthy that his play *Soliman and Perseda* links Catholicism and honour in this eastern context (Degenhardt, pp. 161–2). I return to this point immediately below.
61 This is Wiggins's 'best guess'. The upper and lower limits are 1585–91 (Wiggins, p. 369).
62 Wesley, 218 and (citing previous criticism) 226, note 28.
63 All quotations from *The Spanish Tragedy* are from *The Spanish Tragedy by Thomas Kyd*, ed. by Clara Calvo and Jesus Tronch, Arden Early Modern Drama (London: Bloomsbury, 2013).

Since *The Spanish Tragedy* begins with Andrea's 'rights of funeral not performed' (1.1.21–2), the action of both plays is framed by burial. Tamburlaine's arrangement of hearse and throne indicates the art involved. As a 'parcel' of his funeral (5.3.213), the arrangement is as wrapped-up as a body in a cloth and as closed as a corpse in a coffin. In *Tamburlaine II*, this is the arrangement of the dramatic end, the close of events. Yet it is even more suggestive for *The Spanish Tragedy*. There, the show of the corpse exists in a wider show, which is itself the show of Andrea and Revenge. In *The Spanish Tragedy*, too, the action begins and ends in stories of life underground. Parcelling, here, is a claustrophobic principle of organisation. The 'endless tragedy' (4.5.48) is being continually wrapped up for a funeral.

With rituals of burial as the background, I have argued for a collaboration of ideas of funerary theatre in *Tamburlaine II* and *The Spanish Tragedy*. Yet setting the stage for debate, the plays diverge over funerary religion. Tamburlaine's allusion to 'a tomb as Mausolus", where he and Zenocrate 'will rest and have one epitaph / Writ in as many several languages / As I have conquered kingdoms with my sword' (*Tamburlaine II*, 2.4.133–6) has three important effects on what follows.

First, these lines associate the epitaph over the tomb with the babble of Roman Catholicism in its English, Protestant guise as Babylon, making Catholic memorial, particularly associated with prayer for the purgatorial dead, an incoherence.[64] Second, the lines transform Tamburlaine's conquests leading to Babylon into his and Zenocrate's material epitaph, with the many voices of the conquered cultures evidencing the memorial incoherence. Third, the lines anticipate Tamburlaine's death, where Zenocrate's corpse is a reminder of the ordained funeral and 'here ... all things end'. (*Tamburlaine II*, 5.3.250). Funeral babble leading to Babylon here brings us to the Apocalypse, in a coherent sweep of dramatised Protestant propaganda.[65]

Not that Tamburlaine's empire is straightforwardly a Catholic one; nor is the play straightforwardly anti-Catholic. Though the play's mixed religious

---

64 See Per Siverfors, 'Conflating Babel and Babylon in Tamburlaine 2', *Studies in English Language*, 52/2 (Spring 2012), 293–323, especially 301–2 and 315. The article gives a substantial view of Protestant connections between Babylon and linguistic 'babble'.

65 John Foxe and Marlowe are often connected: for example, David Anderson, *Martyrs and Players in Early Modern England: Tragedy, Religion and Violence on Stage*, Studies in Performance and Early Modern Drama (Farnham and Burlington, VT: Ashgate, 2014), pp. 151–82. Marlowe probably knew Foxe's *Acts and Monuments* from its second edition. See Fuller, 'Introduction', *The Complete Works of Christopher Marlowe, Volume 5: Tamburlaine Parts 1 and 2*, ed. by David Fuller, *The Massacre at Paris*, ed. by Edward Esche (Oxford: Clarendon Press, 1998), p. xxiii.

signals extend incoherence beyond the funerary, they do not do so coherently.[66] Yet the link of dramatic action with funeral and this association with Babylon's end of days is coherent: the dramatic bête noire is the Catholic ritual for the dead.

This is in sharp contrast to *The Spanish Tragedy*, where Babylon receives no mention and is certainly not a geographical locus. Possibly the playlet 'Soliman and Perseda' was performed in sundry languages, according to Hieronimo's promise, and (it has been argued) the playlet signals Babylon. Yet if so, the signal is indirect. At the point of revelation, moreover, God is not revealed, making Babylon anticlimactic.[67] In fact, the extant text of 'Soliman and Perseda' is in English: the claim that it really was performed in sundry languages depends on a single, unusual editorial interpolation.[68] That is suspect – doubly so, since understanding the speeches of 'Soliman and Perseda' is important for the wider play. Kyd's play *Soliman and Perseda* (1588) clarifies his attitude to Catholicism in the playlet: in the play, Knights of Malta regain their honour 'not by shedding their Catholic associations but by re-embracing the virtues of chastity'.[69] *The Spanish Tragedy* probably only became anti-Catholic in its later performances: Elizabethan admiration for Spain is as important to the play as Elizabethan hostility.[70]

The funerary contrast is also sharp in *The Spanish Tragedy*'s presentations of obligations to the dead, which divided Protestants from Catholics. From its first induction, funerary obligation to the dead is central in the play. The Ghost of Andrea says, 'my rites of burial not performed, / I might not sit amongst his [Charon's] passengers' (1.1.21–2). That makes funerals for the dead a supernatural law. It implies that to lessen the suffering of the dead, the living must complete their funerals. In the Virgilian context, in which the English recognised Purgatory, the line drawn makes the complete and

---

66 See Siverfors, 315. On *Tamburlaine II*'s 'several ... religious messages', see also Jeff Dailey, 'Christian Underscoring in *Tamburlaine the Great, Part II*', *The Journal of Religion and Theatre*, 4/2 (Fall 2005), 146–59 (147). For more on Protestant and Catholic influences on Marlowe in the Tamburlaine plays, see Fuller, p. xxiii.
67 Siverfors, 301; Jannette Dillon, *Language and Stage in Medieval and Renaissance England* (Cambridge: Cambridge University Press, 1998), p. 186.
68 The unusualness of the interpolation was noted by S. F. Johnson in '*The Spanish Tragedy*, or Babylon Revisited', in *Essays in Shakespeare and Elizabethan Drama in Honour of Harding Craig*, ed. by Richard Hosley (London: Routledge & Kegan Paul, 1963), pp. 23–36 (23).
69 Degenhardt, pp. 161–2.
70 See especially Eric Griffin, 'Ethos, Empire, and the Valiant Acts of Thomas Kyd's Tragedy of "the Spains"', *English Literary Renaissance*, 31/2 (Spring 2001); and Griffin, 'Nationalism, the Black Legend, and the Revised *Spanish Tragedy*', *English Literary Renaissance*, 39/2 (Spring 2009). Griffin sees sizeable differences between *The Spanish Tragedy* and the so-called Spanish Black Legend. Elizabethan 'Hispanophilia', he argues, is as relevant to the play as Hispanophobia.

Spanish funeral Catholic.[71] None of this is scriptural; all of it is 'Romish' in the relational sense in which the term is used in Article 22 of the *Thirty-nine Articles*, 'Of Purgatory'.

The benefit of funerals for the dead was a way of uniting them with the living.[72] It depended on an idea of community with the dead that changed fundamentally with the rejection of Purgatory by Protestants and the denunciation of Purgatory as 'vainly invented' in Article 22.[73] Watched by the Ghost of Andrea, Horatio's determination to recover Andrea's corpse in battle and sigh and sorrow 'as became a friend' (1.4.37) revives this Catholic idea of community, while his emphasis on an exteriorised grief runs counter to godly discipline. The grief enlarges in Isabella's speeches of mourning for her son, and they become larger still in the speeches of Hieronimo. While the Prayer Book's burial rite of 1559 had removed the reference to 'comfort', Hieronimo enjoins comfort and Isabella openly condoles:

> HIERONIMO: Here, Isabella, help me to lament,
> For sighs are stopped, and all my tears are spent.
> [...]
> ISABELLA: O gush out, tears, fountains and floods of tears!
> Blow, sighs, and raise an everlasting storm,
> For outrage fits our cursed wretchedness!
> (*The Spanish Tragedy*, 2.4.36–46)

Just as it earlier 'became' the friend, mourning the dead here 'fits' the parents. Just as mourning had to be complete, so here it opposes truncation. It is a moving English portrait of Spain's Romish rituals for the dead. Watched by the Ghost of Andrea and the theatrical audience beyond, the moving grief extends to everyone.[74]

---

71 For discussion of early modern readings (following Augustine) of Virgil's underworld as Purgatory, see David Scott Wilson-Okamura, *Virgil in the Renaissance* (Cambridge: Cambridge University Press, 2010), pp, 173–8. Critics who have read Kyd's underworld in these terms include Lucas Erne, *Beyond 'The Spanish Tragedy': A Study of the Works of Thomas Kyd* (Manchester: Manchester University Press, 2002), p. 53; Lorna Hutson, *The Invention of Suspicion: Law and Mimesis in Shakespeare and Renaissance Drama* (Oxford: Oxford University Press, 2007), p. 280.
72 MacCulloch (2003), p. 13.
73 For this distinction between Protestant and Catholic in detail, see Lucy Wooding, 'Remembrance in the Eucharist', in *The Arts of Remembrance in Early Modern England: Memorial Cultures of the Post Reformation*, Material Readings in Early Modern Culture, ed. by Andrew Gordon and Thomas Rist (Burlington, VT: Ashgate, 2013; Routledge, 2016), pp. 19–36.
74 For useful exploration of how mourning extends to theatrical audiences (though focused on *Hamlet*), see Kate Welch, 'Making Mourning Show: *Hamlet* and Affective Public Making', *Performance Research: A Journal of the Performing Arts*, 16/2 (2011), 74–82.

The big question for memorial tragedies like *Tamburlaine II* and *The Spanish Tragedy* is the extent to which grieving commemoration is compromised by its violent outcomes.[75] Critics of revenge tragedy highlight biblical passages seemingly forbidding revenge (Deuteronomy 32:35; Romans 12:19). Yet Christianity is altogether more complex. It is not straightforwardly pacifistic, and it may have been physically militant, in whole or part, from its earliest days.[76] Making Old Testament violence allegory and typology, Origen (c.185–254) spiritualised the violence and by the seventh century Ephesians 6, 11–17 was the key authority:

> Put you on the armour of God, that you may be able to stand against the deceits of the devil. For our wrestling is not against flesh and blood; but against principalities and powers, against the rulers of the world of this darkness, against the spirits of wickedness in the high places. Therefore, take unto you the armour of God, that you may be able to resist in the evil day and to stand in all things perfect. Stand therefore, having your loins girt about you with truth and having on the breastplate of justice. And your feet shod with the preparation of the gospel of peace (*pax*). In all things taking the shield of faith, wherewith you may be able to extinguish all the fiery darts of the most wicked one. And take unto you the helmet of salvation and the sword of the Spirit (which is the Word of God).[77]

It is easy to see how this spiritualised violence, which orders individuals to stand and fight against evil, transfers to commemorative tragedy. Tamburlaine and Hieronimo fight against 'wickedness in high places', as do Titus Andronicus and Hamlet, among others. From the Church Fathers, Christian spiritual warfare divided God's time into two stretches, devoted respectively to war and peace, vengeance and forgiveness; yet importantly, in this typology, one does not have the one without the other.[78] Though commemorators of the dead in English Renaissance tragedy may be compromised by their violence, they are never entirely so in Christian terms. The question, rather, is whether they are (in Lear's phrase) 'more sinned against than sinning'. Yet any such judgement is relative, encouraging audiences to see degrees of merit in characters, rather than to see them as absolute reprobates.[79]

---

75 See Derek Dunne, *Shakespeare, Revenge Tragedy and Early Modern Law: Vindictive Justice*, Early Modern Literature in History (New York: Palgrave Macmillan, 2016), pp. 18–19.
76 See Philippe Buc, *Holy War, Martyrdom and Terror: Christianity, Violence and the West* (Philadelphia: University of Pennsylvania Press, 2015), p. 68.
77 Buc, pp. 72–3.
78 Buc, p. 73. For further discussion of vengeance in Christian history, see pp. 152–74.
79 Questions of human cruelty and even of why the innocent suffer can elicit from audiences 'a complex response'. See David Beauregard, 'Shakespeare's Prayers', *Religion and the Arts*, 22 (2018), 577–97 (584).

Histories and ghosts

Meaning at once 'story' and 'history' in the period, the term 'histories', devised by John Heminges and Henry Condell in Shakespeare's First Folio (1623), shows that what we call the history play today was connected to other dramatic genres. Yet Heminges and Condell clearly understood the past as having special prominence in the plays. Their implicit recognition that the genre concerned the dead is explicit in Thomas Nashe's recollection of *I Henry VI*. His context was plays 'for the most part borrowed out of our English Chronicles, wherein our forefathers' valiant acts, that have lain long buried in rusty brass and worm-eaten books, are revived':

> How would it have joyed brave Talbot, the terror of the French, to think that after he had lain two hundred years in his tomb, he should triumph again on the Stage, and have his bones new embalmed with the tears of ten thousand spectators at least (at several times), who, in the tragedian that represents his person, imagine they behold him fresh bleeding![80]

According to the funerary metaphors here and the rich understanding of impersonation (in which Henry VI and his actor both triumph on the stage) *I Henry VI* was a lively encounter with the dead. If that gets lost in abstract phrases like 'history play' or 'the past', Nashe reminds us that the dead are history's content.[81] The description also makes the actor the commemorator of history, meaning both performer and narrative in the history play are commemorative. *I Henry VI* highlights the actor's role in these terms. An example is Talbot telling the Countess of Auvergne that he is but 'Talbot's shadow' (2.4.45). A debate follows as to whether he is a 'man' (II.iv.47), or she has 'substance' (2.4.49):

> TALBOT No, no, I am but shadow of myself.
> You are deceived; my substance is not here.
> For what you see is but the smallest part
> And least proportion of humanity.
> I tell you, madam, were the whole frame here,
> It is of such a spacious, lofty pitch
> Your roof were not sufficient to contain't.
> COUNTESS This is a riddling merchant for the nonce.
> He will be here, and yet he is not here.
> How can these contraries agree?
> (*I Henry VI*, 2.1.50–9)

---

80 See 'The Defense of Plays' in 'Pierce Penniless', in *Thomas Nashe: The Unfortunate Traveller and Other Works* (London: Penguin, 1972; repr. 1985), pp. 112–14.
81 Robert Harrison, *The Dominion of the Dead* (Chicago and London: University of Chicago Press, 2003).

Talbot here distinguishes between his theatrical 'shadow' (a synonym for a spectre or 'shade') and the substantive Lord Talbot of history.[82] The theatrical riddle highlighted by the Countess is that Talbot is 'here, and yet he is not here'.[83]

Yet the ghosts of the past keep reproducing themselves in *I Henry VI*. When the Earl of Salisbury dies, Talbot seeks to 'be a Salisbury' (1.6.84), but when Talbot dies the young Sir William Lucy is identified as 'old Talbot's ghost' (4.7.87). It is a haunted stage, made Romish by features both smaller and larger. As Salisbury dies, for example, Talbot prays for his soul: 'Heaven, be thou gracious to none alive / If Salisbury wants mercy at thy hands' (1.4.64–5). The larger context of this prayer for the dead is a medieval Europe in which English Catholics fight French ones. There is also the affective dimension of the drama highlighted by Nashe. Salisbury's death is a 'woeful tragedy' (1.6.55), requiring both 'revenge' (2.1.83) and 'comfort' (2.1.68). While the former links the history play to commemorative tragedy, the need for comfort in mourning runs counter to the developing, disciplinary thrust of the Prayer Books we have noticed.

On these points, what is true of *I Henry VI* is true of the history play genre. History plays look backward to move forward. They make the actor a commemorator and they make audiences his commemorative observers. Shakespeare does this pointedly. Every Shakespearean history play except *Henry V* begins with a backward glance, which normally takes the form of a commemorated death. *The First Part of the Contention of the Two Famous Houses of York and Lancaster* begins with the 'grief / Your grief, the common grief of all the land' at the passing away of Henry V with his French legacies, Anjou and Maine (*2 Henry VI*, 1.1.73–4). *The True Tragedy of Richard Duke of York and the Good King Henry the Sixth* initially follows with battle, blood, and the lofted head of the Duke of Somerset. In an image of the dead giving birth to the future, Richard throws the head down saying, 'Thus do I hope to shake King Henry's head' (*3 Henry VI*, 1.1.73–4). Foregrounding the funerary theme, *The First Part of Henry the Sixth* – probably written after the two other plays – opens with Henry V's funeral, which makes the funeral the premise of the sequence. Especially since his image of the risen Talbot recalls one of 'Henry's corpse ... burst[ing] his lead and rise[n] from death' (*I Henry VI*, 1.1.62–6), Nashe's analysis of Shakespeare's history as a dramatic resurrection was precise.[84]

82 For the shadow as spectre and shade, see 'shadow' (noun) in the *OED*, definition 7, which includes several literary examples including by Shakespeare and Marlowe.
83 For more on how Talbot 'haunts' the stage, see Mullaney, pp. 115–22.
84 Nashe's description of Talbot as 'the terror of the French' directly quotes Act 1, Scene 6, line 20. It seems Nashe substituted Shakespeare's image of Henry rising from his tomb for an image of Talbot doing so.

With greater or lesser funerary weight, other Shakespearean histories give the past similarly commemorative forms. *Richard II* opens with 'Old John of Gaunt, time-honoured Lancaster' (*Richard II*, I.i.1). *Richard III* opens with a 'buried' past, where 'arms are hung up for monuments' (I.i.3; 5); *1 Henry IV* opens with King Henry on England's 'blood' (I.i.6) spilt in the 'intestine shock' of civil war (I.i.12); *2 Henry IV* brings Rumour with true and false commemorations of Shrewsbury Field. In this context the Chorus of *Henry V*, focusing on a living king, is novel. Harry, who in the Chorus does not emerge from a past but is instead 'like himself' (I.i.5), is a fresh start. Nevertheless, Act 1, Scene 2 delves deep into his heredity, over which the ensuing drama is a battle. Its conclusion is Shakespearean commemoration at its most formal:

> Do we all holy rites:
> Let there be sung *Non nobis* and *Te Deum*,
> The dead with charity enclosed in clay.
> (*Henry V*, 4.8.122–4)

As nation and religion earlier merged in Henry's commemoration of the day of St Crispin, here history and heredity merge with the grand funerals of Roman Catholicism. At England's high watermark in Shakespeare's cycle and the play's soberest moment of triumph, *Henry V* claims the commemorative unity of its historical and temporal, funerary and religious modes.[85] Returning to lineage in the marriage to Catherine in Act 5 and then looking beyond Henry's death, temporal history seems one long funeral in preparation. Next to the emergence of plays of violent commemoration including *Tamburlaine II* and the revenge tragedies, the emerging history play (as written by Shakespeare and interpreted by Nashe, Heminges and Condell) adds pointedly to the early modern association of theatre and Romish religion.

Comedy and mourning

The commemorative features found both in tragedy and history plays are also in comedies. From the medieval 'boy bishop festivities' to Shakespeare's *Twelfth Night*, English comedy's roots are religious.[86] Especially important was the Christmas season of play, with its Feast of Fools and appointed Lord of Misrule.[87] Yet the jigs which normally ended an early modern play

---

85 My reading of *Henry V* develops that of Philip Schwytzer in *Literature, Nationalism and Memory in Early Modern England and Whales* (Cambridge: Cambridge University Press, 2010), pp. 126–51.
86 See Matthew Smith, pp. 13–51.
87 Smith, p. 15.

had 'trans-Reformational underpinnings'.[88] Jig clowning evolves from medieval theatre's Vice figures, for example, while the fool characters in jigs anticipate the early modern fool on stage.[89] The jig, writes Smith, 'reminds us that the greater atmosphere and history of the early modern playhouse is that of religious festival'.[90]

One question is how these jigs gybed with the playhouse's soberer themes, especially in tragic drama. Including music, dancing, sexuality, deception, rampant wordplay and thwarted ambition, jigs shared many of the thematic and theatrical elements of even the bleakest thematic tragedies.[91] Postlude jigs, therefore, remind audiences that even tragic plays exist in a world of *commedia*, based in a Christian understanding of guilt redeemed by innocence.[92] Yet early modern drama is distinctly aware of transitions between tragedy and comedy and it marks the transitions as matters of funeral.

A striking example is Shakespeare's *A Midsummer Night's Dream*, which opens with an instruction by Duke Theseus to Philostrate. The instruction is to manage the public mood:

> Go, Philostrate,
> Stir up the Athenian youth to merriments.
> Awake the pert and nimble spirit of mirth.
> Turn melancholy forth to funerals –
> The pale companion is not for our pomp.
> (*A Midsummer Night's Dream*, 1.1.12–16)

Philostrate is like a choreographer in a pageant.[93] Yet pageantry is of two kinds: merriment and mirth or melancholy and funerals. The performative distinction underlines the relation of comedy to tragedy, but it also implies comedy is a 'turning forth' of funerals and melancholy by stirring up viewers to happier moods. 'Pyramus and Thisbe' will later show comedy emerging from tragedy (and 'Ninus' tomb') and both cases can be thought instances of tragedy within *commedia*. Yet the consciousness of choreography, in the case of Philostrate, shows the playwright signalling funeral in comedy. As Philostrate stirs youth from funeral to merriment in Act 1, Scene 1, indeed,

---

88 Smith, p. 317.
89 Smith, p. 317.
90 Smith, p. 318.
91 Smith, p. 310.
92 Smith, p. 319.
93 C. L. Barber, *Shakespeare's Festive Comedy: A Study of Dramatic Form and its Relation to Social Custom, with a New Foreword by Stephen Greenblatt* (Princeton and Oxford: Princeton University Press, 1959; repr. 2012), p. 142.

so play and playwright stir the Elizabethan audience to a comedy that will, in fact, prove funerary. Though Theseus would cast off funerals, the play ends 'in remembrance of a shroud' (5.2.8), among graves, sprites and 'the churchyard paths' (5.2.12). Comedy distinguishes itself from funerary tragedy, but it does not escape it.[94]

Twelfth Night works similarly. Mourning her dead brother 'like a cloistress' (I.i.27), Olivia has shut herself off from the world for seven years. Confronted by the clown, Feste, in Act 1, Scene 5, she is teased into cheerfulness and a gradual re-engagement with those around her. Unlike *A Midsummer Night's Dream*, funeral is implicit, rather than explicit, but the juxtaposition of funerary and comic moods is similar. Similar too is that 'good fooling' (1.5.29–30) is an effort. As Philostrate choreographs the mood of Athens, melancholy Feste, appealing to 'Wit' (1.5.29), digs deep to bring merriment to Olivia's house. For Feste, too, jokes are 'revenges' (5.1.373) based in the medieval dramatic tradition:

> Like to the old Vice,
>   Your need to sustain,
> Who with dagger of lath
> In his rage and his wrath
> Cries 'Aha' to the devil,
>   Like a mad lad ...
>   (*Twelfth Night*, 5.1.127–32)

Comedy's function here is to scare away the devil, but its properties (rage, wrath, revenge) are those of revenge tragedy, meaning funerals are never far away. Youth, as Feste knows, does not endure (2.3.51) and for Orsino, at least, the temptation of 'savage jealousy' is to 'Kill what I love' (5.1.117). Love, mirth and laughter are 'present', but not 'hereafter' (2.3.45–6). Though the comedians will 'strive to please you every day', in the end, 'our play is done' (5.1.403–4). Sealing a 'holy close of lips' in marriage (5.1.156), the priest's remark, 'my watch hath told me, towards my grave / I have travelled but two hours' (5.1.160–1) is not just a curiosity. It marks pleasure as limited by time, which is marked in minutes, hours, marriages and funerals.

From the First Folio, the comedies which bring out best the religion in this dynamic are from either end of Shakespeare's career: *Love's Labour's*

---

94 See, further, Tobias Döring, *Performances of Mourning in Shakespearean Theatre and Early Modern Culture*, Early Modern Literature in History (Basingstoke and New York: Palgrave Macmillan, 2006); Matthew Steggle, *Laughing and Weeping in Early Modern Theatres* (Aldershot and Burlington, VT: Ashgate, 2007).

Lost (probably written in 1593–94) and *The Winter's Tale* (from *c.*1610). In the former, again, comedy stops when news of the death of the king of France 'interrupt'st our merriment' (5.2.710), leaving the audience 'under the sign of death' and 'caught between the impossible vows of monasticism and marriage'.[95] Similarly, under a sign of death, in the latter play Paulina fashions the tyrant Leontes into 'the penitent king'.[96] Yet Romish features are easily found in the other comedies. Bounded by time and funeral, for example, the songs of love and death in *Twelfth Night* surround its 'chantry' (4.3.25). Derived from 'cantaria', a place for singing, chantries were so-called from the Catholic convention that Masses were sung.[97] Yet they were also endowments to support perpetual Masses for the soul of their founder, so the agreement of Olivia and Sebastian to plight their troth under a chantry's 'consecrated roof' (4.1.25), before the priest, commemorates their surprising love as religious, harmonious, purgatorial and Catholic.[98] *A Midsummer Night's Dream* is more obliquely Romish. The early modern spirit-world was uncertain, even to leading thinkers. Terms such as 'ghost', 'demon', 'the returned dead', 'apparition', 'phantom', 'shade' and 'spirit' were used interchangeably, but knowing how to respond to spirits meant discerning between their kinds.[99] Often splitting along confessional lines (but not always so), answers ranged from demons, souls from Purgatory and saints to things less orthodox.[100] Yet the challenge of a term like 'fairy' is its ambiguity, especially when fairies are as active and present as in *A Midsummer Night's Dream*. Confronting the audience with fairies, *A Midsummer Night's Dream* invites questions of their discernment. Critics, of late, who have followed the purgatorial and Catholic potential of the play may not demonstrate its doctrinal Catholicism, but they do demonstrate its Romishness.[101]

---

95 Joshua Philips, 'Labor's Lost: The Work of Devotion in Tudor Literature', *Journal of Medieval and Early Modern Studies*, 44/1 (Winter 2014), 45–68 (62). See also Rist, 'Topical Comedy: On the Unity of Love's Labour's Lost', *Ben Jonson Journal*, 7/1 (2000), 65–87.
96 Paul Stegner, 'Masculine and Feminine Penitence in *The Winter's Tale*', in *Renascence: Essays on Values in Literature*, 66/3 (Summer 2014), 189–201 (190).
97 See MacCulloch (2003), p. 12.
98 On chantries, recently, see Barbara Harris, *English Aristocratic Women and the Fabric of Piety, 1450–1550* (Amsterdam: Amsterdam University Press, 2018), pp. 51–70 (p. 52).
99 Kathryn Edwards, 'The History of Ghosts in Early Modern Europe: Recent Research and Future Trajectories', *History Compass*, 10/4 (2012), 353–66 (354 and 358).
100 Edwards, 355, 358.
101 See, notably, Kevin Pask, *The Fairy Way of Writing: Shakespeare to Tolkien* (Baltimore, MD: The Johns Hopkins University Press, 2013), pp. 13–38; Regina Buccola, *Fairies, Fractious Women, and the Old Faith: Fairy Lore in Early Modern British Drama and Culture* (Selinsgrove, PA: Susquehanna University Press, 2006).

The haunted stage

In examples of tragedy, history and comedy, we have observed early modern theatre recalling the dead with Romish implications. The question arising is how pervasive those implications were on the early modern stage. A complete analysis of plays in the period is beyond us. Yet considering the nature of early modern narrative is informative. I return, therefore, to *Hamlet*, especially its theatrical connection of ghosts to stories.

When the Ghost in *Hamlet* says it 'could a tale unfold whose lightest word / Would harrow up thy young blood' (1.5.15–16), it is the preface to his claim to come from Purgatory; yet it is not the first time that stories and ghosts combine in the play, and neither is it the last. In Act 1, Scene 1, Horatio proposes that he, Francisco and the sentinels sit to hear Barnardo's 'story' (1.1.30) of the Ghost just before its appearance, while the play ends with Horatio seeking (in dead Hamlet's words) 'To tell my story' (5.2.301). The 'perfect symmetry' between stories and ghosts in *Hamlet* is striking, but the connection of ghosts and stories is not.[102] Behind *Hamlet*, winters' tales, old wives' tales and purgatorial stories helped generate belief in Purgatory in early modern England.[103] Inadvertently, the Church of England added to this generation. Condemning Purgatory as 'vainly invented', Article 22 of the *Thirty-nine Articles* made Purgatory not just a matter of fiction, but also of imagination at its most active.[104] Early modern England frequently associated invention with acts of imagination; to find out, or devise, by original thought or ingenuity – even to originate – are standard meanings of 'to invent' in the period.[105] In rhetoric, *inventio* is especially linked with the seats of human imagination, from which ideas were drawn and thus in-vented into the world.[106]

Ghostly generations of narrative are common on the Elizabethan stage. Though narrative slightly precedes Ghost at the start of *Hamlet*, in *The Spanish Tragedy* (a model for Shakespeare's play) it is a Ghost that starts. Behind that (among other sources) is the ghost of Seneca and his own, staged ghosts. The Ghost of Andrea that opens *The Spanish Tragedy* (like the spirit of Machevil who opens *The Jew of Malta*, though without the 'evil') is also

---

102 See Catherine Belsey, 'Shakespeare's Sad Tale for Winter: *Hamlet* and the Tradition of Fireside Ghost Stories', *Shakespeare Quarterly*, 61/1 (2010), 1–25 (5).
103 Belsey, 1–25.
104 Medieval ideas of Purgatory were intertwined with imagination. In MacCulloch's phrase, medieval Purgatory was 'a marvellous way of uniting the dead and the living' (MacCulloch [2003], p. 13).
105 See 'invent (verb) in the *OED*, definition 3; see also 2a, 2b, and 2c.
106 See Kirk Dodd, 'What's in a Name? Shakespeare's Inventio and the Topic of 'Notatio' ("Names")', *Early Modern Literary Studies*, 21/1 (2019), 1–35 (1).

a form of prologue. This ubiquitous feature of early modern drama is never just the beginning to a play; its apparent liminal position is 'as a reminiscence of the past, as well as an explanation or comment of what is to come'.[107]

To speak of a haunted early modern stage therefore makes sense; yet to interpret this as the action of a 'memory machine' is not quite right.[108] Early modern examples of the haunting past are both more personal and more literary than a machine implies. Consider Francis Meres's famous comment on Shakespeare's *Venus and Adonis*: 'As the soul of Euphorbus was thought to live in Pythagoras, so the sweet witty soul of Ovid lives in mellifluous and honey-tongued Shakespeare.'[109] This twice presents a dead soul as the source of later human agency. Animation (from the Latin *anima* or soul; but having the sense of 'living' also in the Greek: *psyche*) is here a matter in which the dead are the soul of liveliness.[110]

In theatre, this animation bears emphasis. In *Hamlet*, the Ghost's claim that his story could 'freeze thy young blood' (1.5.16) bring outs early modern versions of physiology derived from Galen (c. AD 130–210).[111] In his physiology, spirits, the energetic faculties that make the body move and feel, animate bodies.[112] In Act 1, Scene 5, Hamlet's ghostly play on 'spirits' – both personal and medical – underlines the importance of animation in the scene, especially in its causes. We may therefore ask: what animates Hamlet, causing him to act? Is it a spirit from the dead or of his physiology? Yet in early modern analysis, Galenic medicine and religion were interdependent.[113]

---

107 Brian Schneider, *The Framing Text in Early Modern English Drama: 'Whining' Prologues and 'Armed' Epilogues*, Studies in Performance and Early Modern Drama (Aldershot and Burlington, VT: Ashgate; 2011; repr. Routledge, 2016), p. 16.
108 See Marvin Carlson, *The Haunted Stage: The Theatre as Memory Machine* (Ann Arbor: University of Michigan Press, 2003).
109 Francis Meres's famous comment on *Venus and Adonis* (1598).
110 For 'anima' as 'soul', see the *OED* etymology for 'anima'. Interestingly, 'anima' contrasts with 'animus', these being the irrational and rational parts of the soul respectively. The *OED* also traces the etymology of 'animation' from Classical Latin, meaning 'form of life', through various early modern examples. Definition 4 specifically pertains to 'Senses relating to life, quickening, bringing into action'.
111 For discussion of Hamlet's 'young blood' in terms of physiology, see Rist, 'Catharsis as "Purgation" in Shakespearean Drama', in *Shakespearean Sensations: Experiencing Literature in Early Modern England*, ed. by Katharine Craik and Tanya Pollard (Cambridge: Cambridge University Press, 2013), pp. 138–54 (p. 149).
112 For this definition of spirits, see Gail Paster, 'Nervous Tension: Networks of Blood and Spirit in the Early Modern Body', in *The Body in Parts: Fantasies of Corporality in Early Modern Europe*, ed. by David Hillman and Carla Mazzio (London: Routledge, 1997), 107–28 (111).
113 See Charles Parker, 'Diseased Bodies, Defiled Souls: Corporality and Religious Difference in the Reformation', *Renaissance Quarterly* 67/4 (Winter 2014), 1265–97, especially 1269.

At root, the cause is theological. Early modern discussions of physiological spirits (even among more material-minded medical theorists) celebrated the breakaway force of *pneuma*.[114] Yet as important as the First Cause are the causal links between it and Hamlet. According to the scenes from *Hamlet* considered here, those links take two forms: the Ghost and the stories of the past. The implication is that ghost, narrative and history are intertwined (the latter connection is implied in the French *histoire*), with each bound up in Purgatory and purging. Yet it is also that ghosts animate historical narratives. That is a claim very close to Nashe's indication (in his analysis of *I Henry VI*) that in Histories the dead 'triumphe againe on the Stage'. What other dramatic precedents exist for the claim that narrative is an active ghost?

One answer is already in *Gorboduc*, in the 'Order and Signification of the Dumb Show Before the Fourth Act'. It explains introducing its Furies and the dead: 'Hereby was signified the unnatural murders to follow' (*Order and Signification*, 13). Spirits stand for narrative in this authorised explanation, especially for a fictional narrative of historical events to come. Well before Shakespeare, this shows, the ghost-as-narrative was fungible. In its prologue, *The Spanish Tragedy* places this fungible property front and centre. Spoken by the Ghost of Andrea, the prologue is at once the opening of the narrative, the story of Andrea's past and, therefore, a dramatised history. That makes the Ghost the voice of history; yet it also makes history the content of the ghost. *The Spanish Tragedy* depends on this opening speech by the Ghost. The ensuing drama, overseen and eventually ended by the Ghost, equates dramatic narrative (in this case a fictional presentation of history) with the dead.

Tamburlaine II presents physiological spirits instead of ghosts. Physicians surround Zenocrate and, also, Tamburlaine's deathbeds. The centre of their practice is 'spirits':

> PHYSICIAN. I viewed your urine, and the hypostasis,
> Thick and obscure doth make your danger great;
> Your veins are full of accidental heat,
> Whereby the moisture of your blood is dried.
> The humidum and calor, which some hold
> Is not a parcel of the elements,
> But of a substance more divine and pure,

---

114 Paster, 'Nervous Tension', p. 115. Explicitly for the author of the *Novum Organum*, Francis Bacon, all the universe besides the 'passive' earth consists of 'pneumatic matter'. See '3.3. Matter Theory and Cosmology' under 'Francis Bacon', in *Stanford Encyclopaedia of Philosophy*, http://plato.stanford.edu/entries/francis-bacon/ (accessed 18.6.2015).

> Is almost clean extinguishèd and spent,
> Which, being the cause of life, imports your death.
> Besides my lord, this day is critical,
> Dangerous to those whose crisis is as yours.
> Your arteries, which alongst the veins convey
> The lively spirits which the heart engenders,
> Are parched and void of spirit, that the soul,
> Wanting those organons by which it moves,
> Cannot endure by argument of art.
> Yet if your majesty may escape this day,
> No doubt but you shall soon recover all.
> *(Tamburlaine II, 5.3. 82–99)*

This detailed and final medical analysis goes to the heart of the liveliness of Tamburlaine. He is animated or dead through a rationale in which spirits move the soul. The analysis defines the play's idea of humanity. It makes the life of the soul the definition of living, explaining action and theatre as the soul's visible manifestations. Although there are no ghosts in *Tamburlaine II*, the souls traditionally emerging as ghosts in death are essential.

Those inner spirits are also in *The Spanish Tragedy*, most obviously in the Ghost of Andrea's introduction of his 'soul': the 'eternal substance' that 'Did live imprison'd in my wanton flesh / Each in their function serving the other's need' (1.1.1–3). The inner spirits equated to action are almost as evident in Revenge. He is both a personified feeling ('vengefulness') and a personified action. The opening of *The Spanish Tragedy* turns inside out the explanation of action in *Tamburlaine II*. Through an external association of spirit, feeling and action, it shows the physiological religion diagnosed by Marlowe in Tamburlaine's body. Yet *The Spanish Tragedy* complements this heightened visibility with another form of spiritual intercession:

> And all the saints do sit soliciting
> For vengeance ...
> *(The Spanish Tragedy, 4.1.33–4)*

The spiritual impetus here is the saints of Roman Catholic Spain.

The example of *Richard III* can show, in conclusion, how the linked forms of spirituality (narratological, physiological, Catholic) explain action. Four short scenes after Buckingham identifies the day of his death as 'All-Souls day' (5.1.12), Act 5, Scene 5 identifies 'Dreams' as part of a spirit's arsenal (5.5.100). From Act 1, Scene 1, where Clarence complained that Edward IV 'hearkens after prophecies and dreams' (1.1.54), the truthfulness of prophetic dreams has been in question. Act 5, Scene 5 provides the answer. Here the ghosts of Clarence, Prince Edward and Rivers tell Richard they will 'sit heavy on thy soul tomorrow' (5.5.71; 85; 93); and in tenor, Richard receives the same message from the ghosts of Henry, Gray, Vaughan, the Princes and Lady Anne. Awaking, Richard's soliloquy of doubt and broken phrases (5.3.131–60) shows his spirit is broken. Also visited by the ghosts, but with encouragement, Richmond, by contrast, awakes in high spirits.

By contrast, then, the two characters illustrate the causal relation of spirits to feeling to action. Stressing the relationship, Richmond comments: 'Methought their souls whose bodies Richard murdered / Came to my tent and cried on victory. / I promise you, my soul is very jocund' (5.6.184–6). This connection of 'their souls' to 'my soul' underlines the connections between ghosts, persons and how they feel. The subsequent success and failure of Richmond and Richard in battle connects these ghost-induced feelings with actions and events, both in the theatre and in its view of English history.

Prominent in these haunted scenes are the interchangeability of terms: 'ghost', 'soul', 'spirit'. The first two remain sub-species of the third in general discourse. As we have seen, the third term (while the focus of more strictly physiological discourse in the period) was connected to the soul, and so the soul in death: the ghost. All three terms (ghost, soul, spirit) can imply religion and the play brings this out not just in 'All-Souls', but also in the prayers its souls offer.

The ghost of Queen Margaret shows proper piety when she prays to 'dear God' (4.6.77) for England's salvation from Richard; indeed, though Richard calls her the 'she-wolf of France', her reputation in the era (far from confirming Richard's view) was contested.[115] Margaret's personal piety is remembered in a role of devotions now in the Bodleian library, where her queenship is strikingly associated with the Virgin Mary, both as a matter of private devotion and as a means of participating in public and political discourse.[116] When, therefore, Margaret states that 'saints pray' for Richard's demise (4.4.75) there are reasons to believe her. In turn, when the Ghost of Lady Anne says to Richmond that she 'pray[s] for thee' (5.6.119), her link with Margaret, in prayer, spirit and intention, gives a reason to believe her too.

Medieval saints and ghosts, then, pray for the freedom of England from Richard's tyranny and the Tudor succession through Henry VII. They support the 'God and good angels' (5.5.129) who bring that about, so that, literally,

---

115 See Carole Levin, 'Queen Margaret in Shakespeare and Chronicles: She Wolf or Heroic Spirit', in *Scholars and Poets Talk about Queens*, ed. by Carole Levin and Christine Stewart Nuñez, Queenship and Power (New York and Basingstoke: Palgrave Macmillan, 2015), pp. 111–32.
116 See Sonja Drimmer, 'Beyond Private Matter: A Prayer Role for Queen Margaret of Anjou', *Gesta*, 53/1 (March 2014), 95–120 (97).

the so-called 'ghosts' of Margaret and Anne are on the side of the angels. They may be saints or, perhaps, souls from Purgatory, where the dead had plenty of time to pray for the living and were expected to do so.[117]

Which of the two, saints or purgatorial souls, is unconfirmed. When Margaret, praying to God for Richard's demise, says not just 'saints pray', but also 'fiends roar' (4.4.75) Purgatory may be suggested: the speech places the speaker between hell and heaven. Yet it is the bigger picture that is clear: the haunted scenes integrate Catholic spirituality in human events and theatrical action, and they do so as a matter of theatrical work. Tragedies, histories and comedies, as we have seen, bear witness to the integration, promoting a theatre 'of Purgatory' according to the Church of England's *Thirty-nine Articles of Religion*, Article 22. Scholarship observes an early modern spirituality in which mingled Galen's physiology, the anatomy derived from Vesalius (1514–64) and prominently Catholic ideas of corporeal sanctity and corruption.[118] As I have shown, early modern theatre animated the Catholic spirits, despite a watchful Church of England.

---

117 See MacCulloch (2003), p. 13.
118 See Parker (2014), 1268, 1266.

4

Catholic worship and devotional poetry

Chapter 3 argued that Romish spirituality haunted the early modern theatre, but this chapter argues that it haunted persons far more intimately connected with the Prayer Book: the English clergymen Richard Crashaw (1612–48), George Herbert (1593–1633), Robert Herrick (1591–1674) and John Donne (1572–1631). Of these English poets, Crashaw converted from the Church of England to Catholicism and John Donne converted the other way. Argument about Catholic dimensions to these poets began with Louis Martz, whose *The Poetry of Meditation*, originally published in 1956, observed from English translations of Spanish Mystics like Luis de Grenada (1504–88) large-scale spiritual formation in England.[1] For devotional poetry, Martz argued the importance of Ignatian meditation. Critical arguments have taken many turns since.[2] My argument is that the institutional church presented through the poetic corpora of the English clergymen, Crashaw, Herbert, Herrick and Donne is in substantial part Roman Catholic. I start with some recent critical claims for these poets, particularly those touching on my wider themes.

---

1 Louis Martz, *The Poetry of Meditation: A Study in English Religious Meditation of the Seventeenth Century* (New Haven, CT, and London: Yale University Press, 1954; revised 1962; repr. 1974), pp. 6–9.
2 I discuss important recent contributions in the following sections. On the literary influence of the Mystics, critical discussion since has been narrower and more equivocal. See Elizabeth Howe, 'Donne and the Spanish Mystics on Ecstasy', *Notre Dame English Journal*, 13/2 (1981), 29–44 (31); Michael Martin, *Literature and the Encounter with God in Post-Reformation England* (London and New York: Routledge, 2016), p. 48; Jennifer Nichols, 'Dionysian Negative Theology in Donne's "A Nocturn Upon S. Lucie's Day"', *Texas Studies in Literature and Language*, 53/3 (2011), 352–67, 363, note 4. These tend to focus on Donne and Saint Teresa: de Grenada disappears. On Teresa's influence beyond Donne, see Jonathan Crewe, 'Reading Rapture: Richard Crashaw's Saint Teresa', *Studies in English Literature*, 59/1 (2019), 135–52.

I have previously noted the conscious juxtaposition of Molly Murray's *The Poetics of Conversion in Early Modern Literature* (2009) with Brian Cummings's *The Literary Culture of the Reformation* (2002), but their rival views of English devotional poetry needs emphasis. Cummings located English poets like Herbert and Donne amid a Protestantism derived from Luther, which searched for a language and logic to encapsulate a 'central paradox': that 'the sinner is never made righteous, he is always being made righteous. Or, alternatively, the sinner is always righteous, but still always sinful.'[3] For Murray, by contrast, devotional paradoxicality in verse reflects the alternative versions of Christianity of the day: far from being 'implicitly Protestant', devotional poetry wrestled with the era's religious alternatives.[4]

The difference between Cummings and Murray stands out in their treatment of Robert Southwell. For Murray, resurgent critical interest in Southwell 'has helped to demonstrate, as Louis Martz suggested half a century ago, that post-Tridentine Catholicism ... encouraged a poetically fruitful "conversion of the heart"'.[5] Yet rather than producing a Catholic dimension to English religious poetry, for Cummings the influence of Southwell was absorbed 'back into English protestantism'.[6] Enabling this conclusion was Cummings's emphasis on penance, repentance and confession in Southwell: since these topics absorbed Protestants, the argument goes, English Protestants could absorb Southwell without disruption to English Protestantism.[7] As my reading of *St Peter's Complaint* implies, there is something to this; yet it is far from a complete picture, either of Southwell or the devotional poets who followed him. Contrition, confession and absolution, as we now know, provoked a long conflict about the conventions of forgiveness in the Church of England; on these topics, there was no simple model of replacement of things Catholic by things Protestant.[8] Moreover, the interests of the devotional poets go well beyond penitential topics. By contrast with the penitential emphasis of Cummings, therefore, this chapter highlights a different side

---

3 Brian Cummings, *The Literary Culture of the Reformation: Grammar and Grace* (Oxford and New York: Oxford University Press, 2002), p. 326.
4 See Molly Murray, *The Poetics of Conversion in Early Modern English Literature: Verse and Change from Donne to Dryden* (Cambridge: Cambridge University Press, 2008), p. 98. I agree with Murray, in this respect, that Cummings 'moves too quickly from noting the poetry's theological "confusion" to assigning to it a more abstract (and implicitly Reformed) notion of ineffable grace' (Murray, p. 98).
5 Murray, pp. 32–3.
6 Cummings (2002), p. 364.
7 Cummings (2002), pp. 339–64.
8 See Sarah Beckwith, *Shakespeare and the Grammar of Forgiveness* (Ithaca and London: Cornell University Press, 2011), pp. 3 and 56.

to devotional poetry: one that (*pace* Cummings) is Catholic in outlook, yet which Catholicism (*pace* Murray) goes beyond poetic style.[9]

Gary Kuchar has recently observed similarities between the depictions of Eucharistic worship of George Herbert and Robert Southwell.[10] Yet critics since Martz have repeatedly noted a pervasive *influence* of Southwell on the devotional poets.[11] I therefore argue that Southwell's Catholic presentation of Eucharistic worship was a pervasive influence on these poets; that despite adherence to the Church of England and its prescribed rituals in the Prayer Book, Crashaw, Herbert, Herrick and Donne celebrated facets of Catholic worship through their poetry.[12] I illustrate this point by identifying the Roman Catholic features of worship in Southwell, which together present worship as an institutional feature of the Catholic Church. Next, I demonstrate the re-presentation of the features in Crashaw, Herbert, Herrick and Donne, so showing that the institutional church of Southwell – a Roman Catholic church – recurs in the subsequent poets.

The features of Eucharistic worship in question are the transubstantiated Eucharist, the church congregation and context, ritual procedures of the Mass, Roman Catholic saints and what Cummings called the 'Petrine' context of Southwell's Catholic Church.[13] Re-collecting these features in their poetry, Crashaw, Herrick, Donne and Herbert differently recollect Southwell's Catholic Church, in a process of literary memorialisation. We begin with Southwell. More than a dozen editions of his *Saint Peter's Complaint* appeared

---

9 Murray argues 'poetic style' in early modern poetry implies 'a movement between churches and not solely a progression toward grace' (Murray, p. 5).
10 See Gary Kuchar, 'Poetry and Sacrament in the English Renaissance', in *A Companion to Renaissance Poetry*, ed. by Katharine Bates (Hoboken, NJ, and Chichester: Wiley Blackwell, 2018), pp. 50–62 (p. 59).
11 Important studies of this influence include Alison Shell's discussion of 'Catholic Poetics and the Protestant Canon', in *Catholicism, Controversy and the English Literary Imagination*, 1558–1660 (Cambridge: Cambridge University Press, 1999), pp. 56–106; Anne Sweeney, *Robert Southwell, Snow in Arcadia: Redrawing the English Lyric Landscape, 1586–95* (Manchester and New York: Manchester University Press, 2006); Sophie Read, *Eucharist and the Poetic Imagination* (Cambridge: Cambridge University Press, 2013), pp. 40–1. For more recent discussion, see, Shaun Ross, 'Robert Southwell: Sacrament and Self', *English Literary Renaissance*, 47/1 (2017), 73–109. The claim here that Southwell 'anticipated and inspired subsequent English poets' regarding their presentations of 'sacramentalism' (Ross, 73–4) is especially relevant to my present argument.
12 The importance of Eucharistic worship in poetic culture (and controversy) is also emphasised by Nandra Perry, in 'Turning the Tables: 'Richard Crashaw Reads the Protestant Altar', *Studies in Philology*, 112/2 (2015), 303–26.
13 Cummings (2002), p. 331.

between 1595 and 1640, of which most were from mainstream Protestant presses.[14]

The institutional church of Robert Southwell

Southwell's poetry reminded his first, Catholic readers of their membership of the one, true Catholic Church, but the poetry also provided Protestant readers in England with the first poetic model for consecrated poetry.[15] The model combined individual and 'corporate' expression, in which the Catholic Church stands out as an institution.[16] This combination of the personal and the institutional is conspicuous in Southwell's poems presenting St Peter.

The self-castigating 792 lines of *Saint Peters Complaint* illustrate the combination. Based in scripture, the poem speaks to the interest in scriptural mosaics of English Protestants.[17] Yet its speaker, St Peter, presents an intense, personal experience of suffering. Images of torture emphasise this. 'I seem to see a messenger from hell, / That my prepared torments comes to tell', says Peter (599–600), despairingly adding: 'Thou has made me to my self a hell' (672).[18] The end of such self-observation is paradoxical. Though there is hope for mercy in the poem's last two stanzas, the speaker's plea to 'Cancell my debtes, sweete *Jesu*' (792) receives no answer and Peter's crucifixion awaits. As an image of Christ's crucifixion, this suggests both salvation and the Eucharist; yet crucifixion is also a torture, meaning personal agony is central in the poem to the end.

The 'corporate' aspect of Peter's narrative is threefold. As a Christian example from scripture, Peter stands for the Christian community which must suffer in Christ's imitation: a concept central to the Reformation's collective argument.[19] Yet Southwell's Catholic example speaks especially to English recusants. Their distinct suffering, as recusants in Protestant England, finds expression in Peter.[20] Moreover, the 'Petrine' dimension of the poem indicates the Catholic Church. Here, Peter points to the Church

---

14 Read, p. 41.
15 Ross (2017), 109.
16 Ross, 108.
17 I discussed these mosaics and the Protestant 'poetics' they gave rise to in the Introduction. See pp. 7–8 and p. 21, note 115.
18 All quotations from Southwell are from *The Poems of Robert Southwell, S.J*, ed. by James McDonald and Nancy Brown (Oxford: Clarendon Press, 1967).
19 On this 'collective argument' of the Reformation, see Peter Marshall, *Heretics and Believers: A History of the English Reformation* (New Haven, CT: Yale University Press, 2017), p. 5.
20 Ross speaks of Southwell's poetry giving recusants 'strategies to perform' their 'identity in an individual way' (Ross, 109).

according to Christ's description of Peter as its foundation (Matthew 16:18). By Catholic interpretation and the tradition for which Southwell died, St Peter is the first Pope and successive Popes are his heirs. The poem thus presents three interrelated ideas of Peter's suffering: the Christian, the recusant and the institutionally Catholic. This last may help to explain the popularity of the poem with Protestants, for it suggests a church which in Peter has betrayed Christ and needs redemption.[21] Nevertheless, in Southwell's poem the Christian, the recusant and the Catholic Church are one body and there are no Christian alternatives.

For Cummings, *St Peters Complaint* brought readers into the metaphorical context of the church of Peter 'without making the connection too obvious'.[22] Yet while *St Peters Complaint* is the longest of Southwell's poems, it is by no means his only poem focusing on St Peter. The recurrence of St Peter in three further poems – 'St Peter's Afflicted Mind', 'St Peter's Remorse' and a second, shorter version of 'St Peter's Complaint' – stresses the importance of Peter, the foundation of the Church, for Southwell's readers. Enhancing Peter's association with Roman Catholicism in Southwell's poetry, moreover, is Southwell's repeated and explicit presentations of Peter as a saint.

The Church of England never decided to create Protestant saints.[23] Moreover, Church of England texts regularly reflect hostility to saints.[24] The three-part sermon 'Against the Peril of Idolatry' in the *Book of Homilies*, for example, echoes Calvin's claim that saint-veneration is essentially polytheism.[25] Saints in England, therefore, and especially saints associated with Southwell, imply controversial Catholic worship: a point of importance for the Protestant poets interested in saints to be considered soon. Yet Southwell's highlight of St Peter, in the poems celebrating him, is just one example of his use of saints to emphasise Catholic identity. Southwell's poems of worship are populated by several religious persons presented as saints, notably St Thomas Aquinas, Mary Magdalene and Mary the mother of Jesus, who is also present as 'Our Lady' and 'The Virgin'.

Like Peter, these saints embody the Church at its best and the importance of saints generally for Southwell is clear. Far more of Southwell's poems

---

21 See, also, Jillian Snyder, 'Pricked Hearts and Penitent Tears', *Studies in Philology*, 117/2 (2020), 313–36 (329).
22 Cummings (2003), p. 331.
23 See Graham Parry, 'Sacred Space in Laudian England', in *Sacred Text – Sacred Space: Architectural, Spiritual and Literary Convergence in England and Wales*, ed. by Joseph Sterrett and Peter Thomas (Leiden and Boston: Brill, 2011), pp. 123–41 (p. 124).
24 See James MacDonald, 'The Redcross Knight and the Limits of Human Holiness', *Spenser Studies*, 30 (2015), 113–31 (118).
25 MacDonald, 118.

address the saints than Christ's crucifixion. Southwell begins *Saint Peters Complaint* with these lines in 'The Author to the Reader':

> Dear eie that daynest to let fall a look,
> On these sad memories of Peters plaints:
> Muse not to see some mud in cleerest brooke,
> They once were brittle mould, that now are Saints.
> Their weaknesse is no warrant to offend:
> Learn by their faults, what in thine owne to mend.
> ('The Author to the Reader', 1–6)

This opening emphasises the saintliness of Peter among others, encouraging the reader to use the saints as exemplary models in their lives, since one can learn from their faults and take heart that saints too were once of 'brittle mould'. Similarly emphasising saints are the fifty-two short lyrics (identically sequenced in four of the five extant manuscripts, with only small variation in the fifth) written by Southwell in English.[26] These begin with a sequence 'On the Virgin Mary and Christ'.

The sequence therefore puts Christ alongside the Queen of Saints, while putting her first. Making her queenship plain, the fourteenth and last poem in the sequence is 'The Assumption of our Lady':

> Gemm to her worth, spouse to her love ascendes,
> Prince to her throne, Queen to her heavenly kinge,
> Whose court with solemne pompe on her attends,
> And Quires of Saintes with greeting notes do singe.
> Earth rendreth upp her undeserved praye,
> Heaven claymes the right and beares the prize awaye.
> ('The Assumption of our Lady', 13–18)

This clearly establishes quires of saints and Mary as their queen, in a figure of holiness signally Catholic. For while the Church of England never formally established saints, as we have seen, the sanctity of Mary was especially problematic for Protestants. So important was Mary, writes Stephen Bates, that radical Mariolatry came to define 'both the limits and hermeneutic of the English Reformation'.[27]

Part of the issue was the limited evidence about Mary in scripture: *sola scriptura* meant Protestants were inclined only to accept claims about Mary which scripture guaranteed.[28] Mary's association with the Mass and Purgatory also made her problematic, while the embrace of Mary by the

---

26 On the manuscripts and their authority over the publications, see MacDonald and Brown, pp. xxxvii and xcii–xciii.
27 See Stephen Bates, 'The Virgin Mary and the Reformation of the Midlands, 1516–1560', *Midland History*, 44/2 (2019), 159–75 (171).
28 See Diarmaid MacCulloch, *All Things Made New: Writings on the Reformation* (London: Penguin, 2017), p. 51.

Counter-Reformation sharpened Protestant anxieties about her.[29] One can multiply examples of the destruction of Marian images in England from the time of Thomas Cromwell, to Edward VI and Elizabeth I.[30] The last official Hail Mary heard in England was in the wake of Queen Mary I; and Mary, the mother of Christ, remained almost entirely absent from official English religion until Arminians, especially Lancelot Andrewes, returned to her in their 'rewriting' of the history and theology of the English Church.[31]

In Southwell's short lyrics, then, one embarks upon religious topics through the Virgin Mary and the saints. Only by going through these saints, sequentially, do readers arrive at the Passion, ensuring the Catholic presentation of Christianity is marked. A still bolder strategy is in *St Peters Complaint*: since it never reaches the Passion, its intense and protracted focus on the suffering saint makes sainthood exemplify Christian holiness. Indeed, there is a sense in which Peter's suffering stands for Christ's, for while Christ's Passion and death are never shown in the poem, every Christian knew it followed in scripture. In 'The Author to his loving Cosen', Southwell wrote of Christ 'making a Himm [hymn], the conclusion of his last Supper, and the Prologue to the first Pageant of his Passion'.[32] In *St Peters Complaint*, similarly, the suffering of Peter functions as a 'Prologue': one never sees Christ's Passion in the poem, but since one knows it follows in scripture, the suffering of the saint, Peter, anticipates the suffering of Christ. Focusing on Peter's suffering, while saying nothing of the suffering of Christ, allows *St Peters Complaint* to stress the sanctity of Peter, especially as a prologue to the Eucharistic suffering of Christ in scripture.

Southwell's poetic church is not only a matter of saints. It is also one of sacraments, materials and ritual. Southwell's Eucharistic poems bring this institutional view of Christianity to the fore. Anticipating several poets of this chapter, 'A Holy Hymne' and 'Of the Blessed Sacrament of the Aulter' are two poems locating a Eucharistic theology of Christ's sacrifice in the ritual action of the priest in church.[33] 'A Holy Hymme' presents this as a matter of shared, Christian faith:

> Christians are by faith assured
> That to flesh the bread is changed,
> The wine to blood most pretious,

---

29 On Mary in regard to the Mass and Counter-Reformation, see MacCulloch (2017), pp. 45 and 52. On Mary's involvement in Catholic theology, 'notably that of the purgatorial system', see Bates, 171.
30 MacCulloch (2017), p. 39.
31 MacCulloch (2017), pp. 52 and 54.
32 MacDonald and Brown (eds), p. 1.
33 Scholars observe the Mass ritually underpinning medieval and early modern literature; for example, Regina Schwartz, 'Tragedy and the Mass', *Literature and Theology*,

> ...
> When the priest the hoast devideth,
> Know that in each part abideth
> All that the whole hoast covered ...
> ('A Holy Hymme', 31–57)

With a similar emphasis on materials of the Eucharist transformed, 'Of the Blessed Sacrament of the Aulter' identifies Christ's sacrifice in the ritual of the Mass:

> The god of hoastes in slender hoste doth dwell,
> Yea god and man, with all to ether dewe:
> That god that rules the heavens and rifled hell,
> That man whose death did us to life renewe,
> That god and man that is the Angells blisse,
> In form of bredd and wyne our nurture is.
> ('Of the Blessed Sacrament of the Aulter', 61–6)

Although Southwell considered it truth, this Eucharistic poetry is polemical. Claiming 'Christians' will recognise transubstantiation makes convinced Protestants un-Christian: a view Protestants rejected. Yet just as important as the Eucharistic theology of each extract is the wholly mediated presentation of Christ's sacrifice, which Southwell never presents directly. Depicting a practising Church, the centre of Christian faith in the poems is the Mass, complete with altar and priest, bread, wine and the Christian congregation.

Presenting anonymous members of that congregation is Southwell's last way of ensuring that the institutional Church mediates Christ's sacrifice. Anonymously, the figures function in Southwell's organisation as lesser versions of his saints. Recalling, for example, Christ carrying the cross (*John* 19: 16–18), the poem 'Sinnes heavie loade' begins not just with Christ but with 'My sinne' (1). A believing Christian, possibly Southwell, thus imagines Christ:

> O LORD my sinne doth overcharge thy breast,
> The poyse thereof doth force thy knees to bow;

19 (June 2005), 139–58; Eamonn O Carragain, *Ritual and the Rood: Liturgical Images and the Old English Poems of the Dream of the Rood Tradition* (London and Toronto: The British Library and University of Toronto Press, 2005); Heather Marring, 'Toward a Ritual Poetics: Dream of the Rood as a Case Study', *Oral Tradition*, 26/2 (2011), 391–410. See also Kimberley Johnson, *Made Flesh: Sacrament and Poetics in Post-Reformation England* (Philadelphia: University of Pennsylvania Press, 2014); Regina Schwartz, *Sacramental Poetics at the Dawn of Secularism: When God Left the World* (Stanford: Stanford University Press, 2008); Robert Whalen, *The Poetry of Immanence Sacrament in Donne and Herbert* (Toronto: University of Toronto Press, 2002); Theresa DiPasquale, *Literature and Sacrament: The Sacred and the Secular in John Donne* (Pittsburgh, PA: Duquesne University Press, 1999).

> Yea flat thou fallest with my faults opprest,
> And bloody sweat runs trickling from thy brow:
> (Sinnes heavie loade, 1–4)

The presence of the Christian believer seeing, experiencing and representing Christ's Passion is vital. Though among Southwell's most direct visualisations of the Passion, 'Sinnes heavie loade' is primarily a Christian's witness, affirming shared Christian beliefs and membership and extending these to the reader. The point bears emphasis, for devotional poets frequently speak in the anonymous first person. First-person speakers affirming Christian tenets highlight their membership in and of the Christian body. Although Crashaw, Herbert, Herrick and Donne do not see Christian features identically, in this feature (as in several others) they retained the Catholic, institutional identity of religious poetry garnered for England by Southwell. Indeed, they retained it precisely as Southwell anticipated. In 'The Author to his loving Cosen', Southwell claimed in his poetry to have 'layd a few course threds together, to invite some skillfuller wits to goe forward in the same'.[34] As we shall now see, those wits included Crashaw, Herbert, Herrick and Donne: these poets replicated many facets of Southwell's institutional church, so going 'forward in the same' as Southwell anticipated. We begin with Richard Crashaw who started life as a member of the Church of England. He became a cleric, but he would eventually convert to the Church of Rome which Southwell advocated.

The institutional church of Richard Crashaw

By contrast with Southwell, Richard Crashaw is noted for extravagant devotional conceits, while the proportion of his poems addressing Christ's sacrifice is greater. Nevertheless, even poems addressing Christ's Passion (for example, 'On the Still Surviving marks of oure Saviour's wounds', 'To Pontious Pilate washing his hands', 'Upon our Saviour's Tombe where never man was laid' and 'Upon the Crowne of Thorns of our B. Lord bloody', 'On our Crucified Lord, naked and bloody' and 'Upon the H. Sepulchre') present it institutionally: the narrative is biblical, but also sanctioned by Christian tradition. To recount the Passion in Christian terms as does Crashaw is to affirm this institutional Christianity or, rather, to reaffirm it. Although there is novelty in his representations, no topic could more affirm the accumulated decisions of the Christian past, and so its institution, than does Crashaw's biblical scene. For Crashaw, institutional Christianity meant first the anti-papalism of his father (William Crashaw, 1572–1625/6), next the

---

34 'The Author to his loving Cosen', in Macdonald and Brown (eds), p. 1.

English Church under Laud and finally the Roman Catholic Church of Counter-Reformation Europe.[35]

This development suggests some truth in evangelical objections to the Laudian Church of England. To its proponents, Laudian ceremonialism was 'the political realisation of Protestant best practices as derived from the Holy Scripture, historical precedent, the Book of Common Prayer and the Thirty-Nine Articles'; to its opponents, it was 'dangerous innovations: Catholic-style impositions of human creativity'.[36] Like others to be observed in this study, Crashaw's move from Laudian ceremonialism to Roman Catholicism suggests that Laud's critics had a point. By the time his poems were published, Crashaw's institutional Christianity meant specifically the Roman Catholic Church.

Though many of his poems were written earlier, Crashaw's conversion to Catholicism (no later than 1645) means the first publication of *Steps to the Temple* (1646) was from a known Catholic exile. The title page highlights this: Crashaw, who had lost his Cambridge living, is presented as 'sometimes of Pembroke hall, and late fellow of S. Peter's Coll. In Cambridge'.[37] In the same year of publication (1646), Queen Henrietta Maria recommended Crashaw to the Pope. Crashaw would repay her in the second edition (1648) with a new poem: 'To the Queen's Majestie upon his dedicating to her the forgoing Hymn'. In that, forgoing 'Hymn for the Epiphanie', Crashaw links Christ with monarchy, but he begins with 'beauty': a topic Henrietta Maria promoted.[38] The 1648 and 1666 editions of Crashaw's poetry are marked by his Catholic status.

---

35 On Crashaw's religion in these respects, see Thomas Healey, 'Richard Crashaw', in *Dictionary of National Biography Online* (2004; accessed 15.4.2020). Healey here aligns Crashaw with John Cosin (1595–1672), but their trajectories are tellingly different: Cosin became bishop of Durham. Healey rightly maintains Crashaw was not a 'ready' convert to Roman Catholicism; but his association of Crashaw with an emerging Anglican view in which Rome was no longer 'a false church or no church at all' but rather 'a true church but in error' is not satisfactory. In converting to Roman Catholicism in the 1640s, Crashaw formally abandoned 'Anglican' positions: an especially serious step for a clergyman. Further criticism of the alignment of Crashaw with Cosin is in Johnson (2014), p. 124.

36 Nandra Perry, 'Turning the Tables: Richard Crashaw Reads the Protestant Altar', *Studies in Philology*, 112 (Spring 2015), 303–26 (305–6).

37 See *Steps to the Temple. Sacred Poems, With other Delights of the Muses. By RICHARD CRASHAW, sometimes of Pembroke Hall, and late fellow of S. Peter's Coll. In Cambridge* (London: 1646), in *EEBO* (accessed 28.5.2020).

38 For the two poems to Henrietta Maria, see *Steps to the Temple, Sacred Poems, With the Delights of the Muses. By RICHARD CRASHAW, sometimes of Pembroke Hall, and late fellow of S. Peters in Cambridge. The Second Edition, wherein are added diverse pieces not before extant* (London: 1648), pp. 48–56, in *EEBO* (accessed 28.5.2020). I consider Henrietta Maria's cult of beauty in Chapter 6, pp. 186–7 and p. 192.

In this context, the importance to Crashaw of the Christian institution, the Church, comes out clearly in the poems 'A Hymn to our Saviour by the Faithful Receiver of the Sacrament' and 'A Hymn on the B. Sacrament'. These poems first appear in Crashaw's *Steps to the Temple* of 1648. If they were written before he converted to Catholicism, then he or others withheld them from the 1646 edition. We can only speculate about why; yet their sensitive, theological subject matter is relevant.

The title page of the 1648 edition only describes 'added diverse pieces, not before extant'. Yet along with the new poems to Henrietta Maria, the Eucharistic poems present a new, Catholic confidence reflecting Crashaw's circumstances. After Henrietta Maria's letter to the Pope, from 1647 Crashaw was employed in the retinue of Cardinal Palotto before being found work at Loretto, again, seemingly, by Palotto. It was a thoughtful appointment for a poet devoted to the Virgin, but income and patronage also gave Crashaw independence from England. Since it is implausible that Crashaw only became familiar with Catholic theology of the Eucharist after his conversion to Rome, one must assume that his poems on the Eucharist, though published after that conversion, reflect an earlier interest in Catholic theology. In this respect, it is important to note that Laudian theology in England, contrasting with Protestant emphasis on scripture, put stress on the Eucharist; for the likes of Lancelot Andrews, who planted the seeds of Laudianism, were influenced in their attention to the Eucharist by their reading in Aquinas.[39] Though he could have embraced Aquinas as a Laudian member of the Church of England, therefore, Crashaw's interest in the saintly Catholic theologian, Aquinas, is consonant with his eventual conversion to the Church of Rome. This means Crashaw's interest in things Catholic began while he was of the Church of England and that his conversion to Rome fulfilled this emerging, Catholic interest.[40] Evangelical concerns that Laudian religion was a Catholic seedbed seem again not unfounded.

As Catholic poems on the Eucharist, both Crashaw's 'A Hymn to our Saviour' and 'A Hymn on the B. Sacrament' recall the Eucharistic poems of Southwell, so recalling one significant figure in the history of the Church. Yet Southwell, who was only formally canonised in 1970, is not the foremost canonised saint of these poems, and so not their foremost instance of Catholic

---

39 For discussion, see Joseph Ashmore, 'Faith in Lancelot Andrewes's Preaching', *The Seventeenth Century*, 32/2 (2017), 121–38, especially 125.
40 Gary Kuchar has argued, similarly, that Crashaw's Eucharistic theology must be situated 'in his Laudian *and* Counter-Reformation contexts' (my emphasis). See Kuchar, 'Poetry and the Eucharist in the English Renaissance', *George Herbert Journal*, 36, 1/2 (Fall 2012–Spring 2013), 128–49 (136); see also Graham Parry, *The Arts of the Anglican Counter-Reformation: Glory, Laud and Honour* (Woodbridge: Boydell Press, 2006), p. 143.

Christianity. As Crashaw's editor of 1652 recognised, 'A Hymn to our Saviour' translates the 'Adoro te devote' ascribed to St Thomas Aquinas.[41] Assuming the persona of this saint to speak from the Christian past, the poem makes first-person, religious experience institutional and Church-sanctioned. The poem also presents Thomas the Apostle (line 23), so that it evokes, at once, the early Church, the medieval Church and the Church of the seventeenth century. Saints standing on saints' shoulders, it is a sweeping presentation of the Church as a collection of saints through the ages. Since the Church of England never endorsed saints but preached against them, this Church through the ages is signally Catholic.

The theology is equally Catholic, recalling both Southwell and Aquinas:

> Rich Royall food! Bountifull Bread!
> Whose use denies us to the dead
> Whose vital gusts alone can give
> The same leave both to eat and live...
> ('A Hymn to our Saviour', 37–40)[42]

As much as of Aquinas, this is the theology of Southwell in 'A Holy Hymn' and 'Of the Blessed Sacrament of the Auter'. Confirming evangelical fears, Crashaw's strong Catholic signal emerges through a combination of Catholic saints with Catholic theology.

There are, of course, distinctive embellishments. Yet these too being Christian, Crashaw's Christian institution predominates. Even Crashaw's oft-embellished imagery of blood, in the closing address to Christ the 'Pelican', subsists in Christian institution:

> O soft *self-wounding Pelican!*
> Whose *Brest* weeps *Balm* for wounded man.
> Ah this way bend thy benigne flood
> To a bleeding Heart that gasps for *Blood*.
> That blood, whose least drops soveraign be

---

41 In the third edition of 1652 (published after Crashaw's death), the editor gives 'A Hymn to our Saviour' a new title: 'The Hymn of Sanite Thomas in Adoration of the Blessed Sacrament. Adoro Te'. See *Carmen Deo Nostro* (Paris: 1652), p. I.ij, in *EEBO* (accessed 27.5.2020). For discussions of the translation of St Thomas, see R. V. Young, *Doctrine and Devotion in Seventeenth Century Poetry: Studies in Donne, Herbert, Crashaw and Vaughan* (Cambridge: D.S. Brewer, 2000), p. 154; and Susannah Monta, 'John Austen's Devotions: Voicing Lyric, Voicing Prayer', in *Early Modern English Catholicism: Identity, Memory and Counter-Reformation*, ed. by James Kelly and Susan Royal (Leiden and Boston: Brill, 2016), pp. 226–45 (p. 244). This second discussion helpfully situates the poem in the saint- and faith-contexts I allude to.

42 *Steps to the Temple* (1648), p. 75.

> To wash my worlds of sin from me.
> Come love! Come Lord! ...
> ('A Hymn to our Saviour', 43–9)

Gasping for blood, here, is striking; it suggests a deprivation of the Mass familiar to English Catholics including, of course, Southwell. Yet gasping for the Mass is a way of signalling desire for its institution. In a poem 'of the Sacrament', which translates Aquinas's poem for the Corpus Christi liturgy, even an image as unusual as longing for Christ's blood is of the institutional Church and the connections with Aquinas and 'Corpus Christi' make that Catholic.

Set at the altar or 'Board' in church (20), Crashaw's second Eucharistic poem of 1648, 'A Hymn on the B. Sacrament', is similar.[43] The Corpus Christi liturgy echoes in its title and the theology is institutionally Catholic. The sacrifice of Christ is 'a well-blessed bread and wine. / Transsum'd, and taught to be divine' (29–30). The sacrifice is also detailed: 'In different species, *Names* not Things, / Himself to me my Saviour brings / As meat in that, as *drink* in This' (39–41).[44] Implying a congregation for this ritual of transubstantiation, the enjoinders 'Lo, the life-food of *Angells*' (61) and 'Lo, the full, finall *sacrifice*' (65) present Christ's sacrifice as a feature looked at by congregations, echoing Southwell. Together, the various components – altar, bread, wine, transubstantiation, congregation – present a full portrait of a Christian church and its Catholic ritual. Naming those at the ritual the 'Coheirs of Saints' (77) joins this church, material and spiritual, to an institutional Christian past which – unlike the Church of England – recognised saints formally.

The saints embody this past and are frequent features of Crashaw's church. Beyond the saints Thomas and martyr Southwell observed, they are the highlights, even the superstars, of 'To the Infant Martyrs' (*Steps to the Temple*, 1646); 'The Flaming Heart, upon the book and picture of TERESA' (*Steps to the Temple*, 1648); and of 'A Hymn to the Name and Honor of the Admirable Sanite [*sic*] Teresa' (*Carmen Deo nostro*, 1652). The physicalised terminology of these poems has been derided and explained.[45] Yet

---

43 For the board meaning 'altar' see under 'board' (noun) in the *OED*, definition 6a. See also 'God's board' under 'God', Compound 2c.
44 For this and the following quotations from 'A Hymn on the B. Sacrament', see *Steps to the Temple* (1648), pp. 76–8.
45 For 'A Hymn to the Name of the Admirable Sainte Teresa', see *Carmen Deo nostro* (1652), pp. 93–100. On the physicalised terminology and its critical history, see Kimberley Johnson (2014), p. 119; and Johnson, 'Richard Crashaw's Indigestible Poetics', *Modern Philology*, 107/1 (August 2009), 32–51 (32–3); also, Young, *Doctrine and Devotion*, p. 156.

their sensuality is functional, bringing dead saints, some of the distant past, to life.

The poetry, as much as the critical responses, attests this. In 'The Flaming Heart', for example, Crashaw insists that Saint Teresa, not the seraph, should hold the dart ('Give *him* the veyl, give her the Dart'). This empowers the 'Woman Saint' (26), contending her agency and precedence. Yet each poem, to martyr or saint, is hagiographic, maintaining Catholic saints through focalisation. Theologically, the saints imitate the sacrificial Christ of Crashaw's sacraments. As in Southwell, they are a means of approaching Christ and experiencing his Passion: visible parts of an institutional Church which the English Church never acknowledged and often condemned.

Conforming to a view of the church past and present are the treatments of faith in Crashaw's Eucharistic poems. 'A Hymn on the B. Sacrament' (1648) introduces Christian faith as 'The Heav'n-instructed House of Faith' (31). This makes faith synonymous with a church material and spiritual; indeed, the phrase 'House of Faith' seems to adapt Spenser's 'House of Holiness', which one critic calls a 'virtual fun-house of seemingly idolatrous Catholic figures'.[46] For Crashaw, of course, Spenser's 'idolatry' is legitimate Catholic worship. More immediately, Crashaw's claim, 'Where Nature's *Lawes* no leave will give, / Bold faith takes *Heart* and dares' (37–8), links Christian faith with the institutional theology of Eucharistic 'species' (39), which is especially of Aquinas and his Catholic Church.[47]

Exploring doubts arising from Christ's hiddenness, 'The Hymn of Sanite [*sic*] Thomas' (1652) is similar.[48] Resolving doubt through the Eucharistic 'memorial' which 'lives still, & allowes us breath' (37–8), this revised version of 'A Hymn to Our Saviour' (itself from Aquinas) explains why 'Adoration of the Blessed Sacrament' is of the title. While Christ's sacrifice redeems us, the poem implies, the Eucharist, which is visible and tangible, counters doubt in the otherwise invisible process of salvation. In this analysis, faith emerges through the institutional Church, which in this case is the Eucharistic Church of St Thomas.

---

46 See James Kearney, 'Enshrining Idolatry in *The Faerie Queene*', *English Literary Renaissance*, 32/1 (Winter 2002), 3–30 (21).

47 For discussion of Aquinas's theory of Eucharistic species, especially as a response to long-standing debates in the Catholic Church about how Christ might be at once in Heaven yet in the Eucharist, see Bernard Prusak, 'Explaining Eucharistic "Real Presence": Beyond a Medieval Conundrum', *Theological Studies*, 75/2 (May 2014), 231–59.

48 Johnson considers these doubts central in Crashaw, but 'Crashaw does not depart from the explanation of transubstantiation that had served Catholic institutional orthodoxy since the Fourth Lateran Council (1215) and was later explicated so clearly by Thomas Aquinas'. See Johnson (2014), p. 120; Johnson (2009), 34.

Crashaw's sacramental poems are vital for understanding his oeuvre. In the light of these poems, a work as seemingly strange as 'On the Wounds of Our Crucified Lord' (which asks if the wounds are eyes, mouths, hands, feet, or lips) is a variation on the Eucharistic theme. The corporeal metaphors support Crashaw's claim in 'A Hymn to our Saviour' that the sensible matter of the Eucharist can ward off doubts about Christ's sacrifice (lines 6–10). In 'Be they mouths or be they eyen / Each bleeding part someone supplies' ('On the Wounds of Our Crucified Lord, 3–4), the sensual 'supply' of the Passion removes Christ's sacrifice from a distant, past event to a tangible present; much as Christ's memorial lives (in 'The Hymn of Sanite Thomas') in the Catholic Church and its saints.

The institutional church of George Herbert

While Crashaw moved from a Laudian version of the Church of England to Rome, Herbert (who never faced the deprivations of the Civil War) remained in the Church of England. Neither of the centre of the Church of England of his day nor a Puritan or Arminian, Herbert wanted distance between Canterbury and Geneva.[49] Many of the religious features found in both Crashaw's and Southwell's poetry are evident in Herbert. For example, the centrality of the Eucharist in Herbert's *The Temple* (published in 1633) is matched only by his representation of church surrounds.[50] As Achsah Guibbory writes: 'The church, as material structure and institution, shapes Herbert's poetry.'[51] The materiality of the Church is evident in the focus of several poems: 'Perirrhanterium', 'Superliminare', 'The Altar', 'Sepulchre', 'Church Monuments', 'Church-Lock and Key', 'The Church-floore', 'The Windows' and also 'The Church-Porch'. Through this last, one enters a collection designed to evoke a materially Christian place of worship.[52] Alongside ritual actions, particular poems catalogue other, lesser material

---

49 Jeremy Morris, *A People's Church: A History of the Church of England* (London: Profile, 2022), p. 101.
50 The Eucharistic centrality is well known. See Johnson (2014), p. 35. I address Herbert's Eucharist, including its theology, in this section.
51 See Achsah Guibbory, 'Devotional Poetry and the Temple of God', *George Herbert Journal*, 37, 1/2 (Fall 2013–Spring 2014), 99–116 (104).
52 For evocation of this design, see Alison Shell, 'Seventeenth Century Poetry 2: Herbert, Vaughan, Philips, Cowley, Crashaw, Marvell', in *The Cambridge History of English Poetry*, ed. by Michael O'Neill (Cambridge: Cambridge University Press, 2010), pp. 211–30 (216). The question of whether the design is to be taken materially or metaphorically has a long critical history addressed in my 'Monuments and Religion: George Herbert's Poetic Materials', in *The Arts of Remembrance in Early Modern England: Memorial Cultures of the Post Reformation*, Material Readings in Early

objects: 'Pulpits and Sundayes ... / Bibles laid open... / Blessings beforehand' ('Sinne I', 5–9).

Many of the feasts celebrated in *The Temple* can be aligned with *The Book of Common Prayer*.[53] Yet material objects in *The Temple* often have a distinct, Catholic ring. This is the case for both details and the bigger picture. For example, in 'Perirrhanterium' in the Williams Manuscript (seemingly from before 1630) we find allusion to 'sprinkling', and so to the Aspergillium: the brush used by Catholic priests to sprinkle foundation stones of churches and worshippers at the start of Mass.[54] Thus blessed from the start, Herbert's readers receive a Catholic initiation into the Williams Manuscript subtly kin to the Christian's entrance to the Church in baptism. Yet the bigger picture also suggests Catholic materials. Herbert's material Church (seen for example in floor and altar) is 'Petrine' in the literal sense of being of rock. This Petrine metaphor, which is pervasive in *The Temple*, adopts and adapts the emphasis on St Peter in Southwell, inscribing the saint into the fabric of Herbert's material church. In an age when Protestants regularly identified Catholicism with idolatry, Herbert shows clear awareness of the idolatrous Catholicism latent in this procedure. In 'The Temper', he frets that his rhymes 'engrave' God's love, drawing attention both to the material basis of his verse and its idolatrous potential.[55] Since Protestants regularly linked idolatry with Catholicism, Herbert here highlights the popish challenges implied in his Petrine construction.

By contrast with Southwell, Herbert's presentation of St Peter is indirect, but it is not alone. Taken at face value, the title of the poem 'To All Angels and Saints' is pointedly inclusive, with Peter among all Catholic saints implied.[56] As we have seen, the Church of England formally recognised no saints, while sermons like 'Against the Peril of Idolatry' in the *Book of*

Modern Literature (Farnham and Burlington, VT: Ashgate, 2013), pp. 105–24. Christopher Waller argues Herbert maintained Laud's appropriation of the 'sacred spaces' of post-Reformation Catholics in England, but argues for Herbert's '"consensual conformism", in opposition to Laud's divisive conformism'. I argued Herbert goes beyond standard 'Arminian' reforms. See Christopher Waller, 'Herbert, The Church and Consensual Conformism: "God is more there, then thou"', *Early Modern Literary Studies*, 20/1 (2018), 1–35 (11); Rist, 'Monuments and Religion', p. 108.

53 See Jeannie Judge, 'Keeping the Major Feasts in George Herbert's The Temple', *George Herbert Journal*, 35, 1/2 (Fall 2011–Spring 2012), 110–26.
54 See Elizabeth McLaughlan and Gail Thomas, 'Communion in *The Temple*', *Studies in English Literature, 1500–1900*, 15/1 (Winter 1975), 111–24 (112).
55 Kuchar (2018), p. 50.
56 I turn to the critical history of this poem, but for inclusive reading of it within that history of debate, see Andrew Harnack, 'Both Protestant and Catholic: George Herbert and "To All Angels and Saints"', in *George Herbert Journal*, 11/1 (Fall 1987), 23–39.

Homilies presented belief in saints as like polytheism. Herbert's comprehensive celebration of 'all ... saints' is therefore outside official English belief.

The presentation is even problematic in Laudian terms. Even Lancelot Andrewes, whom we have observed as part of an English vanguard rewriting the history and theology of the English Church, made standardly Calvinistic statements about saints. In general terms, Andrewes could celebrate saints. In *A Manual of Directions for the Visitation of the Sick*, for example, he speaks of souls in a 'state of joy, bliss and happiness, with all thy blessed Saints, in thy heavenly Kingdome'; while in the 'Confession of Faith' appended to the *Manual*, he notes 'the Communion of Saints'.[57] Yet when he considers the theology of saints, Andrewes's language and attitude are very different. Clearly, he affirms belief in saints, but what they are, strictly, is a million miles not just from Southwell, but also from Herbert:

> All the Merit of a Saint, if it be judged strictly by the eternal Judge, is deformity. And again: we are bound on all sides by the Burden of Corruption, but by no means arrive at perfect Deliverance from it. And all human Righteousness would be found Unrighteousness, if it was to be strictly examined; all our Righteousness would be found Unrighteousness.[58]

This is, to be sure, a relatively early statement by Andrewes. Yet it is also an unusually full and precise statement about saints from him, giving exceptional insight into his thinking about what sainthood means: abject human worthlessness, the standard evangelical view.[59] Importantly, therefore, Andrewes's tone in this precise statement is almost entirely different from that of 'To All Angels and Saints'. The poem opens by praising saints as 'glorious spirits, who after all your bands / See the smooth face of God' (1–2) and stating that 'every one is king, and hath his crown' (3). Nothing could be further from the images of corruption and deformity Andrewes ascribes to saints when considering them 'strictly' and, indeed, theologically. Andrewes's presentation of saints as without 'merit' aligns him with Calvinism.

---

57 Lancelot Andrewes, *A Manual of Directions for the Visitation of the Sick, with sweet meditations to be used in time of sickness whereunto is added a short confession of the faith, with a form of thanksgiving and prayers for morning and evening* (London: 1642), in *EEBO* (accessed 12.11.21), image 58 (unnumbered page); image 93 (unnumbered page).

58 Lancelot Andrewes, *Justification in Christ's Name: A Sermon Preached at Whitehall, November 23, 1600. By Launcelot Andrews, Lord Bishop of Winchester. Extracted from the Second Edition of that Great Prelate's Works and Re-Published by the Reverend Mr Madan* (London, 1765), p. 24, in *Eighteenth Century Collections Online* (accessed 24.9.2022).

59 On this standard view, see James Simpson, *Burning to Read: English Fundamentalism and its Reformation Opponents* (Cambridge, MA, and London: Harvard University Press, 2007), p. 106.

His additional presentation of saints as deformed and corrupt when 'judged strictly' supports the refusal of the Church of England to endorse saints in the seventeenth century.

By contrast with the Church of England standard and Laudian, then, Herbert's poem celebrates the 'glorious spirits' that are 'all' saints. The comprehensiveness, as well as the positive imagery, is important, for it implies the inclusion of Catholic saints. It is the saints inclusively viewed who receive the opening praise as 'glorious spirits' and several following descriptions emphasise the scope of Herbert's praise. Soon after, it is 'ev'ry' saint' who 'is king, and hath his crown' (4); and inclusiveness extends still further, from the male saints each with 'his' crown to the female 'blessed Maid, / And Mother of my God' (9–10). The Catholic associations of this saint have been noted already. Yet Diarmaid MacCulloch makes clear how striking and controversial Herbert's presentation is:

> In England, where the last official Hail Mary was heard in the wake of the death of Queen Mary I, people were discouraged from singing about the Virgin as their ancestors had done. The ballads which were put into print from the London presses, which admittedly may not be identical with those which were actually sung, are notable for what they do not contain: it was God's providence, not Our Lady's, which appeared in the lyrics. Christmas carols, such as Luther loved and amplified, were controversial in England, associated with Catholic survival and infrequently published in Elizabeth's reign, although they began to make a comeback in the early seventeenth century; English publishers produced no picture of the Holy Family before 1637. One might even see the popular carol 'Righteous Joseph' as an attempt to take the spotlight off Our Lady and redirect it onto her husband.[60]

Allowing for the comeback of Mary just beginning in the seventeenth century, the controversial and Catholic dimensions of celebrating her are clear. Yet despite this, hailing Mary is what 'To All Angels and Saints' wishes to do. The collective pressure of the printers and publishers noted by MacCulloch emerges in Herbert in an imagined tension between the speaker and 'our King'. Herbert writes: 'I would address / My vows to thee most gladly, blessed Maid / And Mother of my God' (8–10). Yet the poem continues: 'But now (alas!) I dare not; for our King, / Whom we do all joyntly adore and praise, / Bids no such thing' (16–18). In the Williams Manuscript, 'our King' is instead 'my King'.[61] Yet in what follows, the King's bidding emerges as 'injunction' (19) and 'prerogative' (21). Both terms suggest earthly power is what keeps Herbert from addressing Mary more fully than he does.

---

60 MacCulloch (2017), p. 52.
61 See *The Williams Manuscript of George Herbert's Poems: A Facsimile Reproduction* (Delmar, NY: Scholars' Facsimiles and Reprints, 1977), p. 57.

The importance of this point is reflected in the long critical debate 'To All Angels and Saints' has inspired. The crux is whether the king in question is God or Charles I (regnant 1625–49), for the former implies venerating Mary is ruled out by divine command, while the latter implies it is ruled out by the head of the English Church. The question was first raised by Martz, who observed that the forbidden veneration 'now' points to Herbert's era, rather than to divine and immutable command, making the poem suggest regret for the loss of Marian veneration in the Church of England.[62] Beneath 'our king' (that is, the king of 'Angels, Saints, Herbert, and other human beings') Martz observed the 'earthly king' lurked.[63] That is evidently true for 'my king' in the Williams Manuscript. Yet seventeenth-century readers could also easily have construed 'our king' as referring to themselves, the poet and Charles I; or to Charles as king of the English people ('our' king). In response to Martz, Richard Strier sought to reduce interpretative possibilities, claiming the 'King' referred only to God, that the poem therefore forbade veneration of Mary as a matter of divine command and that this made it strictly Protestant.[64] Yet at no point does the poem name or identify the King, meaning Charles I and English strictures against venerating the saints are context for its entirety.

Herbert's speaker who 'would' venerate Mary, yet does not 'dare' do so, suggests a divided religious outlook: one showing (as Strier feared) 'the most faint-hearted and uneasy of Protestants'.[65] Yet divided outlooks of the kind are recognisable in seventeenth-century poetry. Ben Jonson's 'An Epigram to the Queen' asks 'why may not I, / (Without profanesse) as a Poët, cry / Hail *Mary*'.[66] His next demand that hailing Mary should 'be lawful' echoes one Shakespearean king's reply that kneeling before memorial statues of queens should be 'lawful as eating'.[67] The clash with authority of religious impulses and actions is a literary *topos*.

62 See Martz (1974), pp. 97–8.
63 Martz (1974), p. 98.
64 Richard Strier, '"To All Angels and Saints": Herbert's Puritan Poem', *Modern Philology*, 77/2 (Winter 1979), 132–45.
65 Strier, 132.
66 On 'An Epigram to the Queen' in this respect, see my 'Mary of Recusants and Reform: Literary Memory and Defloration', in *Biblical Women in Early Modern Literary Culture, 1550–1700*, ed. by Victoria Brownlee and Laura Gallagher (Manchester: Manchester University Press, 2015), pp. 162–79 (162–3). I consider this poem in full in Chapter 5, on pp. 141–4.
67 On *The Winter's Tale*, see Susan Dunn-Hensley, 'Return of the Sacred Virgin: Memory, Loss, and Restoration in Shakespeare's Later Plays', in *Walsingham in Literature and Culture from the Middle Ages to Modernity*, ed. by Dominic Janes and Gary Waller (Farnham: Ashgate, 2010), pp. 185–97.

'To All Angels and Saints' itself contrasts the 'crown' of the saints with that of the king (lines 4 and 22), implying a rivalry of authorities enhanced in: 'we dare not from his [the King's] garland steal, / To make a posie of inferiour power' (24–5). Since the crown of the saints threatens that of the King, it is inadmissible in a 'poesie' that has admitted it. Trying to erase the contradiction, Strier imagined a second, Catholic speaker in the poem, creating a debate between denominations in which Herbert's virtuous Protestant triumphs. Yet there is nothing in the poem approaching a defined, second speaker. There is just one speaker in 'To All Angels and Saints'. The contradictions are his.[68]

Nominating Mary as the 'holy mine, whence came the gold' (11), 'To All Angels and Saints' celebrates both Mary and her Son. Yet having to 'mine' for the gold (Jesus) means digging through rock for it. Since Laud promoted the beauty of holiness in English churches, material metaphors of the kind point to a development in the Church of England widely perceived as treasonous popery.[69] Yet Herbert's imagery is even more Catholic than that.[70] Designating Mary a mine is like his blessing of the Church's founding stone in the Williams Manuscript. Both instances highlight the material foundations of the poetic 'Temple', asserting the 'Petrine' basis of the collection. Though the method of presentation differs, *The Temple*'s fundaments are the saints, Mary and Peter: as they are in Southwell.

68 Strier spoke of an 'accuser' who is 'presumably a Papist' (Strier, p. 134). Since there is just one speaker in the poem, the speculation in 'presumably' is notable. The argument leading to the presumption is also suspect. It depends on the observation that the poem 'falls into two halves' (Strier, 133), which is not at all the same as being spoken by two persons. The procedure is characteristic of a reading repeatedly explaining away, rather than explaining, Catholic aspects of the poem. For example: 'Although he chooses to address himself to the angels and saints directly rather than to the (implied) accuser, what Herbert is *basically* doing in lines 1–15 of 'To All Angels and Saints" is defending his character' (Strier, 134; my emphasis). The so-called heresy of paraphrase stands out starkly in this reading, as it does again in: 'The third stanza, *with its handsome praise of the Virgin*, is an attempt to manifest appreciativeness and generosity' (Strier, 134; my emphasis). Martz's point was precisely that the poem is 'modulated' and 'brimful of ambiguity' (Martz [1974], p. 97).

69 On Laudian churches and beauty, see Parry (2011), pp. 123–39; and Ian Atherton, 'Cathedrals, Laudianism and the British Churches', *The Historical Journal*, 53/4 (December 2010), 895–918. On the association of Laudianism with treasonous popery, see Patrick McGrath, 'Reconsidering Laud: Puritans and Anglican Asceticism', *Prose Studies*, 34/1 (2012), 32–49 (38); and Atherton, 913.

70 John Adrian in fact finds in Herbert a 'tacit challenge' to Laudianism. See Adrian, 'George Herbert, Parish "Dexterity" and Laudianism', *The Seventeenth Century*, 24/1 (2009), 26–51 (27).

Herbert also echoes Southwell on the Eucharist. Once again Laudianism is of note, since Laudians set up, decorated and celebrated stone altars.[71] Yet one cannot reduce Herbert to Laudianism, as his poem 'The Altar', which not only discusses an altar but visualises it, shows: 'An altar was, after all, a piece of church furniture, one that for all but the most ceremonial of reformers signified Roman Catholicism'.[72]

Topics including Easter and Christ's sacrifice in *The Temple* all reinforce the importance of 'The Altar' as a central symbol of the collection. Yet it is Herbert's poems on the Eucharist that flesh out the details of his theology. Herbert's pre-eminent poem of the Eucharist, 'The H. Communion', shows his attitude to the sacrament had changed since his days at Cambridge.[73] The poem presents the Eucharist's physical properties as efficacious. Entering human subjects in the Eucharist's 'small quantities' (10), God's powers 'spread their forces into every part / Meeting sinnes force and art" ('The H. Communion', 11–12). Quantification, here, makes the materials of the Eucharist vital in transactions of grace. 'While Calvinist theology demands that the physical elements have no spiritual efficacy, Herbert seems to emphasise the influence of the physical elements in a way that approaches the Catholic theory of transubstantiation.'[74] Taken together, 'The Altar' and 'The H. Communion' make for a Herbert who, beneath his Church of England robes, is distinctly Catholic regarding the Eucharist.

That is important for *The Temple* generally. The ubiquity of the Eucharist in *The Temple* speaks not just to Christ's sacrificial presence in its poems, but also to Herbert's definition of ordinary humanity. While poems including 'The Agonie', 'Good Friday', 'Redemption', 'Sepulchre', 'Easter', 'Easter-wings' and 'The Sacrifice' bespeak Christ's Passion in the gospels, others like 'Grace', 'Affliction', 'Sighs and Grones' and 'The Crosse' present regular human suffering in Christ's imitation. All forms of exchange between humans and God in Herbert constitute verbal 'junctures' suggesting the crucifixion.[75] Making Christ the metaphor for human happiness and His cross the metaphor for human pain, for example, the poem 'Affliction' concludes that as Christ

---

71 See, for example, Atherton, 911–12; Parry (2011), 128.
72 Paul Dyck, 'Altar, Heart, Title Page: The Image of Holy Reading', *English Literary Renaissance* (January 2013), 541–71 (547).
73 See Louis Martz, 'Donne, Herbert and the Worm of Controversy', *Early Modern Literary Studies*, Special Issue 7 (2001), 1–13 (3–4).
74 See Clay Green, 'Our Souls and Fleshy Hearts: The Body, Sacraments and Grace in Herbert's "The H. Communion"', in *Citharia*, 57/2, Special Issue on the Poetry of George Herbert (May 2018), 43–57 (43).
75 Buffy Turner, 'Productive Discord and George Herbert's "Artillerie"', *Citharia*, 57/2, Special Issue on the Poetry of George Herbert (May 2018), 18–42 (21).

is 'All my delight, so all my smart: / Thy cross took up in one' (13–14). Crucially enough, delight and pain, which are human experiences, are both 'one' and 'all' in Christ, whose cross is, etymologically, a *crux*.[76] The poem 'The Crosse' details what this human 'all' entails:

> Ah my deare Father, ease my smart!
> These contraries crush me: these cross-actions
> Do wind a rope about, and cut my heart:
> And yet since these thy contradictions
> Are properly a crosse felt by thy sonne,
> With but four words, my words, *Thy will be done.*
> ('The Crosse', 31–6)

Describing the human, here the cross encompasses feeling ('my smart'), intellectual syntheses ('contraries'), actions ('cross actions') and dictions ('contradictions'). The definition has important consequences for Herbert's theology and style. Since contradictions and contraries are the crux, an unparadoxical theology is improper. A happy consequence, for Herbert, is that Protestant and Catholic positions can coexist, even if incoherently. Yet it is important to understand the basis of the coexistence. As an expression of martyrdom (death in the image of Christ), it was Southwell who put paradox at the centre of English devotional poetry; on this 'formative paradox' portraying Christian sacrifice the Eucharistic paradoxes of Herbert depend.[77]

The haunted church

From the first publication of Southwell's poems in the 1590s, through Herbert's publication in 1633 to Crashaw's publications of 1646–52, there is a span of over 50 years. Yet in their presentations of the Church, time seems oddly to have stood still. This is in part because Southwell's poetry continued to be published deep into the seventeenth century and was widely read by Protestants. Nevertheless, in view of the irreconcilable differences which arose from the Reformation on matters of liturgy and worship, the consistency between the poets is remarkable.[78] Each poet forcefully maintains an institutional Church of received rituals and saints, centred on an efficacious Eucharist and an attendant, sacrificial world view. The temporal advance of 50 years, in this respect, is offset by the poets' repetitions of Church subject matter. Each poet looks backward, as much as forward, with precedent

---

76 On the etymology of a cross as a crux, see 'cross' (noun) in the *OED*.
77 See Read, *Eucharist and the Poetic Imagination in Early Modern England*, pp. 42 and 40.
78 On the 'irreconcilable differences', see Read, p. 1.

driving 'new' poetic figurations. Repeatability, it is observed, is 'the most important' feature of the Eucharist as a ritual model for Herbert's poetry.[79] Revising this, we can now say it was repeating the Eucharistic model of worship provided by Catholic Southwell that governs the Protestant Herbert and eventual Catholic Crashaw in their poetry. Recognising these repetitions of Eucharistic worship, from Southwell to Crashaw to Herbert, brings out the continuity and influence of Roman Catholic religion in early modern England. It also implies how vital the Catholic religion was to professed members of the Church of England.

From Southwell to Herbert, devotional poets reflect on repetition, presenting it as part of the circular temporality of the Church, in which the past always remains present. In 'The Flower', for example, Herbert celebrates the 'returns' (2), each spring, of Christ, in a repetitive, seasonal view of time. 'The Flower' explains this circularity personally, so that hearts are 'recover'd' (9) and 'I bud again' (38). These images of repetition help make the springs of the past 'an houre' (17), making distant pasts and presents one tight unit of time. Importantly, these presentiments of the past are Christian: 'These are thy wonders, Lord' (15). In the universal repetitions of 'The Flower' (as in the cross everywhere in 'The Cross') the historical past is present and recurring. Moreover, as so often in Herbert, it recurs from Southwell.

For Herbert's combined images of nature and time in 'The Flower' are in Southwell, especially his prefiguring treatments of Christian repetition. It is Southwell's premise, in 'Of the Blessed Sacrament of the Autar', that 'In paschal feast the end of aunciert rite / An entrance was to never endinge grace' (1–2). This makes past rites present in the Eucharist, yet 'never ending' in future. On this basis, distinctions between past, present and future collapse. As in Herbert, later, Southwell's Eucharist is everywhere, making spring not just a season but, by definition, 'christian spring' ('The Flight into Egypt', 13). The definition develops in the view of Christ in Southwell's following poem, 'Christ's returne out of Egypt':

> Flowre to a flower he fitly doth retire.
> For flower he is and in a flower he bred,
> And from a thorne now to a flower he fled.
> ('Christ's returne out of Egypt', 10–12)

Defining Christ as a flower, Southwell reinforces his definition of spring's season as Christian. Defining His mother, Mary, and His crucifixion as flowers, he defines the season as a prototype of Christ's life. Noting that Herbert grows from Southwell is more, therefore, than a convenient metaphor. Herbert repeats Southwell from the broad Christian themes of

---

79 Shaun Ross, 'Sacrifices of Thanksgiving: The Eucharist in *The Temple*', *George Herbert Journal*, 40, 1/2 (2016), 1–40 (4).

the trans-historical Eucharist and the omnipresence of Christ's sacrifice to particularisations of these themes through images of flowers and seasons. Indeed, presenting Christ's sacrifice restoring 'us' (37) from Adam's sin, in 'The H. Communion' Herbert sees human history typologically, much as Southwell sees it trans-historically in 'Of the Blessed Sacrament of the Autar'.

Two more English clergymen

In different ways, the English clergymen Robert Herrick and John Donne affirm this trans-historical theology. Donne, famously, was born into a family consciously Roman Catholic, but eventually became a senior member of the Church of England as Dean of St Paul's. Herrick was ordained a deacon and priest of the Church of England in 1623 and was presented with the vicarage of Dean Prior, in the south of Dartmoor, in 1629. As a royalist, he had lost this living by 1646, but he petitioned for it again in 1660 and returned to Dean Prior when he was 69.[80] In *Hesperides* (published 1648), Herrick's royalism connects him to Catholicism through the figure of Queen Henrietta Maria; yet highlighting at the start of *Hesperides* that 'times trans-shifting' is his topic ('The Argument of his Book', 9), Herrick develops the natural typologies of Southwell and Herbert in poems including 'To the Virgins, to Make Much of Time' and 'Corinna's Going a Maying'. In this last, 'Birds' sing 'Mattens' and 'Hymns' and all of nature is engaged in 'Devotion'.[81]

This is not just metaphor. According to Achsah Guibbory, Herrick's turn to religion in nature is a product of the physical destruction of the Church of England during the Civil War: 'Churches and cathedrals had been desecrated by soldiers, and iconoclasts had destroyed their beauty.'[82] Perhaps, but Herrick's 'Corinna' may precede the Civil War.[83] A more reliable context is the 'permanent revolution' of the era, in which attempts to limit iconoclasm enhanced it.[84] Militant Protestants had campaigned against popular festivities

---

80 See 'Robert Herrick', in *Oxford Dictionary of National Biography* (online; accessed 8.3.2023).
81 See Guibbory (2013), 113.
82 Guibbory (2013), 110.
83 See John Creaser, '"Times trans-shifting": Chronology and the Misshaping of Herrick', *English Literary Renaissance*, 39/1 (2009), 163–96 (166, 188). Focused on chronology, Creaser undermines widespread claims that Herrick was 'a committed Laudian'. See Creaser, 173.
84 James Simpson, *Permanent Revolution: The Reformation and the Illiberal Roots of Liberalism* (Cambridge, MA, and London: Harvard University Press, 2019), pp. 161–2; see also Ethan Shagan, *The Rule of Moderation: Violence, Religion and the Politics of Restraint in Early Modern England* (Cambridge: Cambridge University Press, 2011), p. 148; Parry (2006), p. 6.

since the reign of Elizabeth I.[85] Promoting Merry England was a means of countering this campaign.[86] For its defence, seventeenth-century royalism depended on a symbiotic relationship between country and court.[87]

Yet this sustained context for Herrick overlooks the Catholic. As we have seen, the link between Christianity and nature is already in Southwell. Yet sites of Catholic martyrs were 'graced' with the supernatural in the era; texts and stories by both priests and religious laypeople made these spots emotively religious.[88] The effect on natural environments was prodigious.[89] What Alexandra Walsham calls 'vegetative wonders' were an 'index of the resacralization of the natural world that characterised the era of Catholic revival'.[90] This Catholic context, at once natural and literary, speaks to Herrick's *Hesperides*. Southwell's linkage of Christianity with nature (which Herrick recalls) was that of a Catholic martyr. Moreover, Herrick's treatment of 'time trans-shifting' echoes Southwell's trans-historical view of the Eucharist: since time in 'To the Virgins' and 'Corinna' is perpetually disappearing, it is also perpetually present; and since the natural phenomena which mark time – rosebuds, the 'dewbespangling herb and tree' – are seasonal, they recur even as they disappear. To go 'a Maying' means doing so now and every May, in a seasonal view of devotion recognisable from Herbert and Southwell before him. Reading *Hesperides: Or, the Works both Human and Divine of Robert Herrick* (1648) through the natural lens of Southwell and linked Catholic martyrs helps to bridge Herrick's gap between 'human and divine', especially regarding the pious 'Noble Numbers' at the end.

For its exhortation to 'obey' the *Book of Sports* ('the Proclamation made for May', in Herrick's phrase), 'Corinna's Going a Maying' and other poems of the *Hesperides* are associated with Stuart anti-Puritanism.[91] 'Corinna' suggests the girl traditionally worshipped by Propertius, whom Ovid half-seriously

---

85 Peter Stallybrass, '"Wee feaste in our Defense": Patrician Carnival in Early Modern England and Robert Herrick's "Hesperides"', *English Literary Renaissance*, 16/1 (1986), 234–52 (247). Stallybrass is one of Herrick's few 'modern' critics whose arguments Creaser (writing in 2009) absolved of serious problems regarding dates for Herrick's poems. See Creaser, 168.
86 Stallybrass, 251.
87 Stallybrass, 241.
88 Alexandra Walsham, *The Reformation of the Landscape: Religion, Identity, and Memory in Early Modern Britain and Ireland* (Oxford: Clarendon Press, 2011), pp. 225–6.
89 Walsham (2011), p. 227.
90 Walsham (2011), p. 227.
91 For a standard discussion, see Leah Marcus, 'Robert Herrick', in *The Cambridge Companion to English Poetry: Donne to Marvell*, ed. by Thomas Corns (Cambridge: Cambridge University Press, 1993), pp. 171–82 (pp. 174–6), though my interpretation of 'times-trans-shifting' is more extensive than suggested there.

imitated.[92] In Herrick's seventeenth-century Corinna, anti-Puritanism collides with this old and newer veneration from Rome: in the era, Puritans required a total and clean break with Rome's past.[93] Yet published by Charles I in 1633, the *Book of Sports* is certainly no Puritan document: it positions itself between Puritanism and Catholicism. Concerned for what it terms the 'lawful recreations' of 'our good people' taking place on 'Sundayes and other Holy dayes', the *Book of Sports* had emerged from Lancashire, where James I had found 'two sorts of people wherewith that Countrey is much infected (We meane Papists and Puritans)'.[94] In a balancing act between these Christian alternatives, James (and following him, Charles I) rescues the recreations of 'old custome' from Puritan suppression, yet condemns widespread conflations of such custom with papistry.

Recalling the *Book of Sports*, therefore, 'Corrina Going a Maying' recalls Catholic as well as Puritan contexts. Strictly obeying the *Book of Sports*, moreover, entails the difficult proposition of adhering to customs associated with Catholicism while rejecting their Catholic meaning. The instability of the proposition emerges in various poems by Herrick. In 'Corinna', for example, the speaker incites: 'Wash, dress, be brief in praying: / Few Beads are best when once we go a-Maying' (27–8). While brief prayers oppose Puritan zeal, 'Beads' evoke Catholic rituals of the rosary explicitly. Other poems recall Catholic elements similarly. Like 'Corinna', for example, the poem 'The Rosary' links the Catholic instrument of devotion with roses, seasonal budding and florescence. Here nature is Catholic. Similarly in nature again is 'The Fairy Temple, or Oberon's Chapel'. Here, the temple is 'Part pagan, part papistical' (32).

In view of the admiration of Jonson we have observed previously, especially in Herrick's poem 'His Prayer to Ben Jonson', these Catholic interests are unsurprising.[95] Yet explanation also comes from Charles I's marriage to the unapologetically Catholic Queen Henrietta Maria. In the marital scenario, supporting the Stuarts meant at least some toleration of Catholicism. Yet

---

92 On Propertius, Ovid and Corinna, see Kathleen Berman, 'Some Propertian Imitations in Ovid's "Amores"', *Classical Philology*, 67/3 (July 1972), 170–7.
93 See Maggie Kilgour, 'The Poetics of Time: The *Fasti* in the Renaissance', in *A Handbook for the Reception of Ovid*, ed. by John Millar and Carol Newmans (Oxford: Wiley Blackwell, 2014), pp. 217–31 (p. 221).
94 All quotations are from *The Book of Sports, as set forth by K. Charles I. With Remarks* (London: 1633; repr. 1710), in *Eighteenth Century Collections Online* (accessed 8.1.2020). Creaser notes that the specific link with May is stronger in the text of 1618 issued by James I than in Charles I's reissued text of 1633 (Creaser, 166); still, 'Holy dayes' are in both.
95 See Chapter 1, pp. 35–6.

Catholic worship and devotional poetry 131

in 'To the Queen', Herrick not only tolerates but effusively welcomes Henrietta Maria. The tone is far closer to Propertius than Ovid:

> Goddess of youth, and lady of the spring
> Most fit to be the consort to a King,
> Be pleased to rest you in this sacred grove
> Beset with myrtles, whose each leaf drops love.
> Many a sweet-faced wood-nymph here is seen,
> Of which chaste order you are now the queen:
> Witness their homage when they come and strew
> Your walks with flowers, and give their crowns to you.
> Your leafy throne, with lily-work possess
> And be both princess here and poetess.

Praise of the fitness of Henrietta Maria for Charles I here both opposes Puritanism and endorses Catholicism in England's ruling family. Welcoming Henrietta Maria as queen of the Hesperides' 'sacred grove', moreover, places Herrick's poetic and religious domain in her hands. The *Hesperides* here allies itself with a Catholic culture which Henrietta Maria transmitted from the court of Charles I.[96] In 'An Epigram to the Queen', Herrick's hero Ben Jonson wrote of Henrietta Maria in similarly eulogising, yet still more pointedly, Catholic terms.[97]

True to the injunction to be 'brief in praying', Herrick's Christian features tend to be evoked briefly. Nevertheless, they are significant. Altars, for example, are regularly mentioned in the *Hesperides*, according to Guibbory because Puritans feared even the word 'altar' pointed to the Mass.[98] Explaining Herrick's altars as anti-Puritan features in this way is reasonable, but it is also reductive. Frequent Ave Marias, telling of beads, splashings of holy water, incense-burnings, missals and trentals in Herrick commend the Catholic practices.[99] Since various features of Herrick's poetry show 'papistical' interest, it is reasonable to conclude that his focus on altars – like his focus on 'saints' – is also partly papistical.[100]

---

96 See Chapter 6, pp. 186–93.
97 This poem, also mentioned here, is considered in detail in Chapter 5 (see pp. 141–4).
98 For Herrick amid Puritan fears that even the word 'altar' pointed to the Mass, see Achsah Guibbory, *Ceremony and Community from Herbert to Milton: Literature, Religion and Cultural Conflict in Seventeenth-Century England* (Cambridge: Cambridge University Press, 1998), pp. 97–8.
99 Parry (2006), p. 147.
100 For detailed analysis of the Christian aspects of Herrick's classical imagery – including, for example, 'saints' – see Robert Deming, 'Herrick's Funereal Poems', *Studies in English Literature, 1500–1900*, 9/1 (Winter 1969), 153–67, especially 165.

Catholic inflections given to devotional poetry by Southwell are therefore in Herrick. Yet of the poets observed so far, Herrick, whose poems were composed in the trans-shifting era 1610–47, is the most heterodox.[101] Herrick wrote four brief poems on the crucifixion (two poems called 'Crosses', one called 'Comforts in Crosses' and another called 'Patience, or Comforts in Crosses'), and while these broadly recall Herbert (and behind him, Southwell) the poems are too slight to stand for more than general Christian markers. They align, too, with pagan sources and poems on pagan, rather than Christian, sacrifice: 'Sweetness in Sacrifice', 'Steame in Sacrifice', 'The Smell of the Sacrifice'; and also, with poems partly pagan and partly Christian: 'Cheerfulness in Charity; or The Sweet Sacrifice'; 'The Sacrifice by way of Discourse betwixt himself and Julia'.[102] Though consistently anti-Puritan, the religious coordinates of Herrick's poetry point in contrary directions. 'Part pagan, part papistical' – Herrick's own phrase – catches the religious ambiguity.

By contrast, John Donne's exchange of poems 'In Sacram Anchoram Piscatoris' shows how he, like Herbert, considered the cross Christianity's anchor.[103] Donne's poem 'The Cross' is similar. Here Donne presents Christ's cross as a universal order. The poem is filled with the emphatic paradoxicality we have observed in Herbert and Southwell before him:

> Look down, thou spiest out crosses in small things;
> Look up, thou seest birds rais'd on crossed wings.
> All the globes frame, and spheres, is nothing else
> But the meridians crossing parallels.[104]
>
> ('The Cross', 21–4)[104]

In this world of crosses, individual activities such as swimming (19), alchemy (37), crossing your heart (51) and even denying Christ' sacrifice entail that sacrifice, for 'No cross is so extreme, as to have none' (14). The perspective broadly recalls Thomas à Kempis's claim that the cross 'in all things consists'.[105] Yet even as Donne takes the logic of that claim to a seemingly contradictory, cross-ridden, conclusion, he also intensifies the previously

---

101 On the dates, see Creaser, 188–96.
102 On the breadth of Herrick's pagan sources, see Gordon Braden, *The Classics and English Renaissance Poetry: Three Case Studies* (New Haven, CT, and London: Yale University Press, 1978), pp. 154–258.
103 See Christina Malcolmson, *George Herbert: A Literary Life* (Basingstoke: Palgrave Macmillan, 2004), pp. 25–6; and Andrew Harvey, 'Crossing Wits: Donne, Herbert and Sacramental Rhetoric', *Renaissance Papers* (2005), 69–84.
104 All quotations from Donne are from *John Donne's Poetry*, ed. by Donald Dickson (New York and London: Norton, 2007), unless otherwise indicated.
105 Thomas à Kempis, *The Imitation of Christ*, trans. Leo Sherley-Price (Harmondsworth: Penguin, 1952; repr. 1959), p. 84.

observed claim (in Herbert's poem 'The Cross') that crosses are in actions and contradictions. Describing the 'crossing' parallels of the meridian, Donne illustrate Christ's sacrifice in metaphor. When we 'Cross ... dejections / ... Cross and correct concupiscence ... / Cross no man else, but cross thyself' (53–60), the metaphors are obtrusively contradictory.

Importantly, Donne's 'The Cross' is not merely literary. It also addresses contemporary controversies over religious images and the relation of poetic images to material ones. The poem has been connected to the 1604 Hampton Court Conference, especially its debates over making the sign of the cross; but 'The Cross' is also linked with recusant crucifixes, as seen for example in Justus Lipsius's *De cruce libri tre* (Antwerp 1593).[106] The poem begins with the question of whether one might deny not just Christ's 'image' but also 'th' image of his cross' (1–2). The first of these questions receives a developed response. The poem first decides 'Material crosses then, good physic be' (25); then it adds that 'spiritual [crosses] have chief dignity' (26); but then it concludes 'we love harmlessly / The crosses pictures' (62–3). The conclusion answers Protestant claims that religious images are harmful and an argument about poetic images sustains the conclusion. Presenting Christ's cross through metaphors, the poem consistently implies its imagery is unintelligible without a material counterpart. That counterpart includes, besides pictures, an 'Altar' (4) and a 'crucifix' (32). The cross metaphorically organising the poem, it transpires, depends on institutional church materials of a Catholic kind.

Both Herbert and Donne, then, envisage Christ's sacrifice in an institutional church context of sacrificial action. Both poets also present this action in Catholic terms recalling Southwell in the history of devotional poetry. From persons habituated by Jacobean religion, we can expect nothing more theologically explicit. Though the *Thirty-nine Articles* and the Oath of Allegiance spelt out the essentials of English faith and required assent, the English Church under James I (1603–25) forbade explicit discussion of more divisive points of doctrine.[107] The censorship helps explain anxiety in Herbert for *The Temple*: seen, for example, in his never having seemingly shown its poetry to anyone before handing it to Nicholas Ferrar (1593–1637); and in Herbert's instruction to Ferrar to 'burn' the work if he judged it not 'to the advantage of any poor soul'.[108] 'No other poet in the early modern

---

106 See Ceri Sullivan, 'John Donne's "The Cross" and Recusant Graffiti', *Notes and Queries*, 63/3 (September 2016), 458.
107 Brooke Conti, *Confessions of Faith in Early Modern England* (Philadelphia: University of Pennsylvania Press, 2014), p. 50.
108 Helen Wilcox, 'George Herbert', *Oxford National Dictionary of Biography* (online; accessed 31.3.2023).

period' was as scrupulous about his readers as Herbert opening *The Temple*.[109] For Donne (whose poems, like Herbert's, were published posthumously in 1633), the consequence of doctrinal censorship under James I was consistent theological evasion.

That is already seen in 'The Crosse'. To its observed Catholic features, the poem also envisages an alternative, raising questions about its Christian sincerity. In affirming 'No Cross is so extreme, as to have none' (14), the poem suggests that the greatest cross is not having one: a claim at once endorsing crosses and their absence. Although it is claimed this absence is a cross to be borne, envisaged too is a Christianity entirely without Christ's cross, and so without redemption. The poem never confirms this transformed idea of Christianity, but critics have observed similar presentations in Donne elsewhere. Of the image of Christ's death in 'Good Friday, Riding Westward, 1613', for example, Judith Anderson writes: 'Within a few lines ... Donne's speaker discounts the image of Christ the Redeemer that he has realised in the poem.'[110] Indeed, imagining the denial of Christ's image, cross and altar as a 'dare' (1, 4), the opening of 'The Cross' takes its doubtful Christianity seriously. A poem like Holy Sonnet 19 ('O, to vex me') is a counterpart to 'The Cross' in this respect. Heaven, prayer, contrition, God and the fear of Him are all present in the poem, yet Christ, the altar and the cross are not.

Standing in for this last in the sonnet is a relevant emphasis on 'contraries' (1) and 'Inconstancy' (2), for as we have seen, each of these have parallels in Herbert and origins in Southwell. Yet the abstract concepts are unsupported by the image of the cross, the poem instead ascribing their meaning to humours (5) and sickness (13). In stark contrast to any of the poets hitherto, it is notable that no poem by Donne addresses the Eucharist directly.[111]

Donne's view of the saints presents a further contrast but similar evasion. Roman Catholic sainthood underpins 'The Canonization' and 'The Relique' and Donne habitually treats patrons like patron saints.[112] Yet importantly, it is hard to tell how much more these saints are than conceits or vehicles

---

109 A. W. Barnes, 'Editing George Herbert's Ejaculations: Texts, Contexts and Interpretation', *Textual Cultures*, 1/2 (2006), 90–113 (95).

110 See Judith Anderson, 'Working Imagination in the Early Modern Period: Donne's Secular and Religious Lyrics and Shakespeare's Hamlet, Macbeth and Leontes', in *Shakespeare and Donne: Generic Hybrids and the Cultural Imagination* (New York: Fordham University Press, 2013), p. 215.

111 Notice, here, 'directly'. Sacramental poetics (different from poems directly on the Eucharist) have been widely attributed to Donne. See DiPasquale (1999); Whalen (2002); Read (2013), pp. 69–97; Johnson (2014), pp. 89–118.

112 See Alison Chapman, *Patrons and Patron Saints in Early Modern English Literature*, Routledge Studies in Early Modern Literature (New York and London: Routledge, 2013), pp. 119–21.

of praise. Since poems to patrons can be self-serving, Donne's connection of patrons with patron saints stands between true and mock veneration.

In 'A Letter to the Lady Carey, and Mistress Essex Rich, from Amiens', for example, Donne presents a town that is 'HEre, where by All All saints invoked are' (2).[113] Yet he quickly condemns this religion as 'heresie', arguing only veneration of his dedicatees is truthful (4–6). The manner is iconoclastically Protestant, yet (since his praise emerges from Amiens) metaphorically Catholic. His patrons thus positioned as pseudo saints of 'influence' (45), the Catholicism sustains the poem in its praise, intricacy, and obsequiousness – its closing note:

> May therefore this be enough to testifie
> My true devotion, free from flatterie;
> He that beleeves himself, doth never lie. (61–3)

Pleading the poem be taken for 'true devotion' raises doubts, especially since devotion (to the mistresses, to the saints) is the loose pivot on which praise has turned. Finally suggesting the poem could lie (63) adds doubt; and the basis of this last argument for honesty in an idiosyncratic self and its questionable aphorism does not help. Formally patronage poetry, Donne's letter from Amiens is about saints, doubts about saints and doubts about the doubts, hedging at every turn. One cannot write off the Catholicism, but it is a long way from Southwell.

More conventional is 'To Mrs Magdalene Herbert: of St Mary Magdalene'.[114] Here Donne conflates Lady Magdalene (mother to George Herbert, who was Donne's godson) with Mary Magdalene, who was a biblical figure and a saint. Since, Donne maintains, Church Fathers could not believe one woman could do as much as the Magdalene, they wrongly ascribed her 'active faith' (3) to several Marys. Restoring the Magdalene's credit in the poem, therefore, Donne encourages veneration for the saint and her namesake, Lady Herbert, calling for more such Marys: 'Increase their number, Lady, and their fame' (9). The poem lacks the suggestion in 'A Letter to the Lady Carey, and Mistress Essex Rich, from Amiens' that sainthood is foreign; and though by no means strident, it presents sainthood without ambivalence. The saint 'harbour[ed] Christ himself, a guest' (13) and 'More than the Church did know, / The Resurrection' (4–5). With the Church briefly here at fault, the call, for more virtue and, too, more saints, looks for Catholic restoration of a kind.

---

113 All citations of this poem are from *Poems by J.D.* (1635), pp. 198–200.
114 Citations from this poem are from *John Donne: The Major Works*, ed. by John Carey (Oxford: Oxford University Press, 1990), p. 170. The next cited poem ('An Epithalamion … on St Valentines Day') is also from this edition (pp. 238–41).

Yet quite what kind is unclear: evasion runs through Donne like a thread.[115] In his sermons, Donne maintained that just as the Roman Church did not say everything preached by the English Church was wrong, so the English Church did not say everything preached by the Roman Church is false. Donne therefore encouraged parishioners to distinguish between fundamentals and non-fundamentals of religion for themselves.[116] Yet we cannot assume Donne's sermons tell us more about his religious views than his poems. Pulpits produced insincerity. Jacobean divines who exceeded the boundaries of conformity paid the legal and political consequences. Preachers, tailoring their words to the pulpit, exerted laws of self-censorship.[117]

A final example from the patronage poems, 'An Epithalamion, or The Marriage Song of the Lady Elizabeth, and Count Palatine being married on St Valentine's Day' illustrates Donne's evasions about saints and Christ's sacrifice together. Since it celebrates a marriage, the Church is in view.

In 'Hail Bishop Valentine' (1), the poem opens in strident address to that Church. Asserting that the day belongs to the bishop and 'All the air thy diocese is' (1–2), the poem connects the Church, past and present, through its saints as, in turn, did Southwell, Crashaw and Herbert. The fourteenth of February was the feast of three martyrs of the early Church called Valentine. Donne distinctly evokes 'Bishop Valentine' (56) of Interamna (now Terni, in Italy). Yet his extended evocation of 'chirping choristers' (3) broadly evokes the medieval feast of the three saints Valentine, whose shared day (says Chaucer) brings 'every foul … to choose his make'.[118]

The wedding of the Count and Lady allows Donne to address love as a sacrificial sanctity. The couple, unlike ordinary birds, are 'two phoenixes' (18, 23), making fiery death and resurrection central. Yet celebrating by making 'the whole year through, thy day, O Valentine' (28) alters the saints' feast day; and requesting 'all men date records from this day, Valentine' (42) resets the Christian calendar. 'Thy day was but the eve to this, O

---

115 Playing fast and loose with texts, especially by misquotation, is a regular feature of preaching in Donne's era. See Alison Knight, 'The "Very, Very Words": (Mis)quoting Scripture in Lancelot Andrewes's and John Donne's Sermons on Job, 19: 23–27', *Studies in Philology* (2014), 442–69.

116 See William Mueller, *John Donne: Preacher* (Princeton, NJ: Princeton University Press, 1962), pp. 152–4.

117 See Jeanne Shami, *John Donne and Conformity in Crisis in the Late Jacobean Pulpit* (Cambridge: D.S. Brewer, 2003), p. 1; John Waters, 'John Donne's Sermons: Counsell and the Politics of the Dynamic Middle', *English Literary Renaissance*, 50/3 (2020), 391–416 (394).

118 See 'The Parliament of Fowles', line 310, in *The Complete Poetry and Prose of Geoffrey Chaucer*, ed. by John Fisher (New York: Holt, Rinehart and Winston, 1989), p. 572. At lines 320–1, the poem emphasises 'every foul' congregates on St Valentine's day 'fro yer to yeere'.

Valentine' (84) shrinks and displaces the saints and their day; and 'More truth, more courage in these two do shine, / Than all thy turtles have, and sparrows, Valentine' (97–8) makes the couple's new Valentine's Day better than the old one.

Striking sacrificial changes follow: 'by this act of these two phoenixes / Nature again restored is' (99–100). In the poetic church of new Christian days, Christ's salvation goes to the couple. Adding, 'There's but one Phoenix still, as was before' (102) and that we only 'enlarge' (112), rather than displace, Saint Valentine's day, in the end the poem backs away from this blasphemy. Yet vacillation is clear. Here and generally, evading precise views on the Church and its saints is strategic. The observation accounts for the recent claim that firm evidence for Donne's recusant upbringing is 'absent'.[119] Beyond his priesthood (from 1615), firm evidence of Donne's religious convictions is absent in general: he projects evasion.[120] Since his views on the topic are read both ways, Donne is reasonably termed Jesuitical.[121] In *Ignatius his Conclave* (1611), he even used evasive language to condemn Jesuit equivocation.[122] It is true that Donne's religious identity is best understood in his 'casuistical discourse and habits of thought'.[123] Yet the context for this evasive personality is the rejection of precise doctrinal discussion under James I.[124] Barring a find of significance, I do not think we will ever know Donne's precise theological view of the Eucharist or the saints; possibly, he did not know it.

Following Southwell, Crashaw, Herbert and Herrick, Donne is the last, great poetic clergyman of this chapter. Of these poets, Donne's extensively pursued, strategic ambiguity over the Eucharist and the saints puts him

---

119 Mary Morrissey, 'Was Donne a Catholic?' Conversion, Conformity and Early Modern English Confessional Identities', *The Review of English Studies* (2022), 1–14 (14). Morrissey considers Donne's upbringing was 'church papist' (Morrissey, 7).
120 Importantly, in this respect, assessments of Donne's religion largely depend on Donne's accounts (Morrissey, 2). Further evidence presented by Morrissey seems to me problematic. Her readings of sermons, for example, overlook the self-censorship in sermons of the era we have observed.
121 See John Klause, 'Hope's Gambit: The Jesuitical, Protestant, Skeptical Origins of Donne's Heroic Ideal', *Studies in Philology*, 94/2 (Spring 1994), 181–215 (213–15); and Andrew Hadfield, *Lying in Early Modern English Culture: From the Oath of Supremacy to the Oath of Allegiance* (Oxford: Oxford University Press, 2017), pp. 152–7. See also Victor Houliston, 'Paul's Cross and the State Church: The Case of John Donne and the Jesuits', in *Old St. Paul's and Culture*, ed. by Shanin Altman and Jonathan Buckner, Early Modern Literature in History (Cham, Switzerland: Palgrave, 2022), pp. 173–96 (p. 162).
122 Houliston (2022), p. 149.
123 Shami, p. 21.
124 See my comments on this above (citing Brooke, p. 50). See also Shami, p. 21.

most directly at odds with the Catholic presentation of worship in poetry promoted by Southwell. Nevertheless, Christian sacrifice, saints, rituals and materials of worship remain central in Donne's poetry, so that while he develops and adapts Southwell's Catholic presentation of worship, he also follows and responds to it. Herrick, who can seem heterodox, shows distinct interest in features of Catholic worship promoted by Southwell and though these features are mostly presented briefly by Herrick, they are presented without subversion or opposition, and they recur. Crashaw and Herbert echo Southwell extensively: in their combined presentations of the Eucharist, saints and the Church, their poetry carries forward much of the Catholic worship promoted by Southwell. Crashaw does this as a Church of England clergyman who converted to Catholicism; Herbert as a Church of England clergyman who did not. In sum, Southwell's presentations of Catholic worship emerge in some form in every one of the Church of England poets of this chapter. Deep into the seventeenth century, therefore, devotional poetry in English continued to echo Catholic presentations of worship. That this Catholic presentation emerges repeatedly from Church of England priests (including the converts Crashaw and Donne) makes the presentation remarkable. It implies a limited adherence to Church of England worship by its poetic priests and a residual desire in them for Catholic forms of worship, despite the enduring break from Rome of the English Church in 1558.

On that break, publications shed a further light. Published in the same year that William Laud was made Archbishop of Canterbury (1633), Herbert and Donne's poems emerged into a decade unusually inclined to pre-Reformation worship.[125] The trend suggests Herbert's Southwellian poetic (though it does not explain it), while underlining Donne's reservations. First published in 1646 and 1648, by contrast, the poetry of Crashaw and Herrick emerged into an almost entirely different world. Laud was dead: executed in 1645. Between 1646 and 1649, the Prayer Book was banned, traditionalist clergy were ejected from their livings for refusing to take the Covenant and the Negative Oath, and royalists were 'directly subject to Parliament's assault on the traditions of church life'.[126] For royalist religion the outlook was bleak; for some apocalyptic:

> For a few, disestablishment meant that the Church of England no longer existed, and they promptly converted to Rome. For those who did not convert,

---

125 Anthony Milton, *Catholic and Reformed: The Roman and Protestant Churches in English Protestant Thought, 1600–1640* (Cambridge: Cambridge University Press, 1995), pp. 315–20; Milton, *England's Second Reformation: The Battle for the Church of England, 1625–1662*, Cambridge Studies in Early Modern British History (Cambridge: Cambridge University Press, 2021), p. 57.
126 Milton (2021), p. 282.

one answer was exile, where they could hope to observe Prayer Book worship unmolested: although even in the Netherlands; [sic] ministers could find themselves under pressure not to use the Book. For those who remained, the problem of religious identity was acute.[127]

As his poetry reveals, in 1646 Crashaw was intellectually ready for the Catholic move. Remaining in England, Herrick did differently. Publishing his 'loose baggy monster of some 1400 poems' in 1648, Herrick aptly reflected in *Hesperides* the lost identity of the royalist Church of England.[128] Yet in Catholicism, he also put forward the viable alternative.

---

127 Milton (2021), p. 283.
128 Creaser, 170–1; see also Ruth Connolly, 'Print, Miscellaneity and the Reader in Robert Herrick's *Hesperides*', in *Readings on Audience and Textual Materiality*, ed. by Graham Allen, Carrie Griffin, and Mary O'Connell (London and New York: Routledge, 2011), pp. 23–36 (pp. 25–6). *Hesperides* 'lacks a unifying principle' (Connolly, p. 24).

5

Mary of recusants and reform

Among the forms of worship observed in Chapter 4 was the veneration of the saints, which Robert Southwell encouraged in English poetry and which successive poets (Protestant and Catholic) continued and developed. Outstanding among these saints was the Virgin Mary. As we saw, Protestants had many reasons to be suspicious of the Virgin Mary. Saints, generally, were never created by the Church of England and texts like 'Against the Peril of Idolatry' in the *Book of Homilies* echoed Calvin in presenting saint veneration as essentially polytheism. More specifically, the limited evidence about Mary in scripture meant Protestants were inclined only to accept claims about Mary which scripture guaranteed. Mary's association with the Mass and Purgatory also made her problematic for Protestants, while the embrace of Mary by the Counter-Reformation sharpened Protestant anxieties about Mary. There were no official 'Hail Mary' prayers in England after the death of Queen Mary I and there are countless examples of the destruction of Marian images from the time of Thomas Cromwell to that of Elizabeth I (*r.* 1558–1603). Only with the rise of Arminianism in seventeenth-century England did the Church of England begin to reclaim Mary and the development (which was halted at the Interregnum) was slow and piecemeal. In Stephen Bates's words, the Virgin Mary defined 'the limits and hermeneutic of the English Reformation'.[1] Given this central importance, the remainder of this book attends to the Virgin Mary in English literature.

I here consider the Virgin in sixteenth- and seventeenth-century poetry in two ways: as the divisive mother of Christ and the image of England's broken church. Breaking that church apart, forcing it to different shapes, a 'permanent' wave of iconoclastic and counter-iconoclastic turmoil broke on the English Church in the sixteenth and seventeenth centuries.[2] Marian

---

1 See Stephen Bates, 'The Virgin Mary and the Reformation of the Midlands, 1516–1560', *Midland History*, 44/2 (2019), 159–75 (171). With reference to Bates, Diarmaid MacCulloch (2017) and Graham Parry (2011) among others, I established the various points about saints and the Virgin Mary made here in Chapter 4 (see pp. 109, 110, 121–2).

2 See James Simpson, *Permanent Revolution: The Reformation and the Illiberal Roots of Liberalism* (Cambridge, MA, and London: Harvard University Press, 2019); see also my comments on Herrick at the end of Chapter 4 and the Introduction.

Mary of recusants and reform 141

poetry to be considered soon cries out at the experience. Yet since Southwell underpinned the Marian poetics of Chapter 4, I begin by recalling Protestant attitudes to Southwell in England:

> To patriotic Protestants ... Southwell was properly captured, tortured and executed, as one of the instigators of terrorism in the dangerous 1580s and 1590s. His Marian poetry would be seen as blasphemous superstition, the verbal manifestations of his life of subversion and idolatry.[3]

Yet the verbal manifestations of Catholic Mary go beyond Southwell, the poets of the previous chapter or even 'patriotic Protestants'.[4] Popular demand for the Virgin kept her alive even in very unexpected places. For example, some copies of the 1552 Prayer Book contain an image of the Virgin.[5] Her removal from the 1559 edition bespeaks the greater anti-Marianism of the Elizabethan Prayer Book, as well as the developing opposition to Mary in the sixteenth-century Church of England. Early modern English sermons reveal the Virgin Mary functioned in the Church of England as a distastefully gendered means of demonising the Catholic Church.[6] Yet the image of the Virgin in the 1552 Prayer Book shows the willingness even of Protestant printers to produce books for people across sectarian lines.[7] Catering 'for established, as well as emerging readerly tastes', the image of the Virgin in the 1552 Book of Common Prayer bespeaks a popular demand for the Virgin in English religion and among English readers.[8]

Of course, 1552 is neither the 1580s nor 1590s of Robert Southwell, nor the still later periods of a Herbert or Crashaw. Yet Ben Jonson's 'An Epigram to the Queen' of 1630 takes us deep into the seventeenth century. It illustrates both the continued difficulty of venerating the Virgin in England and a continuing desire to practise her veneration:

> HAile *Mary*, full of grace, it once was said,
> And by an Angel, to the Blessed Maid,
> The Mother of our Lord: why may not I,
> (Without prophannesse) as a Poët, cry

---

3 See Gary Waller, *The Virgin Mary in Late Medieval and Early Modern English Literature and Popular Culture* (Cambridge: Cambridge University Press, 2011), p. 119.
4 They also go beyond Waller's study of Marian development, in which Crashaw is the 'climax' (Waller, 2011, p. 200).
5 See Isabel Davies, 'Tales of the Unexpected: A Marian Woodcut in the Book of Common Prayer', *Notes & Queries*, 66/3 (2019), 384–7 (386).
6 Lilla Grindlay, *Queen of Heaven: The Assumption and Coronation of the Virgin in Early Modern English Writing* (Notre Dame, IN: Notre Dame University Press, 2018), p. 43.
7 Davies, 386.
8 Davies, 386.

> Haile *Mary*, full of Honours, to my Queene,
> The Mother of our Prince? When was there seene
> (Except the joy that the first *Mary* brought,
> Whereby the safety of the world was wrought)
> So generall a gladnesse to an Isle,
> To make the hearts of a whole Nation smile,
> As in this Prince? let it be lawfull so
> To compare small with great, as still we owe
> Our thankes to God: then haile to Mary, spring
> Of so much health, both to the Realm, and King!
> (Ben Jonson, 'An Epigram to the Queene, then lying in')[9]

Most important, here, is that as late as 1630, in an author as influential as Jonson, the Virgin is not forgotten but promoted, despite the 'self-evident' problem the Virgin presented to officially Protestant England.[10] As we shall see in Chapter 6, Henrietta Maria promoted a cult of the Virgin Mary, so Jonson's connection of the two queen Marys – the Mary, Queen of Heaven and Henrietta Maria, Queen of England – emerges in part from an active attempt to re-Catholicise English culture by Henrietta Maria.[11] Yet Jonson's openly recusant period (1598–1610), as well as his enduring promotion of theologically Catholic 'works' of literature (see Chapter 2) suggest he was far from an unwilling promoter of the Virgin Mary. The poem merits attention.

From the start, Jonson evokes by direct quotation the opening of the 'Hail Mary', as it was developed into formal prayer from St Luke's gospel.[12] Yet the poem also reflects on a history more recent. As we have seen, the last official Hail Mary was heard in 1558, at the end of Mary Tudor's reign, while as successive scholars have observed, venerations of Mary (the mother of Christ) were outlawed in consciously Protestant practice thereafter.[13] Jonson's last clause in line 1, 'it once was said', therefore, throws the Hail Mary prayer into ironic, historical relief. Before becoming a panegyric to the queen, the poem reflects on the loss of the Hail Mary prayer in formal

---

9 Citation from 'Underwoods: Consisting of Diverse Poems', in *Ben Jonson: The Poems, The Prose Works*, Volume VIII, ed. by C. H. Hereford Percy and Evelyn Simpson (Oxford: Clarendon Press, 1947; repr. 1965), pp. 125–293 (238).

10 Quotation from Christine Peters, *Patterns of Piety: Women, Gender and Religion in Late Medieval and Reformation England* (Cambridge: Cambridge University Press, 2003), p. 212.

11 For further discussion, see Chapter 6, pp. 186–93.

12 For useful discussion of the history of the 'Hail Mary', see 'The Catholic Encyclopedia', http://www.newadvent.org/cathen/07110b.htm (accessed 2.9.2018).

13 See Peters, p. 228; Grindlay, p. 8; Diarmaid MacCulloch, *All Things Made New: Writings on the Reformation* (London: Penguin, 2017), p. 51; George Tavard, *The Thousand Faces of the Virgin Mary* (Minnesota: The Liturgical Press, 1996), p. 135.

English religion. The reflection colours analogies between the Virgin Mary and Henrietta Maria (queen of England from 1625) to follow. Line 4 is not just concerned with the profanity of comparing the sacred Virgin to a human being – a comparison already suggesting a catholic definition of profanity, since Protestants (rejecting Mary as Queen of Heaven) reconfigured her as plainly, if gracefully, human.[14] Since the Hail Mary prayer was 'prophanness' in Protestant England, line 4 recalls the controversial prayer again.

The Marian transgression surfaces again at line 11. Here the allusion to what is 'lawfull' refers not just to the profanity or otherwise of analogies between the queen and the Queen of Heaven, but also to the objectional status of the Hail Mary prayer in Protestant religion. Referring to the prayer to Mary that opened the poem, 'let it be lawfull' (11) is a thinly disguised demand for the return of the Hail Mary in English religious practice.[15] Since Mary often stood for the Catholic Church in Protestant polemic, the appeal for a return to venerating Mary is also interpretable as a call for the return of Roman religion.[16]

Concluding 'then haile to Mary' (13), in the same vein the last couplet hails Henrietta Maria while firmly establishing the Hail Mary prayer. The defiance is characteristically Jonsonian. Having re-established the objectionable prayer, he presents an ambiguous scenario where, alongside Charles I, the 'King' of the last line refers to God the Father or Christ. The wider 'health ... to the realm', therefore (in earlier elaborations the 'gladnesse to an Isle, / To make the hearts of a whole Nation smile' and the 'safety of the world'), presents a transformed Christianity: English, yet also universally 'catholic' and (with Mary at its heart) suggestively Catholic.

Not that a catholic – indeed Roman Catholic – sense of profanity is not also present. The poem celebrates the birth, in 1630, of the future Charles II to Queen Henrietta Maria. It links the notoriously Catholic queen and her son with the Virgin Mary and her Son; Maria with Mary; and the Queen of England with the Queen of Heaven. Yet sensitive to Catholic 'prophannesse', Jonson sidesteps it, stressing he compares 'small with great' (12) and making Henrietta Maria full of 'Honours' (5), rather than grace. The link of Henrietta Maria with the Virgin, in which each reflects on the other, bolsters the Roman Catholic in both. The linking strategy was common at

---

14 See Grindlay, p. 107; Peters, p. 224. I consider this matter further here.
15 As noted previously, parallel connections between Mary and unlawfulness are in Herbert and Shakespeare. See p. 123. These include ambiguity as to which 'king' – the monarch or God – is being addressed.
16 As noted, representation of the Virgin among Protestants often stood for 'a demonizing of the Catholic church' (Grindlay, 43). Celebrating Mary, therefore, can maintain the allusion to the Catholic Church while reversing the demonisation.

the court of Henrietta Maria; yet writers already deployed it for Mary Tudor.[17] The linking strategy has also been claimed for Elizabeth I; yet with Elizabeth, the link entails appropriation of Catholic imagery to bolster royal and Protestant authority.[18] Deployed towards Catholic Henrietta Maria, by contrast, the imagery becomes resoundingly Catholic.

Jonson no doubt recognised the enlarged sympathy for Rome at court and elsewhere in England under Henrietta Maria, behind much of which was the queen herself. The poem testifies to the historical reduction of Marian veneration in England since Mary Tudor. Yet in the formally Protestant country, the poem also testifies to authors and readerships still ready to recognise and venerate the Virgin in older ways.[19] Most obviously these authors included those recusants who 'refused' England's Protestant solutions; in whose number Jonson counted himself for a time and whose complex influence on him Ian Donaldson has brought to life.[20] To discover how traditional salutations to Mary did *not* disappear in the era; to discover their marginal persistence up to and beyond Jonson's poem, observing in detail how they adapted to straitened conditions, we turn to such recusant writing.

---

17 Wizeman observes that praise of Mary Tudor frequently linked her with the Virgin so that 'one Mary possessed an essential role in salvation' and the other possessed 'an essential role in England's participation in salvation'. See William Wizeman, 'The Virgin Mary in the Reign of Mary Tudor', in *The Church and Mary: Papers Read at the 2001 Summer Meeting and the 2002 Winter Meeting of the Ecclesiastical Society*, ed. by R. N. Swanson (London: Institute of Historical Research), 2004), pp. 239–48 (p. 245). Su Fang Ng discusses the promotion of associations between the Virgin and Henrietta Maria as a significant feature of the queen's court in *Literature and the Politics of Family in Seventeenth-Century England* (Cambridge: Cambridge University Press, 2007), pp. 41–2. In these pages she also recalls Erika Veevers's association of masque culture – in which Jonson was the leader – with Marian veneration.

18 See Waller (2011), p. 121. The connection of Elizabeth I to the Virgin was previously explored by Helen Hackett, in *Virgin Mother, Maiden Queen: The Cult of Elizabeth I and the Virgin Mary* (Basingstoke: Macmillan, 1996); see also Anna Riehl, *The Face of Queenship: Early Modern Representations of Elizabeth I* (Basingstoke: Macmillan, 2011). Waller's caution is nevertheless important: 'It is, nevertheless, hard to read the patriotic encomia to Elizabeth without seeing them within the historical context of the Reformation and the crusade carried out by the Protestant regime against the cult of Mary' (Waller, p. 122). MacCulloch considers Elizabeth turned images of the Virgin Queen 'to her own triumphant use'. See Diarmaid MacCulloch, *All Things Made New: Writings on the Reformation* (London: Penguin, 2017), p. 156.

19 Peters, p. 229, notes the generally 'more favourable environment [to 'strongly catholic authors'] of the 1630s'. I discuss the court culture of this period in Chapter 6.

20 See Ian Donaldson's *Ben Jonson: A Life* (Oxford: Oxford University Press, 2011).

Recusant Marys

Since the Church of England never endorsed the veneration of saints, sixteenth and seventeenth-century poetry venerating Mary as a saint, even as 'Queen of Saints', was in a sense recusant by default, because it refused Elizabethan conformity.[21] Not that recusancy equates wholly with subversion. 'Though I am passionately affectionate to my Religion', Henry Constable wrote to the Earl of Essex, 'yet am I not in the number of those who weh [wish] t[h]e restitution thereof w[it]h the servitude of my country to a forrein Tyranny'.[22] Although his conversion to Roman Catholicism meant forfeiting his lands, loss of powerful friends including Essex and Sir Francis Walsingham, and a life spent largely abroad; and despite being imprisoned at various points including in the Tower of London in 1604, Constable (1562–1613) had qualities of open-mindedness and moderation of interest in today's pluralistic England. The opening chapter of his *The Catholic Moderator*, 'To All the Kings Faithful Subjects And Principally to those Faithful Catholikes, that are desirous of the Quiet of the Church and State', gives a taste of the outlook of this gentleman who found his convictions a 'hard hap'.[23] The full title of the work gives somewhat more:

> The Catholic Moderator: Or A Moderate Examination of the Doctrine of the Protestants. Proving against the too rigid Catholikes of the times, especially of the book called, *The Answere to the Catholike Apologie*, That We, Who are Members of the Catholike, Apostolike, and Roman Church, ought not to Condemn the Protestants for Heretikes, until further proof be made.

Not condemning Protestants out of hand; deferring judgement until matters of doctrine are ascertained through reason; even condemning 'too rigid' Romanists from the off. These are features illustrating a desire to moderate and be moderate in the wake of the murder of Henri III of France (1589). How fully Constable's text is a response to that event, or a more general statement of belief, is debatable. Yet being too radical for both most English protestants and Counter-Reformation authorities, it shows a recusant's ability to rise far above the 'charitable hatred' of the day.[24]

---

21 See definition 1a of 'recusant' in the *OED*.
22 See 'Introduction', in *The Poems of Henry Constable*, ed. by John Grundy (Liverpool: Liverpool University Press, 1960), p. 37. All citations from Constable's 'Spiritual Sonnets' will be from this edition. For an overview of Catholic loyalism, see Alison Shell, *Catholicism, Controversy and the English Literary Imagination, 1558–1660* (Cambridge: Cambridge University Press 1999), pp. 107–68.
23 This and subsequent citations from *The Catholic Moderator* are from *EEBO*, 2nd edn (London: 1623) (accessed 1.9.2013).
24 For the 'radical' nature of Constable's text in this respect, see Gary Kuchar, 'Henry Constable and the Question of Catholic Poetics: Affective Piety and Erotic Identification

Since the saints were never formally endorsed by the Church of England, his *Spiritual Sonnetts to The honour of God and hys Sayntes* (c.1593) shows Constable rose above religious hostilities without compromising his beliefs.[25] Yet the poems, including three 'To our blessed Lady', contain an autobiographical bitterness towards Elizabeth I. A contemporary account alleges Constable had been a favourite, but she now blocked his advancement.[26] In contrasts of Mary with Elizabeth I, Constable uses the Virgin to critique a perceived injustice at the very heart of English political life and at its highest echelon. He implies there are more significant loyalties than those even to a monarch. As the poems explain, those loyalties are to the Virgin.

Yet Mary is the means to a much wider critique, which is both theological and religio-political. The poems fulfil various religious functions. The first is to render Mary visible. To maintain her traditional role and image, in a landscape where they had formally and largely disappeared and where her images raised the deepest Protestant hostility.[27] Intensely concerned with religious imagery, 'To our blessed Lady (1)' follows its request to see Christ with an emphatic expression of the poet's need to see the Virgin: 'shewe me thy lovely face; / whose beams the Angells beuty do deface; / and even inflame the Seraphins with love'. All three poems picturing the Virgin, each are expressions of this longing for her un-defaced image.

Each poem also foregrounds the mediation of Mary which English Protestants rejected on the ground that it weakened Christ's mediation with his Father.[28] With tact, therefore, Constable makes Mary mediate between himself and Christ, rather than directly to the Father: avoiding contemporary suggestions that 'Mother Mary' might have authority over her Son.[29] Christ, therefore, is undoubtedly above his mother, in a chain of being where He,

---

in the *Spirituall Sonnettes*', *Philological Quarterly*, Volume 85 (Winter 2006), 69–90 (71). For discussion of its circumstantial history, see Grundy, 'Introduction', pp. 33–4. For 'charitable hatred' as the religious feeling of the day, see Alexandra Walsham, *Charitable Hatred: Tolerance and Intolerance in England, 1500–1700* (Manchester: Manchester University Press, 2006).

25 There is in fact a fourth poem 'To the Blessed Virgin', but I do not consider it in this chapter. In what follows I therefore refer to the three poems of the sequence as the first, second and third poems 'To our blessed Lady'.
26 See Shell, pp. 123–5.
27 Peters claims that images of Mary were the aspect of her cult Protestants most objected to. See Peters, p. 212. The observation is especially relevant to this chapter's concluding view of the English Church.
28 See Peters, p. 219.
29 For discussion of Mary as having authority over her Son in the period, see Sid Ray, *Mother Queens and Princely Sons: Rogue Madonnas in the Age of Shakespeare* (Basingstoke: Palgrave Macmillan, 2012). I discuss this matter further in relation to Constable in what follows.

not she, is the necessary link to the Father. Sovereign of Queens, the first poem begins, approaching Christ through Mary, 'shewe me thy sonne in his imperiall place, whose servants reigne, our kinges & queens above'. This Marian role as 'mediatrix' to Christ is still more explicit in the third poem in the sequence:

> Sweete Queene: although thy beuty rayse upp mee
> from sight of baser beutyes here belowe:
> Yett lett me not rest there: but higher goe
> to hym, who tooke hys shape from God & thee.

This address to the Virgin carefully balances its appeal for help from her with an unambiguous picture of heavenly hierarchy in which Christ is above Mary and God is the ultimate Father. Maintaining Mary's mediation, this responds to Protestant anxieties that Catholics make Mary into God by ensuring she does not threaten Him.

The second poem in the sequence combines the foci on Marian mediation and Marian imagery with impressive complexity. The sestet opens by contrasting sights of the Virgin with 'earthly sight':

> An earthlye syght doth onely please the eye,
> and breedes desire, but doth not satisfye:
> thy sight, gives us possession of all ioye,
> And with such full delyghtes eche sense shall fyll,
> as harte shall wyshe, but for to see thee still,
> and ever seyng, ever shall inioye.

In an era of Marian iconoclasm, the poet wants again to see the Virgin. Yet it is not only seeing her that he wants. Constable also wants to see as through Mary's eyes (with 'thy sight'). Making Mary a mediator once more, an implication of this play on 'seeing' is that it is through Mary's eyes that one finds the 'all ioye' of God. It is a Catholic idea from the early Church that to glimpse Mary with the eyes of faith is to see the love of God.[30] Constable's images of seeing Mary mark his place in the tradition.

They also put Constable amid Reformation debate. Praising Mary, notes Gary Waller, Constable refocused the idealisation of women in Petrarchan poetry onto the Virgin, finding in her the appropriate outlet for female veneration.[31] Yet to equate Mary with 'all joy' links her with God, suggesting the idolatry with which Reformers charged Romanists. Constable invites

---

30 Brian Daley, 'Woman of Many Names: Mary in Orthodox and Catholic Theology', *Theological Studies*, 71 (2010), 846–69 (847, 867, 869).
31 Waller (2011), p. 150.

the consideration. His suggestion that Mary is the divine is still stronger in the opening octave:

> Why should I any love O queene but thee?
>   if favour past a thankful love should breede?
>   thy womb dyd beare, thy brest my saviour feed;
>   and thou dyddest never cease to succour me.
> If Love doe followe worth and dignitye?
>   Thou all in [thy] perfections doest exceed:
>   if Love be ledd by hope of future meede?
>   what pleasure more then thee in heaven to see?

Presenting Mary in her role of Mother of God, bearing Jesus in the womb and suckling Him at her breast, this shows Christ at his most childlike and vulnerable. It also shows Mary at her most powerful. Madonna-and-Child imagery of the kind offended Reformers for the seeming implication that Mary could dominate Christ, relegating him to a position of dependency. John Calvin strongly opposed the imagery.[32] With its query as to whether there is any greater pleasure in heaven than Mary, moreover, the last line of the octave verges on the blasphemy that Mary might be greater than God. Certainly, Constable never states Mary is salvation's primary cause.[33] Yet her greatness develops an imagery insisting Mary ('thy womb ... thy breast ... thou ...') leads to salvation.

Courting Reformation controversy, theology in the poem seems wilfully untidy. That is true in the claim that Mary exceeds 'all ... perfections', as it is in the opening question. Opening with 'Why should I any love O queene but thee?' has Elizabeth I in mind. Yet by championing the Virgin over Elizabeth, so that the English queen comes to stand for 'any' and 'all' other loves, every other love becomes less than love for the Virgin. Importantly, Constable's claims that the poet loves Mary above 'any' and 'all' are conditional: the first claim is part of a hypothetical question and the second is predicated on an 'if' clause. Yet creating a hierarchy where the Virgin looks down on an Elizabeth herself associated with God, even if only implicitly – especially amid images of the Mother of God – is flirting with two blasphemies: that the Queen of England and God can be identified; and that the Virgin is therefore above God.

---

32 See Ray, p. 9.
33 On distinctions between primary and secondary causation, see Craig Boyd and Aaron Cobb, 'The Causality Distinction, Kenosis and a Middle Way: Aquinas and Polkinhorne on Divine Action', *Theology and Science*, 7/4 (2009), 391–406; Peter Frick, 'Johannine Soteriology and Aristotelean Philosophy: A Hermeneutical Suggestion on Reading John 3.16 and 1 John, 4.9', *Biblica*, 88/3 (2007), 415–21; Frick, 'The Means and Mode of Salvation: A Hermeneutical Proposal for Clarifying Pauline Soteriology', *Horizons in Biblical Theology*, 29 (2007), 203–23.

Constable thus presents both striking and problematic illustrations of Mary after 1559. He is important for offering direct, poetic venerations of Mary extant after 1559: a glimpse into continuing contemporary beliefs about her which the official attitudes of the day make unforthcoming. By the same token, however, he is problematic because it is difficult to assess how widely representative his attitudes were. The special circumstance of Constable's Roman Catholicism and alienation from Elizabeth helps create his near-to-idolising of the Virgin in the first 'To our Blessed Lady'. Yet should we infer from this circumstance that the attitude of the poem was unusual, or does it warrant us to imagine other recusant devotees of Mary idiosyncratically diverging from correct theology – and if so, in what numbers? It has been claimed that in the popular piety of late medieval England, imaginative devotion to the Virgin, independent of her Son, 'ran riot', but the perspective seems partial.[34] Providing a mothering, tender and approachable means to the Incarnation, Mary had enabled a medieval Christianity 'very different in feel' from the earlier Church's often stern and frightening portrayal of Christ Pantocrator and Judge.[35] In Constable's case, a clear concern to explain correct veneration of Mary merges with hints of incorrectness to which sensitive readers might easily have objected. Since much Reformation polemic hinges on whether Roman Catholic saints were venerated or idolised, these questions deserve a wider response.

The poetry to Mary of Richard Verstegan is less known than Constable's, and their backgrounds seem initially different. While Constable was a favourite of Elizabeth who fell from grace, with seeming leanings towards ecumenism, Verstegan was a printer who in the wake of Edmund Campion's execution became a leading Counter-Reformation publicist on the continent. Yet there are parallels between the two men. Both were university-educated, converts to Catholicism, sought by the law, and spent large portions of their lives in exile. Verstegan converted to Catholicism while at Oxford and so left the university. To a Catholic literary network at the turn of the sixteenth century connecting England to Europe and the Hapsburg Netherlands, he was crucial.[36] Keenly aware of his responsibility as a clandestine printer, from an underground Catholic press at Smithfield, Verstegan printed an account of the martyrdom of Campion in 1581.[37] He was arrested, escaped and fled

---

34 Waller (2011), p. 32.
35 Eamon Duffy, *A People's Tragedy: Studies in Reformation* (London: Bloomsbury, 2020), p. 33.
36 Marcin Polkowski, 'Richard Verstegan as a Publicist of the Counter-Reformation: Religion, Identity and Clandestine Literature', in *Publishing Subversive Texts in Elizabethan England and the Polish-Lithuanian Commonwealth*, ed. by Theresa Bela, Clarinda Calma and Jolanta Rzegocka (Leiden and Boston: Brill, 2016), pp. 263–88 (p. 263).
37 Polkowski, pp. 269–70.

abroad, settling in Antwerp in 1589. Verstegan remained there until his death in 1640, managing the smuggle of recusant books: a vital task for Catholic England, since books could circulate more freely and extensively than a small number of missionary priests.[38] Verstegan's works circulated widely on the continent, and it is likely his poetry found readerships in England. Published in English in 1601, the *Odes* discussed here anticipate English readers.[39]

On the twenty-fifth page of the *Odes*, there begins a sequence titled 'The Fifteen Mysteries of the Rosary, to our Blessed Lady. Whereof the First are Joyful. The Second Sorrowful. And the Third Glorious'.[40] Though it may sound stodgy, Verstegan introduces the collection in verses emphasising their poetic innovation and sophistication:

> The vaine conceits of loues delight
> I leaue to *Ouids* arte,
> Of warres and bloody broyles to wryte
> Is fit for *Virgils* parte.
>
> Of tragedies in doleful tales
> Let *Sophocles* entreat:
> And how vnstable fortune failes
> Al Poets do repeat.
>
> But vnto our eternal king
> My verse and voyce I frame
> And of his saintes I meane to sing
> In them to praise his name.

This scan of the contemporary literary scene reveals a poet who knows his voice. 'All poets' are doing Ovid, Virgil and Sophocles, Verstegan notes, showing his literary credentials; so, avoiding cliché, Verstegan will do otherwise. Strikingly, Verstegan here uses the Common Metre popularised through Protestant translations of the psalms like those of Thomas Sternhold and John Hopkins; yet here too Verstegan does differently.[41] The difference

---

38 Alexandra Walsham, '"Domme Preachers"?: Post-Reformation English Catholicism and the Culture of Print', *Past & Present*, 168 (2000), 72–123 (80, 85).
39 For fuller biography of Verstegan see Paul Arblaster, *Antwerp and the World: Richard Verstegan and the International Culture of Catholic Reformation* (Leuven: University of Leuven Press, 2004).
40 See Richard Verstegan, *Odes* (Antwerp: 1601), in *EEBO* (accessed 1.8.2013). All subsequent citations from the *Odes* are from this edition.
41 For Sternhold and Hopkins's metre, see for example *Al Such Psalms of Dauid as T. Sternhold didde in his lifetime draw into English metre* (London, 1553), in *EEBO* (accessed 18.11.21). For helpful discussion of their literary influence, see Margaret Hannay, 'Psalms Done Into Metre: The Common Psalms of John Milton and of the Bay Colony', *Christianity and Literature*, 32/3 (1983), 19–29 (23). On the controversial history of Sternhold's Psalms, see Cummings (2003), pp. 236–7.

is not writing religious poetry (hardly a new activity) but honouring the saints in English. That makes room not only for a literary novelty, but also for an anti-establishment aesthetic underscored by Verstegan's status as an exile. This is no mouldy verse (to adapt Jonson), but self-consciously marginal poetry: advertised of the moment, in terms a modern can appreciate. Regrettably, the *Odes* are not in print today.

With a suitable mood for her entrance, the sequence approaches Mary through seven odes based on the Penitential Psalms and a sequence on the 'Sybyllaes Prophesies of Christ'. The last gives the first glimpse of the Virgin in the text, in what is clearly an end-of-section, transitional moment. Mary appears as both Mother of God and *Madonna lactans*:

> **Sibylla Tiburtina.**
> THow Bethlem arte the birth-place of thy Lord,
> That doth from Nazareth assume his name,
> O blessed moother, blis doth thee affoord,
> His loue, that leaues himself pledge of the same
> O blessed bee that sweet milk-yeilding brest,
> To no wrish [nourish] God, right happely adrest.
> FINIS.

Next is a lengthy rosary sequence ending with three stanzas under the heading 'Ave Maria', followed by further sections of similar length called: 'Epithets of Our Blessed Lady', 'Our Blessed Ladies Lullaby' and 'A Reprehension of the Reprehending of our Ladies Praise'. Structurally, Mary is the first and most prominent of the saints the sequence honours, in a volume made to showcase her importance.

The integrated design is visible in Mary's place in the collection. She appears in the observed, transitional moment, where the sequence moves from the pre-Christian (Psalms and Prophesies) to the Christian (beginning in the Virgin). Yet Mary is also the 'door' and 'way' to later, sacred topics showing, for example, Christ crucified and in the sepulchre. Mary is thus not only the mediator to whom we pray, but also the mediator of Christian history.

Linked epithets suggest the self-conscious pivoting of the sequence around her mediation. This is Mary as 'Porta Caeli' and 'Scale Caeli':

> **Porta Caeli.**
> WHen grace came from aboue, then wa'st thou made the gate,
> By which it entred heer, & brought the hope of blis,
> Which hope in hartes of men, remaineth stil in state,
> And stil through faith and loue, aliue preserued is:
> Then since thow wa'st the dore, for grace this to relate,
> So art thow heauens gate, and wel accordeth this,
> That as God vnto men, did thee his entrance make,

> Men entrance vnto God, againe by thee may take.
> **Scale Caeli.**
> HOw may our heauy load, enclyning to descend,
> Ascend vp in the ayre, beyond the egles flight,
> Except by such a guyde, as wil assistance lend,
> And can from step to step, direct the passage right:
> Or rather her owne self, vs better to defend,
> The ladder wil become, that scaleth heauens height,
> By whose degrees of grace, to blis we may attaine,
> And in our mounting vp, not to fall downe againe.

Whether as a stairway to heaven or as its gate, Mary is here what she is in the sequence as a whole: the approach to the sacred. En route, her humanity is important. Images such as of the Virgin breastfeeding humanise and render accessible the theological subject matter; or would have done so for traditionalists. For confirmed Protestants, it was a different matter. As part of his opposition to saints' relics, Calvin expressed a 'raw indignation' at images of the breastfeeding Mary which caught on among Reformers. The bodily and lactating Virgin made her into a milk-cow, he sneered, adding: 'had the Virgin been a wet-nurse all her life, or a dairy, she could not have produced more than is shown as hers in various parts … it is superfluous here to remark that there is no Foundation in the Gospels for these foolish and blasphemous extravagances'.[42] In Verstegan's physicalised Mary, the recusant's Catholic identity shines through. Yet identity and politics are inseparable here, making this a religio-political and even proto-feminist intervention by the standards of the day.

In one respect, too, Calvin might not have objected to the *Odes*. Though Mary is its foremost personality, readers of the sequence move through the poems about her towards those about Christ: His mediating sacrifice is the goal. The sequence thus presents the theological correctness promoted by the Counter-Reformation, as well as evidence (seen also in Southwell) that Mariolatry of the period was not synonymous with idolatry.[43] If distinctions with veneration seem fine, they reflect the tension in Christianity's view that Christ the Redeemer came from Mary through the Incarnation.[44] As stressed

---

42 See Waller (2011), p. 90; and Gary Waller, 'The Virgin's "Pryvytes": Walsingham and the Late Medieval Sexualization of the Virgin', in *Walsingham in Literature and Culture from the Middle Ages to Modernity*, ed. by Dominic James and Gary Waller (Farnham and Burlington, VT: Ashgate, 2010), pp. 125–6.

43 The exclusive direction of Marian veneration towards Christ was an 'imperative' of the Counter-Reformation, though having roots in the fourteenth century. See Wizeman, pp. 247–8. For discussion of Southwell's similarly constructed Mariolatry, see Chapter 4, p. 111.

44 For further details, see Bates, 170–1.

in the twelfth century by St Bernard, Luke 1:38 ('let it be done to me') shows Mary's assent in bearing the Son of God.[45] The narrative gives Mary agency and a role in redemption's process, suggesting her necessity.[46]

Like Constable, Verstegan is substantial evidence of Marian continuity among English recusants. Yet for Protestants, Mary's 'slim scriptural persona' made her difficult.[47] Attacks in England on her cult meant the destruction of her images even including (under Edward VI and Elizabeth I) images of Mary from scripture.[48] In the Catholic poetry of Constable and Verstegan, signs of Mary's material body are signs of praise. Yet English poetry of the post-Reformation altered this sign of Mary's body from praise to violation. As I now show, the violation came to stand for the broken and pained state of England's Church and her Christianity.

Mary deflowered

The movement of Verstegan's sequence on towards Christ through the Virgin carries penetrative connotations that are also sexual in view of Verstegan's physical depictions of Mary. Attesting the Incarnation, Mary's body is highly visible in the *Odes*: in her 'sweet smelling breath' ('Quasi Cypressus'), in her 'womb' ('Ave Maria'), and in the maintained 'maiden' that closes the gynaecologically inflected 'Conteyning the Birth of Christe'. With their emphasis on the physicality of Mary, these poems seem to respond directly to the objection of Reformers that medieval veneration of Mary idolatrously sexualised her body.[49] Mary's sensuality is tangible in the opening of 'Our Blessed Ladies Lullaby', but, importantly, it exists in relation to Christ:

> Vpon my lap my soueraigne sits,
> And sucks vpon my brest,
> Meane whyle his loue sustaines my lyf,
> And giues my body rest.

Here the lap, the breast, the body, the sucking and sitting all give Mary a highly physical, incarnational existence, but the baby, Christ, is explicitly Mary's 'sovereign'. In 'Lilium inter Spinas' (Lily among Thorns) and 'Nauis

---

45 Laura Miles, *The Virgin Mary's Book at the Annunciation: Reading, Interpretation and Devotion in Medieval England* (Cambridge: D.S. Brewer, 2020), pp. 175–6.
46 The importance of the Incarnation cannot be underestimated in Christianity. I consider the Incarnation's impact on the medieval Church (and its survival in the likes of Herbert) on pp. 124 and 158.
47 Bates, 173.
48 Bates, 174.
49 Waller (2011), p. 33.

Institoris' (Merchant Ships), Mary's physicality is sexual and attractive, but as a means toward Christ. Here is 'Nauis Institoris':

> IF certitude of gaine, may stir the searching mynde,
> To venter in the ship, from whence misfortunes flee,
> That gouerneth the tyde, and doth comaund the wynde,
> And speedely returnes, with goodes that pretious bee,
> The barck of blis is shee, and fortunate by kynde,
> With grace shee fraighted is, and is of custome free,
> Taking but for her hyre, and her inritching trade,
> Loue of deuoted myndes, that rich by her are made.

The 'bark of bliss' is a Mary we enter to find grace – something with which Mary has been 'freighted', implying she receives it from elsewhere, as Verstegan maintains his mediating and material theme. Strikingly, the 'bliss' is at least metaphorically sexual in Mary's 'custome free', while her 'inritching trade' connotes prostitution. Yet the controversial point is that Mary is available to us; and because she is a 'bark', or ship, she is a mediator, carrying us to the place of grace. That place, as the collection shows, is Christ. Poems like 'Sacrificium sub lege Euangelica' are explicit on this point.[50] Yet because Mary is the mediator in 'Nauis Institoris', her availability is the height of pleasure; that we must only devote our minds to Mary to have this pleasure is the basis of Verstegan's sexual analogies. As a sensual reflection on Mary, the poem makes Christian theology pleasurable.

'Lilium inter Spinas' takes Mary's sexuality still further:

> AMiddes a gard of thorne, this goodly lilly grew,
> Defended from the foe, that would it faine deface,
> Who neere it to aproche, the entrance neuer knew,
> With poison to infect, where filth had neuer place,
> Yet such might bee the hate, that heeron did ensue,
> That hee reseru'd reuenge, vnto succeeding space,
> What tyme a crowne of thorne, the sonnes head did sustaine,
> To make the mothers hart, be pricked with the payne.

If the innocent reader might miss the eroticism of the opening eight lines praising Mary-the-Lily, the final view of her being 'pricked' should give reason to pause. The word renders the phallic already latent in line one's 'thorn' explicit; so that with hindsight, the garden of Mary whose 'entrance never knew / ... poison' is seen to have faced a sexual threat from the start. That threat is evident in another garden poem by Verstagan, 'Hortus

---

50 Verstegan repeatedly deploys the literary technique of approaching the Passion through Mary's particular, feminine relation to Christ: see, strikingly, the magnificent subsequence of poems 'The Fifteen Mysteries of the Rosary, of Our Blessed Lady' in Verstegan's *Odes*.

Conclusus', which (developing a long tradition from the *Song of Songs*) celebrates Mary as an enclosed garden where 'no serpent can get in, nor shall for evermore'.[51] In 'Lilium inter Spinas', therefore, the contrast of Mary's enclosed body 'pricked' by the crucifixion is startling but has many precedents. Celebrating Christ's death, the Catholic Mass of the fifteenth and sixteenth centuries often venerated Mary, 'the flower of paradise', in adapted songs of secular love.[52] Implying the Fall left nothing untouched, the idea that there is 'no rose without thorn' (*rosa sine spina*) dates from St Ambrose.[53]

In the poetry of Verstegan, then, Mary is paradoxically virginal, sensual and deflowered. Yet her defloration is a sign of the ultimate Christian tragedy, Christ's death, as well as of our redemption, though Verstegan does not dwell on that. What is absent from his treatments of the Virgin's sexuality is any real anger, bitterness or lasting material damage. In this, Verstegan is medieval: in pre-Reformation literature, Mary survived unfazed and amused the attacks of detractors, her virginity intact.[54] Even in 'Lilium Inter Spinas', where Mary's defloration expresses the Christian tragedy of Christ's crucifixion, the horror is offset by the neatness of the conceits. These link garden to thorn, thorn to Christ's death, Christ's death to Mary's defloration, and that to the garden-setting once more. Even as its congruent arrangement of disparate items and ideas (gardens, Christ's Passion, Mary's defloration) teases rather than mourns, the poem is organised with an extreme artful congruence. This proclaims its author not struck down by tragedy, but in full control of his faculties.

Serious treatments of violating Mary, whose inviolate status the early church enshrined, required in early modern authors events of equivalent, iconic destruction. The poem of unknown author, 'The Wracks of Walsingham', provides an example. Medieval Walsingham was one of Europe's two leading sites of Marian devotion: a cultural hub celebrated in 'The Wracks of Walsingham' through lamentation at its loss:

> Level, level with the ground
> The towers do lie,

---

51 On the *Song of Songs* tradition, see, notably, Stanley Stewart, *The Enclosed Garden: The Tradition and the Image in Seventeenth-Century Poetry* (Madison, Milwaukee and London: The University of Wisconsin Press, 1966).
52 See David Rothenberg, *The Flower of Paradise: Marian Devotion and Secular Song in Medieval and Renaissance Music* (Oxford and New York: Oxford University Press, 2011), p. 6.
53 See George Whitling, 'And Without Thorn the Rose', *The Review of English Studies*, 10/37 (February 1959), 60–2.
54 Emma Solberg, *Virgin Whore* (Ithaca and London: Cornell University Press, 2018), p. 155.

> Which with their golden glittering tops
> Pierced once to the sky.
> Where were gates no gates are now,
> The ways unknown
> Where the press of peers did pass
> While her flame far was blown.[55]

This laments the cultural loss of the shrine as a centre whose towers 'Pierced ... the sky', attracting from faraway lands a 'press of peers'. The alliteration conveys the vibrancy of grandees rubbing shoulders in a bustling, Marian municipality.

That is a reminder that, far from just points of religious preference or theological abstraction, what was at stake in the era's changing devotion was the fabric and habits of traditional ways of life.[56] Highlighting that life by contrasting it with a death repeatedly 'bitter', the destruction of the shrine entails 'seely sheep / Murdered' by Reformers and allowing Catholics. The result is a landscape of 'ways unknown': a wasteland contrasting starkly with the former bustle:

> Bitter was it, O, to view
> The sacred vine
> (While gardeners played all close)
> Rooted up by the swine.
> Bitter, bitter, O, to behold
> The grass to grow
> Where the walls of Walsingham
> So stately did show.

'Swine' at once evokes the iconoclastic Reformers who created the ruin and, evoking the landscape, the pigs left rooting in its grounds after the destruction.[57] With a contrasting metonymy, the gardeners playing 'all close' points not just to the unresisting Catholic leaders earlier criticised

---

55 Anonymous, 'The Ruins of Walsingham', in *The New Oxford Book of Sixteenth-Century Verse*, ed. by Emrys Jones (Oxford: Oxford University Press, 1991; repr. 2002), p. 550. I prefer the title 'The Wracks of Walsingham' because the poem as we have it today has no title. 'The Ruins' is an editorial interpolation, while 'In the wracks of Walsingham' is the poem's first line.

56 On this fabric and these habits, notably, see Eamon Duffy, *The Voices of Morebath: Reformation and Rebellion in an English Village* (New Haven, CT, and London: Yale University Press, 2001; repr. 2003).

57 Though Spenser's attitudes to reform and Catholicism are entirely different, the image of swine in a desecrated landscape recalls the end of Book 2 in *The Faerie Queene*. There too, indeed, one finds 'a less than subtle point about pigs with their noses in the trough'. See Gillian Hubbard, 'Stoics, Epicureans and the "sound sincerity of the gospel" in Book 2 of *The Faerie Queen*', *Studies in Philology* (2014), 225–54 (254).

as 'shepherds [who] did sleep' (12). Via the image of gardeners devoted to the upkeep, it also points to the great gardens of the Walsingham estate, as they formerly were.

Yet all of this is a kind of defloration. Contrasting the wild 'grass' of the ruin with the 'sacred vine' of the cultivated site, the passage juxtaposes ideas of flowering. Sixteenth-century Protestants, more and less moderate, feared the idolatrous potential in nature.[58] In the poem, contrastingly, the flowering of the wilderness follows from the deflowering of the sacred.

At the centre is Mary: the 'rose' of the rosary, traditional 'Lilium Inter Spinas' and the famed bloom of Walsingham. English Protestants often labelled the Virgin a whore, William Grey stating in 1563, for example, that our Lady of Walsingham abandoned her pedestal to fornicate with the Rood of Boxley 'very oft'.[59] Yet as the *raison d'être* of the pilgrimage site, in the poem Mary stands in metonymic relation to Walsingham's gardens, whose undefiled *floruit* express her inviolate self.[60] It is the destruction of the gardens, contrarily, which entails her defloration. The idea is all but explicit as the closing poem turns from mournful plaint to increasingly direct invective.[61]

> Weep, weep O Walsingham, Whose dayes are nightes,
> Blessing turned to blasphemies, Holy deedes to dispites
> Sinne is where our Ladye sate, Heaven turned to helle;
> Sathan sittes where our Lord did swaye, Walsingham oh, farewell.

As part of this pattern of ruin where 'Heaven [is] turned to helle' and Satan replaces 'our Lord', a personified Sin – normally a corrupt sexual woman – replaces the Virgin.[62] Though Sin and the Lady are allegorically different, the sitting Lady who is the Virgin gives way to sin with sexual suggestion. Focusing on 'where our Ladye sate' intensifies this, making the contest over Mary's 'seat'. The seat giving way, Mary, her seat in Walsingham, is violated.

---

58 Alexandra Walsham, *The Reformation of the Landscape: Religion, Identity and Memory in Early Modern Britain and Ireland* (Oxford: Oxford University Press, 2011), p. 93.
59 Solberg, p. 151.
60 For wider illustration of Mary as a garden in the period (indeed by Ben Jonson) see Barry Spurr, *See The Virgin Blest: The Virgin Mary in English Poetry* (Basingstoke: Palgrave Macmillan, 2007), pp. 94–7. For discussion of the ways Renaissance gardens entailed symbolic meanings more generally, see Amy Tigner, *Literature and the Renaissance Garden from Elizabeth I to Charles II* (Burlington, VT: Ashgate, 2012).
61 On this 'turn' see James and Waller, 'Walsingham, Landscape, Sexuality, and Cultural Memory', in *Walsingham in Literature and Culture from the Middle Ages to Modernity*, p. 9. For discussion of the poem's dating, see p. 8.
62 For Sin being allegorised as feminine in this way since early Christianity, see *Milton: Paradise Lost*, ed. by Alastair Fowler, 2nd edn (Harlowe: Longman, 2007), pp. 146–47.

The Mary of 'The Wracks' thus raises the historian's question of what the Reformation really was. Implying construction, building and form, 'Reformation' certainly does not reflect the historical testimony of 'The Wracks'. Deformation catches the mood better; indeed, an 'indelible scar' was left on the English landscape by the dissolution of the monasteries in the 1530s which was still the subject of comment, and open memorial, at the close of the sixteenth century.[63] Alexandra Walsham observes: 'The landscape of late sixteenth- and seventeenth-century Britain and Ireland was littered with mutilated remains of the pre-Reformation past – with the hollowed shells of ruined monasteries, battered pilgrimage shrines, crumbling chapels, decapitated crosses, and bare patches of ground which these monuments to Catholic piety had once occupied.'[64] The Reformation chronicled by 'The Wracks' catches the mood evoked by this picture of widespread destruction and deformation, while the poem's attendant imagery of Mary's defloration evokes the completeness of the English and Christian destruction.

The Marian imagery also evokes the Incarnation again. Justification for a material Church depends, theologically, on the Incarnation, where God is made flesh through Mary. Making metaphors of form and violability relevant, the long-standing link of Mary with the Church reflects the materialism in both.[65] The rape of churches found in many English texts of the era testifies to a widespread anxiety that the Reformation had violated the Church. Yet it also attests a more specific anxiety: that this violation was of Mary.[66] Significantly, this anxiety appears not just in Catholic but also in Protestant writings of the era, among Protestants of very different kinds.

Though polemicists painted statues of the Virgin as whoredom, Protestants also reconfigured the Virgin into a model for emulation, mainly, though not exclusively, for women.[67] They adapted The Sorrows of the Virgin into

---

63 See Stuart Mottram, *Ruin and Reformation in Spenser, Shakespeare and Marvell* (Oxford: Oxford University Press, 2019), p. 1.
64 Walsham (2011), p. 233.
65 On Mary, the Church, materialism and the Incarnation, see Sarah Ritchey, *Holy Matter: Changing Perceptions of the Material World in Late Medieval Christianity* (Ithaca and London: Cornell University Press, 2014), pp. 15 and 48–54; Michael Blastic, 'The Virgin Mary in the Writings of Francis and Clare of Assisi', in *Medieval Franciscan Approaches to the Virgin Mary: Mater Sanctissima, Misericordia, et Dolorosa*, ed. by Steven McMichael and Katherine Wrisley Shelby (Leiden and Boston: Brill, 2018), pp. 13–31 (pp. 20–22); Donna Ellington, 'Impassioned Mother or Passive Icon: The Virgin's Role in Late Medieval and Early Modern Passion Sermons', *Renaissance Quarterly*, 48/2 (Summer 1995), 227–61 (229). On the broader association of Mary with the Church, see Miri Rubin, *Mother of God: A History of the Virgin Mary* (London: Allen Lane, 2009), p. 168.
66 See Rubin, p. 168.
67 Solberg, pp. 150–4; Peters, p. 243.

appropriate metaphors for the godly, Protestant women finding in Mary the chaste wife for the godly minister or martyr.[68] Poetic versions of Mary in this mould include 'The Salutation and Sorrow of the Virgin Marie', in Aemilia Lanyer's *Salve Deus Rex Iudaeorum* (1611), where Mary receives 96 lines (12 stanzas); and also *Paradise Regained* (1671), where Mary speaks for 39 lines.[69]

Both these Marys show a suffering woman of the home in which, in Milton's words, 'Motherly cares and fears got head, and rais'd some troubl'd thoughts' (*Paradise Regained*, II, 64–5). Yet the thoughts are limited, bringing out motherhood largely generically; the intense, physical, transformative Mary seen in this chapter is gone. The tiny exceptions in the restriction are Lanyer's allusion to Mary not just as 'Servant, Mother, Wife', but also as 'Nurse / To Heavens bright King': a brief, moment of Mother Mary's subversive revival.[70] There is, too, the facility with which Milton's Mary expresses her sorrow. It gives just enough sense of an unusual mind, perhaps, to make one want more.

Yet if these small hints have significance, it is in their suggestion that the authors knew Mary could be both more and greater than their portraits allow.[71] Lanyer, notably, is considerably more subversive in her prose address 'To the Virtuous Reader' prefacing the poetry than she is in the poetry itself: 'It pleased our Lord and Saviour Jesus Christ, without the assistance of man … to be begotten of a woman, borne of a woman, nourished of a woman, obedient to a woman.'[72] In the poem, therefore, the Virgin's 'contradictory blending of subordination and empowerment' is disappointing.[73] In *Paradise Regained*, according to Mary Beth Rose, Milton presents the Virgin Mary's authority 'in its immensity and also its limits' – but the assessment seems generous: it is hard to agree that 39 lines of speech from Mary early in the poem make her 'a central figure', especially from a Protestant author who 'ardently denied the divinity of Mary, fearing her rivalry with

---

68 Peters, pp. 234 and 226.
69 Lanyer's 'Salutation' is in fact thirteen stanzas long, but the last stanza does not address Mary, so I discount it here.
70 Spurr emphasises the 'conservative cast' of Lanyer's Mary. See Spurr, pp. 83–4. Kuchar observes 'late medieval and Counter-Reformation' features of Lanyer's Mary restricted by Protestantism. See Gary Kuchar, 'Aemilia Lanyer and the Virgin's Swoon: Theology and Iconography in Salve Deus Rex Judaeorum', *English Literary Renaissance*, 37/1 (2007), 47–73 (67–8).
71 Milton's knowledge of Catholic ideas about Mary has been treated by Marjorie O'Rourke Boyle, in 'Home to Mother: Regaining Milton's Paradise', *Modern Philology*, 97/4 (2000), 499–527.
72 See Aemilia Lanyer, 'To The Virtuous Reader', in *Salve Deus Rex Judaeorum* (London: 1611), in *EEBO* (unnumbered page; accessed 25.8.2022).
73 Grindlay, 124.

Christ'.[74] In fact, Mary's appearance in *Paradise Regained* recalls 'On the Morning of Christ's Nativity', where Mary is initially acknowledged but then fades.[75] Limits, in this respect, seems more to the point for Milton than 'immensity'; male fear of female domination arises in Milton's divorce tracts and, even by seventeenth-century standards, *Paradise Lost* is repressive towards Eve.[76] Parodies of Marian hymns in the Eve of *Paradise Lost* imply hostility.[77] For Mary, the second Eve and leading Christian woman, the sense prevails that godliness in Milton came at an imaginative price for Mary.

The tradition of seeing Mary as the Church shows that contemporaries expressed the loss as a Marian violation. A considerable precedent is in Spenser. Making rape and abusing a church synonymous, his 'Kirkrapine' recalls the destruction of churches and holy places by Protestant iconoclasts.[78] The motif of rape as iconoclasm is widespread in English Renaissance literature.[79]

Later examples linking the Church with rape to express Reformations include the accomplished poem of 1649 'The Presbytery: A Satyr'. Writing from an entirely different religious viewpoint from the author of 'The Wracks', in the midst of Civil War the anonymous poet condemns the Presbyterian structure of Government instituted by Parliament in 1645. The main stanza ends:

> Religion, which a blind man well might call
> Immense, but one that's deafe, not finde at all,
> That which the world doth generally disguise,
> That stamp by which all knavery currant is;
> Art thou thy selfe, great Nymph? or else doe some
> Deflowre thee, nay force thee away from home,

---

74 See Mary Beth Rose, *Plotting Motherhood in Medieval, Early Modern and Modern Literature*, Early Modern Cultural Studies (London: Palgrave Macmillan, 2017), pp. 105–22 (pp. 105, 107 and 112).
75 Waller (2011), p. 194.
76 See Thomas Kranidas, 'Milton Rewrites The Doctrine and Discipline of Divorce', *Studies in English Literature*, 1500–1900, 53/1, The English Renaissance (Winter 2013), 117–35 (124); and Shannon Miller, 'Milton and the Seventeenth Century Debate over Women', *Milton Quarterly*, 42/1 (2008), 44–68.
77 Waller (2011), p. 195.
78 Waller (2011), p. 120.
79 On 'rape as iconoclasm', see Anna Swärdh, *Rape and Religion in English Renaissance Literature: A Topical Study of Four Texts by Shakespeare, Drayton and Middleton* (Uppsala: University of Uppsala Press, 2003), especially p. 223; and Stephanie Bahr, '"Ne spared they to strip her naked all": Reading Rape and Reformation in Spenser's Faerie Queene', *Studies in Philology*, 117/2 (2020), 285–312; and my following examples.

> And make thee doe their drudgery? O spleen,
> Couldst thou but rise as some lungs stretch'd ha been,
> Thou mightst boil out more hot, then ere one brother
> Could to pronounce damnation on another.[80]

The polemical targets of this poem are entirely different from those of 'The Wracks'. Yet here the Church is overtly feminine and her abuse (not by Reformers, as in 'The Wracks', but allegedly through a Presbyterian threat parallel with popery) again takes the form of a defloration or rape.

Still further on in the century, in 1679, the royalist debunking of the Popish Plot known only as 'A Ballad Upon the Popish Plot, written by a Lady of Quality', presents the same idea again:

> If our English Church (as he says) be a Whore
> We're sure 'twas Jack Presbyter did her deflower.[81]

Here the connection of the Church with whoredom recalls John Donne in 'Satire 3' and 'Show me dear Christ'.[82] Yet in 'A Ballad Upon the Popish Plot', as in both 'The Presbytery: A Satire' and 'The Wracks', we find not just the whoredom of the Church, but also its defloration. Implying definitions of 'Reform' are contingent on the speaker, moreover, here the Church receives satire from a ceremonialist rather than from a Civil War or Catholic standpoint. Yet despite the gulf between their ideals of religion, these poets of 1649 and 1679 share the key idea with the 'The Wracks': despoilers of a true Church are her rapists. In evoking the feminine Church as ideally inviolate, they each recall two things: St Paul's designation of a Virgin Church (2 Corinthians 11:2); and scriptural allusions to Mary not by name but as 'woman'. This presents Mary as the personification of the messianic people.[83]

Recalling this scriptural Mary, each poet presents the Church as a seventeenth-century Mary without name. Through the terms of rape and defloration, each one implies a loss of Christian community, the metaphor maximising the horror of the loss. As if she could not have birthed Christ, broken Mary poems, from 'The Wracks' to the later seventeenth century, condemn in strongest terms England's Church in pieces. In the trope of

---

80 See 'The Presbytery: A Satire' (London, 1649), in *EEBO* (accessed 1.8.2013).
81 See 'A Ballad upon the Popish Plot, written by a Lady of Quality' (London, 1679), in *EEBO* (accessed 1.8.2013).
82 See John Donne: *The Major Works*, ed by John Carey (Oxford and New York: Oxford University Press, 2000), pp. 29–31 and 288.
83 Spurr, p. 5. For scriptural details, see Cleo Kerns, *The Virgin Mary: Monotheism and Sacrifice* (Cambridge: Cambridge University Press, 2008), especially pp. 155, 158, 164–5. Mary was integrated further into ideas of church genealogy and womanhood in late medieval Christianity. See Ritchey, pp. 49–54.

Marian rape, this broken Church is beyond redemption, its Christianity irredeemable. The verdict on Marian reform is (quite literally) damning.

By contrast, the poems to Mary of Jonson and Verstegan are contented and humane. Linking the Virgin to 'the Queen lying in', Jonson highlights birth- and child-rearing processes also to be found in Verstegan's attention to Mary's womb, her birthing of Christ and lullabies. These are familiar to other women than queens. Since the Reformation undid the long-standing identification with the Virgin of pregnant women, these male poems revive a female culture of giving birth.[84] They did so despite the theological 'discipline' which the Prayer Book's 'Churching of Women' imposed on new mothers.[85]

In view of Henrietta Maria's Catholicism, Jonson's 1630 celebration of her, post-partum, stands out. Yet it is notable that much earlier in his career Jonson had also linked the Virgin with the recent experience of a mother giving birth. Written while still a recusant, his poem 'On My First Daughter' similarly joins young motherhood with Mary:

> Here lyes to each her parents' ruth
> *Mary*, the daughter of their youth:
> Yet, all heaven's gifts, being heaven's due,
> It makes the father lesse to rue.
> At six monthes end, she parted hence
> With safetie of her innocence;
> Whose soule heaven's Queene (whose name she bears)
> In comfort of her mothers teares
> And placed amongst the virgin-traine:
> Where, while that sever'd doth remaine,
> This grave partakes the fleshly birth.
> Which cover lightly, gentle earth.[86]

This epitaphic poem of around 1600 notes that the naming of the child is in honour of the Virgin Mary for the comfort of her mother. She now, with

---

84 On pregnant women identifying with the Virgin and the destruction of this medieval culture by Reformers, see Mary Fissell, *Vernacular Bodies: The Politics of Reproduction in Early Modern England* (Oxford: Oxford University Press, 2004; repr. 2006), pp. 14–89. See also David Cressy, *Birth, Marriage and Death: Ritual, Religion and the Life-Cycle in Tudor and Stuart England* (Oxford: Oxford University Press, 1997), p. 22. Among other evidence, this last notes in the Sarum Missal ('one of the most popular formularies of pre-reformation worship') masses said '"on behalf of women labouring with child" and supplication to St Mary, "the benign assistor of women in travail"'.

85 On the discipline, see David Cressy, 'Purification, Thanksgiving and the Churching of Women in Post-Reformation England', *Past & Present*, 141 (1993), 106–46 (107).

86 *The Complete Poetry of Ben Jonson*, 11–12. All further quotations of this poem are from this edition.

Jonson, sees her daughter in the 'virgin-traine' of the Queen of Heaven. The poem is more than 'a quiet, moving evocation of the Virgin's traditional roles'.[87] It avoids, too, the fanfare of 'An Epigram to the Queene, then lying in'.

Here, instead, Jonson's focus is the everyday: infant mortality, an unnamed mother, a father whose name is only implicit and a child of whom nothing is known but the Christian name. Given in 'comfort' of the mother, that Christian name, Mary, ties mother, child and the Virgin together, in a moving evocation of the Virgin in everyday life far from the corrosive images of whoredom and rape this chapter has explored in the Reformation's aftermath. The name, Mary, ties the family together through the Virgin's Catholic cult of motherhood, but also, underlyingly, through the importance of names as baptismal symbols.[88] For reasons baptismal, Christian and of the Reformation, names were far from neutral in early modern England.[89] In the everyday, as in 'Henrietta Maria', their significance emerges substantially in early modern drama, to which we now turn.

---

87 Waller (2011), p. 188.
88 On naming in baptism and its symbols, see Cressy (1997), p. 100. His observation that normally in post-Reformation England mothers did not attend baptisms since they were lying in (Cressy, pp. 149–50) suggests the baptismal background for Jonson's 'An Epigram to the Queene, then lying in' implicit in my link of that poem to 'On My First Daughter'.
89 Cressy (1997), pp. 97–194. Naming is also vital in early modern literature. See Alastair Fowler, *Literary Names: Personal Names in English Literature* (Oxford: Oxford University Press, 2012), pp. 51–116. Fowler is brief on saints' names, but correctly notes they were standard sources for 'given names' in the Middle Ages (Fowler [2012], p. 21). Remarking on the same page that 'much of life was then allegorical', he observes William Camden's sixteenth-century distaste for 'new names' and his understanding of their 'conceit'. I turn directly to this in Chapter 6.

6

What's in a name?: The Virgin Mary on stage

> If that any among us have named their children *Remedium Amoris, Imago Saeculi*, or with such like names, I know some will thinke it more then a vanitie, as they do but little better of the new names, *Free-gift, Reformation, Earth, Dust, Ashes, Delivery, More Fruite, Tribulation, The Lorde is neare, More trial, Discipline, Joy Againe, From Above*: which have lately beene given by some to their children with no evill meaning, but upon some singular and precise conceit.
> – William Camden, *Remains Concerning Britain* (1605)[1]

> MARIE, Heb: Exhalted. The Name of the blessed Virgine, who was blessed among women, because of the fruit of her womb.
> – Camden, 'Christian names of Women', *Remains* (1605)[2]

The importance of names, as early moderns knew, lies in their import; and the importance of baptismal names lies in their Christian meaning. This is as true of the names of real persons as it is of literary characters. In early modern England, they present allegorical names in a world that was often itself understood allegorically.[3] Illustrating the baptismal import, William Camden's Puritan names from *Remains Concerning Britain* are real-life examples of this understanding. Here, parents seal children with Christian meanings and the children present those meanings thereafter. Far from being neutral, names, as Camden observes, are a 'conceit' indicating a world view.

For the name of Mary, the conceit is important. Chapter 5 presented two poems by Ben Jonson – one to his daughter, the other to Queen Henrietta

---

1 Cited in Alastair Fowler, *Literary Names: Personal Names in English Literature* (Oxford: Oxford University Press, 2012), p. 21.
2 William Camden, *Remains Concerning Britain* (full title: *Remaines of a Greater Work, concerning Britaine, the inhabitants thereof, their languages, names, surnames, empresses, wise speeches, poesies, epitaphs*) (London, 1605), *in EEBO* (accessed 5.2.2020), p. 83.
3 Fowler (2012), p. 21. Puritan names were often of the Old Testament or theophoric. This last was common in the early Church. The son of St Augustine, for example, was Adeodatus: 'Given by God'.

Maria – which link a human Mary on earth with the Queen of Heaven. The early and later dates of these poems (*c.*1600 and 1630) show Marian names continuing as conceits for the Virgin Mary over the course of the first three decades of the seventeenth century. The Marian conceit was deeply exploited by Henrietta Maria, as we shall see further in this chapter. Yet it is worth noting just how widespread this was. Mary I (reigned, 1553–58) was frequently connected to the Virgin Mary through her name.[4] Henry Constable, whose 'Delivery of Conceit' was described as unparalleled in 1621, connected Mary Queen of Scots with the Virgin Mary in his *Spiritual Sonnets*.[5] Generally, Marian imagery empowered regnant queens.[6] Yet as Jonson's poem to his daughter shows, the name, Mary, could also denote the Virgin among commoners and playwrights.

Chapter 5 also showed the Virgin Mary's continuing presence in seventeenth-century poetry. That presence has been found in other seventeenth-century spheres. Anna of Denmark exploited resonance of the Virgin in Jacobean court masques and her anticipation of Henrietta Maria, in this respect, means the Virgin Mary was subversively displayed at court throughout the reigns of James I and Charles I.[7] The Virgin was also the subject of high-profile sermons that went into print. Long after the figure of the Queen of Heaven was wiped from the liturgy, these sermons, at once denouncing and memorialising, show that she continually pervaded Elizabethan and Jacobean England.[8] In court, in print and in the pulpit, therefore, 'overt and not [just] covert or fragmented representations of the Virgin' continued to provide meaningful contexts for literary interpretation in the seventeenth century, even before the flowering of Marian devotion in the 1630s.[9]

---

4 See Sarah Duncan, *Mary I: Gender, Power and Ceremony in the Reign of England's First Queen* (New York: Palgrave Macmillan, 2012), pp. 129–33; and William Wizeman, 'The Virgin Mary in the Reign of Mary Tudor', in *The Church and Mary*, Ecclesiastical History Society (Woodbridge and New York: Boydell Press, 2004), pp. 239–48.

5 See Maria Jesus Perez-Jauregui, 'A Queen in a "Purple Robe": Henry Constable's Poetic Tribute to Mary, Queen of Scots', *Studies in Philology*, 113/3 (2016), 577–94. Quotation from p. 577. For specific treatment of Constable's linkage of Mary Queen of Scots with the Virgin Mary, see pp. 579, 586, 587, 589.

6 Duncan, p. 129.

7 See Susan Dunn-Hensley, *Anna of Denmark and Henrietta Maria: Virgins, Witches and Catholic Queens*, Queenship and Power (London: Palgrave Macmillan, 2017), especially pp. 36, 86, 160.

8 See Lilla Grindlay, *Queen of Heaven: The Assumption and Coronation of the Virgin Mary in Early Modern English Writing*, Reformations: Medieval and Early Modern (Notre Dame, IN: University of Notre Dame, 2018), p. 43.

9 Grindlay, pp. 11 and 6.

This chapter therefore presents a range of Elizabethan and Jacobean plays in which the name of Mary evoked her cultural significance in Catholic terms. The plays are various in focus, suggesting the widespread deployment of images of Mary in drama of different forms. The plays are also of various dates, showing the continuity of dramatic interest in the Virgin across the seventeenth century. I begin with two 'Robin Hood plays', both by Anthony Munday and printed in 1601. Catholicism loomed large in Munday's life (1560–1633), but his religious conscience still puzzles.[10] Seemingly fostered, his 'Janus-faced authorial identity' may be irresolvable.[11]

Munday's inscrutable religious identity is significant for this chapter taking in outwardly Protestant as well as Catholic dramatists depicting Mary. Munday is typical of an early modern English nation normally concealing from authority its deepest religious beliefs.[12] Yet Munday's Robin Hood plays show an evolving author: from anti-Catholic propagandist to critic of Elizabeth I's religious policy.[13]

Robin Hood Marys: Anthony Munday

Robin Hood's devotion to the Virgin is as old as his ballads.[14] Performed on holy days and financed by parish guilds, fifteenth- and early sixteenth-century Robin Hood plays emphasised the devotion.[15] The introduction to the three

10 Elizabeth Evendon-Kenyon, 'Anthony Munday: Eloquent Equivocator or Contemptible Turncoat?', in *Reformation Reputations: The Power of the Individual in English Reformation History*, ed. by David Crankshaw and George Cross (London: Palgrave Macmillan, 2021), pp. 363–92 (p. 363).

11 Evendon-Kenyon, 373, 383. See also Andrew Hadfield, *Lying in Early Modern English Culture: From the Oath of Supremacy to the Oath of Allegiance* (Oxford: Oxford University Press, 2017), p. 8.

12 See Hadfield (2017), pp. 5–14.

13 See Kristin Bezio, '"Munday I sweare shal bee a holliday": The Politics of Anthony Munday, from Anti-Catholic Spy to Civic Pageanteer (1579–1630)', *Études Anglaises*, 71/4 (2018), 473–90.

14 'There is no need to speculate about Robin's devotion to St Mary, to whom an appeal and dedication is made in every early ballad.' See A. J. Pollard, *Imagining Robin Hood: The Late Medieval Stories in Historical Context* (London and New York: Routledge, 2004), p. 112. Besides observing modes and sites of devotion to Mary, Pollard's chapter on 'Religion and the Religious' (pp. 111–34) gives a full view of the Catholic culture of Robin Hood, including the considerable importance of monasteries and the religious. I observe this inherited culture of monasteries and religious in Munday's *The Death* below. Also, on Robin's devotion to the Virgin Mary, see Jim Bradbury, *Robin Hood* (Stroud: Amberley Publishing, 2010), pp. 24, 83, 116, 120, 127, 142–3, 155, 161–2, 209.

15 On the holy day, Robin Hood performances, see Paul Whitfield White, *Drama and Religion in English Provincial Society, 1485–1660* (Cambridge: Cambridge University Press, 2008), p. 57.

masses Robin attends each day in *A Geste of Robin Hood*, the most widely disseminated Robin Hood text in Tudor England, is illustrative:

> The one in the worship of the Fader,
> And another of the Holy Ghost,
> The thirde of Our dere Lady
> That in loved alther moste.[16]

The Virgin is Robin's special love, affecting his behaviour towards women and their friends:

> Robyn loved our dere lady
> For doubte of deadly sinne
> Would he never do company harme
> That any woman was in.[17]

Extending to women generally, Robin's devotion to Mary is focal in his beloved Maid Marian, herself a late sixteenth-century addition to Robin Hood tradition.[18] As her name suggests, Maid Marian is a Marian maid: a maid of the Virgin Mary loved by Robin. Yet in post-Reformation England, Robin's enemy, King John, was a litmus test for confessional difference. While Protestants championed him for resisting the Pope, Catholics condemned the King for oppression and cruelty.[19] In this respect, Shakespeare's *King John* (1595–96) is a play appealing to Catholic loyalists: 'about as far away from a heavily confessionalised, exclusively protestant vision of Englishness as it was possible to get, on the public stage'.[20]

16 Cited by White, p. 60.
17 *A Mery Geste of Robyn Hoode and of his Lyf, with a new play for to be played in Maye games very pleasaunt and full of pastyme* (London, 1560), in EEBO (accessed 30.1.2017).
18 On this historical addition, see Liz Oakley-Brown, 'Anthony Munday's Huntington Plays', in *Robin Hood: Medieval and Post-Medieval*, ed. by Helen Philips (Dublin: Four Courts Press, 2005), pp. 113–28 (p. 125).
19 See Donna Hamilton, *Anthony Munday and the Catholics, 1560–1633* (Aldershot and Burlington, VT: Ashgate, 2005), p. 132; and Bradbury, p. 107. Oakley-Brown observes the plays' relevance to Catholic–Protestant tensions 'to which Munday was personally subject' (p. 123), noting too that the plays 'manipulate historical characters' and 'play with notions of historicity' (p. 118). How entirely responses to King John were driven by sectarianism is in Peter Lake, *How Shakespeare Put Politics on the Stage: Power and Succession in the History Plays* (New Haven, CT, and London: Yale University Press, 2016), pp. 181–94. See also Igor Djordjevic, *King John (Mis) Remembered: The Dunmowe Chronicle, the Lord Admiral's Men, and the Formation of Cultural Memory* (Farnham: Ashgate, 2015), though his claim (argued largely from Drayton's 'Matilda') that the Matilda-John fable is 'completely devoid of any political dimension that could be construed as offensive to the royal prerogative in the Elizabethan context' (p. 56) ignores the Marian of this chapter and seriously underplays the religio-political more generally.
20 Lake (2016), p. 231.

Robin Hood is not in Shakespeare's play, but there is a tantalising trace of Marian in Lady Falconbridge. In the anonymous Robin Hood play *Look About You* (1600), we find the Lady Marian Fauconbridge and this Marian lady is linked to the Virgin. A frequent evoker of 'God's mother', 'God mary mother', 'my hollydam' (Holy Lady), or simply 'Mary', her husband, Lord Fauconbridge, moves easily from the Mass to his wife, to the Virgin. For example: 'By the morrow Masse / You are come as fitly as my heart could wish: / Prince Iohn this night will be a Reueller, / He hath inuited me and Marian. / Gods mary mother goe along with vs, / Its but hard by, close by, at our towne Tauerne.'[21] This shows the Marian association of 'Lady Falconbridge' on stage. While Shakespeare's Lady Falconbridge, the mother of the Bastard, is not the Virgin Mary, her reflection on the Bastard's birth, 'Heaven lay not my transgression to my charge' (1.1.256) is notably pious. Her son exonerates her explicitly:

> Ay, my mother,
> With all my heart I thank thee for my father.
> Who lives and dares but say thou didst not well
> When I was got, I'll send his soul to hell.
> Come, lady, I will show thee to my kin,
> And they shall say, when Richard [Coeur-de-lion] me begot,
> If thou hadst said him nay, it had been sin.
> Who says it was, he lies; I say 'twas not.
> (*King John*, 2.1.269–76)

The defence is questionable, especially in its last line. Yet since the Bastard is 'the play's patriotic hero (in so far as it has one)', his words carry weight, especially since the play constructs England in his image as a 'Bastard Nation'.[22] In this perspective, Lady Falconbridge is at the heart of all, even if her Marianism is only a trace. Though he notes one example, from Yorkshire in 1615, where 'playing Robin Hood' got two servants of the Catholic landowner Richard Cholmeley into trouble with the Archbishop of York's Visitation Court, Paul Whitfield White considers it 'unlikely' Robin Hood's Catholic identity survived in many English communities after the

---

21 See *A pleasant commodie, called Look about you. As it was lately played by the right honourable the Lord High Admirall his servaunts* (London, 1600), in *EEBO* (accessed 22.4.2020).
22 Michael Gadaleto, 'Shakespeare's Bastard Nation: Scepticism and the English Isle in *King John*', *Shakespeare Quarterly*, 96/1 (Spring 2018), 3–34 (31). Gadaleto's reading is similar to Lake's: 'the bastard plays a central role, indeed he emerges as something like the hero' (Lake [2016], p. 198). Like Lake, he also sees the England of *King John* as contrasting with Protestant propagandists (Gadaleto, 28).

What's in a name?: The Virgin Mary on stage   169

Reformation.[23] The Catholicism in Munday's Robin Hood plays, of 1598 and 1601, is therefore important.[24]

The Marianism in these plays is much more than a trace. In Munday's two Robin Hood plays, *The Downfall of Robert, Earle of Huntington* (hereafter *The Downfall*) and *The Death of Robert Earl of Huntington* (hereafter *The Death*) Robin's partner goes under two names, 'Maid Marian' and 'Matilda'. It is not just the first of these names that suggests Catholicism. As in the poem 'Matilda' by Michael Drayton (1563–1631), Matilda was a virgin maiden who found refuge from an oppressive and rapacious king in the Church.[25] There are echoes of Catholic perceptions of King John here. Moreover, Camden notes Matilda is cognate with Hilda, 'the name of a religious lady in the Primitive church of England', and he deciphers the name as 'Noble or honourable Ladie of Maides'.[26] Combining Maid Marian and Matilda, Munday combines two legends, Matilda's and Maid Marian's, in the figure of a holy woman linked with the Virgin against tyranny.

Naming highlights in the titles of both Munday's Robin Hood plays. In *The Downfall*, it is in Huntington being 'afterwards called Robin Hood', while in *The Death* he is 'Otherwise called Robin Hood'. Both titles focus on alternative names and extend the focus to Maid Marian. The full, printed title of *The Downfall* is: *The DOWNFALL OF ROBERT Earl of Huntington, AFTERWARD CALLED Robin Hood of Merrie Sherwode: with his love to chaste Matilda, the lord Fitzwater's daughter, afterward his fair Maid Marian*.[27] The importance of Maid Marian's name develops in the swithering treatment of it on stage.

That begins in a formal, scripted process of renaming which echoes the title:

> JOHN Next tis agreed (if thereto she agrees)
> That faire Matilda henceforth changes her name,
> And while it is the chance of Robin Hood

---

23 White, pp. 64–5.
24 White's brief reading of Munday's *The Downfall of Robert, Earl of Huntington, Afterward Called Robin Hood* is flawed by his view that Munday was a 'serious-minded Protestant' (White, p. 65). As we have seen, this is very far from the mark. White says nothing at all about Munday's other Robin Hood play, *The Death of Robert Earl of Huntingdon*.
25 See, similarly, Hamilton, p. 129.
26 See under 'MAUD for MATILD' in 'Christian names for Women', Camden, *Remaines*, p. 83.
27 Anthony Munday, *The DOWNFALL OF ROBERT Earl of Huntington, AFTERWARD CALLED Robin Hood of Merrie Sherwode: with his love to chaste Matilda, the lord Fitzwater's daughter, afterward his fair Maid Marian* (London: William Leake, 1601), in *EEBO* (accessed 21.4.2020). All citations from this play are from this edition.

> To live in Sherwodds a poor outlawes life
> She, by Maid Marian's name, be only cald.
> MATILDA: I am concluded; read on Little John,
> Henceforth let me be nam'd maid Marian.

As in the title, Matilda here becomes Maid Marian; but the play does not leave the matter there. Having shown the promised change of names, it worries at the discrepancy. A first, straightforward example is the rumination of her father, Fitzwater: 'Is my Matilda cald Maid Marian? I wonder why her name is chang'd thus.' Seeking and finding his lost daughter in Sherwood, but pretending to be blind, Fitzwater provides a second example:

> FITZ But heare me master, can you tell me newes
> Where faire Matilda is, Fitzwater's daughter.
> ROB Why? Here she is this Marian is shee.
> FITZ Why did she change her name?

Again, the focus is the name and the meaning of its change. Yet as Robin leads Fitzwater to recognise his daughter in Marian, the play stresses the identity of the names and persons of the woman, while also presenting their uncertainty. The question 'why did she change her name?' stands out. This is Robin's answer:

> Why? She is cald maid Marian, honest friend,
> Because she lives a spotless maiden life:
> And shall, till Robin's outlawe life have end,
> That he may lawfully take her to wife;

Robin's answer to the title's focus on names and its dramatic development together is that maid Marian is the name of virgin womanhood. That he presents this as self-evident makes sense only in the context of his devotion to the Virgin and the understanding that Maid Marian is an honourable, Marian maid.[28]

The full, printed title of Munday's second Robin Hood play is *The Death of Robert Earl of Huntington, Otherwise Called Robin Hood of merrie Sherwode: with the lamentable death of chaste Matilda, his faire maid Marian, poysoned at Dunmowe by King John*.[29] This too emphasises the

---

28 The spotless imagery here intensifies the link with the Virgin. See Jarosav Pelikan, *The Christian Tradition: A History of the Development of Doctrine, 4: Reformation of Church and Dogma, 1300–1700* (Chicago and London: University of Chicago Press, 1985), pp. 38–9.

29 Anthony Munday, THE DEATH OF ROBERT EARL OF HUNTINGTON, OTHERWISE CALLED *Robin Hood of merrie Sherwodd: with the lamentable Tragedie of Chaste Matilda, his faire maid* MARIAN, *poisoned at Dunmowe by King John* (London, 1601), in *EEBO* (accessed 20.4.2020). All citations from this play are from this edition.

alternative names and identities of its protagonists with the relation of Matilda to maid Marian. Yet there is a difference. The title refers to Matilda as the maid Marian belonging to Robin, making the synonymy of Matilda and Marian his. This is important because Robin dies roughly halfway through *The Death*, suggesting that Matilda's Marianism dies with him. Showing Marian formally take the name of Matilda at Robin's death, the dramatic action demonstrates this. Surviving him, in *The Death* the new-named Matilda replaces Robin as the central figure, making Robin and his Marian devotion of the past and Matilda the future.[30]

Yet giving Matilda the play's second half means showing what Marian becomes. On the face of it, this is a new woman, emerged from Robin and the Virgin's shadow to dominate the stage. The transition is marked. King Richard authorises the new designation of Matilda in a larger process of entitlement:

> Robin, wee see what we are sad to see,
> Death like a champion treading downe thy life:
> Yet in thy end somwhat to comfort thee,
> Wee freely giue to thy betrothed wife,
> Beautious and chast *Matilda*, all those lands,
> Falne by thy folly, to the Priors hands,
> And by his fault now forfetted to mee:
> Earle Huntington, she shall thy Countesse bee,
> And thy wight yeomen, they shall wend with mee,
> Against the faithlesse enemies of Christ.

Complementing the new name of Matilda is the title Countess of Huntington and a new, landed wealth. Removing the merry men (to the Crusades) further removes Matilda from her past and the transition builds on one started by Robin. Seeking peace between Marian, Queen Eleanor and Prince John, with his last words Robin seeks to secure Matilda's identity.

Yet the new identity contains elements of the old. Richard designates her 'chast Matilda' and the new role as Countess he accords is as Robin's widow: 'thy Countesse'. Persuading Eleanor and John to be peaceful, Robin emphasises his 'maiden wife / Chaste Maid Matilda'. In response, the Queen swears 'I will a mother be / To fair Matilda's life and chastitie', guaranteeing

---

30 This replacement is explicit. Following Robin's funeral, the Friar states: 'Robin is deade, that grac'd his entrance: / And being dead he craves his audience, / With this short play they would have patience'; to which Chester replies: 'Nay fryer, at request of thy kind friend, / Let not thy play so soon be at an end / Though Robin Hood be dead, his yeomen gone, / And that thou thinkest there not remains not one / To act another scene or two or three: / Yet knowe full well, to please this company, / We mean to end Matildaes Tragedy.'

the Marian facets without the name. John echoes the guarantee of chastity equivocally:

> When Iohn solicites chast Matildaes eares,
> With lawlesse sutes, as he hath often done:
> Or offers to the altars of her eyes,
> Lasciuious Poems, stuft with vanities,
> He craues to see but short and sower daies,
> His death be like to Robins he desires,
> His periur'd body proue a poysoned prey,
> For cowled Monkes, and barefoote begging Friers.

Drawing her between chastity and his 'lawless suits', John's equivocal avowal frames Matilda's future. At the play's end, therefore, it is her triumph to receive in epitaph a further name: 'Matilda martyred, for her chastite'. Between-times, she is called 'blessed maid', a term for the Virgin used by Protestants. The 1601 text frequently refers to her as 'Ma': equally and ambivalently interpretable as Matilda, Marian or Mary.

Contrasting remembrances of Robin and Matilda in death show how far and how little she travels from being Marian. Robin's death is heavy with Catholic imagery. This is heard in Robin's request to be buried:

> First I bequeath my soule to all soules souer [savor],
> And will my bodie to be buried,
> At Wakefield, vnderneath the Abbey wall:
> And in this order make my funerall;
> When I am dead, stretch me vpon this Beere,
> My beades and Primer shall my pillowe bee:
> On this side lay my bowe, my good shafts here,
> Upon my brest the crosse, and vnderneath,
> My trustie sworde, thus fastned in the sheath.

The Catholic imagery is also in the Friar's eulogy over Robin's corpse. It takes the form of a dirge, in which Robin's men are invited to join:

> Weepe, weepe, ye wod-men waile,
>   Your hands with sorrow wring:
>   Your master Robin Hood lies deade,
>   Therefore sigh as you sing.
>   Here lies his Primer and his beades,
> His bent bowe and his arrowes keene,
> His good sworde and his holy crosse,
> Now cast on flowers fresh and greene:
>   And as they fall, shed teares and say,
> Wella, wella day, wella, wella day:
> Thus cast yee flowers and sing,
> And on to Wakefield take your way.

Amid the imagery of 'all souls', crosses and primers, Robin's tearful funeral procession evokes unreformed burial services in Elizabethan England.[31] Burial at Wakefield stresses this: Yorkshire (in which we find both Wakefield and Huntington) was notable for religious conservatism and recusancy.[32] The image of Robin resting on his beads, or rosary, and the repetition of this image by his men and the presiding friar, mark this funeral at Wakefield Abbey as Catholic.

It also fanfares the end of Robin's Catholic legend. Yet the religion survives the man, including in the form of the send-off. Entailing Hail Marys, Robin's twice-mentioned 'beads' do not disappear from the play any more than do monasteries. A theology of charity, characteristic in the medieval Robin Hood, also emerges.[33]

Allowed by Hubert, King John's representative, to escape to Dunmowe Abbey, Matilda, proposing to 'end my life a votary', gives thanks: 'Kind *Hubert*, many prayers for this good deede, / Shall on my beades be daily numbered'. In this development, the abbey, the nun, good deeds and the rosary stand out. Unlike at Robin's funeral, using the rosary here looks to a future of Marian prayer. It is a cloistered Marianism, rather than of Sherwood or Huntington; yet one which, while precipitated by King

---

31 Medieval society 'looked more tolerantly' on tears than did early modern England. See B. Capp, 'Jesus Wept but did the Englishman? Masculinity and Emotion in Early Modern England', *Past and Present*, 224 (2014), 75–108 (78). Ettenhuber notes that 'there are only two extant sermons on John 11:35 ['Jesus wept']' from early modern preachers. See Katrin Ettenhuber, 'Inordinate Grief: Complicated Grief in Donne and Augustine', in *Passions and Subjectivity in Early Modern Culture*, ed. by Freya Sierhus and Brian Cummings (Farnham and Burlington, VT: Ashgate, 2013), pp. 201–17 (p. 201). Recent work usefully addressing the religious meanings of tears on stage include Katherine Goodland, 'Female Mourning, Revenge and Hieronimo's Doomsday Play', in *The Spanish Tragedy: A Critical Reader*, Bloomsbury Arden Shakespeare, ed. by Thomas Rist (London: Bloomsbury, 2016), pp. 175–96; Laura Gallagher, '*Stabat Mater Dolorosa*: Imagining Mary's Grief at the Cross', in *Biblical Women in Early Modern Literary Culture*, ed. by Victoria Brownlee and Laura Gallagher (Manchester: Manchester University Press, 2015), pp. 180–96.

32 Emma Watson, 'Clergy, Laity and Ecclesiastical Discipline in Elizabethan Yorkshire Parishes', in *Getting Along? Religious Identities and Confessional Relations in Early Modern England – Essays in Honour of Professor W. J. Scheils*, ed. by Nadine Lewycky and Adam Morton (London and New York: Routledge, 2016), pp. 97–114 (p. 99); Victoria Spence, 'Craven and the Elizabethan Settlement: Diverging Confessional Identities, 1580–1603', *Northern History*, 54/1 (2017), 28–58 (29–31); Elizabeth Ferguson, 'Veneration, Translation and Reform: The Lives of Saints and the English Catholic Community, c.1600–1642', *British Catholic History*, 32/1 (2014), 37–65 (42–3).

33 On Robin's medieval charity see A. J. Pollard, p. 114 and White p. 63. I considered this theology of 'good deeds' and its post-medieval continuity earlier in relation to 'works'; see Chapters 1 and 2.

John, is chosen. Moving from popular and public locations to religious seclusion, 'Ma' wrests her Marian identity from Robin, 'Matilda' and merry men.[34]

The final commemoration of Matilda is accordingly Catholic, though combining the convent's exclusion with a renewed, public vision. Bar the brief, four-line epilogue, its last speech eulogises 'this maid':

> Let vs goe on to *Dunmow* with this maid:
> Among the hallowed Nunnes let her be laide:
> Unto her tombe, a monthly pilgrimage
> Doth king *Iohn* vowe in penance for this wrong.
> Goe forward maids: on with Matildaes herse,
> And on her Toombe see you ingraue this verse;
>> Within this Marble monument, doth lye
>> *Matilda* martyrde, for her chastitie.

In this last dramatic view, Dunmowe becomes a shrine maintained by nuns as a place of pilgrimage and veneration of the saint. Taken to the convent and revised for public benefit, the Marian always implicit in Drayton's Matilda gains a new, monarch-chastising purpose. That was lessened by neither the dissolution of the monasteries nor the passing of time. At Dunmowe Abbey, the dissolution brought the Virgin into focus. Becoming the Priory Church of Saint Mary the Virgin, Little Dunmowe, the one building to survive the dissolution was the Lady Chapel of the Priory Church.[35] As a landmark, the Lady Chapel stood out for the Virgin, as contemporaries knew. In the words of Sir William Dugdale (1605–86), 'The Church here was built in Honour of the blessed Virgin Mary.'[36] Burying Matilda and commemorating her sanctity at Dunmowe, *The Death* enshrined her in the church of the Virgin.

Munday's Robin Hood plays emphasise and explore Marian identity as the sixteenth century turned into the seventeenth. In so doing, they bring a medieval and Catholic England into the Protestant England of Elizabeth I. The plays did so against a backdrop in which Catholic ideas of Mary

---

34 The Counter-Reformation brought greater emphasis on Marian purity. See William Wizeman, 'The Virgin Mary in the Reign of Mary Tudor', in *The Church and Mary*, ed. by R. N. Swanson, Studies in Church History (Woodbridge: Boydell Press, 2004), pp. 239–48 (pp. 247–8); and Ulriche Strasse, *State of Virginity: Gender, Religion and Politics in an Early Modern Catholic State* (Ann Arbor: University of Michigan Press, 2004).

35 Djordjevic, p. 47, note 16. The page also shows the church as it stands today.

36 Sir William Dugdale, *Monasticon Anglicanum, or, The history of ancient abbies, and other monasteries, hospitals, cathedral and collegiate churches, in England and Wales* (London: 1693), in *EEBO* (accessed 5.2.2020), p. 136. Dugdale here highlights several customs and historical details of the Abbey.

were at once rejected and remembered and the plays seem, therefore, polemical. Yet their play on Marian identity, the donning and removing of Mary's name, is important too, suggesting Munday's wider style of religious elusiveness.[37] That style, as we have seen, suggests an era in which deepest religious beliefs were often hidden: an era in which religion required disguise and performance.[38] There is vulnerability in Munday's Catholic Marys, therefore, even as there is theatricality. The theatricality emerges with a twist in our next play, *The Roaring Girl*.

The Roaring Girl (1611)

The Roaring Girl by Thomas Dekker and Thomas Middleton was performed about a decade after Munday's Robin Hood plays and can broadly be classed as a city comedy. Set in London, the plot stems from Sebastian, the son of Sir Alexander Wengrave. Forbidden by his father to marry as he wants, Sebastian pretends to love London's notorious cross-dressing woman, Moll, thinking his father will prefer anything to the match and so come round to Sebastian's original love choice: Mary Fitzallard. More immediately, the ruse draws Sir Alexander's ire on Moll. He employs Trapdoor to 'weave fine nets / To ensnare her very life' (1.2.231–2).[39] The snaring is to be sexual: 'Deep spendings / May draw her that's most chaste to a man's bosom' (1.2.220–1).

This focus on sexual traps and integrity established, Moll faces and evades varied attempts on her chastity. In conclusion, Sir Alexander confesses Moll's honesty, as well as his and the wider world's misapprehension of her integrity. Yet aspects of Robin Hood remain in the play. When in *The Roaring Girl* Mrs Openwork and Mrs Gallipot speak of Goshawk, their subject is archery and Bunhill: the legendary site of an archery contest featuring Robin Hood.[40] The incident has resonance for *The Roaring Girl*, with its cross-dressing heroine, for despite puritan disapproval, cross-dressing as 'May Marions' was a feature of early modern Maytime games.[41] The resonance of Robin Hood has also been found in revivals of the play. In the RSC production

---

37 On Munday's style in these terms, see Hadfield (2017), pp. 10–13.
38 See Hadfield (2017), p. 30.
39 See *The Roaring Girl: Thomas Middleton and Thomas Dekker*, A Norton Critical Edition, ed. by Jennifer Panek (New York and London: Norton, 2011). All quotations from the play are from this edition.
40 See *The Roaring Girl*, ed. by Kelly Stage, Broadview Anthology of English Literature (Peterborough: Broadview Press, 2019), p. 111, note 5.
41 David Cressy, 'Gender Trouble and Cross-Dressing in Early Modern England', *Journal of British Studies*, 35/4 (October 1996), 438–65 (459 and 461).

of 1983, Moll was 'a feminist Robin Hood preaching equality of the sexes and an end to poverty and corruption'.[42]

Robin Hood seems, then, one reason for the Marianism of the play this chapter argues for; concern with female chastity is another reason. Yet there are further reasons, which go beyond the continuing pertinence of Mary we have observed in the culture. *The Roaring Girl* is the climax of a set of dramatic collaborations between Thomas Middleton and Thomas Dekker that began with *Caesar's Fall* in 1602.[43] Critics of both dramatists have found a complex, even contradictory, religion. Dekker's post-Gunpowder Plot play *The Whore of Babylon* (1607) is widely (though not universally) considered anti-Catholic and Middleton, famously declared a Puritan by Margot Heinemann, has recently been presented in the alternative guise of a Calvinist by Gary Taylor.[44] Nevertheless, there are problems with these categories. Dekker's *The Virgin Martyr* (1620), which he co-authored with Philip Massinger, is faithful to 'many of the elements of the medieval legend of St Dorothy, including her inviolable virginity'; this is 'striking given the strong cultural mandates against vowed celibacy in Protestant England'.[45]

---

42 See Chi-Fang Sophia Li, '*The Roaring Girl* in Retrospect: The RSC Production of 1983', *New Theatre Quarterly*, 30/3 (2014), 274–97 (275).

43 Michelle O'Callaghan, *Thomas Middleton: Renaissance Dramatist* (Edinburgh: Edinburgh University Press, 2009), pp. 44–45.

44 Jeri Smith-Cronin follows the 'most sustained critical account of *The Whore of Babylon*' of Julia Gasper, reading the play as Dekker's 'definitive militant Protestant play'; see Jeri Smith-Cronin, 'The Apocaplyptic Chivalry of Thomas Dekker's The Whore of Babylon and Anglo-Spanish Diplomacy', *The Journal of Medieval and Early Modern Studies*, 50/3 (September, 2020), 633–57 (636); for the alternative view, see Regina Buccola, 'Virgin Fairies and Imperial Whores: The Unstable Ground of Religious Iconography in Thomas Dekker's *The Whore of Babylon*', in *Marian Moments in Early Modern British Drama*, ed by Regina Buccola and Lisa Hopkins (London and New York: Routledge, 2016), 141–60. For Margot Heinemann's work, see *Puritanism and Theatre: Thomas Middleton and Opposition Drama under the Early Stuarts* (Cambridge: Cambridge University Press, 1980). Taking issue with Heinemann, Taylor notes 'Calvinism was compatible with a life in the theatre; puritanism was not'. Taylor rightly notes the Reformed parish in which Middleton was brought up, but his claim that 'Calvinism is evident through his [dramatic] career' does not imply the religion is present exclusively in Middleton's drama, or that it might not have been moderated by collaboration or context. The precise commitment of Middleton to Calvinism therefore remains in question. See Gary Taylor, 'Thomas Middleton', in *Oxford Dictionary of National Biography* (April 2021; accessed online on 7.6.2022).

45 See Jane Hwang Degenhardt, 'Catholic Martyrdom in Dekker and Massinger's *The Virgin Martyr* and the Early Modern Threat of "Turning Turk"', *English Literary History*, 73 (2006), 83–107 (87); Jane Hwang Degenhardt, *Islamic Conversion and Christian Resistance on the Early Modern Stage* (Edinburgh: Edinburgh University Press, 2010), p. 79.

At the least, in Thomas Moretti's phrase, *The Virgin Martyr* 'broadens the centre' between the era's religious extremes.[46] Middleton, who is 'obsessed with virginity', also defies simple categorisation.[47] Of Middleton's *A Game of Chess* (1624), Stephen Wittek writes: '*Game* makes Catholicism look extremely appealing, not just for "credulous" Catholics but for the Protestants in the audience as well.'[48]

Behind this claim is Jacobean politics, which we have already observed subversively promoting the Virgin in the masques of Anna of Denmark. Together with a degree of tolerance for Catholics by James I, the so-called 'Spanish Match' pursued by the King from 1617 to 1624 sharpened concerns about Catholic Spain's influence on England dating back to the Spanish Armada and the reign of Mary Tudor.[49] Yet the Jacobean era was characterised 'nearly as much' by Hispanophilic admiration as by Hispanophobic resentment, while 'in no sphere of Jacobean life was Hispanophilia more prevalent than in English theatrical culture'.[50] Entailing the consciousness of Catholicism, English Hispanophilia was, too, a means of promoting the religion.[51] In the intertwined Hispanophobia and Hispanophilia of the era, and especially in the Hispanophilic playhouse, we should not be surprised to find Catholic meanings emerging from Jacobean plays by Dekker, Middleton or others. In the reign of James I, we must distinguish the divisive ways of the court and church from the more inclusive, less sectarian way of the theatre.[52]

Yet *The Roaring Girl* is distinctly Catholic. Evidently, cross-dressing was condemned by Puritans, but a scenario where it was 'permissible to cross-dress

---

46 See Thomas Moretti, 'Via Media Theatricality and Religious Fantasy in Thomas Dekker and Philip Massinger's The Virgin Martyr', *Renaissance Drama*, 42/2 (2014), 243–70 (253). Catholic and Protestant sources for the play are possible. See Julia Gasper, 'The Sources of the Virgin Martyr', *The Review of English Studies*, 42/165 (1991), 17–31. Moretti reads the play as both echoing and deviating (in a Catholic direction) from Foxe's Protestant account (Moretti, 258–64).

47 Kim Jaecheol, 'The Price of Virginity in the Early Modern Theatre: Middleton and Rowley's *The Changeling*', *Women's Studies: An Interdisciplinary Journal*, 50/7 (2021), 709–26 (709).

48 Stephen Wittek, 'Middleton's *A Game of Chess* and the Making of A Theatrical Public', *Studies in English Literature, 1500–1900*, 55/2 (2015), 423–46 (434).

49 Wittek, 427.

50 Eric Griffin, 'Dramatizing the Black Legend in Post-Armada England', in *Espana ante Las Criticos: Las Claves de la Leyenda Negra*, ed. by Yolanda Rodríguez Pérez, Antonio Sánchez Jiménez and Harm den Boer (Madrid: Iberoamericana; Frankfurt: Vervuert, 2015), 209–27 (224).

51 See Miriam Castillo, 'Catholic Translation and Protestant Translation: The Reception of Luis de Granada's Devotional Prose in Early Modern England' *Translation and Literature*, 26/2 (2017), 145–61, especially 147–8.

52 Moretti, 250. Witteck similarly makes this distinction. See especially his discussion of 'Theatre as Event' (Wittek, 435).

on the green, but offensive if the celebrants came unchanged to church' means cross-dressing was contrary to the 'order and discipline' of the Church of England.[53] The distinctiveness of this religion is clear, for early and medieval Christianity abounds with virgin, transvestite saints.[54] St Margarita-Pelagius, for example, avoided marriage, dressed as a male and was sometimes presented in medieval art as bearded. 'Legends, carvings, paintings and prints depicting this venerated virgin were created and circulated throughout Europe from about 1400 on.'[55] In *The Roaring Girl*'s masculine, cross-dressing woman, Moll, Dekker thus seems involved in a similar, medieval world of virgin sanctity as he would later present in *The Virgin Martyr*. Collaborating with him, Middleton (1580–1627) also engaged in that world, especially in Moll's heroic figure. His positive view of things Catholic in 1626 (as noted by Wittek) thus dates from as early as 1611.

Contemporaries recognised the Catholicism in London's notoriously cross-dressing Mary Frith: the source for 'Moll' by critical consensus. Frith was compared with Pope Joan and her haunts were 'alike both sacred and profane, nunneries and monasteries as well as the common places of prostitution'.[56] Slurs of the kind have history. Pope Joan was conventionally linked to the Whore of Babylon in Protestant polemic.[57] Links of the Virgin Mary with Mary Magdalene, and so purity and the 'penitent whore', provided for medieval women's needs.[58] Yet according to the *Oxford English Dictionary*, the first use of the name 'Moll' to mean prostitute is in Middleton's *The Ant and the Nightingale* (1604).[59] That means Middleton was pivotal in pejoratively transforming Moll's innocent name. Seemingly, he regretted it. In Middleton's *A Chaste Maid in Cheapside* (1613), 'Moll' is 'the chaste maid with a wrong address'.[60] In *The Roaring Girl* (1611), Moll is equally chaste; yet her chastity receives a careful investigation.

As I now show, *The Roaring Girl* doubts, tests and eventually proves Moll's integrity, especially her chastity and forthrightly claimed virginity.

---

53 Cressy (1996), 463.
54 Ilse Friesen, 'Virgo Fortis: Images of the Crucified Virgin Saint in Medieval Art', in *Virginity Revisited: Configurations of the Unpossessed Body*, ed. by Judith Fletcher and Bonnie MacLachlan (Toronto: University of Toronto Press, 2007), pp. 116–27 (p. 117).
55 Friesen, p. 117.
56 See 'The Life and Death of Mrs Mary Frith', in Panek (ed.), pp. 163–6.
57 Craig Rustici, *The Afterlife of Pope Joan: Deploying the Popess Legend in Early Modern England* (Ann Arbor: University of Michigan Press, 2006), p. 69.
58 Charles Freeman, *Holy Bones, Holy Dust: How Relics Shaped the History of Medieval Europe* (New Haven, CT, and London: Yale University Press, 2011), p. 185.
59 See 'Moll' (noun), definition 1, in the *OED* (online; accessed 21.4.2023).
60 Swapan Chakravorty, *Society and Politics in the Plays of Thomas Middleton* (Oxford and New York: Oxford University Press, 1996; repr. 2002), p. 96.

The play thus dispels allegations of 'common' sexuality while clearing the Marian name: 'Moll' is a synonym for Mary. Yet Moll is also said to be a common kind of woman found in London, both when the Prologue says, 'of that tribe [of Molls] are many' (Prologue, 16) and Sebastian refers to 'all Molls' (II.ii.182). In 1611, the lines affirm a widespread Marianism in London at once connected with Catholicism and whorish slurs, especially regarding the places of the play. Published at the 'Pope's head palace, near the Royal Exchange', the title page of *The Roaring Girl* highlights locales in London that were known for 'Catholikes of the English'.[61]

Yet by 1611, Catholic Marianism in London had gone much further. In 1609, the English Ladies of Mary Ward (1585–1645) set up residence in the Strand.[62] Known as the Scola Beata Mariae (today, the Institute of the Blessed Virgin Mary), the lives and reputations of these Ladies devoted to the Virgin are an overlooked dimension of 'Moll', even as they speak to the observed, Catholic dimensions of Mary Frith. A cadre of virgins and girls, the English Ladies moved between female and male spheres, without fixed home, ethos or identity.[63] Importantly, in 1611 *The Roaring Girl* was not a self-evident referent: the *Oxford English Dictionary* notes the phrase only came into use with the play, so its connotations were broad. Yet the ascribed meaning is 'a noisy, bawdy, or riotous woman or girl', especially 'one who takes on a masculine role'.[64] The earliest biography of Ward (1650) called her a 'holy Amazon'.[65] Condemned for partaking in 'the fight for the breeches', Ward's English Ladies usurped male roles and were said to change 'ground and habit at will'.[66] The Ladies moved easily

---

61 See Thomas Scott, *The Second Part of Vox Populi* (London: 1624), p. 19 in *EEBO* (accessed 30.6.2019). Though this is dated thirteen years later than *The Roaring Girl*, the Royal Exchange had long been associated with popery. See Helen Pierce, 'Unseemly Pictures: Political Graphic Satire in England, c.1600–c.1650' (PhD thesis, University of York, 2004), especially its chapter on 'Graphic Satire and the Threat of Popery' (pp. 63–90).
62 Lowell Gallagher, 'Mary Ward's "Jesuitresses" and the Construction of a Typological Community', in *Maids and Mistresses: Cousins and Queens: Women's Alliances in Early Modern England*, ed. by Susan Frye and Karen Robertson (New York and Oxford: Oxford University Press, 1999), pp. 199–220 (p. 202).
63 Lowell Gallagher, pp. 200 and 207.
64 See 'roaring girl' (noun) in the *OED* under 'roaring' (adjective and adverb). The novelty of the phrase in 1611 is underlined by the *OED*'s suggestion that 'roaring boy' too dates from 1611.
65 Lowell Gallagher, p. 205.
66 Lisa McClain, 'On a Mission: Priests, Jesuits, "Jesuitresses," and Catholic Missionary Efforts in Tudor-Stuart England', *The Catholic Historical Review*, 101/3 (2015), 437-62 (446); Laurence Lux-Sterrit, 'An Analysis of the Controversy Caused by Mary Ward's Institute in the 1620s', *Recusant History*, 25/4 (2001), 636-47 (640-1); Lowell Gallagher, p. 203.

among the poor.[67] To detractors, they frequented inns and were 'esteemed curtisans and suspected for hoores'.[68] Used to the Catholic categories of priest and nun, Protestant authorities struggled to identify Ward's unenclosed Ladies.[69]

In *The Roaring Girl*, Catholic Marianism may centre on Mary Frith: 'Moll'. Yet swirling around these Marys are therefore Catholic and anti-Catholic meanings exploited by the play, especially in its focus on the name Mary. Mary Frith's conjunction of the religious and profane is heard in Laxton's instruction to take Moll to 'Marybone Park – a fit place for Moll to get in' (3.1.4). In a play precise on bawdy and locales, the name 'Marybone' combines the London church of St Mary le Bourne with Laxton's desire to eat (have sex with) Moll like a 'marrowbone' (2.1.181).[70] Moll, as Laxton explains, has the spirit 'of four great parishes' (2.1.177–8). Yet the claim that St Mary le Bourne is the 'fit place' for Moll marks her not just as attractive and religious, but also of St Mary.

A similar mixing of place, Catholicism and Moll's identity is a few lines on. Asked 'what house you're of' (3.1.164), Moll replies: 'One of the Temple, sir' (3.1.165). Her questioner assents: 'Mass, so methinks' – to which Moll replies: 'And yet sometimes I lie about Chick Lane' (3.1.166–7). The repartee joining house, Temple, the Mass and Chick Lane (one's dwelling, the Inns of Court, a church, its Catholic ritual, and the rough and bawdy 'Chick Lane') highlights Moll's evasively suggestive identity. As her place of origin, her 'house' is each of these things, the Mass included. The reason St Mary le Bourne is the 'fit place' for Moll is that her name is Mary; its religious house is her own. Linked to cross-dressing and virginity – of which more soon – Moll presents a female, Catholic sacredness that is Marian in name.

The play's wide concern with Moll's identity is in her contrast with its one other unmarried young woman: Mary Fitzallard. Giving Marianism a pronounced emphasis, this second Mary plays on the first in name and action. Refused marriage to Mary Fitzallard by Sir Alexander, Sebastian courts Moll to goad his father into changing his mind, guessing Sir Alexander will prefer anything for his son to marriage with Moll. The plot thus depends on distinctions between two forms of Mary, with even Sebastian at first thinking Moll a 'mad girl' whom only the 'blind' might love (2.2.198 and 192). Nevertheless, the synonymy between Mary and Moll is heard when Sebastian calls Mary Fitzallard 'sweet Moll' (1.1.170) and says, 'I court

---

67 McClain, 448–9.
68 McClain, 446.
69 McClain, 446–7.
70 For this reading, see Panek (ed.), p. 41, note 4.

another Moll' (1.1.171). Since Sebastian courts both, the synonymy of Mary and Moll is enhanced as the plot develops, especially as Sebastian comes to appreciate Moll's integrity.

The treatment of clothing, so important in Moll's cross-dressing persona (as in Mary Frith's and Mary Ward's) helps blur the distinctions between the Marys onstage. Though clearly different from Moll, Mary Fitzallard first appears disguised as a sempster (1.1. SD). Like Moll's, her persona is malleable through disguise. Their cross-dressing connection emerges fully when Mary and Moll appear on stage at once, Moll as a man and Mary 'as a page' (4.1.40. SD). Male sexuality could be inflamed by cross-dressing in the era and Sebastian responds accordingly: 'So methinks every kiss she gives me now / In this strange form is worth a pair of two' (4.1.57–8).[71] Yet 'a pair of two' describes the cross-dressing Marys onstage, extending the desirability of Mary Fitzallard to Moll. As in a mirror, where one reflects on the other, the two Marys ask not just what it means to be male or female, but also what it means to be Mary. It is a question with moral as well as religious facets; and it is here that the test (promoted by Sir Alexander) of Moll's integrity comes into focus.

Beyond the religion already observed, *The Roaring Girl* contains frequent, Catholic imprecations, for example: "Sdeath' (God's death), 'Zounds' (God's wounds) and 'Foot' (God's foot).[72] The first two acts alone sound the word 'Mass' four times and, pointedly, they sound 'Marry' four times.[73] 'By' Lady' (3.2.250: 'by Our Lady') is a variant. To court Moll, say both Sir Alexander and Sebastian, is to bow to her idol (1.1.118; 1.2.153); and when Sir Alexander asks Moll whether she teaches singing she replies, 'Marry, do I, sir (4.1.196), identifying her music with the Virgin.

This speaks to the Catholic, Marian contexts identified. Yet sounds, in Renaissance drama, are essential.[74] In *The Roaring Girl* (which promotes female sound) a religious soundscape of London extends beyond the chatter and singing observed to the ringing of church bells. 'Marry amen, say I' and 'So say I too' is one moment of prayer (4.1.126–7) in the din. 'Zounds, now hell roars' is another (4.2.172). In a play telling time by London's bells (2.1.374 SD–375), the text sounds, beside St Mary le Bourne, 'Saint Kathern's' (4.1.109), 'Saint Antholin's Bell' (2.1.288) and 'Bow Church': an abbreviation of St Mary le Bow, where Gallipot is to appear 'upon *Crastino*, do you see,

---

71 On male sexuality inflamed by female cross-dressing, see Cressy (1996), 459.
72 See for example, 1.1.229; 4.2.72; 4.2.180; 5.1.165 and 275. See also 'Ud's so' (4.2.182, 5.1.10) and 'Ud's light' (3.2.205): God's Soul and God's Light.
73 See Act 1, Scene 2, lines 5, 50 and 93; and Act 2, Scene 1, lines 28, 147, 231, 261 and 327.
74 Allison Deutermann, *Listening for Theatrical Form in Early Modern England* (Edinburgh: Edinburgh University Press, 2016), p. 2.

Crastino sancti Dunstani, this Easter term' (4.2.256–8).[75] That refers to 20 May, the day after St Dunstan's day, while evoking the legal authority of England's Church.[76] Yet among each church bespeaking saints, the bells also sound anxiety: 'The jingling of golden bells, and a good fool with a hobbyhorse, will draw all the whores in the town to dance in a morris' (1.2.222–4).

This from Trapdoor links the ringing city of saints with the moral concern for Moll, whose name itself is cross-dressed: it sounds (that is, signifies) Mary without sounding it out, being no more transparent than Moll's clothing.[77] The moral concern is widespread: notable, for example, in Sir Alexander's response to Moll singing. True to Protestant conjunctions of Catholicism and corrupt sex in the Whore of Babylon, Alexander associates this music linking her to the Virgin with 'prick-song', 'The Witch' and 'a company of whoremasters' (4.1.198, 203, 194).[78] That recalls once more the links of Mary Frith with nunneries, monasteries, prostitution and Pope Joan; and similar slurs on Mary Ward's Ladies. Yet *The Roaring Girl* pursues its moral anxiety through an extended dramatic trial of Moll eventually clearing her Marian name. In this, it is like the Consistory Court of the Bishop of London, which in 1612 remanded Mary Frith to Bridewell. Yet the play reverses the Bishop's judgement, championing Moll by upholding her virginity. It thus upholds for Moll the claim on which Mary Frith insisted. For while Frith 'voluntarily confessed' cross-dressing (notably at St Paul's), singing on stage, immodesty and what the ecclesiastical court called 'tearing God out of His kingdom', 'when pressed to declare whether she had not been dishonest with her body' Frith 'absolutely denied' it.[79]

The sign both of Marianism and her integrity, Moll's name is made central from the start of *The Roaring Girl*. The Prologue invites the audience to 'know what girl this roaring girl should be', adding: 'Would you hear her name? / She is called Mad Moll' (Prologue, 15, 29–30). Focus on, and uncertainty about, the name develops. 'There's a wench', says Sebastian, 'called Moll, Mad Moll, or Merry Moll – a creature / So strange in quality,

---

75 On Bow Church as St Mary le Bow, see Panek (ed.), p. 82, note 259.
76 Panek (ed.), p. 82, note 258.
77 On 'sound' (verb) meaning to signify, see the OED definition 4a.
78 On the corrupt sexuality and Catholicism, see Emma Solberg, *Virgin Whore* (Ithaca and London: Cornell University Press, 2018), pp. 148–66; Frances Dolan, *Whores of Babylon: Catholicism, Gender and Seventeenth-Century Print Culture* (Ithaca: Cornell University Press, 1999; repr. University of Notre Dame Press, 2005); Alison Shell, Catholicism, *Controversy and the English Literary Imagination* (Cambridge: Cambridge University Press, 1999), pp. 23–55.
79 See 'Mary Frith's Appearance at the Consistory Court January 27, 1612' in Panek (ed.), pp. 147–8.

a whole city takes / Note of her name and person (1.1.99–102). Since Merry and Mary are near homonyms, another play on the name of the Virgin intrudes.[80] Yet taking note of the name of Moll is now not just for the audience, but also for the city. The point returns with Sir Alexander: 'Didst never as thou walkst about this town, hear of a wench called Moll, Mad, Merry Moll?' (1.2.199–200); and we see it in the city still later:

> GOSHAWK Life, yonder's Moll.
> LAXTON Moll? Which Moll?
> GOSHAWK Honest Moll.
> LAXTON Prithee, let's call her – Moll.
> ALL Moll, Moll, psst, Moll!
> (*The Roaring Girl*, 2.1.165–9)

Amid the jangling of her name another homonym, of the bells and the *belle*, suggests itself. Yet the focus on Moll's name and its, here moral, meaning resounds. Unquestionably, this play intends names meaningfully. There are not just Goshawk, Laxton and Moll, but other names too: Wengrave (older and younger), Neatfoot, Sir Adam Appleton, Sir Davy Dapper, Sir Beauteous Ganymede, Sir Thomas Long, Greenwit, Tiltyard, Openwork (Mr and Mrs.), Hippocrates Gallipot, Ralph Trapdoor, Curtalax and Hanger.[81] Names, here, have meaning.

Importantly, therefore, Moll defies Sir Alexander, calling 'whore' 'a name which I'd tear out' (3.1.89). To do so, she affirms her virginity: 'I keep my legs together' (4.1.130) and 'never yet / Had angling rod cast towards me' (3.1.102–3). Moll is, therefore, a virgin Mary; yet it is necessary to clear her name because she is thought disreputable, because Sebastian uses her disrepute to marry Mary Fitzallard and because the focus on her bad name (meaning both her disrepute and 'Moll') is intense throughout the play. Expressing that disrepute, Sir Alexander calls Moll 'a thing / One knows not how to name' (1.2.129–30), telling Sebastian that marrying her will 'confound thy name' (2.2.145) and adding: 'Methinks her very name should fright thee from her' (2.2.152). To this, Sebastian replies leadingly: 'Why, is the name of Moll so fatal, sir?' (2.2.155). By reputation, the answer to this Marian question is evidently yes.

The play thus presents two views of Moll. One centres on her virgin Mary honesty, the other on her public reputation, reflecting the Virgin Mary's

---

80 On this homonym pointing to the Virgin in previous early modern drama, see Rist, '"Merry, Marry, Mary: Shakespearean Wordplay and *Twelfth Night*', *Shakespeare Survey*, 62 (2009), 81–91.
81 Consider, further, Sir Alexander's question to Trapdoor, 'How is thy name?' (I.ii.241) and, discovering it is 'Trapdoor', his following 'Trapdoor, be like thy name' (1.2.243). Wengrave Senior, similarly, states he is old and going to his grave (2.2.127–32).

wider divisiveness in the seventeenth century, as well as divisions over the likes of Mary Frith and Mary Ward.[82] As in a trial, the play must decide which view to uphold. Sebastian announces the need for proof in Act 3:

> And for her honesty, I have made such proofs on't,
> In several forms, so nearly watched her ways,
> I will maintain that strict against an army.
> (*The Roaring Girl*, 3.2.174–6)

This emphasis on proof echoes Moll's own claim regarding Jack Drapper's wench: 'the purity of your wench would I fain try' (2.1.309–10). According to Moll, ''tis impossible to know what woman is thoroughly honest, because she's ne'er thoroughly tried' (2.1.304–5). The play offers a thorough trial of Moll in response.

Thinking a demonstration of Moll's bad character will clear his son's mind, in Act 2 Sir Alexander renews his plot to 'pursue her [Moll] to shame' (2.2.189). Yet Moll is aware of the dangers of lost reputation, in turn challenging the sexual traps set for women. As she says to Laxton: 'How many of our sex by such as thou / Have their good thoughts paid with a blasted name / That never deserved loosely or did trip / In path of whoredom? … What durst move you, sir, to think me whorish?' (3.1.81–9). Laxton proves no match for Moll: neither sexually nor in sparring. In the lax town of London, so prove everyone else.

Highlighting the abuse to Moll, and women's, sexual reputation is one form of defence in *The Roaring Girl*, but other defences are also offered. Goshawk's appellation 'Honest Moll' (2.1.167) is a simple example. Yet arguing 'the name neither saves nor condemns' (2.2.173), her pretend lover Sebastian makes an eloquent case for 'Moll':

> Put case a wanton itch runs through one name
> More than another, is that name the worse
> Where honesty sits possessed in it?
> (*The Roaring Girl*, 2.2.164–6)

This distinguishes between the associations of a name and a person's integrity. Moll develops the distinction sincerely later, in a parallel challenge to honesty and 'shame' (5.1.302). Accused of being a thief, Moll Cutpurse, she responds: 'A name, methinks, damned and odious' (5.1.296). Acknowledging she has sat with thieves – including 'in full playhouses' (5.1.301) – Moll admits that she 'in that stream met an ill name' (5.1.303). Yet rather than for theft, she says, she was condemned only by association. Echoing Sebastian's

---

82 On that divisiveness, see especially Chapter 5, pp. 110–11.

distinction between reputation and integrity, Moll asks: 'must you have / A black ill name because ill things you know?' (5.1.324). In theft as in sexuality, the play repeatedly tests Moll's honesty. Yet it also allows her to defend herself, before eventually vindicating her claims.

Aside, in Act 2, Sir Alexander already admits, 'I wrong this girl!' (2.2.65). Yet the proof is in the pudding. In the end, Sir Alexander first forgives Mary Fitzallard because 'I see the brightness of thy worth appear' (5.2.200). Having been her most outspoken critic, he then outspokenly forgives and re-evaluates Moll, 'cast[ing] the world's eyes from me, / And look[ing] upon thee freely with mine own' (5.2.252–3). Climactic, in this transformation, is his public avowal: 'I'll nevermore / Condemn by common voice, for that's the whore' (5.2.255–6). Tried and found out by the play, fault ultimately lies in the common voice of popular opinion, not in the name of Moll, which is especially exonerated of sexual corruption. That is as Moll wished when she sought to 'tear out' (3.1.89) her name of 'whore', and the Catholic dimensions of the removal are clear. In the new, public moral order, Moll's cross-dressing, manly virgin Mary is forgiven demonstratively. Cross-dressing, medieval saints like Margarita-Pelagius and Catholic devotees of the Virgin like Mary Ward are absolved by extension.

The Roaring Girl thus draws on the transvestism of the female Catholic religious, both medieval and early modern, in a Marian representation of virginity. The play challenges the Marian persona, especially in her virginity, but it ultimately endorses the honesty of both. It does this through dramatised tests which demonstrate Moll's integrity to the satisfaction of her fiercest critic, Sir Alexander. Importantly, by making Moll vital in the Mary Fitzallard–Sebastian marriage plot, the play also eventually makes Moll integral in comedy: where 'the happiness of this day shall be remembered / At the return of every smiling spring' (5.2.271–2). Comic happiness, it transpires, depends on virgin Mary.

The Epilogue accepts audiences in 1611 might 'wonder that a creature of her [Moll's] being / Should be the subject of a poet' (Epilogue, 19–20), but it does so only before an appeal for applause which will 'beckon her [Moll] to you' (Epilogue 38). Extending Sir Alexander's endorsement of Moll to the audience, these very last lines turn dramatic applause into applause for Moll. If some withheld that applause (the only seventeenth-century record of performance for *The Roaring Girl* is from 1611), they did so against the grain of the play: five acts increasingly affirming virgin Mary. Though the promise to bring 'The Roaring Girl herself' to the stage 'some few days hence' (Prologue, 35) is taken to refer to Mary Frith, it also suggests Mary Ward. The reference point ('The Roaring Girl') is opaque. Just possibly (as in *The Winter's Tale*, which was also performed in 1611) it portends staging a truly Marian 'idol' (1.1.118; 1.2.153).[83] Otherwise Ward, not Frith, was the standout virgin.

Historically important are ramifications in 'a creature of her being' (Epilogue, 19). That highlights Moll is a type, much as the Prologue highlighted in London a plurality of 'roaring girls' (Prologue, 25), stating 'of that tribe are many' (Prologue, 16). A question arises: beyond Ward's English Ladies (or even Marian images) how truly representative of London women was Marian 'Moll'? As a genre, city comedy is representative of, and biased about, early modern London.[84] We may never discover, therefore, how 'many' Molls inhabited the city; yet the play is a snapshot from 1611 of how prominent they seemed. Emily Vine observes: 'the awareness that certain streets or areas of the city were inhabited by religious minorities … influenced the means by which urban space [in London] was experienced'.[85] Highlighting Moll, Mary Fitzallard, Mary Frith and even Mary Ward amid Moll's 'tribe', *The Roaring Girl* exhibited in 1611 a London Catholic in its Marianism.

What's in her name? The England of Henrietta Maria

Hard on the heels of the Spanish Match (1617–24), Charles I married Henrietta Maria of France in 1625. Instead of a prospective Catholic queen from Spain, England now had a real Catholic queen from France. We enter, therefore, a critical field in which Marian influence on drama is better understood. Critics from Erika Veevers to Rebecca Bailey and Susan Dunn-Hensley have stressed the projection of queenship and Catholicism in Henrietta Maria's Caroline masques, seeing it as partly a matter of the masques' Marian iconography. Yet the precise Marianism of these occasions needs emphasising. For Veevers, Marianism (and Catholicism) were expressions of fashionable *Préciosité* from France.[86] Saying less about Mary, Bailey extended Veevers's thesis to the Counter-Reformation and Roman Catholic

---

83 On the Marianism of *The Winter's Tale*'s statue, see Susan Dunn-Hensley, 'Return of the Sacred Virgin: Memory, Loss and Restoration in Shakespeare's Later Plays', in *Walsingham in Literature and Culture from the Middle Ages to Modernity*, ed. by Dominic Janes and Gary Waller (Farnham: Ashgate, 2010), pp. 185–97.

84 See Robert Hume, 'The Socio-Politics of London Comedy from Jonson to Steele', *Huntingdon Library Quarterly: Studies in English and American History and Literature*, 74/2 (2011), 177–217, especially 217.

85 Emily Vine, '"Those Enemies of Christ, if they are Suffered to Live Among Us": Locating Religious Minority Homes and Private Space in Early Modern London', *The London Journal: A Review of Metropolitan Society, Past and Present*, 43/3 (2018), 197–214 (211).

86 Erica Veevers, *Images of Love and Religion: Queen Henrietta and Court Entertainments* (Cambridge: Cambridge University Press, 1989), pp. 2–3.

hopes in Europe.[87] Dunn-Hensley more recently acknowledges both Marianism and Catholicism, yet her focus on 'the female sacred as a source of authority' in a 'patriarchal divine right monarchy' is both more recognisably feminist and more nebulously religious.[88] None of these perspectives are wrong, but each downplays important components. Veevers and Bailey's emphasis on the French salons and the continent as the source of Henrietta Maria's Catholicism misses the readiness of English drama for the kind of playing on Mary which the Caroline masques project. This is implicit in Dunn-Hensley's study, which presents the masques of Henrietta Maria as extensions of those of Anna of Denmark and the court of James I, but it is explicit in this chapter.[89] For as we have seen, English drama was a fertile field for Marian representation in the public theatre before the queen's arrival in England; and as we shall see further, the masques of Henrietta are embedded in a calendar of religious ritual with deep English roots. Dunn Hensley's emphasis on 'the female sacred' which 'evoked Marian imagery', meanwhile, seems back to front.[90] As I now show, Marianism is a main basis from which female, royal and Catholic power in the masques of Henrietta Maria emerges. As in the preceding English plays, the basis for this dramatised Marianism is the name of Mary, though in the case of Henrietta, that name was a reality, as much as an aspect of dramatic plot.

At the wedding of her daughter in 1625, Marie de Medici wrote to Henrietta Maria, emphasising she owed the Virgin 'une devotion particulière' (special devotion) because she was 'mère de son âme' (the mother of her soul).[91] One Mary conjuring the Virgin Mary to another Mary, a queen invoking the Queen of Heaven to a queen to be, the conceit of names stands out. A fuller view of the letter reveals in the conceit a basis for Henrietta's identity:

> Je ne finirais j'amais si je narrêtais les mouvements de mon coeur, tant je suis émue et remplie de diverses pensées; mais il faut achever, il faut que je vous laisse partir, que je donne lieu à mes pleurs et que je prie Dieux de vous inspirer pour moi ce que mes larmes effaceraient, si je pensais l'écrire. Ma fille, je vous laisse et vous livre à la guarde de Dieux et de son ange; je vous donne a Jésus-Christ, votre, Seigneur et Rédempteur; je supplie la Vierge, de laquelle

---

87 Rebecca Bailey, *Staging the Old Faith: Queen Henrietta Maria and the Theatre of Caroline England, 1625–1642* (Manchester: Manchester University Press, 2009), p. 149; for Bailey's debt to Veevers, see especially pp. 143–5.
88 Dunn-Hensley (2017), p. 143.
89 For more general observation of the continuity of masques 'across the seventeenth century', see Lauren Shohet, *Reading Masques: The English Masque and Public Culture in the Seventeenth Century* (Oxford: Oxford University Press, 2010), p. 43.
90 Dunn-Hensley (2017), p. 143.
91 Veevers, p. 94; Bell, p. 93.

vous portez le non, de daignez être mère de votre Ame et l'honneur de ce qu'elle est mère de votre Dieu et votre Sauveur. Adieu, encore une et plusieurs foi! vous êtes a Dieu, demeurez à Dieu pour jamais.[92]

[So moved and full of diverse thoughts am I that I shall never finish [this letter] unless I stop the movements of my heart; but I must stop, I must let you go, that I give place to my tears, and that I pray God to inspire in you, for me, what my tears will efface if I thought to write it. My daughter, I leave you and I leave you to the protection of God and his angel; I give you to Jesus Christ, your God and Saviour; I supplicate the Virgin, whose name you bear, to deign to be the honourable mother of your soul as she is mother of your God and your Saviour. Goodbye [literally: To God], once and many times more; you are God's, stay with God always.]

As 'mother of your soul', the Virgin here is both essential in Henrietta Maria and a substitute mother for Marie de Medici. Both are one in the Virgin. The sign is in Henrietta Maria's baptismal name ('laquelle vous portez le non'). Henceforth in Christian life, Henrietta Maria carries forward the Virgin in name.

Contemporaries recognised her Marian mission. Later playing on Mary in the names 'Mariadulus' and 'Mariamastix', the dedication to the anti-Puritan *Maria Triumphans* (1635) made Henrietta Maria's identity with the Virgin a matter of her name:

She, whome it chiefly concerns, will a new become your Patronesse: And thus will *Mary* intercede for *Mary*, the *Queen of Heaven* for a great *Queene* upon *earth*; the Mother of our *Celestial King*, for the mother of our future terrene *King*.[93]

On similar grounds of Marian identity, Henrietta Maria evoked Puritan condemnation. Condemning praise of the queen in *The Female Glory* (1635), Henry Burton warned: 'The author glorieth that he is the first who hath written (as he saith) in our vulgar tongue, on this our Blessed Virgin. And God grant he be the last.'[94] Charles I made the same connection, preferring

---

[92] Tanneguy Leveneur, *Mémoires Inédites du Conte Leveneur de Tillières, Ambassadeur en Angleterre sur le Cour de Charles I et son Marriage avec Henriette de France* (Paris: Poulet-Mallassis, 1862), pp. 77–8.

[93] See *Maria Triumphans. Being a Discourse, wherein (by way of Dialogue) the B. Virgin Mother of God, is Defended and Vindicated, from all such Dishonours and Indignities, with which the Precisions of these our days, are accustomed unjustly to charge her* (Saint Omer, 1635), p. 5.

[94] Henry Burton, *For God and the King. The Summe of two sermons preached on the fifth of November last in saint matthewes Friday street. 1636* (Amsterdam: 1636), p. 126. Burton is especially appalled that Mariolatry is professed by one alleging membership of the Church of England, the catalogue of Roman Catholic practices he advances making a reasonable case that this really is writing of 'a tried Champion of *Rome*' (Burton, p. 126). In noting the author 'glorieth that he is the

to call his queen Marie, rather than Henrietta, 'because the land should find a blessing in that name'.[95]

The public recognition reflects Henrietta Maria's performances of Marianism; for the Queen performed the Marian role accorded by her mother in varied venues and forms. The larger part of the religious images in Henrietta Maria's private chapels represented the Virgin.[96] Dedicated to the Virgin, the private chapel Henrietta Maria built at Somerset House made her dedication to the Virgin entirely apparent.[97] Including side-chapels and a vestry, the chapel complex contained two large statues of the Virgin and Child, a painting of the *Crucifixion* by Rubens over the main altar and two paintings of the Virgin and St Francis. The ceiling showed *The Assumption of the Virgin*, by Matthew Goodrich and Thomas de Critz.[98] At its public opening in December 1636, the chapel was a visual wonder, as the queen's Capuchin preacher, Father Cyprien, recorded:

> Those who were in the chapel had great difficulty to leave it on account of the crowd of people who were bent on forcing their way in to see the magnificence displayed there. The crush lasted so long that it was impossible to close the doors of the church till the third night, when the King gave orders that it should be cleared of strangers, for he was desirous himself to be a spectator of that magnificent representation ... He admired the composition, kept his eyes fixed upon it for a very long time, and said aloud that he had never seen anything more beautiful or more ingeniously designed. To satisfy the curiosity of the Catholics and the curiosity of the Protestants, who never ceased coming from all parts to behold this wonder, the report of which had spread in all quarters, from the 8th of December, the day consecrated to the immaculate conception of the Blessed Virgin, the Queen, with great prudence, ordered the chapel to be left with all its decorations till Christmas.[99]

---

first who hath written ... on this our Blessed Virgin', Burton quotes *The Female Glory* directly. See Anthony Stafford, *The Female Glory, or The Life and Death of Our Blessed Lady, the holy Virgin Mary, God's own Incarnate Mother* (London, 1635), c2. *The Female Glory* is dedicated to Lady Theophila Coke. Henrietta Maria is in reference, though, for example when it states the Virgin Mary deserves 'a Quire of Queenes here, and another of Angels in Heaven' (*The Female Glory*, p. 248). Citations from *EEBO* (accessed 21.4.2020).

95 Lucy Hutchinson, *Memoirs of the Life of Colonel Hutchinson, Governor of Nottingham Castle and Town* (London: Henry G. Bohn; New York: Covent Garden, 1863), p. 89. The original text is dated between 1664 and 1668.
96 See R. Malcolm Smuts, *Court Culture and the Origins of a Royalist Tradition in Early Stuart England* (Philadelphia: University of Pennsylvania Press, 1999), p. 228.
97 Jessica Bell, 'The Three Marys: The Virgin, Marie de Medicis and Henrietta Maria', in *Henrietta Maria*, pp. 89–114 (p. 112).
98 Details of the Marian artworks from Bell, p. 112.
99 *The Court and Times of Charles the First ... Including Memoirs of the Mission in England of the Capuchin Friars*, Volume 2, ed. by Thomas Birch (London: Henry Colburn, 1848), p. 314.

With statues and paintings of her attracting crowds, the theatrical, public display, from 'the day consecrated to the immaculate conception of the Virgin', is evident in the King: a 'spectator' at a 'magnificent representation'.

Inigo Jones (1573–1652) worked on the Somerset House chapel and also on Henrietta Maria's court masques. No evidence confirms Jones joined the noble stream of converts in the 1630s court (including Walter Montagu, Kenelm Digby, Lady Purbeck and two daughters of Lord Falkland) or indeed beyond: in 1637, petitioners in St Giles parish complained Catholics 'were so exceedingly multiplied in that part of the parish called Bloomsbury that there are as many or more than Protestants'.[100] Nevertheless, Jones, who might reasonably be described as an Italophile, was clearly ready to participate in Catholic construction. The scenic and architectural parallels between the Somerset House chapel and the court masques have been well described:

> The altar [in the chapel] is placed beneath a proscenium arch in the centre of a raised stage, and the priests come and go to it by passages at the sides of the scene; in performing the service they use the fore-stage with its setting of the altar, much as the fore-stage is used for the action of a masque. The 'picture' beyond the proscenium arch forms the background for this action, and the raised stage is connected with the nave by steps 'in theatrical form'. The queen in the chapel has a special seat prepared for her, the equivalent of the State prepared for the King or Queen at a masque, so placed that it has a perfect view into the perspective scene. The main scene over the high altar is placed behind the proscenium arch, arranged 'according to the rules of perspective', and ablaze with colour and light, similar to the scenes in the heavens or upper stage of Jones's spectacular masques. The scene is covered initially by two curtains, and the congregation becomes the audience who applaud the magnificent sight. The whole performance is accompanied by a wealth of vocal and instrumental music.[101]

Imaging Mary everywhere, the Somerset House chapel was a religious theatre of Capuchins performing to royal and wider audience-congregations. In *Chlorida*, *Tempe Restored*, *Luminalia* and *The Temple of Love*, masques of the 1630s, in which Henrietta Maria starred, the queen correspondingly appeared on stage as the Virgin. The conceit of her name stood out in the masques' emblematic settings.[102]

Heightening the presentation was another dramatic backdrop: the dates of the masques' original performances. Masques generated meaning in relation to their times and occasions.[103] The religious dates of these masques are

---

100 Bailey (2009), pp. 140–1.
101 Veevers, p. 167.
102 On the emblematic settings of the Virgin in the masques, see Veevers, p. 122; Bailey (2009), pp. 181 and 200; Dunn-Hensley (2017), p. 160.
103 Shohet, p. 125.

therefore important. The opening of Ben Jonson and Inigo Jones' *Chloridia* (1630) observes it was performed on Shrovetide; *Tempe Restored* (1631) was on 'shrove Tuesday' and *The Temple of Love* (1634) was the same. *Luminalia* (1637) took place on 'shrovetuesday night'.[104] The dates indicate the masques formed an opening part of the court's Lenten rituals prefiguring Easter: linking them with Crucifixions like those at Somerset House, in which Mary stands beside Christ (John 19:25–7). With Henrietta Maria thus giving birth to the crucified Christ, the start of Lent appears incarnational, in a celebration of the Virgin decidedly Catholic. Even while stressing confession to a priest in shriving, court ritual incorporated the Virgin Mary into the Lenten and Easter celebrations of Henrietta Maria through the masques.

Yet the religious dates of these masques also link the genre to the religious calendar underlying English drama generally. Early modern drama derives from the medieval, sacred drama of feast days. Performed as an extension of religious life, this remained part of early modern theatre's organised culture of performance.[105] The culture has been observed previously in this chapter, in the echoes of early modern, cross-dressing May Marions in *The Roaring Girl*. Yet in the aforesaid masques of Shrovetide, the religious context is no echo but the occasion itself: the Marian masques firmly resituate drama in the religious calendar, ensuring religious meanings stand out.

Francis Lenton's masque *Great Britains Beauties* (1638) illustrates Henrietta Maria's complex Marian figurations on stage. This masque, 'Presented at Whitehall on Shrove Tuesday at Night, by the Queen's Majesty and her Ladies', immediately brings forward the Duchess of Lennox as the second masker, following the queen.[106] Having praised the queen as our 'Magnificent

104 See *Chloridia. Rites to Chloris and her nymphs. Personated in a masque, at court. By the Queenes Majesty and her ladies. At Shrove Tide. 1630* (London, 1631); *Tempe restrd. A Masque presented by the Queene, and fourteen ladies, to the King's Majestie at Whitehall on Shrove Tuesday. 1631* (London, 1632); *The temple of love. A masque presented by the Queenes Majesty, and her ladies, on Shrove-Tuesday. By Inigo Jones, surveyor of his Maties works, and William Davenant, her Maties. servant* (London, 1634); *Luminalia, or The festivall of light. Personated in a masque at court, by the Queenes Majestie, and her ladies. On Shrovetuesday night, 1637* (London, 1638), in *EEBO* (accessed 22.4.2020).

105 On the 'cohesive performance culture', see Matthew Smith, *Performance and Religion in Early Modern England: Stage, Cathedral, Wagon Street* (Notre Dame, IN: University of Notre Dame Press, 2019), p. 2. On the origins of medieval drama, an 'extension' of religious life, in relation to early modern drama, see also White, p. 66. Shohet presents masques as cohesive in wider performance culture on pp. 63–6.

106 Quotations from Francis Lenton, *Great Britains beauties, or, The female glory epitomized, in encomiastick anagramms, and acrostiches, upon the highly honoured names of the Queenes most gracious Majestie, and the gallant lady-masquers in her Graces glorious grand-masque. Presented at White-Hall on Shrove-Tuesday at night, by the Queenes Majestie and her ladies* (London: 1638), in *EEBO* (accessed 22.3.2017).

Queene MARY', the text turns to Lennox, calling her 'A Trusty Arm' (an anagram of Mary Stuart) before adding: 'This gracious Rib is proved a Trusty Arme'. The celebrations make Lennox not only the queen's trusted limb, but, in the imagery of the rib, the first Eve to Mary's second. The imagery climaxes in a poem acrostically spelling 'Mary' and beginning 'MARY's blest name you have, and Mary's grace'. Lennox is thus a limb of Mary, who in turn is both the onstage queen and the Virgin, the Second Eve 'full of grace' (Luke 1:28). The name of the queen and its complex figurations of the Virgin here stand out. In a high-class figuration of the Marian conceit seen earlier in city comedy and in Robin Hood, the person of the Virgin Mother extends outward to other women.

The expansive potential of the figuration stands out in the pastoral play *The Shepherd's Paradise* (1633), by Walter Montagu. This was commissioned by Henrietta Maria and she played the leading female role Bellessa: a remodelled Divine Beauty (also her role) from *Tempe Restored*.[107] The play is mostly set in an enclosed community of celibate women. Taking monastic vows, the community functions on the rules and terminology of Catholic convents.[108] Votorio, the priest, officiates amid tombs and sculptures in rituals including for the community's founder – probably in Catholic priest's garb.[109] Circling the Marian Queen Henrietta Maria, the community suggests the Catholic Church with which both the Marys were synonymous.[110]

Henrietta Maria's persona in this setting is mobile. As Saphira, her first role, she is the Princess of Navarre oppressed by male attention at court and finding refuge in the convent as Bellessa. In this second role, she becomes head of the convent, remaining mother superior for most of the play, in a Neoplatonic equation of beauty and virtue.[111] In the end she adjusts to marriage, the convent continuing under another head: the ideal of vowed virginity goes on.[112] Yet as queen on stage, Henrietta Maria shines through her roles, figuring Mary to the court in an enclosed garden itself figuring Mary.[113] Since seventeenth-century Europe increasingly linked the May Queen

---

107 See Sophie Tomlinson, *Women on Stage in Stuart Drama* (Cambridge: Cambridge University Press, 2005), p. 59.
108 Karin Britland, *Drama at the Courts of Queen Henrietta* (Cambridge: Cambridge University Press, 2006), p. 127.
109 In masques, ostensibly classical priests appeared as Catholic ones. See Veevers, p. 155.
110 Dunn-Hensley, therefore, refers to the play as presenting a 'Catholic Utopia'. See Dunn-Hensley (2017), p. 173.
111 On the Neoplatonism, see Poynting, p. 79.
112 Dunn-Hensley (2017), p. 177.
113 On the association of enclosure with chastity, see extract 2.2.66–71, that follows. The hortus conclusus was the *topos* of the English convents in Holland, to which I return in this study. See Nicky Hallett, 'Philip Sidney in the Cloister: The Reading Habits of English Nuns in Seventeenth-Century Antwerp', *Journal for Early Modern*

to the Virgin, Henrietta Maria's election to queen of the community on 'the first of May' (2.1.42) again expands her Marian resonance.[114]

Yet the expansive Marian figuration also dovetails with Henrietta Maria's marriage to Charles I and performance to his court. The natural walls of the convent present a chink:

> The peace and settledness of this place is secured by nature's enclosure of it on all sides by impregnableness, as if it was meant for chastity only to make a plantation here. At one passage only, the rocks seem to open themselves, so as to let in the King's care in a garrison, which he maintains for safety of the place, which delivers all strangers to us as suitors, not invaders. (2.2.66–71)

Chastity is assured in this symbolic convent through rocky enclosure and natural plantation: impregnation seems impossible. Yet the design betokening its inmates includes 'one passage only', where 'rocks seem to open themselves' to the 'King's care'. Responding to the paradox of a famous queen playing a role, enclosure here is in one respect open. Though nun-like and chaste, Henrietta Maria is wife to the King: Virgin Mother made flesh.

After the Queen: 1: Robert Davenport's *King John and Matilda*

In the preceding analysis, two Marian formulae stand out: Robin Hood and the convent. The latter innately suggests Mary, for as *inventrix virginitatis*, Mary was Christianity's first nun.[115] Yet while the former formula links Munday with Mary Frith and *The Roaring Girl*, the latter links each to Henrietta Maria and her varied performances of Mary. According to Lucy Hutchinson in the mid-seventeenth century, through Henrietta Maria 'the court was replenished with papists, and those who sought to advance themselves by the change turned to that religion. All the papists in the kingdom were favoured, and, by the king's example, matched into the best families.'[116]

Cultural Studies, 12/3 (Summer 2012), 88–116 (102). As noted by Horacio Sierra and in discussion of the play below, connections between female monasteries, the *hortus conclusus* and the Virgin Mary have been observed in *The Convent of Pleasure* by Margaret Cavendish, who was lady-in-waiting to Henrietta Maria. See Horacio Sierra, 'Convents as Feminist Utopias: Margaret Cavendish's *The Convent of Pleasure* and The Potential of Closeted Dramas and Communities', *Women's Studies*, 38/6 (July 2009), 647–69 (660). The fullest discussion of the *hortus conclusus* in early modern literature remains Stanley Stewarts's *The Enclosed Garden in English Literature, 1600–1650* (Los Angeles: University of California Press, 1961); see also Mark Jones, 'Some Versions of the *Hortus Conclusus* in Elizabethan Landscape and Literature', *Literature Compass*, 6/2 (March 2009), 349–61.

114 On the association of the May Queen with the Virgin, see Poynting, pp. 78–9.
115 See Solberg, p. 102.
116 See Hutchinson, p. 85.

The legacy was Catholic sympathy among courtiers, royalists and Roman Catholics, ultimately including Charles II and James II.[117] As we shall see, Marian concerns, including Robin Hood and convents, continued too.

The remaining discussion illustrates this in two plays connecting Henrietta Maria with the Restoration and its drama, before concluding with a view of Aphra Behn. The chapter thus establishes continuities between English theatre in its pre- and post-Revolutionary forms. Framed by the Exclusion Crisis (1677–82) Restoration drama was once characterised as an opposition: between a king and court enjoying the send-up of Whiggery at the Duke of York Theatre and the pageants of pope-burning a few streets away.[118] Yet a more complex picture has emerged: 'it is very likely that for the entire Restoration period, the theatre served as a crucial, continuously operating venue for the political public sphere.'[119] Most importantly: 'Plays like Settle's [*The Empress of Morocco*, of 1673] suggest that from the very beginning of the succession crisis, York's defenders and other members of the establishment were making sophisticated appeals to the public to defend their position.'[120] These developments are important for what follows in two ways. First, they present the theatre as a place of 'open discussion of matters of state'.[121] Second, they suggest the place of Catholic argument in Restoration drama: 'By supporting writers like Settle, many supposed enemies of the public sphere – "loyalists" Catholics, the Stuart brothers, and their supporters – were themselves making sophisticated appeals to the public.'[122] Setting the theatrical scene, the point has a special relevance to the readings of Aphra Behn that follow.

The full title of Robert Davenport's play *King John and Matilda* states it was acted in the Cock Pit, Drury Lane, 'by Her Majesties' servants with great applause'.[123] Her Majesty, here, is Henrietta Maria. The play has been

---

117 For the account of the conversion of Charles II on his deathbed, see Raymond Crawford, *The Last Days of Charles II* (Oxford: Clarendon Press, 1909). Charles II was married to the Catholic Catherine of Braganza in a Catholic ceremony at Portsmouth. In 1670 he had promised (to Louis XIV of France) to convert to Roman Catholicism.
118 See Odai Johnson, 'Pope-Burning Pageants: Performing the Exclusion Crisis', *Theatre Survey*, 37/1 (May 1996), 35–57 (36).
119 William Bulman, 'Publicity and Popery on the Restoration Stage: Elkanah Settle's "The Empress of Morocco" in Context', *Journal of British Studies*, 51/2 (April 2012), 308–39 (338).
120 Bulman, 338.
121 Bulman, 309.
122 Bulman, 309.
123 See Robert Davenport, *King John and Matilda a tragedy: as it was acted with great applause by Her Majesties servants at the Cock-pit in Drury-Lane* (London, 1655), in *EEBO* (accessed 20.2.2020). All textual citations are from this edition.

dated from between 1628 and 1635, but it was not printed until 1655. A second printing of 1662 implies early Restoration interest.[124]

The play reworks Munday's *The Death* in a provocatively Catholic direction.[125] As in *The Death*, King John rapaciously desires Matilda, pursuing her against her will and his marriage vow to Dunmowe Abbey, where she becomes a nun. The event is celebrated as 'chaste Matilda's marriage day' and the Abbess suggests it is both natural and an outgrowth of court corruption: 'See where she walks, souls to heavenly simple / It seems the Court digests not, and (being cloy'd,) / Commends them to the Cloyster'.

Matilda and John's good and bad names stand out. In Act 5, Scene 1, King John stands 'branded in our Chronicles / By the black name of a Wed-lock breaker' and:

> When men shall read the Conquerors great name,
> Voluptuous *Rufus*, that unkind brother *Beauclark*,
> Comely King *Steven*, *Henry* the Wedlock-breaker,
> And Lyon-hearted *Richard*; when they come
> unto his name, with sighs it shall be said,
> *This was King John – the murderer of a Maid;*

Matilda, conversely, is repeatedly a 'saint', 'immaculate', 'immaculate Matilda' and a 'martyr'. In death, says the Chorus: 'Heaven hath her pure part, whilst on Earth her name / Moves in the Sphere of a refulgent Fame.' The play ends with a procession: '*King* and *Lords*, the Lady *Abbess*, Ushering *Matilda*'s Hearse, born by Virgins, this motto fastened unto it – *To Piety and Chastity*. The Body of *Matilda* lying on the hearse, and attended by the *Queene*' (SD). A song of Matilda 'Amongst heavens fair Ones' concludes. Although 'Matilda was her name indeed', the text calls her 'Ma' and the Marian sanctity in both Robin Hood drama and the theatre of Henrietta Maria is evident.

Making the Marianism especially provocative is the play's exceptional treatment of relations between England and Rome. As Act 2, Scene 1 highlights, in its dealings between John and the papal legate Pandulpho, the Pope of the era is Innocent III. The name is resonant in a play about innocence and villainy, especially when innocence (Matilda) finds refuge in a church and villainy (John) pursues. Yet most provocative is the treatment of whether king or Pope has religious authority. Dating back to the coronation of Charlemagne (AD 800), the question was central in Henry VIII's break from Rome.

124 See Robert Davenport, *King John and Matilda a tragedy. As it was acted at the private house in Drury-lane with great applause* (London, 1662), in *EEBO* (accessed 20.2.2020).
125 On the relation to Munday, see David Kathman, 'Davenport, Robert', in *Oxford Dictionary of National Biography Online* (accessed 10.2.2020).

In the play, the question arises when King John, seeking to invalidate Magna Carta and a barons' rebellion, strategically weakens their opposition by having his excommunication removed. As Winchester advises, the legate, 'has power / From his holiness to reinvest your temples / With the rich Diadem; and withal pronounce you / Again admitted to the Church … // … remove all obstacles / Twixt you and the high calling of a King, / which by the reason you stood Curst at Rome, / Receiv'd affronts so frequent.' Like royal authority, the name of the king here depends on the Pope.

To remove the obstacle of papal interdiction, John agrees to be stripped of his crown by the Pope, in the person of his legate, on the condition that he is then reinvested, and his excommunication lifted. This arrangement affirming papal authority over the king is then enacted on stage, beginning with King John:

> Lo in the sight of Prelates Peers,
> Of Earth and Heaven, of all that heares
> My words; I *John Plantagaent*,
> (VVith all submissive reverence,) set
> My Crowne at the most sacred foot
> Of Innocent the Third, unto't
> I joyne my Kingdom, giue them free
> Unto his pious clemencie:
> And for the follies of my Raigne,
> Heats of my youth, and the rough straine
> Of riper years, my Rebellions, my high hand,
> My six yeares Interdictien [sic], and
> Al my mis-doings; I this, and those,
> Submit to the Popes power to disclose.

This scene of John's submission at length concludes with the papal re-investiture:

> Ascend your now true Seat sir, and from the hand
> Pan. gives John the Chair.
> Of my selfe *Pandulph*, Legate for the Pope,
> Observing the due payments specified,)
> Receive your Crown and Kingdoms; and with them
> We here pronounce your absolute readmission
> Into the Church, and from his holinesse
> We re-invest you, with all Powers, Prerogatives,
> Freedomes, Communities (and in the strength of effecacy,)
> That constantly adhears to lawfull Princes,
> And an obedient Son unto the Church,
> Long life to *John* of *England*, VVales and *Ireland*,
> The lawfull King!

The ritual significance of this investiture, in which kings submit to Popes and Popes anoint kings, is unmissable. Prior staging of *King John* had veered from the 'hot Protestant take' of *The troublesome reign of King John* to the dramatic appeal to Catholic loyalists by Shakespeare that we have noticed.[126] By contrast, Davenport's scene puts Shakespeare's careful Catholicism in the shade, for it has no truck with Protestant takes at all. The only objection to this scene's demonstration of papal authority over English kings comes from Fitzwater. He counsels John not to proceed with the investiture, urging that English 'bickerings' be resolved internally ('This is our Countries cause') and urging, too, that the Church wrongs itself by interfering: 'do not wrong that mother [Church], / Apparelling her comely holy face, / With a forehead full of frowns, pleited proceedings'. Yet it is the 'proceedings' of the Church that are objected to rather than her holiness and, like John, Fitzwater allows both 'filial love to our Mother Church' and 'his Holiness command'. The power of the Pope to 'pronounce' a lawful king, in Winchester's phrase, is never in doubt. Performed by the 'servants' of Henrietta Maria, the play demonstrates the dramatization of King John's reign, and the Marianism of Robin Hood plays at their most polemically Catholic. The publication of the play in 1662 shows Catholic and Marian continuity from Munday, at the turn of the seventeenth century, to the early Restoration via Henrietta Maria.

After the Queen: 2: *The Convent of Pleasure* of Margaret Cavendish

In *King John and Matilda*, the Queen's Men joined Dunmowe Abbey with Mary, innocence with Pope Innocent. Yet it was a queen's lady who developed Marian convents in *The Convent of Pleasure*. First printed in 1668, this play by Margaret Cavendish, maid of honour to Queen Henrietta Maria from 1643 and wife to William Cavendish (marquess of Newcastle-upon-Tyne, the defeated royalist commander at Marston Moor) conjures its sexual politics of the seventeenth century through religion and Catholic sympathy.[127] It places the convent centre stage. As elsewhere in this chapter, the convent evokes Mariology: not just in its heterosexual, virginal community, but also in its interpretation of the *hortus conclusus*.[128]

The blend of secular and religious in *The Convent of Pleasure* reflects three liminal experiences of Cavendish's life: her birth and early life at St

---

126 Lake (2016), p. 195.
127 On the sexual politics and Catholic sympathy, see Sierra, 647–69. See also Erna Kelly, 'Playing with Religion: Converts, Cloisters, Martyrdom, and Vows', *Early Modern Literary Studies* 14 (May 2014), 1–24.
128 Sierra, 660.

John's Abbey near Colchester in Essex, the county of Dunmowe; her residence across the garden from the Carmelite convent in Antwerp, at which she assisted in the clothing ritual of Sister Mary of the Blessed Trinity (baptised Mary Cotton); and her role as maid of Honour to Queen Henrietta Maria from 1643.[129] This last provides more than just Marian culture for *The Convent of Pleasure*, for the queen's interest in convents was a constant through her life. On the eve of her marriage, by proxy, to Charles I, Henrietta Maria retreated to the Carmelite convent of the Incarnation in Paris.[130] According to evidence from the 1620s from Alessandro Antelminelli (the representative at the English court of the Grand Duke of Tuscany) Henrietta Maria habitually went into seclusion at Denmark House: 'a long gallery was divided and fitted up with cells, and a refectory, and an oratory, in the manner of a Monastery. There they sang the hours of the Virgin and lived together like nuns.'[131] From 1644, she made frequent retreats into the Carmelite convent in Paris until, no longer satisfied with a life 'half in and half out of the world', in 1651 she founded a house of the 'Filles to Sainte Marie' at Chaillot, Paris, where she then spent weeks at a time.[132]

Devotion to the Virgin here is an opportunity for female community and the exclusion of men: both themes of *The Convent of Pleasure*.[133] The desire of Catholic women to embrace this seclusion is notable, as is the double

---

129 On her residence across the garden from the convent, see Nicky Hallett, *The Senses of Religious Communities, 1600–1800: Early Modern 'Convents of Pleasure'*, Women and Gender in the Early Modern World (Farnham and Burlington, VT: Ashgate, 2013), pp. 13–15. See also J. P. Vander Motten and Katrien Daemen-de Gelder, 'Margaret Cavendish, the Antwerp Carmel and The Convent of Pleasure', *Archiv für das Studium der neueren Sprachen und Literaturen* (2014), 1–13. Worth noting, too, is the 'curiously catholic' iconography of William Cavendish's Bolsover Castle, 'a place for pleasurable retirement'. See Timothy Raylor, '"Pleasure Reconciled to Virtue": William Cavendish, Ben Jonson, and the Decorative Scheme of Bolsover Castle', *Renaissance Quarterly*, 52/2 (Summer 1999), 402–39 (402, 418).
130 Bailey (2009), p. 37.
131 See *Historical Manuscripts Commission: Eleventh Report, Appendix, Part 1: The Manuscripts of Henry Duncan Squire: Salvetti Correspondence* (London: Her Majesty's Stationery Office, 1887), p. 57, recording practice on 17 April 1626. That the practice was repetitive can be seen from the account of 10 July 1626 (*Salvetti*, p. 77). Antelminelli adopted the name 'Amerigo Salvetti'.
132 See 'A Holy Court, 1651–1654', in 'Henrietta Maria' (2008), in *Oxford Dictionary of National Biography* (accessed 17.6.2022).
133 The opportunity devotion to the Virgin afforded women is noted by Strasser, who records the 'popular piety' in early modern Europe where women drove in a carriage around a statue of the Virgin three times before embracing the virginal life of the cloister. 'Through their actions, they asserted a connection between the example of the Divine Virgin and their chosen way of life.' See Ulrike Strasser, *State of Virginity: Gender, Religion and Politics in an Early Modern State* (Ann Arbor: University of Michigan Press, 2004), p. 2.

life, both nun and wife, withdrawn and available to Charles I, of Henrietta Maria. The convent and the Virgin are here devout mechanisms for female self-government in marriage: exploiting a long-standing paradox, since the *hortus conclusus*, the 'spring shut up', the 'fountain sealed' is also 'my spouse' (Song of Solomon, 4.12). In female culture, the Virgin was malleable to strict enclosure, motherhood and so wedlock, the freedom of a Moll Cutpurse or varieties of dependence and independence between. Like Bellessa in *The Shepherd's Paradise*, for example, in *The Convent of Pleasure* the freedom of Lady Happy to come and go from her convent suggests not just Henrietta Maria, but also the English Ladies of Mary Ward (1585–1645), whom we encountered earlier in this chapter as the Scola Beata Mariae. Henrietta Maria met Ward in 1639.[134] By turns famous and notorious, in the seventeenth century the 'English Ladies' were unenclosed, governed by a woman and without rule, habit or perpetual vows.[135]

Cavendish's play presents ladies' sequestration variously. To join a convent, in the opening scene, is to 'incloister' oneself (1.1.15 and 36), connecting self-segregation and a convent's sanctum as if the walls guarantee the person.[136] Distinctions of the convent from the wider world are marked. Suggesting female opportunity in a convent is greater, Lady Happy asks: 'What is there in the public world that should invite me to live in it?' (1.1.16–17). Suggesting opportunity may be less, Lady Moderator replies: 'Those that incloister themselves bar themselves from all other worldly pleasures' (1.1.36–7). What the play shows is a convent of pleasure eventually including the Prince who will take Lady Happy from it. Yet that paradox is answered by another.

---

134 Patricia Harriss, 'Mary Ward in her own Writings', *Recusant History*, 30/2 (2010), 229–39 (237).

135 See Susan O'Brien, 'Ward, Mary, 1585–1645', in *Oxford Dictionary of National Biography* (2005) (accessed 13.2.2020). Ward's career took her from Yorkshire to Europe, where she travelled widely. She sought a rule like that of the Jesuits but did not establish it. Martine Van Elk considers Ward, 'a powerful example of how early modern women could refashion prescribed gender roles and enact prescient models of female community'. See Martine Van Elk, 'Mary Ward and the Society of Jesus', in Early Modern Women: Lives, Texts and Objects' (April 2017), https://martinevanelk.wordpress.com/2017/04/24/mary-ward-and-the-society-of-jesus/ (accessed 13.2.2020). Ward's relevance to seventeenth-century literature is highlighted in Susan Goulding, 'Aphra Behn's "Stories of Nuns": Narrative Diversion and "Sister Books"', *Interdisciplinary Literary Studies* 10/1 (Fall 2008), 38–55 (38). The article highlights the need for 'focused study of Behn's attitude towards religious orders and religious practice'. See reference to 'Aphra Behn's "Stories of Nuns": Narrative Diversion and "Sister Books"', in *The Scriblerian and the Kit-Cats*, 44/1 (2011), 2.

136 All quotations from *The Convent of Pleasure* are from *Three Seventeenth-Century Plays on Women and Performance*, ed. by Hero Chalmers, Julie Sanders and Sophie Tomlinson, The Revels Plays Companion Library (Manchester and New York: Manchester University Press, 1988), pp. 267–308.

The play resolves its dilemma of cloister or public life by giving Lady Happy the convent for as long as she wants, before then giving her marriage. In the retreat from what Shakespeare calls 'the world', there are echoes of *Love's Labour's Lost*, but Cavendish's is a feminine retreat, not a masculine one, and it is explicitly rather than quietly conventual.[137] Henrietta Maria's life combining marriage and the convent is a closer model for *The Convent of Pleasure*.

The 'bar' of the convent separating it from the world is an emphatic aspect of plot. It materialises in the treatment of grates in the convent wall. Ungrated walls conspicuously protect women from men, who are encroaching, randy and, above all, outside:

> COURTLY But is there no place where we may peek into the convent?
> ADVISER No, there are no grates, but brick and stone walls.
> FACIL Let us get out some of the bricks or stones.
> ADVISER Alas, the walls are a yard thick!
> (*The Convent of Pleasure*, 2.4.29–33)

Emphasising a life of consecrated virgins, brick and stone walls, a yard thick, keep the convent women free of men who are Courtly, Facil and, elsewhere, 'Dick'. Though marriage comes in the end, to 'ne'er be a wife / But live a maid' (4.1.44–5) is the watchword. Again, and for most of the play, that commitment links the convent with virgin freedoms. The convent's contrast with the 'public world', so dreary to Lady Happy, is sharp. Under her care, in the convent, women flourish.

Parallels broad and particular with Montagu and Henrietta Maria's *The Shepherd's Paradise* are evident; and Cavendish's acknowledgement of John Fletcher among her influences in 'A General Prologue to all my Playes' suggests his *Monsieur Thomas* (1615, published 1639; republished and performed 1660).[138] Deriving from the pastoral romance *L'Astrée*, by L'Honoré d'Urfé, Fletcher's play also shows men infiltrating a convent.[139] Centring

---

137 See *Love's Labour's Lost* (1.1.30), in *The Oxford Shakespeare: The Complete Works*, ed. by Stanley Wells and Gary Taylor (Oxford: Clarendon Press, 1988; repr. 1995), p. 281. On the play's monasticism, see Joshua Phillips, 'Labor's Lost: The Work of Devotion in Tudor Literature', *Journal of Medieval and Early Modern Studies*, 44/1 (Winter 2014), 45–68 (60–3).

138 On the acknowledged dramatists in Cavendish's 'General Prologue', see Tomlinson, p. 169. For these editions, see John Fletcher, *Monsieur Thomas, A comedy acted at the Private House in Blackfriars. The author John Fletcher, Gent.* (London: 1639); Fletcher, *Father's Own Son. A Comedy. Formerly Acted at the Private House in Black Fryers; and now at the Theatre in Vere street by His Majesties Servants* (London: 1660), in *EEBO* (accessed 23.5.22). Following quotations from the play are from the 1639 edition.

139 Tomlinson, p. 257, note 45.

on two women, Celia and, inevitably, Mary, the play's Catholic nuance is seen, for example, in sympathetic presentations of convent rituals such as matins and choral singing. Appearing only at the end and so less central, Fletcher's convent is also less strongly fortified, less seemingly impregnable than in *The Convent of Pleasure*. Yet in Celia's hope, as in Cavendish, it is a refuge for maids escaping men, as the distraught account of Celia joining the convent shows:

> Her face slubber'd o're with tears, and troubles,
> Me thought she cry'd unto the Lady Abbess,
> For charity receive me holy woman,
> A Maid that has forgot the worlds affections,
> Into thy virgin order: me thought she took her,
> Put on a Stole, and sacred robe upon her,
> And there I left her.
> (*Monsieur Thomas*, 4.1)

Convent and Virgin are in this play's denouement. Suffering like Celia from a troublesome man, eventually Mary teaches Thomas to respect and marry her in a bed-trick highlighting the Virgin. Thomas's response, 'Holy saints defend me ... I am abused ... but I'll vex you' (5.4) receives from Mary short shrift: 'By'r Lady, but you shall not, Sir, but I'll watch you' (5.4). Vexing the man, as patron saint the Virgin helps Mary master Thomas, a rogue evoking lesser saints. Avoiding the wit and with more attention to convent freedom, *The Convent of Pleasure* echoes the Marian format. Though sunny, its portrait reflects the romance-like experience of seventeenth-century nuns.[140] With a last jibe at male misbehaviour from Cavendish, the play's closing mention of convents 'for married men as mad men' (5.3.20–1) affirms the idea of conventual seclusions in married life: like that required through her life by Henrietta Maria and recalling Cavendish's own marital reclusion.[141]

---

140 On the experience of seventeenth-century nuns as 'akin to romance' see Elizabeth Rapley, 'Women and the Religious Vocation in Seventeenth-Century France', *French Historical Studies*, 18/3 (Spring 1994), 613–31 (626). On the 'rich and detailed map of the emotional paths religious women took on their route towards contemplative perfection', see Lawrence Lux-Sterrit, *English Benedictine Nuns in the Seventeenth Century: Living Spirituality* (Oxford: Oxford University Press, 2017), p. 155.

141 Cavendish claimed she had 'made her house her Cloyster, inclosing herself' and that she was 'Inclosing herself like an Anchoret, wearing a Fritz-gown, tied with a cord about my waste'. Waller's interpretation of these claims, that they focus 'on fashion and image and not religious dedication', is reductive. See Gary Waller, *The Female Baroque in Early Modern English Literary Culture: From Mary Sidney to Aphra Behn*, Gendering the Late Medieval and Early Modern World (Amsterdam: Amsterdam University Press, 2020), p. 237. On Henrietta Maria's spells of nun-like seclusion while married to Charles I, see the account of Alessandro Antelminelli above.

After the Queen: 3: Aphra Behn

In Aphra Behn, the convent stands in opposition to the rake, a defining male figure of Restoration comedy with antecedents in the theatre of Beaumont and Fletcher.[142] Showing heaven punish a nun who absconds from a convent to marry, Behn's novel *The History of the Nun: Or the Fair Vow Breaker* (1689) upholds and takes seriously conventual vows.[143] Behn's knowledge of Catholicism, which she encountered in Antwerp, a centre of the Counter-Reformation, was substantial. Her epistolary novel, *Love Letters Between a Nobleman and his Sister* (1684–87), as well as her short story set entirely in Antwerp, *The Fair Jilt* (1688), suggest a thorough appreciation and knowledge of monastic orders.[144] There have been various surmises for the presence and attraction of Catholic features in Behn's work: that they represent a religious 'excess' akin to the aristocratic excesses Behn was attracted to in men like the Earl of Rochester, for example, or that they were a means of turning a profit, in an era fearing the seductive power of popery.[145] Melinda Zook notes that Behn was perhaps born into or converted to Catholicism; but 'even if she remained a member of the Church of England, she certainly retained strong sympathies for the sheer beauty of Counter-Reformation Catholicism'.[146]

Yet this aesthetic reading of Catholicism in Behn's works does not square with our earlier view of Restoration theatre, in which loyalist Catholics, the Stuart brothers and their supporters were 'making sophisticated appeals to the public'. As this view of the theatre implies, it is reductive to consider Catholicism in Behn's plays a simple appeal to the fear of popery, just as it is reductive to consider it a money-making device only. Since Catholics and their sympathisers made their case through the theatre, we must allow for the possibility that Catholic meanings on stage made Catholic appeals to theatrical audiences. In Behn's case this looks especially likely, since as Zook observes, Behn presents Catholicism beautifully.

Behn had various Catholic and recusant connections, but already there is reason to see a political aspect in her Catholic presentations. In this

---

142 Maximilian Novak, 'Libertinism and Sexuality', in *A Companion to Restoration Drama*, ed. by Susan Owen (Malden, MA; Oxford and Victoria, Australia: Blackwell, 2001), pp. 53–68 (pp. 55–6).
143 See Margarete Rubic, 'Excess and Artifice: The Depiction of the Emotions in Aphra Behn's Amatory Fiction', *Women's Writing*, 27/3 (2020), 372–92 (379–80); and Jane Spenser, *Aphra Behn's Afterlife* (Oxford: Oxford University Press, 2000), pp. 127–8.
144 Melinda Zook, *Protestantism, Politics and Women in Britain, 1660–1714*, Early Modern History: Society and Culture (London: Palgrave Macmillan, 2013), p. 102.
145 Zook, pp. 102–3.
146 Zook, pp. 102–3.

respect, her detailed knowledge of monastic orders is important. On stage, nuns feature in *The Dutch Lover* (1673), *The Rover* (1677), *The City Heiress* and *The False Count* (1681–82), *The Emperor of the Moon* (1687?) and *The Younger Brother* (1696). The mentions are sometimes brief, illustrating conflicted idealisations of virginity and marriage and sometimes linking convents with punishment. In *The False Count*, for example, Francisco gives a twist both more brutal and religiously precise to Theseus's threat to Hermia to marry or be 'in shady cloister mewed' (*A Midsummer Night's Dream*, 1.1.71). Francisco's version of this is: 'you are like to wed, or beat the hoof, Gentle-woman, or turn poor Clare, and die a Begging-Nun' (*The False Count*, 1.2.171).[147] In *The Dutch Lover*, by contrast, Silvio curses his beloved for a dissembling chastity: 'Danm her for a dissembler: / Is this the chaste, the excellent Clarinda, / Whom whilst I courted was as cold and nice / As a young Nun the day she is invested?' (1.2.80–2).[148] Here the virgin nun is the man's ideal, which the woman does not live up to.

The Silvio plot of *The Dutch Lover* is linked to the contested religious politics of the period. According to Judy Hayden, it suggests 'a reference to contemporary attempts to have James Duke of Monmouth legitimized and declared heir to the throne, thus by-passing the Catholic James Duke of York'.[149] If so, the noted nun imagery, which is ambiguous, also suggests hesitation over contemporary anti-Catholicism. Yet more important is the bigger picture. The Exclusion Crisis (1679–81) and the Popish Plot (1678–81) seem to have focused Behn's thinking. Monmouth's rapprochement with the Whigs and alliance with the Earl of Shaftesbury cost him support from royalists, Behn included.[150] 'At least by the time she wrote *The Second Part of the Rover* (1681), Behn appears to have decided for the King's brother, since she dedicated the play to the Duke of York, "the Royal Son of a Glorious Father".'[151]

The dedication also links the Catholic Duke of York with *The Rover*, in which convents stand out. Published in 1677, this play twice performed at court was evidently enjoyed by York, who wanted more. The dedication to *The Second Part* notes the encouragement the duke 'was pleas'd to give the

---

147 See Aphra Behn, *The False Count, or, A New Way to Play an Old Game. As it is acted at the Duke's Theatre* (London, 1682), in EEBO (accessed 23.4.2020).
148 See Aphra Behn, *The Dutch Lover: A Comedy Acted at the Duke's Theatre* (London, 1673), in EEBO (accessed 23.4.2020).
149 Judy Hayden, *Of Love and War: The Political Voice in the Early Plays of Aphra Behn* (Amsterdam and New York: Brill, 2010), p. 151.
150 Hayden, p. 151. Janet Todd notes that Behn 'took many opportunities to attack the Duke of Monmouth' during this period, seeing him as 'a danger to legitimacy and national stability'. See Todd, 'Career as a Playwright', in 'Aphra Behn', in *Oxford Dictionary of National Biography* (online, 2004; accessed 20.6.2022).
151 Hayden, p. 152.

Rover at his first appearance and the concern you were pleas'd to have for his second'. Even more strikingly, the dedication identifies the figure of the rover with the duke, since 'he is a wanderer too, distress'd, beloved, tho' unfortunate'.[152] This phrase glances at the Exclusion Crisis, when between March and September 1679, James was required to leave England. The dedication makes similar glances elsewhere; for example, in reference to the 'New Perils and New Exiles' of 'Your Royal Person'. Yet the bigger picture emerging from the dedication of 1681 is of a strong sympathy between Behn, the Duke of York and *The Rover* no later than 1677, when *The Rover* was published.

The Catholic context is important. Standing against a libertine way of life truly worldly, in *The Rover* convents are a basic proposition. The *dramatis personae* describes Hellena, who will eventually marry the rover, Wilmore, as, 'A gay Young Woman design'd for a nun'.[153] This identifies Hellena with the convent. It is also one means by which Behn's play adapts the portrait of Serulina in her source, Thomas Killigrew's *Thomaso*, to give the enclosed life greater prominence. Behn's two young women, Hellena and Florinda, represent the two sides of Serulina: one designed for the convent and the other for marriage.[154] Embodying these designs in different actors, Behn makes the convent, and its contrast with marriage, stand out. They do so in a play in which, generally, there are more virgins and fewer courtesans than in Killigrew.[155]

There are other means by which Behn makes the convent stand out. The *dramatis personae* of *Thomaso* describes Serulina only as 'A beauteous virgin, sister of Don Pedro', so the link of Hellena with the convent in *The Rover*'s *dramatis personae* is Behn's invention: a part of the process of distinguishing Hellena and Florinda from the 'composite' figure of Serulina.[156] Nevertheless, the basis of Behn's young women in Serulina is noteworthy; for the name of Killigrew's beautiful virgin, Serulina, means 'heavenly' (from 'cerulean').[157] Like the Virgin, Serulina is a heavenly virgin. There is no

---

152 See the dedication, 'To His Royal Highness the Duke', in Aphra Behn, *The Second Part of the Rover* (London: 1681), in *EEBO* (accessed 20.6.2022).

153 See Aphra Behn, *The rover, or, The banish'd cavaliers as it is acted at His Royal Highness the Duke's Theatre* (London: 1677), in *EEBO* (accessed 23.4.2020). All citations from the play are from this edition.

154 See Elaine Hobby, '"No Stolen Object but her Own: Behn's Rover and Killigrew's Thomaso', *Women's Writing*, 6/1 (1991), 113-27 (116).

155 J. P. Vander Motten, 'Recycling the Exile: Thomas, The Rover and the Critics', in *Thomas Killigrew and the Seventeenth Century English Stage: New Perspectives*, ed. by Philip Major (London and New York: Routledge, 2016; previously Ashgate, 2013), pp. 126- 41 (128).

156 Hobby (1991), 116.

157 Hobby (1991), 115.

consensus over Killigrew's religious convictions.[158] Yet he was a member of Henrietta Maria's retinue from at least 1632, when he acted in *Tempe Restor'd*, and he was a companion of Walter Montagu, the author of *The Shepherd's Paradise*.[159] A portrait of Killigrew from the 1670s, *The Rover*'s first decade, shows him in a Catholic pose, with the hat, staff, gourd and scallop shells of a pilgrim of St James.[160] For Restoration theatre, the pose is suggestive: from 1660, Killigrew's playhouse was one of just two licensed in London.

The contrasting presentations of Serulina and Hellena on stage is a third means by which Behn makes the convent stand out. While Serulina, in *Thomaso*, only appears on stage in Act 3, Helena is in Act 1, Scene 2 of *The Rover*, where her proposed life as a nun is discussed extensively. It is Florinda's opening assumption that 'a Maid design'd for a Nun, ought not to be so Curious in a discourse of Love'; and while Hellena rejects her designation, others in the scene share Florinda's assumption that Hellena is for the convent. The effect is to normalise and give prominence to the convent, even while suggesting (according to romance convention) that it will not be for Hellena. Hellena, we here learn, has had 'Nunnery breeding'. As late as Act 3, she notes that the abbess loves her, adding she would therefore choose the convent if, in choices for life, the loves of another were decisive.

The second aspect of Hellena's persona highlighted by the *dramatis personae*, her gaiety, is relevant to this decision. A figure of romance, Hellena is nevertheless subject to Behn's tendency to equate marriage with death and erotic love with violence.[161] Instead of the convent, therefore, Hellena pursues and wins Wilmore, but the triumph is equivocal. Wilmore is debauched. Mostly drunk, he confuses the difference between drink and passion, and he is careless of his friend Belvile's plans to marry. Wilmore wants instant sexual gratification, and vows and marriage mean nothing to him.[162] Even as Hellena embarks on marriage in Act 5, Wilmore remarks it is a 'brave Girle' who marries him. In what the play notes is 'Popish Carnival' (Epilogue, 2), Hellena's choice in love against the convent and its

---

158 See John Callow, 'Thomas Killingrew and the Seventeenth Century English Stage: New Perspectives', *The Seventeenth Century*, 31/4 (2016), 496–8 (498).
159 Karen Britland, 'Henry Killigrew and Dramatic Patronage at the Stuart Courts', in *Thomas Killigrew and the Seventeenth Century English Stage: New Perspectives*, pp. 91–108 (pp. 91–2).
160 Vander Motten (2016), p. 137.
161 See Eun Kyung Min, 'Fictions of Obligation: Contract and Romance in Margaret Cavendish and Aphra Behn', *Eighteenth Century Fiction*, 32/2 (2020), 245–69 (269).
162 On Wilmore in these terms, see H. James Jensen (ed.), *The Sensational Restoration* (Bloomington and Indianapolis: Indiana University Press, 1996), p. 285.

abbess looks fatal.[163] The unflattering portrait of Wilmore explains why the dedication of *The Second Part of the Rover* makes very clear that, while James and The Rover are both 'wanderers', they are different people: the duke is the Rover's 'Prince and Master'.[164] The Stuarts did not mind being generously satirised.[165]

The convent figures differently in *The Younger Brother*. Here the Prince falls in love with the simulacrum of a nun entering a Dutch convent in Ghent, in a passage recalling investitures like that witnessed by Margaret Cavendish. Behn might also have witnessed (and certainly knew of) the clothing rituals from her travels in Holland. While in Ghent, Behn borrowed money from John Butler and this Catholic recusant provides a direct link between Behn, Devonshire royalists and the exiled, Catholic communities of Flanders.[166] Most relevantly, for *The Younger Brother*, Butler's will of 1667 gave 500 guilders to the English Benedictine monastery of Ghent, with 200 guilders specifically for Dame Ursula Butler, one of the convent's nuns.[167] At present, Ursula is the only and therefore best candidate for the nun entering the Dutch convent of Ghent in *The Younger Brother*. At very least, Ursula establishes a direct connection between Behn's Catholic networks and the play's convent.

In *The Younger Brother*, the description of the nun entering the convent in Ghent is given by the Prince. Nun and convent initiate the comic love plot to follow. Male, libertine objectification colours the description:

> Arriv'd at Ghent, I went to see an English nun initiated, where I beheld the pretty innocent deliver'd up a Votress to Foolish Chastity; but among the Relation, then attending the Sacrifice, was a Fair Sister of the Young Votress, but so surpassing all I'd seen before, that I neglecting the Dull Holy Business, Pay'd my Devotion to that Kneeling Saint.[168]

As in *The Rover*, this glimpse into convent walls contrasts a dilemma of women's options and lives, enclosed or unenclosed, while also contrasting solemn and foolish venerations. While the Prince thinks convents foolish,

---

163 Behn's texts tend at once to 'revel in' and show the 'fatal potential' of passionate emotion. See Rubic, 379.
164 See the dedication, in *Second Part of the Rover* (London, 1681).
165 Adam Beach, 'Carnival Politics, Generous Satire and Nationalist Spectacle in Behn's *The Rover*', *Eighteenth Century Life*, 28/3 (2004), 1–19 (5).
166 See Karen Britland, 'Aphra Behn's First Marriage', *The Seventeenth Century*, 36/1 (2021), 33–53 (44).
167 Details of the will from Britland, 'Aphra Behn's First Marriage?', 44. The connection of the will to *The Younger Brother* and its convent in Ghent is mine.
168 See *The younger brother, or the amorous jilt. A comedy acted at the Theatre Royal by His MAJESTY, servants* (London: 1696), I.ii.11–13, in EEBO (accessed 23.4.2020). All quotations from this play are from this edition.

the play shows that his 'saint', Mirtilla, is anything but. Mirtilla chooses a different husband and then various lovers, turning the Prince into a fool with poor judgement.

The satire of his limited understanding is sharp in Act 2, when he tries to persuade Mirtilla (now married to Sir Morgan) that his 'devotion' to her in the convent, in Ghent, constituted a marriage: 'Witness the Priest, witness the Sacred Altar where we kneeled, when the blest silent Ceremony was performed' (2.2.97–8). The consensus on stage that he is mad illustrates the Prince's inability to distinguish different women and different professions of vows. Yet Ghent's Catholic convent hangs over all this as the context of love, the two sisters and the comedy of the Prince's stupidity. In particular, the Prince's speech forgets that, compounding the sisters, it was he who dismissed the nun's profession of vows, even though it was the source of his infatuation. The comedy thus illustrates a nobleman's confusion of erotic and Catholic devotion. Yet while it satirises the man, it says nothing bad of the nun or convent persisting in the background. Indeed, the 'Sacred Altar' and 'blest silent Ceremony' of the church leave its convent a tantalising choice.

Parallels between religious ecstasy and amorous passion recur in Behn.[169] In particular, the scene recalls the admission of Octavio to a monastic order in *The Fair Jilt*. Subtitled 'The History of Prince Tarquin and Miranda', the story is connected to Francois Louis Tarquini, a member of the Order of Christ by papal appointment, who resided in Antwerp between 1660 and 1665.[170] Undressed to receive his monastic vestments, *in The Fair Jilt* the figure of Octavio is viewed erotically by the congregation before a magnificent altar and 'the whole atmosphere in church' is like the ecstasy craved by lovers.[171] *The Younger Brother* reworks this religious depiction, so that a woman's clothing as a nun sets the scene for a watching man's erotic awakening. The similarities of theme resound in the recusant connection of both works. Published in 1688, *The Fair Jilt* is dedicated to Henry Pain, remembered today as Henry Payne, the 'veteran Catholic playwright, polemicist and agitator'.[172] In 1690, Payne was arrested in Scotland as 'a traffiqueing papist', to be tortured mainly on encouragement from London.[173] Once again, through a dedication, the connection of Behn's drama to Catholicism is political,

---

169 Rubic, 388.
170 J. P. Vander Motten and René Vermeir, 'Reality, and Matter of Fact': Text and Context in Aphra Behn's *The Fair Jilt*', *The Review of English Studies*, 66/274 (2014), 280–99 (281–2).
171 Rubic, 388.
172 Clare Jackson, 'Judicial Torture, the Liberties of the Subject, and Anglo-Scottish Relations, 1660–1690', in *Anglo-Scottish Relations from 1603–1900*, ed. by T. C. Snout (Oxford and New York: Oxford University Press, 2005), pp. 75–102 (p. 94).
173 Jackson, p. 94.

rather than just aesthetic, and Catholic connections seemingly go further. In 1656, Tarquini married Maria Theresia, whose sister, Anna Louisa, remained unmarried.[174] As women designed for and against marriage, the two sisters provide shadowy templates for the alternative sisters of *The Rover* and *The Younger Brother*.

In *The Younger Brother*, the direct alternative is between Mirtilla's faithless marriage and the convent life of her sister. With its contrast between Mirtilla and the nun established, *The Younger Brother* remains ambivalent about their choices and values. It punishes neither the stupidity of the Prince nor the unchastity of Mirtilla in the end, where it is equivocal about committed enclosure, committed marriage or a dissembling compromise between. In the end, Sir Morgan gives permission for the Prince to visit Mirtilla, the suggestion being that Morgan will wink at impropriety. In the compromise, the foolishness of the Prince's convent-inspired passion looks likely to be rewarded in married Mirtilla's continuing unchastity. The view of both the convent and the holy chastity related to it is thus paradoxical, at least from these two. Nothing more is said of the nun, though as her simulacrum, Mirtilla's presence on stage recalls her in the undying devotion of the Prince. The closing terms of impropriety are relevant too, for these depend on the play's earlier terms of propriety: committed marriage or the convent. Alongside Mirtilla, Sir Morgan and the Prince, these two ideas create the ironic denouement. According to its Epistle Dedicatory, *The Younger Brother* was met 'with very partial judges in the Acting' and received 'unjust Sentence'. Yet if libertines might have enjoyed the play's closing picture of a marriage subverted, the definition of propriety outside marriage through Ghent's Catholic convent for women would have delighted recusants of Behn's circle.

---

174 Vander Motten and Vermier, 281.

Concluding thoughts:
Works of literature again

This book has demonstrated the continuity of Roman Catholicism in English Literature from the accession of Elizabeth I in 1558 to the abdication of James II in 1689. In this literature, the Catholicism has emerged especially in reference to Purgatory, Christian worship, the Virgin Mary and the theology of works. The theology of works has been demonstrated in literary works spanning the period and is inextricable, I have argued, from the early modern idea of poetry and plays as works of literature. Works of literature, in this sense, are inherently theological and the theology worked towards producing the literature. The literary works are inherently Catholic in theology, in contravention to the prevailing religion of Prayer Book England.

The claims for Purgatory, Christian worship and the Virgin Mary have been more limited than those made for works. As discussed here, the three topics figure in a wide range of sixteenth- and seventeenth-century literature and are important contexts for the understanding of literature in the era. Purgatory has been argued entirely to haunt the early modern stage. Nevertheless, for the forms of Catholicism observed in this study an important distinction should be drawn between context and text. While Purgatory, Christian worship and the Virgin form contexts for literature in this study, every work of literature points to the work it does and is. I have especially linked this work with Ben Jonson, but we have noticed the theological consciousness of it as early as Sidney and as late as Dryden. Inherently, rather than as matters of context alone, works of English literature in the Prayer Book eras between Sidney and Dryden are theologically Catholic, therefore, regardless of additional religious features, whether Catholic or Protestant.

Past critics, of course, have stressed Protestant features in literary works of the era, and critics will no doubt do so again. Yet if at all linked to salvation, these features are always parts of the literary work in which the Catholic theology of work inheres. The features are additional to and may modify or subvert the work, but they cannot erase it. The modifications and subversions may only function, moreover, if they also draw attention to the work. In Purgatory, Christian worship and the Virgin Mary, this book has drawn attention to features which in the era enhance, rather than subvert, the literary theology of works. With works at the core, nevertheless, it would seem time to start thinking of English Literature of the era as always Catholic more or less.

An objection intrudes. What about literary works by authors who were Protestant? The answer to this question is twofold. First, recall that English Protestants normally confined their writings to scriptural patchworks and mosaics. Questions of religious sincerity and commitment therefore arise for outwardly Protestant authors deviating from this practice. No one can be sure how many people in England were true Protestant converts and how many continued to think and practise their traditional and ancestral devotions.[1] As observed in 1681, the 'frightful Face of the Law' encouraged a 'defensive Masque of the Gospel'.[2]

The second point takes us deeper into Protestant history, especially to the centrality in it of scripture. Martin Luther's *sola scriptura* is exemplified in his translations of the Bible. They are foundational documents of the Reformation, important for its success in propagating the Gospel.[3] Yet they propagated something else, too. In his own words, Luther's Bible was 'Luthers buch': 'an ultimately quite individual imprint has been made on God's word – that of the artist-translator Martin Luther'.[4] Luther presented this translation as one people could take, leave or improve on if they were able.[5] Originally constructed, here, is the literary and philological culture not just of English Protestants, but also of Calvin and most sixteenth-century evangelicals.[6] It is what Luther meant when he called theology the 'grammar of the language of Holy Writ', which should not be confused with wider grammatic and literary culture.[7] Following Luther, Protestant creativity was a scriptural

---

1 Andrew Hadfield, *Lying in Early Modern English Culture: From the Oath of Supremacy to the Oath of Allegiance* (Oxford: Oxford University Press, 2017), p. 1.
2 Anonymous, 'The Character of a church papist' (London, 1681), pp. 1–2 (p. 1), in *EEBO* (accessed 18.3.2024). See, too, Alexandra Walsham, *Church Papists: Catholicism, Conformity and Confessional Polemic in Early Modern England*, RHS Studies in History, 68 (Woodbridge: Boydell Press, 1993).
3 See Gordon Jensen, 'Embedded Commentary in Luther's Translation of Romans 3' in *The Unfolding of Words: Commentary in the Age of Erasmus*, ed. by Judith Henderson (Toronto, Buffalo and London: University of Toronto Press, 2012), pp. 118–40 (p. 118).
4 See Will Hasty, 'The Singularity of Aura and the Artistry of Translation: Martin Luther's Bible as Artwork', *Monatschefte*, 101/4 (2009), 457–68 (453–4).
5 Hasty, 462.
6 On Calvin and the evangelicals, see Barbara Pitkin, *Calvin, the Bible and History* (New York: Oxford University Press, 2020), p. 2.
7 Luther, cited in Maya Halpern, 'Religion, Grammar and Style: Wittgenstein and Hamman', *European Review*, 27/2 (2019), 195–209 (198).

creativity, which in England is well represented by the Prayer Book, among other scriptural mosaics. Yet this Protestant culture of the word is at odds with literary mosaics of other kinds, of which drama and poetry provide countless examples.

By contrast with the scriptural culture of Protestants, this book has linked the literary theology of works with echoes and treatments of Purgatory, Christian worship and the Virgin in poetry and on the stage. The literary universe indicated joins the living and the dead, the material and the spiritual. In the broadest sense, it is religious and, we can say, Christian, though from the point of view of the Prayer Book, or Protestants who wished to go still further in reform, it is a literary universe saturated with superstition: not Christian at all, especially in its deviations from scripture, but also in its intellectual debts to Catholic ideas of works, Purgatory, the Virgin and worship. Since Purgatory and the Virgin are features of the Catholic geography of the afterlife and works and worship are the means to that life, one can properly speak of this literary universe as Catholic. Nevertheless, one must repeat 'more or less'. Not only do Catholic emphases differ on stage from in poetry, but they also differ within the dramatic and poetic genres. Though the focus of the study has been English Literature's monumental Catholicism, one must also acknowledge that Church of England (and probably atheistic) elements are afloat in this universe.

Might one argue this the other way: that the Catholic features observed in this study are afloat in a literary universe of the Church of England? No; and not just because literary works tend to salvific works. As we have seen during this study, the Church of England of 1559–1689 was (in the main) Biblicist, subordinating reason to biblical literalism. In the etymological sense of 'universal', the Church was thus not 'catholic' (despite the word's use in the Creed), unless one defines the universe by what is in the Bible.[8] Yet for Calvin, and thence normatively in 1559–1689 Church of England theology, that was precisely how the universe was defined.[9] Objectivity in this view emerged from the 'data of the Holy Scripture'; if a wider data contradicted this, that just signified our fallen condition.[10] Notably, this was not the view of a medieval like Aquinas.[11] Yet in a Biblicist age of the Church of England, English Literature during 1558–1689 argued a universe

---

8 'Catholic' derives from 'catholicus' (Latin), meaning 'universal' or 'general'. See the etymology in the *OED*. For 'catholic' in the 1559 Creed, see *The Book of Common Prayer: The Texts of 1549, 1559, and 1662*, ed. by Brian Cummings (Oxford: Oxford University Press, 2011), p. 127. Notably, here, beliefs are 'according to the Scriptures'.
9 See Paul Helm, *Calvin at the Centre* (Oxford and New York: Oxford University Press, 2010), pp. 64–97.
10 Helm, p. 68.
11 Helm, pp. 68–9.

irreducible to biblical data.[12] If scripture from Tyndale to late Milton was (in Thomas Fulton's phrase) 'the Book of Books', plays and poems of the era were not scripture: neither in themselves (as material objects) nor largely in their meanings.[13] Indeed, in this last they tended to an entirely more catholic (that is, universal *and* Roman Catholic) view.

A few other points to emerge from the study deserve comment. One is the importance of the author, who as 'artifex' returns in considerations of his or her work. Unifying author and works, 'The Works of Ben Jonson' is in this respect totemic. In contrast to Sidney, for example, Jonson did as much as possible to imprint his personality in his works.[14] Nevertheless, literary study identifies the originality of early modern authors with their history, genealogy and origins, distinguishing what Foucault called 'the name of the author' at the 'contours' of works from the works themselves.[15] Like many studies of early modern literature today, this study has broadly embraced this approach, seeing the origins of sixteenth- and seventeenth-century literature in post-Reformation religion, especially its Catholic survivals. Yet a vital part of that survival is the theology of works itself, which is only meaningful when it refers to persons, and so (in literary study) to authors. In early modern literary study, in this respect, to lose sight of the work of the author is to lose from view an aspect of originality of precisely the kind Foucauldian approaches would recover. The loss of perspective explains, in part, why previous scholars have failed to see the theological significance of works of literature in early modern England. It suggests the need for a greater attention to authorial works in early modern study (especially regarding theology), within a more general consideration of what the death of the author occludes from literary study.

Another more general consideration is the Virgin Mary, especially as an example for early modern women. Mary was a key female example of the period.[16] Yet as we have seen, Protestants tended to restrict Mary's example,

---

12 Simpson observes an English tradition of anti-literalist, literary artists including 'at least' William Langland, Geoffrey Chaucer and William Shakespeare. See James Simpson, *Permanent Revolution: The Reformation and the Illiberal Roots of Liberalism* (Cambridge, MA, and London: Harvard University Press, 2019), p. 313.

13 On 'the Book of Books', see Thomas Fulton, *The Book of Books: Biblical Interpretation, Literary Culture and the Political Imagination from Erasmus to Milton* (Philadelphia: University of Pennsylvania Press, 2021).

14 See Ghosh Ranjan, 'Ben Jonson and his Reader: An Aesthetics of Antagonism', *The Comparatist*, 37 (2013), 138–56 (140–2).

15 For example, Kurt Schreyer, *Shakespeare's Medieval Craft: Remnants of the Mysteries on the London Stage* (Ithaca and London: Cornell University Press, 2014), p. 162.

16 Gary Waller, *The Female Baroque in Early Modern English Literary Culture: From Mary Sidney to Aphra Behn*, Gendering the Late Medieval and Early Modern World (Amsterdam: Amsterdam University Press, 2020), p. 52.

fashioning her into a role model for godly wives. The reformation of Mary is thus important in the history of women's studies.[17] Two points stand out from this book. First are the examples of real and literary women like Henrietta Maria and Moll (in *The Roaring Girl*). In different ways, these suggest that Mary in a Catholic form could empower women of different social strata. Second is the overlap between Marian veneration and Petrarchan veneration of women – seen, for example, in Behn's *The Younger Brother*. While critical models today distinguish between these venerating forms, Behn stresses commonality as much as difference.[18] She should not be ignored.[19] Since Catholic Mary empowered women, her presence in Petrarchism (and so aspects of the genre) could have empowered women too. We must reassess if truthfully Petrarchism only produced the 'oppression [of women] through [their] exaltation'.[20]

The Roaring Girl also invites questions of sanctity, cross-dressing and theatre. As we saw, Moll's masculine, cross-dressing persona evokes medieval ideas of female sanctity among others. These medieval ideas are given special emphasis in the play. Yet womanly cross-dressing is a regular feature of Renaissance drama: how do these cross-dressers on stage develop medieval ideas of the female saint? Suggesting links with Moll and the Marian maids of Munday, for example, in *As You Like It* Rosalind and Celia connect with Robin Hood and religion.[21] What other means exist to intensify links between sanctity and cross-dressing in the theatre?

The last, general question this study of Catholicism and English Literature 1558–1689 provokes is: what happens next? Detailed answers are beyond our scope, but the question is important, and one can suggest some outlines.

17 Mary's liberating potential for women is a current question in women's studies. See for example, Carolina del Rio Mena, 'Latin American Women: In Mary's Footsteps or in her Shadow?', in *Catholic Women Speak: Bringing our Gifts to the Tables* (New York and Marwah, NJ: Paulist Press, 2015, pp. 40–2; Pekka Metso, Nina Maskulin and Teuvu Laitila, 'Tradition, Gender and Empowerment: The Birth of Theotokos Society in Helsinki, Finland', in *Orthodox Christianity and Gender: Dynamics of Tradition, Culture and Lived Practice*, ed. by Helen Kupari and Elina Vuola, Routledge Studies in Religion (London and New York: Routledge, 2020), pp. 131–46 (p. 134).
18 On the critical distinctions, see Waller (2020), pp. 52 and 63.
19 See Elaine Hobby, 'Review: The Female Baroque in Early Modern English Literary Culture', *Tulsa Studies in English Literature*, 40/2 (2021), 395–8 (397).
20 See Waller (2020), p. 63.
21 See especially Robert Leach, 'As You Like It: A Robin Hood Play', *English Studies: A Journal of English Language and Literature*, 82/5 (2001), 393–400; Tom Rutter, in *Shakespeare and the Lord Admiral's Men: Reading Across Repertories on the London Stage, 1594–1600* (Cambridge: Cambridge University Press, 2017), pp. 165–96 ('Chapter 5: "Not Pure Religion by their Lips Profaned": Old Castle, Robin Hood and *As You Like It*'); also Anne Barton, *The Shakespearean Forrest* (Cambridge: Cambridge University Press, 2017), pp. 70–92.

Especially for English Catholicism, 1689 is a moment of real historical rupture. Yet it was neither the end of Catholic literature nor of the wider literary and cultural history to which we are heirs. The grandest narratives address this culture. Yet even today, they downplay Catholic influence. Tracing the 'illiberal roots of liberalism', for example, James Simpson says nothing of Southwell.[22] Yet Alexander Pope (1688–1744) was an heir to Dryden; and continuities exist between Crashaw, Donne and Dryden.[23] Observed inspiring Donne and Crashaw (among others) in Chapter 4, Southwell thus seems a significant, overlooked source for Pope's eighteenth-century Catholic 'inclusivism'.[24] From Southwell to Pope, Catholic literary history thus appears an important antidote to the illiberalism historically underpinning modernity; a source, that is, of our liberalism and our liberty. We might characterise the development as from peaceful resistance (Southwell), through phases of accommodation more and less successful (Donne, Herrick, Crashaw) to a marginal, severely limited Catholicism seeking wider inclusion (Pope).[25] That Catholic Emancipation occurred in 1829 (and the Universities Tests Act, allowing Catholics to attend universities, in 1871) shows how far ahead of his time Pope was.[26] That its tolerance emerged from outspoken resistance shows how very far ahead was Southwell.

And yet: the central consideration of this book is the association of English Literature with Catholicism, 1558–1689. That sets literature at odds with what the era's historians still refer to as 'Protestant England', raising

---

22 See Simpson (2019). I am not the first to suggest Simpson's history of illiberalism underplays the Catholic. See Peter Marshall's review of Simpson (2019) in *Journal of British Studies*, 59/1 (January 2020), 172–4 (173).
23 See G. Douglas Atkins, *Alexander Pope's Catholic Vision: 'Slave to No Sect'* (New York: Palgrave Macmillan, 2013), pp. 9 and 42–4; Molly Murray, *The Poetics of Conversion in Early Modern English Literature: Verse and Change from Donne to Dryden* (Cambridge: Cambridge University Press, 2009), pp. 138–9. Continuities also exist between Pope and the Reformation. See Alex Eric Hernandez, 'Commodity and Religion in Pope's "The Rape of the Locke"', *Studies in English Literature, 1500–1900*, 48/3 (Summer 2008), 569–84 (573–7).
24 On Pope's inclusivism, see Atkins, p. 46; also p. 59.
25 On the severe restriction, see Pat Rogers, 'Alexander Pope: Religion, Politics, and Poetry', in *A Companion to British Literature, III: Long Eighteenth-Century Literature, 1660–1837*, ed. by Robert DeMaria, Heesog Chang and Samantha Zacher (Chichester: Wiley Blackwell, 2014), pp. 128–42 (pp. 128–34).
26 Davidson observes the 'almost-anachronistic' professions of tolerance in Pope. See Peter Davidson, 'Pope's Recusancy', *Studies in the Literary Imagination*, 38/1 (2005), 63–76 (66). For more on eighteenth-century toleration, see Martin Fitzpatrick, 'From Natural Law to Natural Rights? Protestant Dissent and Toleration in the Late Eighteenth Century', *History of European Ideas*, 42/2 (2016), 195–221, especially 213–15; Ulrich Lehner, *The Catholic Enlightenment: The Forgotten History of A Global Movement* (Oxford: Oxford University Press, 2016), pp. 47–71.

Concluding thoughts: Works of literature again 215

again the question of how Protestant the country really was. Important here is the largely unenthusiastic churchgoing of English men and women, at least until the 1640s.[27] This lukewarm embrace of Protestantism by much of the English populace suggests their openness to alternative religious ideas, especially when communicated through media other than the church. A particular problem for Reformers seeking to replace Catholic habits with scriptural reading was the resistance their encouragement could create: 'in the sixteenth century, rural populations that had developed relatively independently were being forced to conform to institutions controlled from London. Resistance might well be expected from people whose cognitive patterns probably differed markedly from those of their urban cousins.'[28] In assessing England's religion, 1558–1689, these cognitive patterns should not be undervalued. A country divided by a 'social hierarchy of literacy' is not easily (or perhaps ever) made Biblicist.[29]

Yet with England divided in literacy, one must be cautious about equating literary Catholicism with the populace. Since levels of literacy rise with social rank in early modern England, Catholicism in its poetry reflects the interests of the higher strata of contemporary society. Drama, which does not require literacy, is a different matter. Implying drama's popularity, the growth of London's theatres depended on the city's growth and its capacity to sustain the theatres.[30] There is a real case, therefore, for the representative value of Catholicism in the London theatres. Yet authors like Jonson wrote poetry and plays for the public theatres, as well as court masques. Between the elite viewers of these last, the higher-strata readers of poetry and the widely popular plays of the London stage (which could be taken elsewhere), the literature of this study suggests a considerable appetite for literary Catholicism in England's early modern populace. The legacy is an English literary culture immeasurably richer than the scripturalism that might have been.

We owe this legacy to the cool embrace by the English populace of Prayer Book religion. In part, I have suggested, that derives from conflicts of illiteracy

---

27 See Alec Ryrie, *Being Protestant in Reformation Britain* (Oxford: Oxford University Press, 2013), pp. 318–23; see also, Ethan Shagan, *The Rule of Moderation: Violence, Religion and the Politics of Restraint in Early Modern England* (Cambridge: Cambridge University Press, 2011), pp. 112–13.
28 Ellen Spolsky, 'Literacy after Iconoclasm in the English Reformation', *The Journal of Medieval and Early Modern Studies*, 39/2 (2009), 305–30 (312).
29 On the 'social hierarchy of literacy', see David Cressy, *Literacy and the Social Order: Reading and Writing in Tudor and Stuart England* (Cambridge: Cambridge University Press, 1980; repr. 2006), p. 118.
30 José Martin and Stephen Wittick, 'Introduction: Conversion, Cities and Theatre in the Early Modern World', in *Performing Conversion: Cities, Theatres and the Early Modern World*, ed by José Martin and Stephen Wittick (Edinburgh: Edinburgh University Press, 2021), pp. 1–11 (p. 8).

with Biblicism. Yet in *Religio Laici*, Dryden identified it with the commonsensical view of laypeople that one's deeds are important in salvation. More sophisticated versions of Dryden's anti-Calvinist outlook recognised the problem artistically. Reasoning that the Calvinist downplaying of human agency in favour of God's will degrades God and downplays the responsibility humans have in their salvation, the Neoplatonist Ralph Cudworth (1617–88) is illustrative.[31] In *A Sermon Preached Before the Honourable House of Commons at Westminster* (1647), Cudworth took issue through artistic metaphors with the 'many that speak of new glimpses and discoveries of Truth, of Gospel-light', arguing for a 'Divine Light in our minds' since 'no body counts it unlawful, to hear a Lesson played upon the lute or to smell at a Rose'.[32] Arguing for an 'inward Self-moving Principle' in humans, he claimed the principle 'is as if the Soul of Musick, should incorporate itself within the Instrument, and live in the Strings, and make them of their own accord, without any touch, or impulse from without, dance up and down, and warble out their Harmonies'.[33] This joy and melody free of external and salvific determinism embraces the artistic works of humans. As Hamlet suggested more famously, in the theatre, the 'piece of work' that is man is also godlike: 'in form and moving how express and admirable' and in action, as in other works, 'how like an angel'.[34]

---

31 See Benjamin Carter, 'Ralph Cudworth', *Early Modern Philosophy of Religion*, ed. by Graham Oppy and N. Drakakis, The History of Western Philosophy of Religion, 3 (London and New York: Routledge, 2013), pp. 113–25 (p. 115).
32 Ralph Cudworth, *A Sermon Preached Before the Honourable House of Commons at Westminster, March 31, 1647* (London: 1647), in EEBO (accessed 5.9.2022), p. 2 and unnumbered page, image 5.
33 Cudworth, p. 74.
34 *Hamlet*, 2.2.303–5, in *The Oxford Shakespeare: The Complete Works*, ed. by Stanley Wells and Gary Taylor (Oxford: Clarendon Press, 1988; repr. 1995), p. 666.

Bibliography

A Ballad upon the Popish Plot, Written by a Lady of Quality. 1679. (London)
A Mery Geste of Robyn Hoode and of His Lyf, with a New Play for to Be Played in Maye Games Very Pleasaunt and Full of Pastyme. 1560. (London)
A Pleasant Commodie, Called Look about You. As It Was Lately Played by the Right Honourable the Lord High Admirall His Servaunts. 1600. (London)
Adrian, John. 2009. 'George Herbert, Parish "Dexterity and Laudianism"', *The Seventeenth Century*, 24/1: 26–51
Aers, David. 2009. *Salvation and Sin: Augustine, Langland, and Fourteenth-Century Theology* (Notre Dame, IN: University of Notre Dame Press)
Aers, David. 2020. *Versions of Election: From Langland and Aquinas to Calvin and Milton*, ReFormations: Medieval and Early Modern (Notre Dame, IN: University of Notre Dame Press)
Al Such Psalms of David as T. Sternhold Didde in His Lifetime Draw into English Meter. 1553. (London)
Alford, Stephen. 2008. *Burghley: William Cecil at the Court of Elizabeth I* (New Haven, CT, and London: Yale University Press)
Allott, Nicholas, and Benjamin Shaer. 2017. 'Inference and Intention in Legal Interpretation', in *The Pragmatic Turn in Law*, ed. by Janet Giltrow and Dieter Stein (Boston and Berlin: De Gruyter Mouton), pp. 83–118
An Epitaph, or Funeral Inscription, upon the Godlie Life and Death of the Right Worshipfull Maister William Lambe Esquire, Founder of the New Conduit in Holborne, &C. Deceased the One and Twentieth of April, and Intumbed in S. Faiths Church under Powles, the Sixt of Maie next and Immediately Following. Anno. 1580. Devised by Abraham Fleming. 1580. (London)
Anderson, David. 2014. *Martyrs and Players in Early Modern England: Tragedy, Religion and Violence on Stage*, Studies in Performance and Early Modern Drama (Farnham and Burlington, VT: Ashgate)
Anderson, Judith. 2013. *Shakespeare and Donne: Generic Hybrids and the Cultural Imagination* (New York: Fordham University Press)
Anderson, Justin. 2020. *Virtue and Grace in the Theology of Thomas Aquinas* (Cambridge: Cambridge University Press)
Andrewes, Lancelot. 1642. *A Manual of Directions for the Visitation of the Sick, with Sweet Meditations to Be Used in Time of Sickness Whereunto Is Added a Short Confession of the Faith, with a Form of Thanksgiving and Prayers for Morning and Evening* (London)

Andrewes, Lancelot. 1765. *Justification in Christ's Name: A Sermon Preached at Whitehall, November 23, 1600. By Lancelot Andrews, Lord Bishop of Winchester. Extracted from the Second Edition of That Great Prelate's Works and Re-Published by the Reverend Mr Madan* (London)

Angus, Bill. 2019. 'The Night, the Crossroads and the Stake: Shakespeare and the Outcast Dead', in *Reading the Road, from Shakespeare's Crossroads to Bunyan's Highways*, ed. by Lisa Hopkins and Bill Angus (Edinburgh: Edinburgh University Press), pp. 51–70

"Aphra Behn's 'Stories of Nuns': Narrative Diversion and 'Sister Books".' 2011. *The Scriblerian and the Kit-Cats*, 44/1: 2

Arblaster, Paul. 2004. *Antwerp and the World: Richard Verstegan and the International Culture of Catholic Reformation* (Leuven: University of Leuven Press)

Arthur, James. 2021. *A Christian Education in the Virtues: Character Formation and Human Flourishing* (London: Routledge)

Atherton, Ian. 2010. 'Cathedrals, Laudianism and the British Churches', *The Historical Journal*, 53/4: 895–918

Atkins, Douglas. 2013. *Alexander Pope's Catholic Vision: 'Slave to No Sect'* (New York: Palgrave Macmillan)

Augustine, Saint. 1610. *Saint Augustine, Of the Citie of God: With the Learned Comments of Ioannes Ludovicus Vives*. 2nd edn (London)

Bahr, Stephanie. 2020. '"Ne spared they to strip her naked all": Reading Rape and Reformation in Spenser's Faerie Queene', *Studies in Philology*, 117/2: 285–312

Bailey, Rebecca. 2009. *Staging the Old Faith: Queen Henrietta Maria and the Theatre of Caroline England, 1625–1642* (Manchester: Manchester University Press)

Bailey, Rebecca. 2017. 'James Shirley', in *The Encyclopedia of English Renaissance Literature*, ed. by Alan Stewart and Garrett Sullivan (Malden. Oxford and Chichester: Wiley-Blackwell)

Barber, C. L. 1959. *Shakespeare's Festive Comedy: A Study of Dramatic Form and Its Relation to Social Custom, with a New Foreword by Stephen Greenblatt*, ed. by Stephen Greenblatt (Princeton and Oxford: Princeton University Press)

Barducci, Marco. 2013. 'Clement Barksdale, Translator of Grotius: Erastianism and Episcopacy in the English Church, 1651–58', *The Seventeenth Century*, 25/2: 265–80

Barish, Jonas A. 1981. *The Antitheatrical Prejudice* (Berkerley: University of California Press)

Barksdale, Clement. 1670. *A Remembrancer of Excellent Men* (London)

Barnes, A. W. 2006. 'Editing George Herbert's Ejaculations: Texts, Contexts and Interpretation', *Textual Cultures*, 1/2: 90–113

Barton, Anne. 2017. *The Shakespearean Forrest* (Cambridge: Cambridge University Press)

Bates, Stephen. 2019. 'The Virgin Mary and the Reformation in the Midlands, 1516–1560', *Midland History*, 44/2: 159–75

Bayley, Merridee, and Katie Barclay (eds). 2019. *Emotion, Ritual and Power in Europe: Family, State and Church* (Cham, Switzerland: Palgrave Macmillan)

Beach, Adam R. 2004. 'Carnival Politics, Generous Satire, and Nationalist Spectacle in Behn's *The Rover*', *Eighteenth Century Life*, 28/3: 1–19

Beauregard, David. 2018. 'Shakespeare's Prayers', *Religion and the Arts*, 22: 577–97
Beckwith, Sarah. 2017. *Shakespeare and the Grammar of Forgiveness* (Ithaca, NY: Cornell University Press)
Behn, Aphra. 1673. *The Dutch Lover: A Comedy Acted at the Duke's Theatre* (London)
Behn, Aphra. 1677. *The Rover, or, The Banish'd Cavaliers as It Is Acted at His Royal Highness the Duke's Theatre* (London)
Behn, Aphra. 1681. *The Second Part of the Rover* (London)
Behn, Aphra. 1682. *The False Count, or, A New Way to Play an Old Game. As It Is Acted at the Duke's Theatre* (London)
Behn, Aphra. 1696. *The Younger Brother, or the Amorous Jilt. A Comedy Acted at the Theatre Royal by His MAJESTY, Servants* (London)
Bell, Jessica. 2008. 'The Three Marys: The Virgin; Marie de Medicis; and Henrietta Maria', in *Henrietta Maria: Piety, Politics and Patronage*, ed. by Erin Griffey (London: Routledge), pp. 89–114
Belsey, Catherine. 2010. 'Shakespeare's Sad Tale for Winter: *Hamlet* and the Tradition of Fireside Ghost Stories', in *Shakespeare Quarterly*, 61/1: 1–25
Benson, David. 2017. 'Statues, Bodies and Souls: St Cecilia and Some Medieval Attitudes to Ancient Rome', in *Medieval Women and Their Objects*, ed. by Jenny Adams and Nancy Mason Bradbury (Ann Arbor: University of Michigan Press), pp. 267–89
Bennett, Kate. 2004. 'Thomas Shadwell', in *Oxford Dictionary of National Biography*
Berman, Kathleen. 1972. 'Some Propertian Imitations in Ovid's "'Amores'"', *Classical Philology*, 67/3: 170–7
Bezio, Kristin. 2018. '"Munday I Sweare Shal Bee a Holliday": The Politics of Anthony Munday, from Anti-Catholic Spy to Civic Pageanteer (1579–1630)', *Études Anglaises*, 71/4: 473–90
Binns, James W. 1994. 'John Parkhurst and the Traditions of Classical Latin Poetry in Sixteenth-Century England', *International Journal of the Classical Tradition*, 1/1: 52–61
Birch, Thomas. 1848. *The Court and Times of Charles the First* (London: Henry Colburn), II
Blastic, Michael. 2018. 'The Virgin Mary in the Writings of Francis and Clare of Assisi', in *Medieval Franciscan Approaches to the Virgin Mary: Mater Sanctissima, Misericordia, et Dolorosa*, ed. by Steven Mcmichael and Katherine Wrisley Shelby (Leiden and Boston: Brill), pp. 13–31
Blayney, Peter. 2022. *The Printing and the Printers of the Book of Common Prayer, 1549–1561* (Cambridge: Cambridge University Press)
Blidstein, Moshe. 2017. *Purity, Community, and Ritual in Early Christian Literature*, Oxford Studies in Abrahamic Religions (Oxford: Oxford University Press)
Bolton, W. F. (ed.). 1966. *Ben Jonson: Sejanus His Fall* (London: Benn)
Boyd, Craig, and Aaron Cobb. 2009. 'The Causality Distinction, Kenosis and a Middle Way: Aquinas and Polkinhorne on Divine Action', *Theology and Science*, 7/4: 391–406
Bradbury, Jim. 2010. *Robin Hood* (Stroud: Amberley Publishing)

Braden, Gordon. 1978. *The Classics and English Renaissance Poetry: Three Case Studies* (New Haven, CT, and London: Yale University Press)

Brietz Monta, Susannah. 2018. '"A Sweetness Ready Penn'd?" English Religious Poetics in the Reformation Era', in *A Companion to Renaissance Poetry*, ed. by Catherine Bates (Hoboken, NJ, and Chichester: Wiley Blackwell), pp. 63–77

Britland, Karen. 2006. *Drama at the Courts of Queen Henrietta Maria* (Cambridge: Cambridge University Press)

Britland, Karen. 2016. 'Henry Killigrew and Dramatic Patronage at the Stuart Courts', in *Thomas Killigrew and the Seventeenth Century English Stage: New Perspectives*, ed. by Philip Major (London and New York: Routledge), pp. 91–108

Britland, Karen. 2021. 'Aphra Behn's First Marriage?', *The Seventeenth Century*, 36/1: 33–53

Bruhn, Karen. 2003. 'Pastoral Polemic: William Perkins, The Godly Evangelicals, and the Shaping of a Protestant Community', *Anglican and Episcopal History*, 72/1 102–27

Buc, Philippe. 2015. *Holy War, Martyrdom and Terror: Christianity, Violence and the West* (Philadelphia: University of Pennsylvania Press)

Buccola, Regina. 2006. *Fairies, Fractious Women, and the Old Faith: Fairy Lore in Early Modern British Drama and Culture* (Selinsgrove, PA: Susquehanna University Press)

Buccola, Regina. 2016. 'Virgin Fairies and Imperial Whores: The Unstable Ground of Religious Iconography in Thomas Dekker's The Whore of Babylon", in *Marian Moments in Early Modern British Drama*, ed. by Regina Buccola and Lisa Hopkins (London and New York: Routledge), pp. 141–60

Bulman, William. 2012. 'Publicity and Popery on the Restoration Stage: Elkanah Settle's "The Empress of Morocco" in Context', *Journal of British Studies*, 51/2: 308–39

Burton, Henry. 1636. *For God and the King. The Summe of Two Sermons Preached on the Fifth of November Last in Saint Matthewes Friday Street* (Amsterdam)

Butler, Martin, and Jane Rickard. 2020. 'Introduction: Immortal Ben Jonson', in *Ben Jonson and Posterity: Reception, Reputation, Legacy*, ed. by Martin Butler and Jane Rickard (Cambridge: Cambridge University Press), pp. 1–22

Cain, Tom. 2004. 'Robert Herrick', in *Oxford Dictionary of National Biography*

Callow, John. 2016. 'Thomas Killigrew and the Seventeenth Century English Stage: New Perspectives', *The Seventeenth Century*, 31/4: 496–8

Camden, William. 1605. *Remaines of a Greater Work, Concerning Britaine, the Inhabitants Thereof, Their Languages, Names, Surnames, Empresses, Wise Speeches, Poesies, Epitaphs* (London)

Capp, Bernard. 2012. *England's Culture Wars: Puritan Reformation and Its Enemies in the Interregnum, 1649–1660* (Oxford and New York: Oxford University Press)

Capp, Bernard. 2014. '"Jesus Wept" but Did the Englishman? Masculinity and Emotion in Early Modern England', *Past & Present*, 224/1: 75–108

Carlson, Andrew. 2019. 'Monstrous Length in Spenser's Faerie Queene', *English Literary History*, 86: 441–65

Carlson, Marvin. 2003. *The Haunted Stage: The Theatre as Memory Machine* (Ann Arbor: University of Michigan Press)

Carter, Benjamin. 2013. 'Ralph Cudworth', in *Early Modern Philosophy of Religion*, ed. by Graham Oppy and N. Drakakis (London and New York: Routledge), pp. 113–25

Castillo, Miriam. 2017. 'Catholic Translation and Protestant Translation: The Reception of Luis de Granada's Devotional Prose in Early Modern England', *Translation and Literature*, 26/2: 145–61

Cauthen, Irby (ed.). 1970. *Gorboduc or Ferrex and Porrex*, Regents Renaissance Drama Series (London: Edward Arnold)

Cavendish, Margaret. 1653. *Poems, and Fancies Written by the Right Honourable, the Lady Margaret Newcastle* (London)

Chakravorty, Swapan. 1996; repr. 2002. *Society and Politics in the Plays of Thomas Middleton*. Oxford English Monographs (Oxford and New York: Oxford University Press)

Chalindor, Jennifer. 2020. 'Jonson's Ghost and the Restoration Stage', in *Ben Jonson and Posterity: Reception, Reputation, Legacy*, ed. by Jane Rickard and Martin Butler (Cambridge: Cambridge University Press), pp. 105–24

Chalmers, Hero, Julie Sanders and Sophie Tomlinson (eds). 1988. *Three Seventeenth-Century Plays on Women and Performance*, The Revels Plays Companion Library (Manchester and New York: Manchester University Press)

Chapman, Alison. 2013. *Patrons and Patron Saints in Early Modern English Literature*, Routledge Studies in Early Modern Literature (New York and London: Routledge)

Chaucer, Geoffrey. 1989. *The Complete Poetry and Prose of Geoffrey Chaucer*, 2nd edn, ed. by John H. Fisher (Taipei, Taiwan: Cengage Learning)

Chernaik, Warren. 2013. *The Myth of Rome in Shakespeare and His Contemporaries* (Cambridge: Cambridge University Press)

Chloridia. Rites to Chloris and Her Nymphs. Personated in a Masque, at Court. By the Queenes Majesty and Her Ladies. At Shrove Tide. 1630. 1631. (London)

Clegg, Cyndia. 1997. *Press Censorship in Elizabethan England* (Cambridge: Cambridge University Press)

Clegg, Cyndia. 2007. *Press Censorship in Jacobean England* (Cambridge: Cambridge University Press)

Clegg, Cyndia. 2011. *Press Censorship in Caroline England* (Cambridge: Cambridge University Press)

Clegg, Cyndia. 2016. 'The 1559 Books of Common Prayer and the Elizabethan Reformation', *The Journal of Ecclesiastical History*, 67/1: 94–121

Collinson, Patrick. 1988. *The Birthpangs of Protestant England: Religious and Cultural Change in the Sixteenth and Seventeenth Centuries* (Basingstoke: Palgrave Macmillan)

Collinson, Patrick. 2009. 'The Politics of Religion and the Religion of Politics in Elizabethan England', *Historical Research: The Bulletin of the Institute of Historical Research*, 82: 74–92

Conn Liebler, Naomi. 1995. *Shakespeare's Festive Tragedy: The Ritual Foundations of Genre* (London and New York: Routledge)

Connolly, Margaret. 2019. *Sixteenth-Century Readers, Fifteenth-Century Books: Continuities of Reading in the English Reformation*, Cambridge Studies in Palaeography and Codicology (Cambridge: Cambridge University Press)

Connolly, Ruth. 2011. 'Miscellaneity and the Reader in Robert Herrick's *Hesperides*', in *Readings on Audience and Textual Materiality*, ed. by Graham Allen, Carrie Griffin and Mary O. Connell (London and New York: Routledge), pp. 23–36

Connolly, Ruth, and Tom Cain (eds). 2013. in *The Complete Poetry of Robert Herrick* (Oxford: Oxford University Press)

Conti, Brooke. 2014. *Confessions of Faith in Early Modern England* (Baltimore, MD: University of Pennsylvania Press)

Cooper, Helen. 2014. *Shakespeare and the Medieval World* (London: Bloomsbury)

Cooper, Kate. 2007. '"Only Virgins Can Give Birth to Christ": The Virgin Mary and the Problem of Authority in Late Antiquity', in *Virginity Revisited: Configurations of the Unpossessed Body*, ed. by Bonnie Malachlan and Juidth Fletcher (Toronto, Buffalo and London: University of Toronto Press), pp. 100–115

Corthell, Ronald. 2008. 'Writing Back: Robert Persons and the Early Modern English Subject', *Philological Quarterly*, 87/3: 277–97

Cox, John D. 2016. 'Stage Prayer in Marlowe and Jonson', *Comparative Drama*, 50/1: 63–80

Craig, D. H. (ed.). 1995. *Ben Jonson: The Critical Heritage* (New York: Routledge)

Crashaw, Richard. 1642. *Carmen Deo Nostro* (Paris)

Crashaw, Richard. 1646. *Steps to the Temple. Sacred Poems, With Other Delights of the Muses. By RICHARD CRASHAW, Sometimes of Pembroke Hall, and Late Fellow of S. Peter's Coll. In Cambridge* (London)

Crashaw, Richard. 1648. *Steps to the Temple, Sacred Poems, With the Delights of the Muses. By RICHARD CRASHAW, Sometimes of Pembroke Hall, and Late Fellow of S. Peters in Cambridge. The Second Edition, Wherein Are Added Diverse Pieces Not before Extant* (London)

Crawford, Raymond. 1909. *The Last Days of Charles II* (Oxford: Clarendon Press)

Creaser, John. 2009. '"Times Trans-Shifting": Chronology and the Misshaping of Herrick', *English Literary Renaissance*, 39/1: 163–96

Cressy, David. 1980. *Literacy and the Social Order: Reading and Writing in Tudor and Stuart England* (Cambridge: Cambridge University Press)

Cressy, David. 1993. 'Purification, Thanksgiving and the Churching of Women in Post-Reformation England', *Past & Present*, 141/1: 106–46

Cressy, David. 1996. 'Gender Trouble and Cross-Dressing in Early Modern England', *The Journal of British Studies*, 35/4: 438–65

Cressy, David. 1997. *Birth, Marriage and Death: Ritual, Religion and the Life-Cycle in Tudor and Stuart England* (Oxford: Oxford University Press)

Crewe, Jonathan. 2019. 'Reading Rapture: Richard Crashaw's Saint Teresa', in *Studies in English Literature*, 59/1: 135–52

Cudworth, Ralph. 1647. *A Sermon Preached Before the Honourable House of Commons at Westminster, March 31, 1647* (London)

Cummings, Brian. 2002. *The Literary Culture of the Reformation: Grammar and Grace* (Oxford and New York: Oxford University Press)

Cummings, Brian. 2011a. 'Introduction'. *The Book of Common Prayer: The Texts of 1549, 1559 and 1662*, ed. by Brian Cummings (Oxford: Oxford University Press)

Cummings, Brian (ed.). 2011b. *The Book of Common Prayer: The Texts of 1549, 1555, and 1662* (Oxford: Oxford University Press)

Cummings, Brian. 2013. *Mortal Thoughts: Religion, Secularity, & Identity in Shakespeare and Early Modern Culture* (Oxford: Oxford University Press)

Dailey, Jeff. 2005. 'Christian Underscoring in Tamburlaine the Great, Part II', *The Journal of Religion and Theatre*, 4/2: 146–59

Daley, Brian. 2010. 'Woman of Many Names: Mary in Orthodox and Catholic Theology', *Theological Studies*, 71/4: 846–69

Danou, Photini. 2010. 'Catholic Treason Trials in Elizabethan England. Complexities and Ambiguities in the Stage Management of a Public Show: The Case of William Parry', *Journal of Early Modern History*, 14/5: 393–415

Davenant, William. 1673. *The Works of Sir William Davenant, Kt. Consisting of Those Which Were Formerly Published and Those Which He Design'd for the Press: Now Published out of the Authors Original Copies* (London)

Davenport, Robert. 1655. *King John and Matilda a Tragedy: As It Was Acted with Great Applause by Her Majesties Servants at the Cock-Pit in Drury-Lane* (London)

Davenport, Robert. 1662. *King John and Matilda a Tragedy. As It Was Acted at the Private House in Drury-Lane with Great Applause* (London)

Davidson, Peter. 2005. 'Pope's Recusancy', *Studies in the Literary Imagination*, 38/1: 63–76

Davies, Isabel. 2019. 'Tales of the Unexpected: A Marian Woodcut in the Book of Common Prayer', in *Notes & Queries*, 66/3: 384–7

Dawson, Anthony. 2008. 'Shakespeare and Secular Performance', *in Shakespeare and the Cultures of Performance*, ed. by Paul Yachnin and Patricia Badir (Farnham and Aldershot, VT: Ashgate)

De Mézerac-Zanetti, Aude. 2017. 'A Reappraisal of Liturgical Continuity in the Mid-Sixteenth Century: Henrician Innovations and the First Book of Common Prayer', *French Journal of British Studies*, 22/1, The Book of Common Prayer: Studies in Religious Transfer: 1–11

Degenhardt, Jane Hwang. 2015. *Islamic Conversion and Christian Resistance on the Early Modern Stage* (Edinburgh: Edinburgh University Press)

Rio Mena, Carolina del. 2015. 'Latin American Women: In Mary's Footsteps or in Her Shadow?' in *Catholic Women Speak: Bringing Our Gifts to the Tables* (New York; Marwah NJ: Paulist Press), pp. 40–42

Deming, Robert H. 1969. 'Herrick's Funereal Poems', *Studies in English Literature 1500–1900*, 9/1: 153–67

Derings, M. 1614. *Works* (London)

Deutermann, Allison. 2017. *Listening for Theatrical Form in Early Modern England* (Edinburgh: Edinburgh University Press)

Dickson, Donald (ed). 2007. *John Donne's Poetry* (New York and London: Norton)

Dillon, Janette. 1998. *Language and Stage in Medieval and Renaissance England* (Cambridge: Cambridge University Press)

Dipasquale, Theresa. 1999. *Literature and Sacrament: The Sacred and the Secular in John Donne* (Pittsburgh, PA: Duquesne University Press)

Djordjevic, Igor. 2015. *King John (Mis) Remembered: The Dunmowe Chronicle, the Lord Admiral's Men, and the Formation of Cultural Memory* (Farnham and Aldershot, VT: Ashgate)

Dodd, Kirk. 2019. 'What's in a Name? Shakespeare's Inventio and the Topic of 'Notatio', in *Early Modern Literary Studies*, 21/1: 1–35

Donaldson, Ian. 2011. *Ben Jonson: A Life* (Oxford and New York: Oxford University Press)

Donne, John. 2008. *John Donne – The Major Works* (London: Oxford University Press)

Döring, Tobias. 2006. *Performances of Mourning in Shakespearean Theatre and Early Modern Culture*, Early Modern Literature in History (New York: Palgrave Macmillan)

Drimmer, Sonja. 2014. 'Beyond Private Matter: A Prayer Role for Queen Margaret of Anjou', *Gesta*, 53/1: 95–120

Dryden, John. 1682. *Religio Laici, or a Layman's Faith* (London)

Dryden, John. 1691. *The Works of Mr John Dryden* (London)

Dryden, John. 1882. *The Works of John Dryden: Illustrated with Notes, Historical, Critical and Explanatory and a Life of the Author, by Sir Walter Scott, revised and corrected by George Saintsbury* (London)

Dryden, John. 1695. 'An Essay of Dramatic Poesie', in *The Dramatic Works of John Dryden, in Three Volumes* (London)

Duffy, Eamon. 2012. *Sacrilege and Sedition: Religion and Conflict in the Tudor Reformations* (London, Berlin, New York and Sidney: Bloomsbury)

Duffy, Eamon. 2001; repr. 2003. *The Voices of Morebath: Reformation and Rebellion in an English Village* (New Haven, CT and London: Yale University Press)

Duffy, Eamon. 2020. *A People's Tragedy: Studies in Reformation* (London: Bloomsbury)

Dugdale, William. 1963. *Monasticon Anglicanum, or, The History of Ancient Abbies, and Other Monasteries, Hospitals, Cathedral and Collegiate Churches, in England and Wales* (London)

Duncan, Sarah. 2012. *Mary I: Power and Ceremony in the Reign of England's First Queen* (New York: Palgrave Macmillan)

Dunne, Derek. 2016. *Shakespeare, Revenge Tragedy and Early Modern Law: Vindictive Justice*, Early Modern Literature in History (New York: Palgrave Macmillan)

Dunn-Hensley, Susan. 2010. 'Return of the Sacred Virgin: Memory, Loss, and Restoration in Shakespeare's Later Plays', in *Walsingham in Literature and Culture from the Middle Ages to Modernity*, ed. by Dominic Janes and Gary Waller (Farnham and Burlington, VT: Ashgate), pp. 185–97

Dunn-Hensley, Susan. 2017. *Anna of Denmark and Henrietta Maria: Virgins, Witches and Catholic Queens* (London: Palgrave Macmillan)

Duppa, Brian. 1648. *Angels Rejoicing for Sinners Repenting, Delivered in a SERMON by the Right Reverend Father in God, Brian Duppa, now Bishop of Salisbury* (London)

Dyck, Paul. 2013. 'Altar, Heart, Title Page: The Image of Holy Reading', in *English Literary Renaissance*, 43/3: 541–71

Edwards, Kathryn. 2012. 'The History of Ghosts in Early Modern Europe: Recent Research and Future Trajectories', *History Compass*, 10/4: 353–66

Ellington, Donna Spivey. 1995. 'Impassioned Mother or Passive Icon: The Virgin's Role in Late Medieval and Early Modern Passion Sermons', *Renaissance Quarterly*, 48/2: 227–61

Elliott, Dyan. 2017. 'Violence against the Dead: The Negative Translation and *Damnatio Memoriae* in the Middle Ages', *Speculum: A Journal of Medieval Studies*, 92/4: 1020–55

Emily, O. 2009. 'Arms and Letters: Julius Caesar, the Commentaries of Pope Pius II and the Politicization of Papal Imagery', *Renaissance Quarterly*, 62/4: 1057–97

Erne, Lukas. 2009. *Beyond the Spanish Tragedy: A Study of the Works of Thomas Kyd* (Manchester: Manchester University Press)

Ettenhuber, Katrin. 2013. 'Inordinate Grief: Complicated Grief in Donne and Augustine', in *Passions and Subjectivity in Early Modern Culture*, ed. by Freya Sierhus and Brian Cummings (Farnham and Burlington, VT: Ashgate), pp. 201–17

Evendon-Kenyon, Elizabeth. 2021. 'Anthony Munday: Eloquent Equivocator or Contemptible Turncoat?', in *Reformation Reputations: The Power of the Individual in English Reformation History*, ed. by David Crankshaw and George Gross (London: Palgrave MacMillan), pp. 363–92

Fantazzi, Charles. 2013. 'Vives, Juan Luis', in *The Oxford Guide to the Historical Reception of Augustine*, ed. by Willemien Otter (Oxford: Oxford University Press), III, pp. 1876–8

Ferguson, Elizabeth, 'Veneration, Translation and Reform: The Lives of Saints and the English Catholic Community, c.1600–1642', in *British Catholic History*, 32/1 (2014): 37–65

Fincham, Kenneth, and Nicholas Tyacke. 2007. *Altars Restored: The Changing Face of English Religious Worship, 1547–c.1700* (Oxford: Oxford University Press)

Fissell, Mary E. 2007. *Vernacular Bodies: The Politics of Reproduction in Early Modern England* (Oxford: Oxford University Press)

Fitzpatrick, Martin Hugh. 2016. 'From Natural Law to Natural Rights? Protestant Dissent and Toleration in the Late Eighteenth Century', *History of European Ideas*, 42/2: 195–221

Fletcher, John. 1639. *Monsieur Thomas; A Comedy Acted at the Private House in Blackfriars. The Author John Fletcher, Gent* (London)

Fletcher, John. 1660. *Father's Own Son. A Comedy. Formerly Acted at the Private House in Black Fryers; and Now at the Theatre in Vere Street by His Majesties Servants* (London)

Foster, Michael. 2004. 'Digby, Sir Kenelm', in *Oxford Dictionary of National Biography*

Fowler, Alastair. (ed.). 2007. *Milton: Paradise Lost*, 2nd edn (London and New York: Pearson Longman)

Fowler, Alastair. 2012. *Literary Names: Personal Names in English Literature* (Oxford: Oxford University Press)

Freeman, Charles. 2011. *Holy Bones, Holy Dust: How Relics Shaped the History of Medieval Europe* (New Haven, CT, and London: Yale University Press)

Frick, Peter. 2007a. 'Johannine Soteriology and Aristotelean Philosophy: A Hermeneutical Suggestion on Reading John 3.16 and 1 John, 4.9', *Biblica*, 88/3: 415–21

Frick, Peter. 2007b. 'The Means and Mode of Salvation: A Hermeneutical Proposal for Clarifying Pauline Soteriology', *Horizons in Biblical Theology*, 29/2: 203–22

Friesen, Ilse. 2007. 'Virgo Fortis: Images of the Crucified Virgin Saint in Medieval Art', in *Virginity Revisited: Configurations of the Unpossessed Body*, ed. by Bonnie Malachlan and Juidth Fletcher (Toronto, Buffalo and London: University of Toronto Press), pp. 116–27

Fuller, David. 1998. 'Introduction', in *The Complete Works of Christopher Marlowe : Tamburlaine Parts 1 and 2*, ed. by David Fuller (Oxford: Clarendon Press), v

Fulton, Thomas. 2021. *The Book of Books: Biblical Interpretation, Literary Culture, and the Political Imagination from Erasmus to Milton* (Philadelphia: University of Pennsylvania Press)

Gadaleto, Michael. 2018. 'Shakespeare's Bastard Nation: Scepticism and the English Isle in *King John*', *Shakespeare Quarterly*, 96/1: 3–34

Gadamer, Hans-George. 1997. 'Rhetoric and Hermeneutics', trans. Joel Weinsheimer, in *Rhetoric and Hermeneutics in our Time*, ed. by Walter Jost and Michael Hyde (New Haven, CT: Yale University Press)

Gallagher, Laura. 2015. '"Stabat Mater Dolorosa": Imagining Mary's Grief at the Cross', in *Biblical Women in Early Modern Literary Culture*, ed. by Victoria Brownlee and Laura Gallagher (Manchester: Manchester University Press), pp. 180–96

Gallagher, Lowell. 1999. 'Mary Ward's "Jesuitresses" and the Construction of a Typological Community', in *Maids and Mistresses, Cousins and Queens: Women's Alliances in Early Modern England*, ed. by Susan Frye and Karen Robertson (New York and Oxford: Oxford University Press), pp. 199–220

Gasper, Julia. 1991. 'The Sources of the Virgin Martyr', *The Review of English Studies*, 42: 17–31

Gazzard, Hugh. 2010. 'An Act to Restrain Abuses of Players (1606)', *The Review of English Studies*, 61: 495–528

Gerrish, B. A. 1993. *Grace and Gratitude: The Eucharistic Theology of John Calvin* (Minneapolis: Fortress Press)

Giddens, Eugene. 2003. 'The Final Stages of Printing Ben Jonson's Works, 1640–1', *The Papers of the Bibliographical Society of America*, 97/1: 57–68

Kilgour, Maggie. 2014. 'The Poetics of Time: The *Fasti* in the Renaissance', in *A Handbook for the Reception of Ovid*, ed. by John Millar and Carol Newmans (Oxford: Wiley Blackwell), pp. 217–31

Goodland, Katharine. 2005. *Female Mourning in Medieval and English Renaissance Drama: From the Raising of Lazarus to King Lear* (Aldershot and Burlington, VT: Ashgate)

Goodland, Katharine. 2016. 'Female Mourning, Revenge and Hieronimo's Doomsday Play', in *The Spanish Tragedy: A Critical Reader, Arden Early Modern Drama Guides*, ed. by Thomas Rist (London; Bloomsbury), pp. 175–96

Goodrich, Jaimie. 2014. *Faithful Translators: Authorship, Gender and Religion in Early Modern England* (Evanston, ILL: Northwestern University Press)

Goulding, Susan. 2008. 'Aphra Behn's "Stories of Nuns": Narrative Diversion and "Sister Books"', *Interdisciplinary Literary Studies*, 10/1: 38–55

Gouws, John. 2010. 'Nicholas Oldisworth and William Davenant: Moors and Slaves in Early Modern England', *Notes and Queries*, 57/1: 36–7

Gouws, John. 2005. 'Nicholas Oldisworth, Richard Bacon, and the Practices of Caroline Friendship', *Texas Studies in Literature and Language*, 47/4: 366–401

Gray, Patrick. 2016. 'Caesar as Comic Anti-Christ: Shakespeare's Julius Caesar and the Medieval English Stage Tyrant', *Comparative Drama*, 50/1: 1–31

Green, Clay. 2018. '"Our Souls and Fleshy Hearts": The Body, Sacraments and Grace in Herbert's "The H. Communion"', *Citharia*, 57/2: 43–57

Gregory, Brad, '"The True and Zealous Service of God": Robert Persons, Edmund Bunny, and the First Book of the Christian Exercise', in *Journal of Ecclesiastical History*, 45/2 (1994): 238–68

Griffin, Eric. 2001. 'Ethos, Empire, and the Valiant Acts of Thomas Kyd's Tragedy of "the Spains"', *English Literary Renaissance*, 31/2: 192–229

Griffin, Eric. 2015. 'Dramatizing the Black Legend in Post-Armada England', in *Espana Ante Sus Criticos: Las Claves De La Leyenda Negra*, ed. by Yolanda Rodríguez Pérez, Antonio Sanchez Jiménez and Harm den Boer (Madrid and Frankfurt: Iberoamericana and Vervuert), pp. 209–27

Griffin, Eric. 2009. 'Nationalism, the Black Legend, and the Revised *Spanish Tragedy*', *English Literary Renaissance*, 39/2: 336–70

Grindlay, Lilla. 2018. *Queen of Heaven: The Assumption and Coronation of the Virgin in Early Modern English Writing* (Notre Dame, IN: Notre Dame University Press)

Grundyn John (ed.). 1960. *The Poems of Henry Constable* (Liverpool: Liverpool University Press)

Guibbory, Achsah. 1998. *Ceremony and Community from Herbert to Milton: Literature, Religion and Cultural Conflict in Seventeenth-Century England* (Cambridge: Cambridge University Press)

Guibbory, Achsah. 2013. 'Devotional Poetry and the Temple of God', *George Herbert Journal*, 37/1–2: 99–116

Gunter, Stephen (ed.) 2012. *Arminius and his Declaration of Sentiments: An Annotated Translation with Introduction and Theological Commentary* (Waco, TX: Baylor University Press)

Ha, Polly. 2017. 'Introduction', in *The Puritans on Independence: The First Examination, Defence and Second Examination* (Princeton: Princeton University Press)

Hackett, Helen. 1996. *Virgin Mother, Maiden Queen: Elizabeth I and the Cult of the Virgin Mary* (New York: Palgrave Macmillan)

Hadfield, Andrew. 2011. 'Spenser and Religion – Yet Again', *Studies in English Literature*, 51/1: 21–46

Hadfield, Andrew. 2017. *Lying in Early Modern English Culture: From the Oath of Supremacy to the Oath of Allegiance* (Oxford: Oxford University Press)

Haigh, Christopher. 1993. *English Reformations: Religion, Politics and Society under the Tudors* (Oxford: Oxford University Press)

Haigh, Christopher. 2007. *The Plain Man's Pathways to Heaven: Kinds of Christianity in Post-Reformation England, 1570–1640* (Oxford: Oxford University Press)

Haigh, Christopher. 2016. '"Theological Wars": "Socinians" v. "Antinomians" in Restoration England', *Journal of Ecclesiastical History*, 67/2: 325–50

Hallett, Nicky. 2012. 'Philip Sidney in the Cloister: The Reading Habits of English Nuns in Seventeenth-Century Antwerp', *Journal for Early Modern Cultural Studies*, 12/3: 88–116

Hallett, Nicky. 2013. *The Senses of Religious Communities, 1600–1800: Early Modern Convents of Pleasure* (Farnham and Burlington, VT: Ashgate)

Halpern, Maya. 2019. 'Religion, Grammar and Style: Wittgenstein and Hamman', *European Review*, 27/2: 195–209

Hamill, Graham. 2012. 'Blumenberg and Schmitt on the Rhetoric of Political Theology', in *Political Theology and Early Modernity*, ed. by Graham Hamill and Julia Reinhart Lupton (Chicago: University of Chicago Press), pp. 84–103

Hamilton, Donna B. 2005. *Anthony Munday and the Catholics, 1560–1633* (Farnham and Burlington, VT: Ashgate Publishing)

Hamlin, Hannibal. 2013. *The Bible in Shakespeare* (London: Oxford University Press)

Hannay, Margaret. 1983. 'Psalms Done Into Meter: The Common Psalms of John Milton and of the Bay Colony', *Christianity and Literature*, 32/3: 19–29

Harnack, Andrew. 1987. 'Both Protestant and Catholic: George Herbert and "To All Angels and Saints"', *George Herbert Journal*, 11/1: 23–39

Harris, Barbara. 2018. *English Aristocratic Women and the Fabric of Piety, 1450–1550* (Amsterdam: Amsterdam University Press)

Harrison, Robert. 2003. *The Dominion of the Dead* (Chicago and London: University of Chicago Press)

Harriss, Patricia. 2010. 'Mary Ward in Her Own Writings', *Recusant History*, 30/2: 229–39

Harvey, Andrew. 2005. 'Crossing Wits: Donne, Herbert and Sacramental Rhetoric', in *Renaissance Papers 2004*, ed by Christopher Cobb and Thomas Hester (Woodbridge and Rochester, NY: Boydell & Brewer), pp. 69–84

Hasty, Will. 2009. 'The Singularity of Aura and the Artistry of Translation: Martin Luther's Bible as Artwork', *Monatschefte*, 101/4: 457–68

Havens, Earl, and Elizabeth Patton. 2017. 'Underground Networks: Prisons and the Circulation of Counter-Reformation Books in Elizabethan England', in *Early Modern English Catholicism: Identity, Memory and Counter-Reformation* (Leiden and Boston: Brill), pp. 165–89

Hayden, Judy. 2010. *Of Love and War: The Political Voice in the Early Plays of Aphra Behn* (New York: Brill)

Healey, Thomas. 2004. 'Richard Crashaw', in *Dictionary of National Biography*

Hefling, Charles. 2021. *The Book of Common Prayer: A Guide* (New York: Oxford University Press)

Heinemann, Margot. 1980. *Puritanism and Theatre: Thomas Middleton and Opposition Drama under the Early Stuarts* (Cambridge: Cambridge University Press)

Helgerson, Richard. 1988. *Forms of Nationhood: The Elizabethan Writing of England* (Chicago and London: The University of Chicago Press)

Helm, Paul. 2010. *Calvin at the Centre* (London and New York: Oxford University Press)

Henry, John. 2022. 'Sir Kenelm Digby, the Immortality of the Soul, and Philosophical Theology in Seventeenth-Century England', *The Philosophy of Kenelm Digby,*

1603–65, ed. by Laura Georgescu and Hans Adriaenssen (Cham, Switzerland: Springer International Publishing), pp. 89–112

Hernandez, Alex. 2008. 'Commodity and Religion in Pope's "The Rape of the Locke"', in *Studies in English Literature*, 48/3: 569–84

Hibbard, Caroline. 2004. 'Henrietta Maria', in *Oxford Dictionary of National Biography*

Historical Manuscripts Commission: Eleventh Report, Appendix, Part 1: The Manuscripts of Henry Duncan Squire: Salvetti Correspondence. 1887 (London: Her Majesty's Stationery Office)

Hobby, Elaine. 1991. '"No Stolen Object but Her Own": Behn's Rover and Killigrew's Thomaso', *Women's Writing*, 6/1: 113–27

Hobby, Elaine. 2021. 'Review: *The Female Baroque in Early Modern English Literary Culture*', *Tulsa Studies in English Literature*, 40/2: 395–8

Hopkins, Lisa. 1994. *John Ford's Political Theatre* (Manchester: Manchester University Press)

Hopkins, Lisa. 2000. *Christopher Marlowe: A Literary Life* (Basingstoke: Palgrave)

Hopkins, Lisa. 2008. *The Cultural Uses of the Caesars on the English Renaissance Stage* (Aldershot and Burlington, VT: Ashgate)

Hopkins, Lisa. 2019. 'Beautiful Polecats: The Living and the Dead in *Julius Caesar*', in *Shakespeare Survey*, 72: 160–70

Sierra, Horacio. 2009. 'Convents as Feminist Utopias: Margaret Cavendish's *The Convent of Pleasure* and The Potential of Closeted Dramas and Communities', *Women's Studies*, 38: 647–69

Horsfield, Peter. 2015. *From Jesus to the Internet: A History of Christianity and Media* (Chichester: Wiley-Blackwell)

Houliston, Victor. 2022. 'Paul's Cross and the State Church: The Case of John Donne and the Jesuits', *Old St. Paul's and Culture*, ed. by Altman Shanyn and Jonathan Buckner, Early Modern Literature in History (Cham: Palgrave Macmillan), pp. 173–96

Houliston, Victor. 2021. 'Rehabilitating Robert Persons: Then and Now', in *Reformation Reputations: The Power of the Individual in English Reformation History*, ed. by David Crankshaw and George Gross (Cham, Switzerland: Palgrave Macmillan), pp. 421–47

Hrdlicka, Steven. 2019. 'Laborious Ben Jonson', *Ben Jonson Journal*, 26/1: 21–39

Hubbard, Gillian. 2014. 'Stoics, Epicureans, and the "Sound Sincerity of the Gospel" in Book 2 of Edmund Spenser's *The Faerie Queene*', *Studies in Philology*, 111/2: 225–54

Hui, Andrew. 2017. 'The Soundscape of the Dying Pagan Gods in Milton's Nativity Ode', *Modern Language Quarterly*, 78/3: 349–72

Hui, Andrew. 2020. *The Poetics of Ruins in Renaissance Literature* (New York: Fordham University Press)

Hulse, Lynne. 2004. 'Cavendish, William, First Duke of Newcastle upon Tyne', in *Oxford Dictionary of National Biography*

Hume, Robert. 2011. 'The Socio-Politics of London Comedy from Jonson to Steele', *The Huntington Library Quarterly*, 74/2: 187–217

Hunt, Maurice. 2016. 'Jonson vs. Shakespeare: The Roman Plays', *Ben Jonson Journal*, 23/1: 75–100
Hutchins, Christine. 2012. 'English Anti-Petrarchism: Imbalance and Excess in "the Englishe Straine" of the Sonnet', *Studies in Philology*, 109/5: 552–80
Hutchinson, Lucy. 1863. *Memoirs of the Life of Colonel Hutchinson, Governor of Nottingham Castle and Town* (London and New York: Henry G. Bohn and Covent Garden)
Hutson, Lorna. 2007. *The Invention of Suspicion: Law and Mimesis in Shakespeare and Renaissance Drama* (Oxford: Oxford University Press)
Howe, Elizabeth. (1981). 'Donne and the Spanish Mystics on Ecstasy', in *Notre Dame English Journal*, 13/2: 29–44
Hwang, Jane. 2006. 'Catholic Martyrdom in Dekker and Massinger's *The Virgin Martyr* and the Early Modern Threat of "Turning Turk"', *English Literary History*, 73/1: 83–107
Hwang, Jane. 2010. *Islamic Conversion and Christian Resistance on the Early Modern Stage* (Edinburgh: Edinburgh University Press)
Hwang, Su-Kyung. 2016. 'From Priests' to Actors' Wardrobe: Controversial, Commercial, and Costumized Vestments', *Studies in Philology*, 113/2: 282–305
Jackson, Clare. 2005. 'Judicial Torture, the Liberties of the Subject, and Anglo-Scottish Relations, 1660–1690', in *Anglo-Scottish Relations from 1603–1900*, ed. by T. C. Snout (Oxford and New York: Oxford University Press), pp. 75–102
Jaecheol, Kim. 2021. 'The Price of Virginity in the Early Modern Theatre: Middleton and Rowley's *The Changeling*', in *Women's Studies*, 50/7: 709–26
Janes, Dominic, and Gary Waller (eds). 2010. *Walsingham in Literature and Culture from the Middle Ages to Modernity* (Farnham and Burlington, VT: Ashgate)
Jensen, Gordon. 2012. 'Embedded Commentary in Luther's Translation of Romans 3', in *The Unfolding of Words: Commentary in the Age of Erasmus*, ed. by Judith Henderson (Toronto, Buffalo and London: University of Toronto Press), pp. 118–40
Jensen, H. James. 1996. *The Sensational Restoration* (Bloomington, IN: Indiana University Press)
Johnson, Kimberley. 2014. *Made Flesh: Sacrament and Poetics in Post-Reformation England* (Philadelphia: University of Pennsylvania Press)
Johnson, S. F. 'The Spanish Tragedy, or Babylon Revisited', in *Essays in Shakespeare and Elizabethan Drama in Honour of Harding Craig*, ed. by Richard Hosley (London: Routledge & Kegan Paul), pp. 23–36
Johnson, Kimberly. 2009. 'Richard Crashaw's Indigestible Poetics', *Modern Philology*, 107/1: 32–51
Johnson, Odai. 1996. 'Pope-Burning Pageants: Performing the Exclusion Crisis', *Theatre Survey*, 37/1: 35–57
Jones, Elisabeth. 2009. 'From Chamber to Church: The Remarkable Emergence of Thomas Sternhold as Psalmist for the Church of England', *Reformation and Renaissance Review*, 11/1: 29–56
Jones, Emrys (ed.). 1991; repr. 2002. *The New Oxford Book of Sixteenth-Century Verse* (London: Oxford University Press)
Jones, Mark. 2009. 'Some Versions of the Hortus Conclusus in Elizabethan Landscape and Literature', *Literature Compass*, 6/2: 349–61

Jones, Norman, and Paul Whitfield White. 1996. 'Gorboduc and Royal Marriage Politics: An Elizabethan Playgoer's Report of the Premiere Performance', *English Literary Renaissance*, 26/1: 3–16

Jonson, Ben. 1616. *The Workes of Beniamin Jonson* (London)

Jonson, Ben. 1947; repr. 1965. *The Poems, The Prose Works*, ed. by C.H. Hereford Percy Simpson and Evelyn Simpson (Oxford: Clarendon Press)

Judge, Jeannie. 2011. 'Keeping the Major Feasts in George Herbert's the Temple', *George Herbert Journal*, 35/1–2: 110–26

Kathman, David. 2004. 'Davenport, Robert', in *Oxford Dictionary of National Biography*

Kaula, David. 1981. '"Let Us Be Sacrificers": Religious Motifs in Julius Caesar', *Shakespeare Studies*, 14: 197–214

Kearney, James. 2002. 'Enshrining Idolatry in the Faerie Queene', *English Literary Renaissance*, 32/1: 3–30

Kearney, Michael. 2022. 'Melanchthon's Dialectic Genre and the Rhetoric of Reformation', in *Rhetorica*, 40/1: 23–42

Kelly, Erna. 2014. 'Playing with Religion: Converts, Cloisters, Martyrdom, and Vows', *Early Modern Literary Studies*, 14: 1–24

Kempis, Thomas à. 1952; repr. 1959. *The Imitation of Christ*, trans by Leo Sherley-Price (Harmondsworth: Penguin)

Kerrigan, John. 1996. *Revenge Tragedy: Aeschylus to Armageddon* (Oxford: Clarendon Press)

Kilroy, Gerard. 2015. *Edmund Campion: A Scholarly Life* (London: Routledge, 2015)

Klause, John. 1994. 'Hope's Gambit: The Jesuitical, Protestant, Skeptical Origins of Donne's Heroic Ideal', *Studies in Philology*, 94/2: 181–215

Knight, Alison. 2014. 'The "Very, Very Words": (Mis)Quoting Scripture in Lancelot Andrewes's and John Donne's Sermons on Job, 19: 23–27', *Studies in Philology*, 111/3: 442–69

Koch, Jonathan. 2019. '"The Phanaticks Tyring Room": Dryden and the Poetics of Toleration', *Studies in Philology*, 116/3: 539–66

Kranidas, Thomas. 2013. 'Milton Rewrites *the Doctrine and Discipline of Divorce*', *Studies in English Literature 1500–1900*, 53/1: 117–35

Kuchar, Gary. 2006. 'Henry Constable and the Question of Catholic Poetics: Affective Piety and Erotic Identification in the Spirituall Sonnettes', in *Philological Quarterly*, 85/1, 69–90

Kuchar, Gary. 2007. 'Aemilia Lanyer and the Virgin's Swoon: Theology and Iconography in Salve Deus Rex Judaeorum', in *English Literary Renaissance*, 37/1: 47–73

Kuchar, Gary. 2013. 'Poetry and the Eucharist in the English Renaissance', *George Herbert Journal*, 36/2: 128–49

Kuchar, Gary. 2018. 'Poetry and Sacrament in the English Renaissance', in *A Companion to English Poetry*, ed. by Catherine Bates (Hoboken, NJ, and Chichester: Wiley Blackwell), pp. 50–62

Kuhn, John. 2017. 'Sejanus, the King's Men Altar Scenes, and the Theatrical Production of Paganism', *Early Theatre*, 20/2: 77–98

Kuin, Roger. 2021. 'Philip Sidney's Travels in the Holy Roman Empire', *Renaissance Quarterly*, 74/3: 802–28

Kurzon, Denis. 2018. 'Literal Interpretation and Political Expediency: The Case of Thomas More', in *Pragmatics and Beyond*, New Series, 288, ed. by Dennis Kurzon and Barbara Kryl-Kastovsky (Amsterdam and Philadelphia: John Benjamins Publishing Company), pp. 81–97

Kyd, Thomas. 2013. *The Spanish Tragedy, by Thomas Kyd*, ed. byClara Calvo and Jesus Tronch, *Arden Early Modern Drama* (London: Bloomsbury)

Lake, Peter. 2012. 'Ben Jonson and the Politics of Conversion: *Catiline* and the Relocation of Roman (Catholic) Virtue', *Ben Jonson Journal*, 19/2: 163–89

Lake, Peter. 2015. 'Shakespeare's Julius Caesar and the Search for a Usable (Christian?) Past', *Shakespeare and Early Modern Religion*, ed. by David Lowenstein and Michael Whitmore (Cambridge: Cambridge University Press), pp. 111–30

Lake, Peter. 2016. *How Shakespeare Put Politics on the Stage: Power and Succession in the History Plays* (New Haven, CT, and London: Yale University Press)

Lake, Peter. 2020. *Hamlet's Choice: Religion and Resistance in Shakespeare's Revenge Tragedies* (New Haven, CT, and London: Yale University Press)

Lane, Calvin. 2016. 'John Milton's Elegy for Lancelot Andrewes (1626) and the Dynamic Nature of Religious Identity in Early Stuart England', *Anglican and Episcopal History*, 85/4: 468–91

Lanyer, Aemilia. 1611. *Salve Deus Rex Judaeorum* (London)

Leach, Robert. 2001. 'As You Like It: A Robin Hood Play', *English Studies: A Journal of English Language and Literature*, 82/5: 393–400

Lehner, Ulrich. 2016. *The Catholic Enlightenment: The Forgotten History of A Global Movement* (Oxford: Oxford University Press)

Lenton, Francis. 1638. *Great Britains Beauties, or, The Female Glory Epitomized, in Encomiastick Anagramms, and Acrostiches, upon the Highly Honoured Names of the Queenes Most Gracious Majestie, and the Gallant Lady-Masquers in Her Graces Glorious Grand-Masque. Presented at White-Hall on Shrove-Tuesday at Night, by the Queenes Majestie and Her Ladies* (London)

Leone, Anna. 2013. *The End of the Pagan City: Religion, Economy, and Urbanism in Late Antique North Africa* (Oxford: Oxford University Press)

Lester, G. A. (ed.). 1981. *Three Late Medieval Morality Plays: Mankind, Everyman, Mundus et Infans* (New York and London: Norton)

Leveneur, Tanneguy. 1862. *Mémoires Inédites Du Conte Leveneur de Tillières, Ambassadeur En Angleterre Sur Le Cour de Charles I et Son Marriage Avec Henriette de France* (Paris: Poulet-Mallassis)

Levin, Carole. 2015. 'Queen Margaret in Shakespeare and Chronicles: She Wolf or Heroic Spirit' in *Scholars and Poets Talk about Queens*, ed. by Carole Levin, Christine Stewart Nuñez, Queenship and Power (New York and Basingstoke: Palgrave Macmillan), pp. 111–32

Lewalski, Barbara. 1979. *Protestant Poetics and the Seventeenth Century Religious Lyric* (Princeton: Princeton University Press)

Li, Chi-Fang Sophia. 2014. 'The Roaring Girl in Retrospect: The RSC Production of 1983', *New Theatre Quarterly*, 30/3: 274–97

Llewellyn, Nigel. 1996. 'Honour in Life, Death and in the Memory: Funeral Monuments in Early Modern England', *Transactions of the Royal Historical Society*, 6: 179–200

Lovascio, Domenico. 2017. 'Rewriting Julius Caesar as a National Villain in Early Modern English Drama', *English Literary Renaissance*, 47/2: 218–50

Lovelace, Richard. 1649. *Lucasta Epodes Odes, Sonnets, Songs &c. To Which Is Added Aramantha, A Pastorall. By Richard Lovelace, Esq* (London)

Loxley, James. 2012. 'Echoes as Evidence in the Poetry of Andrew Marvell', *Studies in English Literature 1500–1900*, 52/1: 165–85

Luminalia, or The Festivall of Light. Personated in a Masque at Court, by the Queenes Majestie, and Her Ladies. On Shrovetuesday Night, 1637. 1638. (London)

MacCulloch, Diarmaid. 1990. *The Later Reformation in England, 1547–1603* (Basingstoke: Palgrave Macmillan)

MacCulloch, Diarmaid. 2003. *Reformation: Europe's House Divided, 1490–1700* (London: Penguin)

MacCulloch, Diarmaid. 2017. *All Things Made New: Writings on the Reformation* (Falkirk: Penguin)

Macdonald, James Ross. 2015. 'The Redcrosse Knight and the Limits of Human Holiness', *Spenser Studies: A Renaissance Poetry Annual*, 30: 113–31

Mack, Charles. 2012. 'Beyond the Monumental: The Semiotics of Papal Authority in Renaissance Pienza', *Southeastern College Art Conference Review*, 16: 124–50

Mack, Peter. 2011. *A History of Renaissance Rhetoric* (Oxford and New York: Oxford University Press)

Madsen, Frank. 2017. 'Damnatio Memoriae', in *Europe in Crisis: Crime, Criminal Justice and the Way Forward: Essays in Honour of Nestor Courakis*, ed. by C. D. Spinellis, Nikolaos Theodokaris, Emmanoüil Billis, and George Papadimitrakopoulos (Athens: Ant. N. Sakkoulas Publishers), pp. 1217–33

Majumder, Doyeeta. 2017. 'Absolutism Without Tyranny in *Gorboduc*: The Changing Poetics of Tudor Political Drama', *Renaissance Studies*, 32/2: 201–18

Malcolmson, Christina. 2004. *George Herbert: A Literary Life* (New York: Palgrave Macmillan)

Marcus, Leah. 1993. 'Robert Herrick', in *The Cambridge Companion to English Poetry: Donne to Marvell*, ed. by Thomas Corns (Cambridge: Cambridge University Press), pp. 171–82

Maria Triumphans. Being a Discourse, Wherein (by Way of Dialogue) the B. Virgin Mother of God, Is Defended and Vindicated, from All Such Dishonours and Indignities, with Which the Precisions of These Our Days, Are Accustomed Unjustly to Charge Her. 1635. (Saint Omer)

Marlowe, Christopher. 1593. *Tamburlaine the Great. With His Impassionate Furie, for the Death of His Ladie and Love Faire Zenocrate: His Forme of Exhortation and Discipline to His Three Sons, and the Manner of His Own Death. The Second Part* (London)

Marlowe, Christopher. 2003. *The Complete Plays* (London: Penguin Classics)

Marring, Heather. 2011. 'Toward a Ritual Poetics: Dream of the Rood as a Case Study', *Oral Tradition*, 26/2: 391–410

Marshall, Peter. 2004. *Beliefs and the Dead in Reformation England* (London: Oxford University Press)

Marshall, Peter. 2012. 'The Naming of Protestant England', *Past & Present*, 214/1: 87–128

Marshall, Peter. 2017. *Heretics and Believers: A History of the English Reformation* (New Haven, CT: Yale University Press)

Marshall, Peter. 2020. 'Review: Permanent Revolution: The Reformation and the Illiberal Roots of Liberalism', *Journal of British Studies*, 59/1: 172–4

Martin, José, and Stephen Wittick. 2021. 'Introduction: Conversion, Cities and Theatre in the Early Modern World', in *Performing Conversion: Cities, Theatres and the Early Modern World*, ed. by José Martin and Stephen Wittick (Edinburgh: Edinburgh University Press), pp. 1–11

Martin, Michael. 2016. *Literature and the Encounter with God in Post-Reformation England* (London and New York: Routledge)

Martz, Louis. 2001. 'Donne, Herbert and the Worm of Controversy', *Early Modern Literary Studies*, 7: 1–13

Martz, Louis. 1954 rev. 1962 repr. 1974. *The Poetry of Meditation: A Study in English Religious Meditation of the Seventeenth Century* (New Haven, CT and London: Yale University Press)

Maslan, R. W. (ed). 2002. *An Apology for Poetry, or The Defence of Poesy: Sir Philip Sidney* (New York: Manchester University Press)

May, Susan. 2005. 'The Piccolomini Library in Siena Cathedral: A New Reading with Particular Reference to Two Compartments of the Vault Decoration', *Renaissance Studies: Journal of the Society for Renaissance Studies*, 19/3: 287–324

McClain, Lisa. 2015. 'On a Mission: Priests, Jesuits, "Jesuitresses," and Catholic Missionary Efforts in Tudor-Stuart England, *The Catholic Historical Review*, 101/3: 437–62

McCoag, Thomas, '"Guiding Souls to Goodness and Devotion": Clandestine Publications and the English Jesuit Mission', in *Publishing Subversive Texts in Elizabethan England and the Polish Commonwealth*, ed. by Theresa Bela, Clarinda Calma and Jolanta Rzegocka (Leiden and Boston: Brill, 2016), pp. 93–109

McDowell, Nicholas. 2006. 'Early Modern Stereotypes and the Rise of English: Jonson, Dryden, Arnold, Eliot', *The Critical Quarterly*, 48/3: 25–34

McFarlane, Ian, David Ferguson, Karen Kilby and Iain Torrance (eds), *The Cambridge Dictionary of Christian Theology* (Cambridge: Cambridge University Press, 2011)

McGrath, Patrick. 2012. 'Reconsidering Laud: Puritans and Anglican Asceticism', *Prose Studies*, 34/1: 32–49

McJannet, Linda. 2006. *Dialogue in English Plays and Histories about the Ottoman Turks* (New York: Palgrave MacMillan)

McLaughlan, Elizabeth, and Gail Thomas. 1975. 'Communion in The Temple', in *Studies in English Literature, 1500–1900*, 15/1: 111–24

McPherson, David. 1974. 'Ben Jonson's Library and Marginalia: An Annotated Catalogue', *Studies in Philology*, 71/5: 1–106

Melville, Charles. 2019. 'Visualising Tamerlane: History and Its Image', *Iran*, 57/1: 83–106

Mentzer, Raymond. 2014. 'Reformed Liturgical Practices', in *A Companion to the Eucharist in the Reformation*, ed. by Wandel Lee Palmer (e-book: Brill), pp. 231–50

Meskill, Lynn. 2008. 'Ben Jonson's 1616 Folio: A Revolution in Print?', *Études Épistémè: Revue de Littérature et de Civilisation*, 14

Metso, Pekka, Nina Maskulin, and Teuvu Laitila. 2020. 'Tradition, Gender and Empowerment: The Birth of Theotokos Society in Helsinki, Finland', in *Orthodox Christianity and Gender: Dynamics of Tradition, Culture and Lived Practice*, ed. by Helen Kupari and Elina Vuola (London and New York: Routledge), pp. 131–46

Michelle, O., and Thomas Callaghan. 2009. *Thomas Middleton: Renaissance Dramatist* (Edinburgh: Edinburgh University Press)

Middleton, Thomas, and Thomas Dekker. 2011. *The Roaring Girl*, ed. by Jennifer Panek (New York: W.W. Norton)

Miles, Laura. 2020. *The Virgin Mary's Book at the Annunciation: Reading, Interpretation and Devotion in Medieval England* (Cambridge: D.S. Brewer)

Miller, Shannon. 2008. 'Serpentine Eve: Milton and the Seventeenth Century Debate over Women', *Milton Quarterly*, 42/1: 44–68

Millett, L. 1999. 'Construing Statutes', in *Statute Law Review*, 20/2: 107–10

Milton, Anthony. 2011. *Catholic and Reformed: The Roman and Protestant Churches in English Protestant Thought, 1600–1640*, Cambridge Studies in Early Modern British History (Cambridge: Cambridge University Press)

Milton, Anthony. 2015. 'Arminians, Laudians, Anglicans, and Revisionists: Back to Which Drawing Board?' *The Huntington Library Quarterly*, 78/4: 723–42

Milton, Anthony. 2021. *England's Second Reformation: The Battle for the Church of England*, Cambridge Studies in Early Modern History (Cambridge: Cambridge University Press)

Min, Eun Kyung. 2019. 'Fictions of Obligation: Contract and Romance in Margaret Cavendish and Aphra Behn', *Eighteenth-Century Fiction*, 32/2: 245–69

Miner, Robert. 2009. *Thomas Aquinas on the Passions: A Study of Summa Theologiae 1a2ae 22–48* (Cambridge: Cambridge University Press)

Moore, A. T. (ed). 2002. *Love's Sacrifice: John Ford* (New York: Manchester University Press)

Moretti, Thomas. 2014. 'Via Media Theatricality and Religious Fantasy in Thomas Dekker and Philip Massinger's The Virgin Martyr', *Renaissance Drama*, 42/2: 243–70

Morris, Jeremy. 2022. *A People's Church: A History of the Church of England* (London: Profile)

Morrissey, Mary. 2022. 'Was Donne a Catholic?' Conversion, Conformity and Early Modern English Confessional Identities', in *The Review of English Studies*, 74: 64–77

Mottram, Stuart. 2019. *Ruins and Reformation in Spenser, Shakespeare and Marvell* (Oxford: Oxford University Press)

Moul, Victoria. 2010. *Jonson, Horace and the Classical Tradition* (Cambridge: Cambridge University Press)

Mueller, William. 1962. *John Donne: Preacher* (Princeton, NJ: Princeton University Press)

Mullaney, Stephen. 2015. *The Reformation of the Emotions in the Age of Shakespeare* (Chicago and London: University of Chicago Press)

Munday, Anthony. 1601. *THE DEATH OF ROBERT EARL OF HUNTINGTON, OTHERWISE CALLED Robin Hood of Merrie Sherwodd: With the Lamentable Tragedie of Chaste Matilda, His Faire Maid MARIAN, Poisoned at Dunmowe by King John* (London)

Munday, Anthony, 1601. *The DOWNFALL OF ROBERT Earl of Huntington, AFTERWARD CALLED Robin Hood of Merrie Sherwode: with his love to chaste Matilda, the lord Fitzwater's daughter, afterward his fair Maid Marian* (London)

Munroe, Lucy. 2019. 'The Queen and the Cockpit: Henrietta Maria's Theatrical Patronage Revisited', *Shakespeare Bulletin*, 37: 25–45

Murakami, Ineke. 2011. *Moral Play and Counterpublic: Transformations in Moral Drama, 1465–1599* (New York and London: Routledge)

Murray, Molly. 2009. *The Poetics of Conversion in Early Modern English Literature: Verse and Change from Donne to Dryden* (Cambridge: Cambridge University Press)

Neill, Michael. 1992. 'Feasts Put Down as Funeral', in *True Rites and Maimed Rites: Ritual and Anti-Ritual in Shakespeare and His Age*, ed. by Linda Woodbridge and Edward Berry (Urbana, IL, and Chicago: University of Illinois Press), pp. 47–74

Newstok, Scott. 2009. *Quoting Death in Early Modern England: The Poetics of Epitaphs Beyond the Tomb*, Early Modern Literature in History (London: Palgrave Macmillan)

Nichols, Jennifer. 2011. 'Dionysian Negative Theology in Donne's "A Nocturn Upon S. Lucie's Day', *Texas Studies in Literature and Language*, 53/3: 352–67

Novak, Maximilian. 2001. 'Libertinism and Sexuality', in *A Companion to Restoration Drama*, ed. by Susan Owen (Malden, MA; Oxford and Victoria, Australia: Blackwell), pp. 53–68

Oakley-Brown, Liz. 2005. *Robin Hood: Medieval and Post-Medieval*, ed. by Helen Philips (Dublin: Four Courts Press), pp. 113–28

O'Brien, Susan. 2004. 'Ward, Mary, 1585–1645', in *Oxford Dictionary of National Biography*

O'Carrigain, Eamonn. 2005. *Ritual and the Rood: Liturgical Images and the Old English Poems of the Dream of the Rood Tradition*. (London and Toronto: Toronto Press)

O'Neill, Michael (ed.). 2010. *The Cambridge History of English Poetry* (Cambridge: Cambridge University Press), II

O'Rourke, Marjorie. 2000. 'Home to Mother: Regaining Milton's Paradise', *Modern Philology*, 97/4: 499–527

Orgel, Stephen. 2022. *The Idea of the Book and the Creation of Literature* (London: Oxford University Press)

Outterson-Murphy, Sarah. 2016. '"Remember Me": The Ghost and Its Spectators in Hamlet', in *Shakespeare Bulletin: The Journal of Early Modern Drama in Performance*, 34: 253–75

Palmer, Ada. 2020. 'Gods in the Garden: Visions of the Pagan Other in the Rome of Julius II', *Journal of Religion in Europe*, 12/3: 285–309

Parker, Barbara. 2011. '"Cursed Necromancy": Marlowe's Faustus as Anti-Catholic Satire', *Marlowe Studies*, 1: 59–77

Parker, Charles. 2014. 'Diseased Bodies, Defiled Souls: Corporality and Religious Difference in the Reformation', *Renaissance Quarterly*, 67/4: 1265–97

Parry, Graham. 2006. *The Arts of the Anglican Counter-Reformation: Glory, Laud and Honour* (Woodbridge: Boydell Press)

Parry, Graham. 2011. 'Sacred Space in Laudian England', in *Sacred Text – Sacred Space: Architectural, Spiritual and Literary Convergence in England and Wales*, ed. by Joseph Sterrett and Peter Thomas (Leiden and Boston: Brill), pp. 123–41

Pask, Kevin. 2013. *The Fairy Way of Writing: Shakespeare to Tolkien* (Baltimore, MD: The Johns Hopkins University Press)

Paster, Gail. 1997. 'Nervous Tension: Networks of Blood and Spirit in the Early Modern Body', in *The Body in Parts: Fantasies of Corporality in Early Modern Europe*, ed. by David Hillman and Carla Mazzio (London: Routledge), pp. 107–28

Pelikan, Jarosav. 1985. *The Christian Tradition: A History of the Development of Doctrine, 4: Reformation of Church and Dogma, 1300–1700* (Chicago: University of Chicago Press)

Perez-Jauregui, Maria Jesus. 2016. 'A Queen in a "Purple Robe": Henry Constable's Poetic Tribute to Mary, Queen of Scots', *Studies in Philology*, 113/3: 577–94

Perry, Nandra. 2015. 'Turning the Tables: Richard Crashaw Reads the Protestant Altar', *Studies in Philology*, 112/2: 303–26

Persons, Robert, SJ, *The Christian Directory (1582), The First Book of the Christian Exercise Appertayninig to Resolution*, ed. by Victor Houliston (Leiden, Boston and Cologne: Brill, 1998)

Peters, Christine. 2009. *Cambridge Studies in Early Modern British History: Patterns of Piety: Women, Gender and Religion in Late Medieval and Reformation England* (Cambridge: Cambridge University Press)

Phillips, Joshua. 2014. 'Labor's Lost: The Work of Devotion in Tudor Literature', *Journal of Medieval and Early Modern Studies*, 44/1: 45–68

Pierce, Helen. 2004. 'Unseemly Pictures: Political Graphic Satire in England, c.1600–c.1650' (PhD thesis, University of York)

Pitkin, Barbara. 2020. *Calvin, the Bible, and History* (New York: Oxford University Press)

Pollard, A. J. 2004. *Imagining Robin Hood: The Late Medieval Stories in Historical Context* (London and New York: Routledge)

Pollard, Tanya. 2010. 'Tragedy and Revenge', in *The Cambridge Companion to English Renaissance Tragedy*, ed. by Emma Smith and Garett Sullivan (Cambridge: Cambridge University Press), pp. 58–72

Pollard, Tanya. 2012. "What's Hecuba to Shakespeare?," *Renaissance Quarterly*, 65/4: 1060–93

Prince, Michael. 2013. 'Religio Laici v. Religio Laici: Dryden, Blount and the Origin of English Deism', *Modern Language Quarterly*, 74/1: 29–66

Prusak, Bernard. 2014. 'Explaining Eucharistic "Real Presence": Moving beyond a Medieval Conundrum', *Theological Studies*, 75/2: 231–59

Pudney, Eric. 2019. *Scepticism and Belief in English Witchcraft Drama, 1538–1681* (Lund: Lund University Press)

Questier, Michael (ed.). 2015. 'Historical Introduction', in *The Limits of Conformity in Elizabethan England: A Plea for a Priest*, ed. by Michael Questier, Camden Fifth Series, 48 (2015), 103–20

Ramachandran, Ayesha. 2015. 'Humanism and Its Discontents', *Spenser Studies A Renaissance Poetry Annual*, 46/1: 3–18

Ranjan, Ghosh. 2013. 'Ben Jonson and His Reader: An Aesthetics of Antagonism', *The Comparatist*, 37: 138–56

Rankin, Mark. 2019. 'Richard Topcliffe and the Book Culture of the Elizabethan Catholic Underground', *Renaissance Quarterly*, 72: 492–536

Rapley, Elizabeth. 1994. 'Women and the Religious Vocation in Seventeenth-Century France', *French Historical Studies*, 18/3: 613

Ray, Sid. 2012. *Mother Queens and Princely Sons: Rogue Madonnas in the Age of Shakespeare* (New York: Palgrave Macmillan)

Raylor, Timothy. 1999. '"Pleasure Reconciled to Virtue": William Cavendish, Ben Jonson, and the Decorative Scheme of Bolsover Castle', *Renaissance Quarterly*, 52/2: 402–39

Read, Sophie. 2013. *Eucharist and the Poetic Imagination in Early Modern England* (Cambridge: Cambridge University Press)

Rees, Graham, and Maria Wakely. 2010. *Publishing, Politics and Culture: The King's Printers in the Reign of James I and VI* (Oxford: Oxford University Press)

Reinhart Lupton, Julia. 2018. *Shakespeare Dwelling: Designs for the Theatre of Life* (Chicago and London: The University of Chicago Press)

Rex, Richard. 2017. *The Making of Martin Luther* (Princeton: Princeton University Press)

Rickard, Jane. 2020. 'Ben Jonson and Posterity: Redeption, Reputation, Legacy', in *Seventeenth-Century Readers of Jonson's 1616 Works*, ed. by Martin Butler and Jane Rickard (Cambridge: Cambridge University Press), pp. 85–104

Rickard, Matt. 2022. 'Milton and the Education Monopoly', *Studies in Philology*, 119/3: 495–525

Rieger, Gabriel. 2016. *Sex and Satiric Tragedy in Early Modern England: Penetrating Wit* (New York: Routledge)

Riehl, Anna. 2011. *The Face of Queenship: Early Modern Representations of Elizabeth I* (Basingstoke: Palgrave Macmillan)

Rist, John. 2014. *Augustine Deformed: Love, Sin and Freedom in the Western Moral Tradition* (Cambridge: Cambridge University Press)

Rist, Thomas. 2000. 'Topical Comedy: On the Unity of Love's Labour's Lost', *Ben Jonson Journal*, 7/1: 65–87

Rist, Thomas. 2009. 'Merry; Marry, Mary: Shakespearean Wordplay and *Twelfth Night*', *Shakespeare Survey*, 62: 81–91

Rist, Thomas. 2013a. 'Catharsis as 'Purgation' in Shakespearean Drama', in *Shakespearean Sensations: Experiencing Literature in Early Modern England*, ed. by Katharine Craik and Tanya Pollard (Cambridge: Cambridge University Press), pp. 138–54

Rist, Thomas. 2013b. 'Monuments and Religion: George Herbert's Poetic Materials', in *The Arts of Remembrance in Early Modern England: Memorial Cultures of the Post Reformation*, ed. by Andrew Gordon and Thomas Rist, Material Readings in Early Modern Literature (Farnham and Burlington, VT: Ashgate), pp. 105–24

Rist, Thomas. 2015. 'Mary of Recusants and Reform: Literary Memory and Defloration', in *Biblical Women in Early Modern Literary Culture*, ed. by Victoria Brownlee and Laura Gallagher (Manchester: Manchester University Press), pp. 162–79

Rist, Thomas. 2016. '"Those Organnons by Which It Mooves", Shakespearean Theatre and the Romish Cult of the Dead', in *Shakespeare Survey*, pp. 228–42

Ritchey, Sarah. 2014. *Holy Matter: Changing Perceptions of the Material World in Late Medieval Christianity* (Ithaca and London: Cornell University Press)

Robertson, Randy. 2006. 'Lovelace and the "Barbed Censurors": Lucasta and Civil War Censorship', in *Studies in Philology*, 103/4: 465–98

Robey, Tracy. 2013. 'Damnatio Memoriae: The Rebirth of Memory in Renaissance Florence', *Renaissance and Reformation / Renaissance et Réforme*," 36/3: 5–32

Rogers, Pat. 2014. 'Alexander Pope: Religion, Politics, and Poetry', in *A Companion to British Literature*, ed. by Robert Demaria, Heesog Chang and Samantha Zacher (Chichester: Wiley Blackwell), pp. 128–42

Rose, Mary Beth. 2017. *Plotting Motherhood in Medieval, Early Modern and Modern Literature*, Early Modern Cultural Studies (London: Palgrave Macmillan)

Rosendale, Timothy. 2007. *Liturgy and Literature in the Making of Protestant England* (Cambridge: Cambridge University Press)

Rosendale, Timothy. 2018. *Theology and Agency in Early Modern Literature* (Cambridge, England: Cambridge University Press)

Ross, Shaun. 2016. 'Sacrifices of Thanksgiving: The Eucharist in the Temple', *George Herbert Journal*, 40/1-2: 1–40

Ross, Shaun. 2017. 'Robert Southwell: Sacrament and Self', *English Literary Renaissance*, 47/1: 73–109

Rothenberg, David. 2011. *The Flower of Paradise: Marian Devotion and Secular Song in Medieval and Renaissance Music* (Oxford: Oxford University Press)

Rubic, Margeret. 2020. 'Excess and Artifice: The Depiction of the Emotions in Aphra Behn's Amatory Fiction', *Women's Writing*, 27/3: 372–92

Rubin, Miri. 2009. *Mother of God: A History of the Virgin Mary* (London: Allen Lane)

Rustici, Craig. 2006. *The Afterlife of Pope Joan: Deploying the Popess Legend in Early Modern England* (Ann Arbor: University of Michigan Press)

Rutter, Tom. 2017. *Shakespeare and the Lord Admiral's Men: Reading Across Repertories on the London Stage, 1594–1600* (Cambridge: Cambridge University Press)

Ryrie, Alec. 2013. *Being Protestant in Reformation Britain* (London: Oxford University Press)

Ryrie, Alec. 2017. *Protestants: The Radicals Who Made the Modern World* (London: William Collins)

Schaffauer, Thomas. 2014. 'From Sacrifice to Supper: Eucharistic Practice in the Lutheran Reformation', in *A Companion to the Eucharist in the Reformation*, ed. by Wandel Lee Palmer (Leiden: Brill), pp. 205–30

Schneider, Brian. 2011. *The Framing Text in Early Modern English Drama: 'Whining' Prologues and 'Armed' Epilogues*, Studies in Performance and Early Modern Drama," (Farnham and Burlington, VT: Ashgate)

Schreyer, Kurt. 2014. *Shakespeare's Medieval Craft: Remnants of the Mysteries on the London Stage* (Ithaca and London: Cornell University Press)

Schwartz, Regina. 2005. 'Tragedy and the Mass', *Literature and Theology*, 19/2: 139–58

Schwartz, Regina. 2008. *Sacramental Poetics at the Dawn of Secularism: When God Left the World* (Stanford: Stanford University Press)

Schwytzer, Philip. 2010. *Literature, Nationalism and Memory in Early Modern England and Whales* (Cambridge: Cambridge University Press)

Scodel, Joshua. 1991. *The English Poetic Epitaph: Commemoration and Conflict from Jonson to Wordsworth* (Ithaca and London: Cornell University Press)

Scott Kastan, David. 2013. *A Will to Believe: Shakespeare and Religion* (Oxford: Oxford University Press)

Scott, Thomas. 1626. *The Second Part of Vox Populi* (London)

Searle, Alison. 2013. 'Ben Jonson and Religion', *The Oxford Handbook of Ben Jonson*, ed by Eugene Giddens (online edition: Oxford Academic, https://doi.org/10.1093/oxfordhb/9780199544561.001.0001)

Shagan, Ethan. 2011. *The Rule of Moderation: Violence, Religion and the Politics of Restraint in Early Modern England* (Cambridge: Cambridge University Press)

Shagan, Ethan, and Debora Shuger (eds). 2016. *Religion in Tudor England: An Anthology of Primary Sources* (Texas: Baylor University Press)

Shami, Jeanne. 2003. *John Donne and Conformity in Crisis in the Late Jacobean Pulpit* (Cambridge: D.S. Brewer)

Shell, Alison. 1999. *Catholicism, Controversy and the English Literary Imagination* (Cambridge: Cambridge University Press)

Shohet, Lauren. 2010. *Reading Masques: The English Masque and Public Culture in the Seventeenth Century* (Oxford: Oxford University Press)

Shufran, Lauren. 2018. 'At Wit's End: Philip Sidney, Akrasia, and the Postlapsarian Limits of Reason and Will', *Studies in Philology*, 115/4: 679–718

Shwartz, Kathryn. 2013. 'Marlowe and the Question of Will', in *Christopher Marlowe in Context*, ed. by Emily Bartels and Emma Smith (Cambridge: Cambridge University Press), pp. 192–201

Sidney, Philip. 2008. *Sir Philip Sidney: The Major Works*, ed. by Katherine Duncan-Jones (Oxford: Oxford University Press)

Sidney, Sir Philip. 1973. *An Apology for Poetry, or The Defence of Poesy*, ed. by R. W. Maslen (Manchester: Manchester University Press)

Siemon, James R. 2013. 'Marlowe and Social Distinction', in *Christopher Marlowe in Context*, ed. by Emily Bartels and Emma Smith (Cambridge: Cambridge University Press), pp. 155–68

Simpson, James. 2007. *Burning to Read: English Fundamentalism and Its Reformation Opponents* (Cambridge, MA, and London: Harvard University Press)

Simpson, James. 2011. *Under the Hammer: Iconoclasm in the Anglo-American Tradition* (Oxford: Oxford University Press)

Simpson, James. 2019. *Permanent Revolution: The Reformation and the Illiberal Roots of Liberalism* (Cambridge, MA, and London: Harvard University Press)

Sivefors, Pers. 2012. 'Conflating Babel and Babylon in Tamburlaine 2', *Studies in English Language*, 52/2: 293–323

Sloan, Michael. 2013. 'Modern Reception: De Civitate Dei', in *The Oxford Guide to the Historical Reception of Augustine, Volume 3*, ed. by Willemien Otter (Oxford: Oxford University Press)

Smith, Matthew. 2019. *Performance and Religion in Early Modern England: Stage, Cathedral, Wagon, Street*, Re-Formations: Medieval and Early Modern (Notre Dame, IN: University of Notre Dame Press)

Smith-Cronin, Jeri. 2020. 'The Apocaplyptic Chivalry of Thomas Dekker's *The Whore of Babylon* and Anglo-Spanish Diplomacy', *The Journal of Medieval and Early Modern Studies*, 50/3: 633–57

Smuts, R. Malcolm. 1999. *Court Culture and the Origins of a Royalist Tradition in Early Stuart England* (Baltimore, MD: University of Pennsylvania Press)

Snyder, Jillian M. 2020. 'Pricked Hearts and Penitent Tears: Embodying Protestant Repentance in Robert Southwell's Saint Peter's Complaint (1595)', *Studies in Philology*, 117/2: 313–36

Solberg, Emma. 2018. *Virgin Whore* (Ithaca and London: Cornell University Press)

Southwell, Robert. 1967. *The Poems of Robert Southwell*, ed. by J. H. McDonald and N. P. Brown (London: Oxford University Press)

Spence, Victoria, 'Craven and the Elizabethan Settlement: Diverging Confessional Identities, 1580–1603', *Northern History*, 54/1 (2017): 28–58

Spolsky, Ellen. 2009. 'Literacy after Iconoclasm in the English Reformation', *Journal of Medieval and Early Modern Studies*, 39/2: 305–30

Spurr, Barry. 2007. *See The Virgin Blest: The Virgin Mary in English Poetry* (Basingstoke: Palgrave MacMillan)

Stafford, Anthony. 1635. *The Female Glory, or The Life and Death of Our Blessed Lady, the Holy Virgin Mary, God's Own Incarnate Mother* (London)

Stallybrass, Peter. 1986. '"Wee Feaste in Our Defense": Patrician Carnival in Early Modern England and Robert Herrick's "Hesperides"', *English Literary Renaissance*, 16/1: 234–52

Stanford Encyclopaedia of Philosophy, https://plato.standford.edu

Steggle, Matthew. 2007. *Laughing and Weeping in Early Modern Theatres* (Aldershot and Burlington VT: Ashgate)

Stegner, Paul D. 2014. 'Masculine and Feminine Penitence in *The Winter's Tale*', *Renascence*, 66/3: 189–201

Sterrit, Lawrence Lux. 2017. *English Benedictine Nuns in Exile in the Seventeenth Century: Living Spirituality* (Oxford: Oxford University Press)

Stewart, Stanley. 1966. *The Enclosed Garden: The Tradition and the Image in Seventeenth-Century Poetry* (Los Angeles: University of California Press)

Stoyle, Mark. 2022. *A Murderous Midsummer: The Western Rising of 1549* (London: Yale University Press)

Strasse, Ulriche. 2004. *State of Virginity: Gender, Religion and Politics in an Early Modern Catholic State* (Ann Arbor: University of Michigan Press)

Streete, Adrian. 2017. *Apocalypse and Anti-Catholicism in Seventeenth-Century English Drama* (Cambridge: Cambridge University Press)

Strier, Richard. 1979. '"To All Angels and Saints": Herbert's Puritan Poem', *Modern Philology*, 77/2: 132–45

Su Fang Ng. 2007. *Literature and the Politics of Family in Seventeenth-Century England* (Cambridge: Cambridge University Press)

Sullivan, Ceri. 2016. 'John Donne's "The Cross" and Recusant Graffiti', *Notes and Queries*, 63/3: 458

Swärdh, Anna. 2003. *Rape and Religion in English Renaissance Literature: A Topical Study of Four Texts by Shakespeare, Drayton, and Middleton* (Uppsala: University of Uppsala Press)

Sweeney, Anne. 2006. *Robert Southwell: Snow in Arcadia: Redrawing the English Lyric Landscape, 1586–95* (New York: Manchester University Press)

Swift, Daniel. 2012. *Shakespeare's Common Prayers: The Book of Common Prayer and the Elizabethan Age* (Oxford: Oxford University Press)

Tavard, George H. 1996. *The Thousand Faces of the Virgin Mary* (Wilmington, DE: Michael Glazier)

Taxidou, Olga. 2004. *Tragedy, Modernity and Mourning* (Edinburgh: Edinburgh University Press)

Taylor, Gary. 2004. 'Thomas Middleton', in *Oxford Dictionary of National Biography*

Tempe Restrd. A Masque Presented by the Queene, and Fourteen Ladies, to the King's Majestie at Whitehall on Shrove Tuesday. 1631. 1632 (London)

The Book of Sports, as Set Forth by K. Charles I. With Remarks. 1633; repr. 1710 (London)

'The Catholic Encyclopedia', https//www.catholic.org/encyclopedia

The Character of a church papist. 1681 (London)

'The Defense of Plays' in "Pierce Penniless"', *Thomas Nashe: The Unfortunate Traveller and Other Works.* 1972, ed. by J. Steane (London), pp. 112–14

The Presbytery: A Satire. 1649. (London)

The Temple of Love. A Masque Presented by the Queenes Majesty, and Her Ladies, on Shrove-Tuesday. By Inigo Jones, Surveyor of His Maties Works, and William Davenant, Her Maties. Servant. 1634. (London)

The Virgin Mary: Monotheism and Sacrifice. 2008. (Cambridge: Cambridge University Press)

The Whole Workes of W. Tyndall, John Frith and Doct. Barnes. 1573. (London)

The Williams Manuscript of George Herbert's Poems: A Facsimile Reproduction. 1977. (Delmar, NY: Scholars' Facsimiles and Reprints)

The Workes of That Famous Worthy Minister of Christ in the University of Cambridge, M. William Perkins. 1631. (London)

Thomas Adriaenssen, Hans, and Laura Georgescu. 2022. 'Introduction: The Digbean Way, or Navigating Between the Old and the New', *International Archives of the History of Ideas*, ed. by Laura Georgescu and Hans Thomas Adriaenssen (Cham, Switzerland: Springer), pp. 1–33

Thomas, Keith. 2009. 'The Perception of the Past in Early Modern England', in *The Creighton Century*, ed. by David Bates, Jennifer Wallis, and Jane Winters (London, Institute of Historical Research: University of London Press), pp. 185–218

Bennett, Kate. 2004-. 'Thomas Shadwell', in *Oxford Dictionary of National Biography*

Tiffany, Grace. 2018. 'Paganism and Reform in Shakespeare's Plays', *Religions*, 9/7: 214, https://doi.org/10.3390/rel9070214

Tigner, Amy. 2012. *Literature and the Renaissance Garden from Elizabeth I to Charles II* (Farnham and Burlington, VT: Ashgate)

Todd, Janet. 2004. 'Aphra Behn', in *Oxford Dictionary of National Biography*

Tomlinson, Sophie. 2005. *Women on Stage in Stuart Drama* (Cambridge: Cambridge University Press)

Turner, Buffy. 2018. 'Productive Discord and George Herbert's "Artillerie"', *Citharia*, 57/2: 18–42

Van Elk, Martine. 2017. 'Mary Ward and the Society of Jesus', *Early Modern Women: Lives, Texts and Objects*, https://martinevanelk.wordpress.com/2017/04/24/mary-ward-and-the-society-of-jesus/

Vander Motten, J. P. 2016. 'Thomas Killigrew and the Seventeenth Century English Stage: New Perspectives', in *Recycling the Exile: Thomaso, The Rover and the Critics*, ed. by Philip Major (London: Routledge), pp. 126–41

Vander Motten, J. P., and Katrien Daemen-de Gelder. 2014. 'Margaret Cavendish, the Antwerp Carmel and the Convent of Pleasure', *Archiv für das Studium der neueren Sprachen und Literaturen*, ed. by Jens Haustein, 251/1, 134–45

Vander Motten, J. P., and René Vermeir. 2014. '"Reality, and Matter of Fact": Text and Context in Aphra Behn's *The Fair Jilt*', *The Review of English Studies*, 66: 280–99

Veevers, Erica. 1989. *Images of Love and Religion: Queen Henrietta and Court Entertainments* (Cambridge: Cambridge University Press)

Verstegan, Richard. 1601. *Odes* (Antwerp)

Vine, Emily. 2018. '"Those Enemies of Christ, If They Are Suffered to Live Among Us": Locating Religious Minority Homes and Private Space in Early Modern London', *The London Journal: A Review of Metropolitan Society, Past and Present*, 43/3: 197–214

Visser, Arnoud. 2019. 'Juan Luis Vives and the Organisation of Patristic Knowledge', in *Confessionalisation and Erudition in Early Modern Europe*, ed. by Nicholas Hardy and Dmitri Levitin (Oxford: Oxford University Press), pp. 96–114

Voak, N. 2008. 'Richard Hooker and the Principle of Sola Scriptura', *The Journal of Theological Studies*, 59/1: 96–139

Waller, Christopher. 2018. 'The Church and Consensual Conformism: "God Is More There Then Thou,"' *Early Modern Literary Studies*, 20/1: 1–35

Waller, Gary. 2011. *The Virgin Mary in Late Medieval and Early Modern English Literature and Popular Culture* (Cambridge: Cambridge University Press)

Waller, Gary. 2020. *The Female Baroque in Early Modern English Literary Culture: From Mary Sidney to Aphra Behn*, Gendering the Late Medieval and Early Modern World (Amsterdam: Amsterdam University Press)

Walsh, Brian. 2016. *Unsettled Toleration: Religious Difference on the Shakespearean Stage* (Oxford: Oxford University Press)

Walsham, Alexandra. 1993. *Church Papists: Catholicism, Conformity and Confessional Polemic in Early Modern England*, RHS Studies in History, 68 (Woodbridge: Boydell Press)

Walsham, Alexandra. 2000. '"Domme Preachers"?: Post-Reformation Catholicism and the Culture of Print', *Past & Present*, 168: 72–123

Walsham, Alexandra. 2006. *Charitable Hatred: Tolerance and Intolerance in England, 1500–1700* (Manchester: Manchester University Press)

Walsham, Alexandra. 2003. 'Preaching without Speaking: Script, Print and Religious Dissent', in *The Uses of Script and Print, 1300–1700*, eds Julia Crick and Alexandra Walsham (Cambridge: Cambridge University Press), pp. 211–34

Walsham, Alexandra. 2011. *The Reformation of the Landscape: Religion, Identity, and Memory in Early Modern Britain and Ireland* (Oxford: Oxford University Press)

Waters, John. 2020. 'John Donne's Sermons: Counsell and the Politics of the Dynamic Middle', *English Literary Renaissance*, 50/3: 391–416

Watson, Emma, 2016. 'Clergy, Laity and Ecclesiastical Discipline in Elizabethan Yorkshire Parishes', in *Getting Along? Religious Identities and Confessional Relations in Early Modern England – Essays in Honour of Professor W. J. Scheils*, ed. by Nadine Lewycky and Adam Morton (London and New York: Routledge), pp. 97–114

Welch, Kate. 2011. 'Making Mourning Show: Hamlet and Affective Public Making', *Performance Research: A Journal of the Performing Arts*, 16/2: 74–82

Wells, Stanley, and Gary Taylor (eds). 1988; 1995. *The Oxford Shakespeare: The Complete Works* (Oxford: Clarendon Press)

Wesley, John. 2020. 'Quintilian's Forensic Grief and the Spanish Tragedy', *Studies in English Literature 1500–1900*, 60/2: 209–28

Whalen, Robert. 2002. *The Poetry of Immanence: Sacrament in Donne and Herbert* (Toronto: University of Toronto Press)

White, Paul Whitfield. 2008. *Drama and Religion in English Provincial Society, 1485–1660* (Cambridge: Cambridge University Press)

Whitling, George. 1959. 'And Without Thorn the Rose', *The Review of English Studies*, 10: 60–2

Wiggins, Martin (ed). 2012. *British Drama: A Catalogue* (Oxford: Oxford University Press), II

Wilcox, Helen. 2004. 'George Herbert', in *Oxford National Dictionary of Biography*

Williams, Ian. 2011. 'A Medieval Book and Early Modern Law: Bracton's Authority and Application in the Common Law, *c.*1550–1640', *The Legal History Review*, 79/1: 47–80

Williams, James A. 2009. 'Erected Wit and Effeminate Repose: Philip Sidney's Postures of Reader-Response', *The Modern Language Review*, 104/3: 640–58

Wilson-Okamura, David Scott. 2010. *Virgil in the Renaissance* (Cambridge: Cambridge University Press)

Winston, Jessica. 2005. 'Expanding the Political Nation: *Gorboduc* at the Inns of Court and Succession Revisited', *Early Theatre*, 8.1: 11–34

Winston, Jessica. 2019. '*Gorboduc* Now!: The First English Tragedy in Modern Print in Performance', *English*, 68/261: 184–203

Wittek, Stephen. 2015. 'Middleton's *A Game at Chess* and the Making of a Theatrical Public', *Studies in English Literature 1500–1900*, 55/2: 423–46

Wizeman, William. 2004. 'The Virgin Mary in the Reign of Mary Tudor', in *The Church and Mary: Papers Read at the 2001 Summer Meeting and the 2002 Winter Meeting of the Ecclesiastical Society*, ed. by R. N. Swanson (London: Boydell Press), pp. 239–48

Wooding, Lucy. 2013. 'Remembrance in the Eucharist', *The Arts of Remembrance in Early Modern England: Memorial Cultures of the Post Reformation*, Material Readings in Early Modern Culture, ed. by Andrew Gordon and Thomas Rist (Farnham and Burlington VT), pp. 19–36

Woods, Gillian. 2013. 'Marlowe and Religion', in *Christopher Marlowe in Context*, ed. by Emily Bartels and Emma Smith (Cambridge: Cambridge University Press), pp. 222–31

Woodward, Jennifer. 1997. *The Theatre of Death: The Ritual Management of Royal Funerals in Renaissance England, 1570–1625* (Woodbridge: Boydell Press)

Wright, Thomas. 1604. *The Passions of the Minde in Generall* (London)

Yamamoto-Wilson, John. 2015. 'Robert Persons's *Resolution* (1582) and the Issue of Textual Piracy in Protestant Editions of Catholic Devotional Literature', in *Reformation & Renaissance Review*, 15/2: 177–98

Young, Francis. 2016. *English Catholics and the Supernatural 1553–1827* (Oxford and New York: Routledge)

Zim, Rivkah. 2006. 'A Poet in Politics: Thomas Sackville, Lord Buckhurst and First Earl of Dorset (1536–1608)', *Historical Research: The Bulletin of the Institute of Historical Research*, 79/204: 199–223

Zim, Rivkah. 2019. 'Thomas Sackville, Lord Buckhurst's Letters from the Low Countries, the 'Quarrels of My Lord Leicester' and the Rhetoric of Political Survival', *Historical Research*, 92/255: 73–96

Zook, Melinda. 2013. *Protestantism, Politics and Women in Britain, 1660–1714*, Early Modern History: Society and Culture (London: Palgrave Macmillan)

Index

abbess 195, 201, 205, 206
abbot 68, 69, 70, 71
Abbott, George 9
abstinence 69, 70, 72
Act of Supremacy 2, 12
Act of Uniformity 10, 11, 12, 21
action 1, 2, 12, 30, 42, 47, 48, 52, 54, 55, 56, 57, 60, 61, 63, 64, 66, 67, 71, 72, 82, 88, 89, 90, 100, 102, 103, 104, 111, 119, 123, 126, 133, 148, 171, 180, 190, 198, 216, 219
'Against the Perils of Idolatry' 19, 109, 120, 140
All Souls 103, 173
Altar 35, 36, 54, 57, 58, 59, 50, 67, 71, 107, 112, 114, 117, 119, 120, 125, 131, 133, 134, 172, 189, 190, 207, 224, 225, 231, 237
analogical 51, 62, 63, 65, 67
Andrewes, Launcelot 25, 37, 111, 115, 121, 136, 217, 218, 231, 232
Anna of Denmark 165, 177, 187, 224
anti-Calvinist 20, 216
anti-Christ 5, 51, 220
anti-papal 5, 8, 9, 36, 112
anti-Puritanism 129, 130, 131, 132
Antwerp 133, 150, 192, 198, 202, 207, 218, 228, 243
Aquinas, Thomas 14, 18, 26, 109, 115, 116, 117, 118, 148, 211, 217, 219, 235
Arminian 20, 25, 33, 111, 119, 120, 140, 235
Arminius, Jacobus 6, 227 (*see also* Arminianism)

Article 22 ('Of Purgatory') 18, 74, 75, 76, 77, 86, 87, 91, 99, 104 (*see also* Thirty-nine Articles)
Augsburg confession 17

Babylon 89, 90, 176, 178, 182, 220, 230, 241
Bailey, Rebecca 68, 71, 186, 187, 190, 198, 218
'A Ballad Upon the Popish Plot, written by a Lady of Quality' 161
baptism 7, 40, 120, 163, 164, 188
Barksdale, Clement 38, 218
beads 130, 131, 172, 173
Beaumont, Francis and John Fletcher 202
Becket, Thomas 28, 29
Behn, Aphra 19, 194, 199, 202–208, 212, 213, 218, 219, 220, 227, 228, 229, 235, 239, 243
  The City Heiress 203
  The Dutch Lover 203, 219
  The Emperor of the Moon 203
  The Fair Jilt 202, 207
  The False Count 203, 219
  The History of the Nun: Or the Fair Vow Breaker 202
  Love Letters Between a Nobleman and his Sister 202
  The Rover 19, 203–206, 208, 218
  The Younger Brother 19, 203, 206–208, 213, 219
Bellarmine, Robert 39
Bible, the 3, 8, 13, 15, 16, 17, 18, 51, 63, 86, 120, 210, 211, 228, 237 (*see also* scripture)

Index

Biblicism 8, 15, 17, 18, 216
blessed maid 122, 141, 172
Book of Homilies 19, 20, 109, 120–21, 140
Book of Sports, the 129, 130, 242
Burton, Henry 188, 189, 220

Calvinism 20, 28, 33, 78, 79, 121, 125, 176
Calvin, John 9, 18, 20, 44, 55, 109, 140, 148, 152, 210 (*see also* Calvinism)
Camden, William163 164, 169, 220
Campion, Edmund 2, 3, 149, 231
Carey, Lucius 40, 190
Caroline England 13, 18, 19, 35, 186, 187, 218, 221, 227
Cavendish, Margaret 19, 42, 193, 197–201, 205, 221, 229, 235, 243
  The Convent of Pleasure 193, 197–201, 229
Cavendish, William 42, 68, 197, 198, 238
ceremony 63, 71, 75, 131, 165, 194, 207, 224, 227
Charlemagne 195
Charles I 5, 6, 15, 17, 37, 42, 72, 123, 130, 131, 143, 157, 165, 186, 188, 193, 194, 198, 199, 200, 222, 232, 242, 243
chaste 40, 131, 159, 169, 170, 171, 175, 178, 193, 195, 203, 235, 236
Cholmeley, Richard 168
Church of England 3, 4, 6, 9, 10, 18, 19, 20, 21, 22, 23, 33, 36, 37, 40, 41, 43, 44, 46, 47, 48, 74, 75, 76, 99, 104, 106, 107, 109, 110, 113, 114, 115, 116, 117, 119, 120, 122, 123, 124, 125, 127, 128, 138, 139, 140, 141, 145, 146, 178, 189, 202, 211, 230, 235
Church of Rome 9, 75, 88, 113, 115, 145, 147
'Churching of Women' 162, 222
Civil War 4, 15, 19, 41, 119, 128, 160, 161, 239
classical tragedy 80

collaboration 4, 81, 88, 89, 176, 178
Collinson, Patrick 12, 15
commemorative tragedy 92
communion tables 71
Condell, Henry 93, 95
conformity 3, 4, 5, 6, 58, 136, 137, 145, 210, 235, 237, 240, 243
congregation 107, 112, 117, 190, 207
Constable, Henry 19, 145–49, 153, 165, 227, 231, 237
convent 19, 174, 192, 193, 194, 202, 203, 205, 206, 207, 229, 229, 243 (*see also* Cavendish, *The Convent of Pleasure*)
convert 33, 41, 71, 106, 113, 139, 190, 194, 197, 202, 210, 231
Counter-Reformation 1, 64, 111, 114, 115, 116, 140, 145, 152, 159, 174, 186, 228, 236
court 11, 59, 81, 110, 129, 131, 133, 144, 165, 168, 177, 180, 182, 186, 187, 189, 190, 191, 192, 193, 194, 195, 198, 200, 203, 205, 215, 219, 220, 221, 233, 241, 243
Cranmer, Thomas 4, 6, 7, 8, 9
Crashaw, Richard 18, 105, 107, 113–19, 126, 127, 136, 137, 138, 139, 141, 214, 222, 228, 230, 237
  'The Flaming Heart' 117, 118
  'The Hymn of Sanite Thomas' 116, 119
  'A Hymn on the B. Sacrament' 115, 117, 118
  'A Hymn to our Saviour by the Faithful Receiver of the Sacrament' 115
  'A Hymn to the Name and Honor of the Admirable Sanite Teresa' 116, 117, 118
  'On the Wounds of Our Crucified Lord' 119
  Steps to the Temple 114, 115, 116, 117, 222
  'To the Infant Martyrs' 117
Crashaw, William 113
Cromwell, Thomas 111, 140
cross-dressing 175, 177, 178, 180, 181, 182, 185, 191, 213, 222

Cudworth, Ralph 216
Cummings, Brian 3, 4, 5, 8, 9, 21, 22, 26, 54, 55, 74, 75, 78, 79, 106, 107, 109, 115, 173, 211, 222, 223, 225

Davenant, William 35, 42, 68, 191, 223, 227, 242
Davenport, Robert 19, 193–97, 223
De Grenada, Luis 105
Declarations of Indulgence 6
Dekker, Thomas
  The Roaring Girl 19, 175–86, 191, 193, 213, 232, 235
  The Virgin Martyr 19, 175, 176, 177, 178, 220, 230, 235, 241
  The Whore of Babylon 176, 220, 241
Digby, Kenelm 33, 36, 37, 68, 190, 225, 228
dissenters 6
Donne, John
  'Amicissimo & meritissimo' 31, 34, 35
  'The Cross' 132–3, 134, 242
  'An Epithalamion, or The Marriage Song of the Lady Elizabeth, and Count Palatine being married on St Valentine's Day' 135, 136–7
  'Good Friday, Riding Westward 1613' 125, 134
  'Holy Sonnet 19'('O, to vex me') 134
  'A Letter to the Lady Carey, and Mistress Essex Rich, from Amiens' 135
  'In Sacram Anchoram Piscatoris' 132
  'To Mrs Magdalene Herbert: of St Mary Magdalene' 135
dramatic theology 72–3
Drayton, Michael 160, 169
Dryden, John
  'Eleonora: A Panegyrical Poem, Dedicated to the Memory of the late Countess of Abington' 48
  'An Epitaph on Sir Palmes Fairbourne's Tomb in Westminster Abbey' 48
  'Epitaph on the Monument of the Marquis of Winchester' 47
  An Essay of Dramatic Poesie 47, 224
  Religio Laici 43–7, 48, 216, 224, 237
Dudley, Robert 81
Duffy, Eamon 15, 24, 149, 156, 224
Duke of York Theatre 194
Dunmowe Abbey 173, 174, 195, 197
Dunn-Hensley, Susan 123, 165, 186, 187, 190, 192, 224
Duppa, Brian
  Angels rejoicing for sinners repenting 38, 39, 40, 224
  Jonsonus Virbius 37, 38, 39–40

Elizabeth I 1, 2, 6, 11, 15, 17, 18, 19, 37, 46, 58, 75, 111, 129, 140, 144, 146, 148, 153, 157, 166, 174, 209, 217, 227, 238, 243
English Ladies 19, 179, 186, 199 (see also Mary Ward)
epitaphs vii, 18, 22, 23–49, 86, 89, 162, 164, 172, 217, 220, 236, 240
Eric, King of Sweden 81, 82
Eucharist, the vii, 9, 16, 18, 49, 50–73, 91, 107, 108, 111, 112, 115, 117, 118, 119, 120, 126, 127, 128, 129, 134, 137, 138, 226, 231, 234, 237, 238, 239, 245
evangelical 10, 30, 114, 115, 116, 121, 210, 220
Everyman 27, 31, 32, 232
Exclusion Crisis, the 19, 194, 203, 204, 230

Ferrar, Nicholas 133
Fletcher, John 55, 201, 202, 225
Ford, John 18, 49, 50, 68, 69, 71, 229, 235
  Love's Sacrifice 18, 49, 50, 67–72, 73, 235
Foucault, Michel 212
Francis Lenton 191, 232
Fulton, Thomas 8, 13, 15, 16, 21, 44, 212, 226
funeral 27, 40, 78, 79, 81, 82, 84, 85–6, 88–91, 94–6, 98, 171–3, 217, 232, 236, 245

Galen 100, 104
Ghent 206, 207, 208
ghost 41, 76, 77, 90, 91, 93–8, 99–104, 167, 219
Giraldus, Giglio 58
Globe Theatre, the 31
godly, the 5, 30, 79, 80, 82, 86, 91, 159, 213, 220
good deeds 31, 32, 38, 173
Gorboduc 80–4, 88, 101, 221, 231, 233, 244
grace 7, 8, 9, 13, 14, 20, 24, 25, 28, 33, 34, 38, 39, 55, 56, 64, 79, 106, 107, 125, 127, 129, 141, 143, 149, 151, 152, 154, 191, 192, 217, 222, 226, 227, 232

Hamlin, Hannibal 16, 63, 64, 66, 228
Handbook of Gregoria, the 70
haunt 94, 99–104, 105, 126–28, 178, 209, 221
Heinemann, Margot 176, 228
Hemmings, John 93, 94
Henrietta Maria, Queen 15, 19, 42, 67, 68, 114, 115, 128, 130, 131, 142, 143, 144, 162, 163, 165, 186–93, 194, 197, 198, 199, 200, 201, 205, 213, 218, 219, 220, 224, 229, 236
Henry VIII 53, 195
Herbert, George 18, 40, 105, 107, 115, 119–28, 132, 133, 134, 135, 217, 218, 227, 228
  'Affliction' 125
  'The Crosse' 125, 126
  'The Flower' 127
  'The H. Communion' 125, 128
  'Perirrhanterium' 219, 220
  The Temple 10, 120, 124, 125, 127, 133, 134, 227, 231, 234, 239
  'To all Angels and Saints' 121–24, 228, 242
  Williams manuscript, the 120, 122, 123, 124, 242
Herrick, Robert 18, 35, 36, 40, 105, 107, 113, 128–32, 137, 138, 139, 140, 214, 220, 222, 223, 233, 241
  'Corinna's Going a Maying' 128, 129, 130

Hesperides 35, 128, 129, 131, 139, 222, 241
  'His Prayer to Ben Jonson' 35–6, 130
  'To the Queen' 131
  'To the Virgins, to Make Much of Time' 128, 129
Heywood, John 63
Hooker, Richard 38, 44, 243
human 7, 9, 10, 14, 20, 21, 26, 28, 30, 34, 39, 41, 43, 44, 52, 55, 63, 67, 78, 92, 93, 99, 100, 102, 104, 109, 114, 121, 123, 125, 126, 128, 129, 143, 152, 162, 165, 216, 218
humanism 17, 22, 53, 59, 61, 80, 237
Hunt, Maurice 51

iconoclasm 9, 16, 19, 128, 147, 160, 215, 240, 241
idolatry 7, 11, 16, 19, 27, 29, 41, 58, 109, 118, 120, 140, 141, 147, 152, 231 (*see also* monuments)
Ignatian meditation 105
images 57, 59, 74, 86, 87, 111, 112, 133, 140, 146, 148, 152, 153, 166, 178, 186, 189, 226, 236
imagination 3, 8, 9, 10, 15, 24, 30, 44, 47, 49, 76, 77, 99, 107, 126, 134, 182, 212, 214, 217, 223, 226, 238, 240
Incarnation, the 149, 152, 153, 158, 191, 198
Inns of Court 81, 180, 244
Italianate tragedy 68
Italy 67, 72, 136

Jacobean 13, 18, 19, 52, 54, 133, 136, 165, 166, 177, 221, 240
Jacobean canons 54
James I 3, 5, 6, 15, 130, 133, 134, 137, 165, 177, 187, 218
James II 1, 19, 194, 209 (*see also* James Stuart)
Jones, Inigo 190, 191, 242
Jonson, Ben 18, 19, 24, 25, 26, 27, 28, 29, 30, 31, 32, 33, 34, 35, 36, 37, 39, 40, 41, 42, 43, 46, 47, 48, 49, 50, 52, 53, 54–62, 68, 72, 78, 98, 123, 130, 131,

141–44, 151, 157, 162, 163, 164, 165, 186, 191, 198, 209, 212, 215, 219, 220, 221, 222, 224, 226, 229, 230, 231, 232, 234, 235, 238, 240 (*see also* masques)
'An Epigram to the Queen' 19, 123, 131, 141, 142–44, 163
Every Man in his Humour 31, 32, 62
Everyman out of his Humour 32
'Of Life and Death' 32–33, 34
'On my first daughter' 19, 162, 163
Sejanus his Fall 18, 30, 49, 50, 54–62, 72, 219
'The Sinner's Sacrifice' 33–34
'Underwoods' 31, 33, 142
Works of Ben Jonson, The 18, 24, 26, 27, 29, 30, 31, 32, 33, 48, 50, 72
judicial murder 5, 6
Juvenal 60

Kempis, Thomas à 132, 231
Killigrew, Thomas 19, 204, 205, 220, 229, 243
King, Henry 40
Kyd, Thomas 73, 84, 88, 90, 91, 225
Soliman and Perseda 80, 90
The Spanish Tragedy 69, 73, 80, 84, 88–92, 99, 101, 102, 173, 225, 226, 230, 232

Lambe, William 27–28, 218
Lancashire 46, 130
Laud, William 20, 37, 114, 115, 120, 124, 138, 234, 236
Laudianism 19, 24, 25, 37, 38, 109, 114, 115, 119, 121, 122, 124, 125, 128, 217, 218, 235, 237 (*see also* William Laud)
Lenton, Francis 191, 232
libertine 19, 204, 206, 208
Liebler, Naomi Conn 62, 63, 221
Lipsius, Justus 133
liturgy 2, 3, 5, 7, 20, 117, 126, 165, 239
Lovelace, Richard 41, 42, 233, 239
Lutheran 17, 20, 24, 25, 67, 78, 239 (*see also* Martin Luther)

Luther, Martin 14, 17, 20, 25, 32, 33, 45, 55, 59, 67, 106, 122, 210, 228, 230, 238, 239

Magdalene, Mary 109, 135, 178
Maid Marian 19, 167, 169–171, 235, 236
Maria Triumphans 199, 233
Marlowe, Christopher 31, 77, 84–88, 89, 90, 94, 102, 222
  Dr Faustus 70, 75, 77, 78, 80
  Tamburlaine 84, 85, 226, 233
  Tamburlaine II 84–8, 89, 90, 92, 101, 223, 226, 233, 241
Martz, Louis 105, 106, 107, 123, 124, 125, 234
Mary I 53, 111, 122, 140, 165, 165, 224
masques 144, 145, 186, 187, 190, 191, 192, 215, 221, 232, 233, 240, 242
  Chlorida 190
  Great Britains Beauties 191–2, 232 (*see also* Francis Lenton)
  Luminalia 190, 191, 233
  Tempe Restored 190, 191, 192, 205, 242
  The Temple of Love 190, 191, 242
Mass, the 11, 18, 63, 67, 71, 75, 79, 98, 107, 110, 112, 117, 120, 131, 141, 155, 162, 167, 168, 180, 181, 239
Massinger, Philip 176, 177, 230, 235
Matilda 19, 167, 169–74, 193–95, 223, 225, 236
May Marion 175, 191
mediatrix 147
medical 100, 101, 102
Medici, Marie de 187, 188, 189, 219
medieval 1, 11, 14, 15, 19, 21, 31, 32, 51, 59, 60, 62, 64, 70, 72, 75, 78, 80, 91, 94, 96, 97, 98, 99, 103, 111, 116, 118, 136, 141, 142, 149, 152, 153, 155, 158, 159, 160, 161, 162, 165, 166, 167, 173, 174, 176, 178, 175, 191, 200, 201, 211, 212, 213, 214, 217, 219, 220, 222, 223, 225, 226, 232, 235, 236, 239, 241, 243, 244

medieval drama (*see also* moral plays) 31, 62, 80, 97, 191
Melanchthon, Philipp 31, 17, 30
Meres, Francis 100
Middleton, Thomas 16, 19, 160, 175–86, 221, 228, 230, 235, 242, 244
  Caesar's Fall 176
  A Chaste Maid in Cheapside 178
  A Game of Chess 177
  The Roaring Girl 19, 175–86, 191, 193, 213, 232, 235
Milton, John 13, 18, 21, 44, 55, 131, 150, 157, 159, 160, 212, 217, 225, 226, 227, 228, 229, 231, 232, 235, 236, 238
  'On the Morning of Christ's Nativity' 160
  Paradise Lost 13, 157, 160, 225
  Paradise Regained
  A Treatise of Civil Power in Ecclesiastical Causes 44
Montagu, Walter 190, 192, 200, 205
monument 3, 16, 17, 18, 19, 22, 23, 24, 25, 27, 28, 29, 35, 36, 37, 40, 41, 43, 44, 47, 48, 49, 52, 57, 58, 59, 72, 78, 79, 89, 95, 118, 158, 174, 232, 233, 238
moral goods 65, 66
moral plays 31, 70, 72, 236
More, Thomas 11, 14, 53, 232
mourning 71, 80–84, 85, 86, 91, 94, 95–8, 173, 224, 226, 242, 244
Munday, Anthony 19, 166, 167, 169, 170, 174, 175, 193, 195, 197, 213, 219, 225, 228, 235, 236
  The Death of Robert, Earl of Huntington 169, 170–74
  The Downfall of Robert, Earl of Huntington, 169–70
Murray, Molly 9, 23, 106, 214, 236

Nashe, Thomas 16, 93, 94, 95, 101, 242
nature 13, 21, 25, 76, 99, 118, 127, 128, 129, 130, 137, 145, 157, 193, 232
Newstok, Scott 22, 24, 27, 28, 29, 236
Norton, Thomas 80, 82

nun 16, 173, 174, 178, 180, 182, 192, 195, 198, 199, 201, 202, 204, 206, 207, 219, 227, 228, 232, 253

Oath of Allegiance 5, 133, 137, 166, 210
Oldisworth, Nicholas 35, 40, 227
Ordinance for the Taking Away of the Book of Common Prayer 4
Ovid 100, 129, 130, 131, 150, 219, 216

Palotto, Giovanni 115
papistry 114, 130 (*see also* popery)
Parliament 3, 4, 6, 10, 11, 12, 41, 136, 138, 160
Passion 111, 113, 118, 119, 125, 154, 155, 158, 225 (*see also* sacrifice)
Pelagianism 20, 28
Pelagius 25
Perkins, William 24, 25, 26, 30, 33, 38, 220, 242
Persons, Robert 2, 15, 16, 222, 227, 229, 245
Peter (Saint) 59, 106, 107–11, 114, 120, 124, 222, 241
Petrarchism 14, 213, 230
Plutarch 50
polytheism 109, 121, 140
pope-burning 194, 230
Pope, Alexander 214, 218, 223, 229, 239
Pope Joan 178, 182, 239
popery 45, 52, 58, 124, 161, 179, 194, 202, 220 (*see also* papistry)
Popes 15, 35, 51, 59, 77, 109, 114, 115, 157, 179, 195, 196, 197
Popish Plot 19, 46, 161, 203, 218
post-Reformation 1, 2, 16, 23, 34, 78, 79, 105, 112, 120, 150, 153, 162, 163, 167, 212, 222, 227, 234, 244
prayers 9, 23, 31, 92, 103, 121, 130, 140, 173, 213, 219, 242
predestination 5, 6, 20, 24, 25, 219
Preface (*Book of Common Prayer*) 8, 9, 21, 29
Presbyterian 41, 160, 161
'Presbytery: A Satyr, The' 160

priest 3, 4, 18, 26, 34, 53, 58, 59, 60, 65, 68, 97, 98, 111, 112, 120, 128, 129, 137, 138, 150, 179, 190, 191, 192, 207, 230, 234, 237
printers 2, 3, 4, 7, 123, 141, 149, 219, 238
prison 1, 4, 11, 34, 76, 102, 145, 228
Propertius 129, 130, 131
Purgatory vii, 1, 2, 14, 15, 18, 49, 74–104, 110, 140, 209, 211

rake 202
rape 158, 160, 161, 162, 163
recusancy vii, 5, 15, 19, 24, 29, 35, 108, 109, 123, 133, 137, 140–63, 173, 179, 199, 202, 206, 207, 208, 214, 223, 228, 238, 242
repentance 38, 39, 40, 68, 69, 72, 106, 241
reprobate 73, 92 (*see also* reprobation)
reprobation 5
reputation 2, 24, 103, 166, 179, 183, 184, 185, 220, 221, 225, 229, 230
Restoration 6, 19, 23, 41, 44, 45, 57, 123, 194, 195, 197, 202, 205, 220, 221, 227, 230, 236
rhetoric 1, 9, 17, 32, 80, 81, 99, 132, 226, 228, 231, 233, 245
rite 3, 36, 58, 59, 62, 73, 75, 79, 81, 90, 91, 95, 127, 191, 221, 236
Roaring Girl, The 219, 175–86, 191, 193, 213, 232
Robin Hood 19, 166–75, 175, 176, 192, 193, 194, 195, 197, 213, 219, 232, 236, 237 (*see also* Robert Davenport; Anthony Munday)
  A Geste of Robin Hood 167, 217
  Look About You 168, 217
Roman plays 14, 15, 50–67, 230
Romish 18, 74, 75, 76, 77, 80, 82, 86, 87, 88, 91, 94, 95, 98, 99, 105, 239
rosary (*see also* beads) 130, 150, 151, 154, 157, 173
Rosendale, Timothy 1, 15, 16, 18, 23, 29, 63, 239

Royal Shakespeare Company 175, 176, 232
Ryrie, Alec 6, 8, 27, 36, 39, 69, 75, 215, 239

Sackville, Thomas 80
sacrifice 18, 33, 24, 49, 50–73, 85, 111, 112, 113, 117, 118, 119, 156, 126, 127, 128, 132, 133, 136, 138, 152, 161, 206, 231, 235, 239, 242
saint 10, 15, 19, 23, 29, 35, 36, 39, 40, 42, 48, 64, 65, 67, 70, 71, 74, 98, 102, 103, 104, 105, 107, 108, 109, 110, 111, 112, 115, 116, 117, 118, 119, 120, 121, 122, 123, 124, 126, 131, 134, 135, 136, 137, 138, 140, 145, 146, 149, 150, 151, 152, 163, 173, 174, 178, 181, 182, 185, 188, 195, 198, 201, 206, 207, 213, 218, 220, 221, 222, 224, 225, 226, 228, 233, 241, 242
St Ambrose 40, 155
St Augustine 18, 25, 26, 39, 52, 53, 59, 61, 67, 91, 164, 173, 217, 218, 225, 238, 241
St Bernard 39, 153
salvation 2, 5, 7, 18, 19, 20, 24, 25, 26, 27, 28, 29, 30, 31, 32, 34, 37, 38, 39, 41, 42, 43, 44, 47, 48, 49, 50, 52, 54, 55, 61, 62, 64, 67, 69, 71, 72, 92, 103, 108, 118, 137, 144, 148, 210, 216, 217, 226
Scodel, Joshua 32, 33, 240
scripture 7, 8, 9, 13, 14, 17, 19, 20, 27, 30, 38, 39, 41, 44, 45, 46, 47, 49, 74, 79, 108, 110, 111, 114, 115, 136, 140, 153, 210, 211, 212, 231 (*see also* Bible)
Shakespeare, William 4, 16, 17, 18, 23, 49, 50, 51, 52, 54, 62–7, 63, 64, 65, 67, 73, 76, 77, 78, 80, 81, 90, 91, 93–5, 96–8, 91–104, 106, 123, 124, 143, 146, 158, 160, 167, 168, 173, 183, 186, 197, 200, 212, 213, 216, 217, 218, 219, 220, 221, 222, 223, 224, 226, 228, 229, 230,

231, 232, 236, 237, 238, 239,
 240, 242, 243, 243, 244
As you Like It 213, 232
First Folio 93, 97
Hamlet 75, 76, 77, 78, 80
Henry IV (Part 1) 95
Henry IV (Part 2) 95
Henry V 94, 95
Henry VI (Part 1) 93, 94, 101
Henry VI (Part 2) 94
Henry VI (Part 3) 94
Julius Caesar 18, 49, 50, 51, 52,
 53, 54, 62–7, 72, 73, 74, 220,
 225, 229, 231, 232, 233
King John 167, 168
Love's Labour's Lost 97–98, 200,
 238
A Midsummer Night's Dream 96,
 97, 98, 203
Richard II 95
Richard III 95, 102
Twelfth Night 95, 97, 98, 183,
 238
'Venus and Adonis' 100
The Winter's Tale 98, 185, 186,
 241
shame 40, 70, 184
Shirley, James 68, 71, 218
shrine 28, 71, 75, 155, 156, 158, 174
Sidney, Philip 21, 22, 28, 29, 80, 81,
 82, 83, 193, 210, 209, 212, 228,
 231, 234, 240, 243, 244
Sloan, Michael 53, 240
Smith, Matthew 78, 95, 96, 191, 237,
 240, 241
Smithfield 149
sola fide 7, 20, 28
sola gratia 7, 20
sola scriptura 7, 17, 20, 28, 44, 110,
 210, 243
Somerset House 189, 190, 191
soteriology 20, 52, 62, 148, 226
soul 2, 21, 31, 37, 47, 38, 49, 59, 66,
 76, 85, 94, 98, 100, 102, 103,
 104, 121, 125, 133, 162, 168,
 172, 173, 181, 187, 188, 195,
 216, 219, 227, 228, 234, 236
Southwell, Robert 1, 2, 15, 18, 106,
 107, 108–113, 115, 116, 117,
 118, 119, 120, 121, 124, 125,
 126, 127, 128, 129, 132, 133,
 134, 135, 136, 137, 138, 140,
 152, 214, 239, 242
'The Assumption of our Lady' 110
'The Author to his loving Cosen'
 111, 113
'The Author to the Reader' 110
'Christ's returne out of Egypt' 127
'The Flight into Egypt' 127
'A Holy Hymme' 111–12
'Of the Blessed Sacrament of the
 Autar' 127, 128
'Sinnes Heavie loade' 112–13
St Peters Complaint 106, 109
Spanish Match, the 177, 186
Spenser, Edmund 13, 14, 15, 16, 17,
 18, 22, 109, 118, 156, 158, 160,
 218, 220, 227, 229, 233, 235,
 237
spirit 7, 12, 26, 33, 34, 41, 56, 61, 66,
 76, 92, 98, 99, 102, 102, 103,
 104, 105, 109, 117, 118, 121,
 122, 125, 133, 145, 146, 165,
 180, 201, 211, 231, 232, 237,
 241
statue 57, 59, 123, 158, 186
Strier, Richard 123, 124, 241
Stuart, James 6, 203, 204 (*see also*
 James II)
Stuart, Mary 81, 82, 165, 192, 237
superstition 11, 29, 63, 64, 141, 211

Tacitus 51
Taylor, Gary 65, 76, 176, 200, 216,
 240, 244
theatre 2, 11, 12, 18, 19, 30, 31, 49,
 54, 50–73, 74–104, 105,
 164–208, 213, 215, 216
theology 15, 5, 7, 8, 12, 16, 18, 20,
 23, 24, 25, 26, 28, 29, 30, 31,
 32, 33, 34, 35, 37, 38, 43, 45,
 46, 47, 48, 49, 63, 72–3, 80,
 111, 112, 115, 116, 118, 119,
 121, 125, 126, 128, 147, 148,
 149, 154, 159, 173, 209, 210,
 211, 212, 217, 219, 223, 226,
 228, 231, 234, 236, 239 (*see also*
 anti-Calvinist, Arminian,
 Calvinism, grace, Laudianism,
 Lutheran, Pelagianism)

Thirty-nine Articles of Religion 9, 20, 21, 28, 67, 72, 74, 75, 76, 77, 88, 99, 104, 114, 133
Thomas, Keith 15, 242
tomb 22, 23, 36, 71, 72, 85, 89, 93, 94, 106, 113, 174, 192, 236
torture 5, 108, 141, 207, 230
transvestite 19, 178
treason 11, 52, 56, 124, 223
typology 92

Urfé, L'Honoré d' 200

Vatican 59, 77
Veevers, Erika 144, 186, 187, 190, 191, 192, 243
Vega, Andreas 39
Verstegan, Richard 19, 149–53, 154, 155, 162, 218, 243
  'Lilium inter Spinas' 153 154, 155, 157
  'Nauis Institoris' 153–4
  Odes 150–53
  'Our Blessed Ladies Lullaby' 151, 153
  'Porta Caeli' 151–52
  'Scale Caeli' 151, 152
  'Sibylla Tiburtina' 151
Vesalius 104
Vine, Emily 186
virginity 70, 155, 174, 176, 177, 178, 180, 182, 183, 185, 192, 198, 203, 222, 226, 230, 241
virtue 14, 20, 26, 30, 39, 41, 48, 52, 56, 57, 63, 66, 68, 87, 88, 90, 135, 192, 198, 217, 218, 232, 238
Vives, Juan Luis 18, 52, 53, 54, 58, 60, 67, 91, 173, 218, 225, 243
  City of God 18, 52, 53, 54, 58, 67
  Opera Omnia 53

Waller, Gary 14, 123, 141, 144, 147, 149, 152, 153, 157, 160, 163, 186, 201, 212, 213, 224, 230, 243
Walsham, Alexandra 2, 14, 17, 129, 146, 150, 157, 158, 210, 243, 244
Walsingham, Sir Francis 145
Ward, Mary 19, 179, 180, 181, 182, 184, 185, 186, 199, 226, 228, 243
White, Paul Whitfield 78, 82, 166, 168, 169, 173, 231, 244
whore 155, 157, 158, 161, 163, 176, 178, 182, 183, 184, 185, 220, 241 (*see also* Thomas Dekker)
Wilmot, John 202
Wittek, Stephen 177, 178, 244
worship vii, 1, 2, 6, 18, 19, 27, 54, 61, 74, 86, 87, 106–139, 140, 162, 167, 210, 211, 217, 225
'*Wracks of Walsingham, The*' 19, 155, 156, 158, 160, 161
Wright, Thomas 26, 245

Yorkshire 168, 173, 199, 244

Zook, Melinda 202, 245

EU authorised representative for GPSR:
Easy Access System Europe, Mustamäe tee 50,
10621 Tallinn, Estonia
gpsr.requests@easproject.com